**FROM UNION HALLS
TO THE SUBURBS**

A Volume in the Series
CULTURE AND POLITICS IN THE COLD WAR AND BEYOND
Edited by
Edwin A. Martini and Scott Laderman

FROM UNION HALLS TO THE SUBURBS

AMERICANS FOR DEMOCRATIC ACTION AND THE TRANSFORMATION OF POSTWAR LIBERALISM

SCOTT KAMEN

University of Massachusetts Press
AMHERST AND BOSTON

Copyright © 2023 by University of Massachusetts Press
All rights reserved
Printed in the United States of America

ISBN 978-1-62534-761-9 (paper); 762-6 (hardcover)

Designed by Sally Nichols
Set in Minion Pro by Westchester Publishing Services
Printed and bound by Books International, Inc.

Cover design by adam b. bohannon
Cover photo by Alan Kolnik, *2020 USA election yard signs in a neighborhood in North Bethesda*. © Alan Kolnik, photo 199470272 Dreamstime.com.

Library of Congress Cataloging-in-Publication Data
Names: Kamen, Scott, 1986– author.
Title: From union halls to the suburbs : Americans for Democratic Action and the transformation of postwar liberalism / Scott Kamen.
Other titles: Americans for Democratic Action and the transformation of postwar liberalism
Description: Amherst : University of Massachusetts Press, [2023] | Series: Culture and politics in the cold war and beyond | Includes bibliographical references and index.
Identifiers: LCCN 2023013533 (print) | LCCN 2023013534 (ebook) | ISBN 9781625347626 (hardcover) | ISBN 9781625347619 (paper) | ISBN 9781685750404 (ebook)
Subjects: LCSH: Americans for Democratic Action. | Liberalism—United States—History—20th century. | United States—Politics and government—20th century.
Classification: LCC E743 .K34 2023 (print) | LCC E743 (ebook) | DDC 320.510973—dc23
LC record available at https://lccn.loc.gov/2023013533
LC ebook record available at https://lccn.loc.gov/2023013534

British Library Cataloguing-in-Publication Data
A catalog record for this book is available from the British Library.

For Caitlin

CONTENTS

ACKNOWLEDGMENTS ix
LIST OF ABBREVIATIONS xiii

INTRODUCTION
FROM UNION HALLS TO THE SUBURBS VIA THE NEW POLITICS MOVEMENT
1

CHAPTER 1
THE ORIGINS OF A LIBERAL DIVIDE
Debating the Politics of Growth and Qualitative Liberalism in the Affluent Society
17

CHAPTER 2
RETHINKING THE COLD WAR
The Vital Center and the Vietnam War
59

CHAPTER 3
BEYOND THE WAR ON POVERTY
The Civil Rights Movement, Social Democracy, and the Struggle for Racial Equality
92

CHAPTER 4
THE COMING OF THE NEW POLITICS MOVEMENT
The Vietnam War and the Promise of the New Class
127

CHAPTER 5
THE EVOLUTION OF THE NEW POLITICS
A Broader Movement, Neoconservatives, and the Struggle for the Mantle of Liberalism
166

CHAPTER 6
FROM NEW POLITICS TO NEOLIBERALISM
Atari Democrats and the Dual Legacies of the New Politics Movement
206

EPILOGUE
NEW POLITICS, NEW DEMOCRATS, AND AMERICAN LIBERALISM IN THE TWENTY-FIRST CENTURY
245

NOTES 257

INDEX 301

Photo gallery follows page 126

ACKNOWLEDGMENTS

The writing of a book entails many hours alone in front of a computer screen. The journey that accompanies the writing of a book, however, depends on many people. I am grateful to the mentors, archivists, librarians, editors, friends, and family whose help and support made the completion of this book possible. Gary Huey, a longtime family friend and history professor at Ferris State University, first sparked my interest in pursuing a career in history. My undergraduate thesis supervisor at Western Michigan University, Edwin Martini, inspired me through his example as a scholar and a teacher to pursue graduate study in history. Ed has continued to support my work as an editor for the series in which this book is being published. When I began graduate school at the University of Maryland, Saverio Giovacchini guided me through the challenges of writing a master's thesis and impressed upon me the importance of taking ideas seriously.

This book began its life under the guidance of Daniel Geary at Trinity College Dublin. Dan's thorough emails and willingness to work through issues over the phone helped to get this project off the ground during the early stages of my work on it, when we were on opposite sides of the Atlantic Ocean. His challenging comments, timely encouragement, and sense of the relevance of my research improved this work in countless ways. Dan continued to provide critical support and advice throughout the long process of work and revision. Quite simply, this book would not have been possible without his guidance and support.

Its completion also owes much to financial support provided by Trinity College Dublin and the University of New Mexico. A Postgraduate Studentship from Trinity gave me the funding for three years of my work on this project. Generous grants from the Trinity Department of History's Grace Lawless Lee Fund enabled me to make essential research trips to Boston, New York, and Philadelphia. Professional development funds from the University of New Mexico–Valencia allowed me to hire on-site researchers when travel and in-person research were not possible at the onset of the COVID-19 pandemic, while a grant from the University of New Mexico Research Allocation Committee provided me with the funds to hire a professional indexer to produce the index for this book. The research leave granted to me during the 2021–22 academic year by University New Mexico–Valencia Dean of Instruction Laura Musselwhite let me focus on this project at a pivotal stage.

I also thank the numerous archivists and librarians who assisted my research. The staff at the John F. Kennedy Presidential Library, Library of Congress, New York Public Library Manuscripts and Archives Division, Swarthmore College Peace Collection, Wilson Library at the University of North Carolina, and Wisconsin Historical Society were generous with their time and uniformly helpful. Lisa Marine at the Wisconsin Historical Society graciously found an image file that I mistakenly deleted from my computer. Tal Nadan at the New York Public Library helped me track down a stubbornly difficult-to-find pamphlet and did well to remind me that sometimes a document simply is not in the collection no matter how hard you look for it.

Friends across the world have helped me in innumerable ways. Jane Burns provided a place to stay and human interaction outside the archive over the course of numerous research trips to Wisconsin. Marie Mapes and Seth Gitter gave me a place to sleep during a research trip to Washington, DC. Friends in the Department of History at Trinity College Dublin were a continual source of support and helped me to retain some sense of sanity while I was working on this project. Lunchtime conversations on the blocks in the Arts Building were a necessary reprieve from research and writing. I am grateful to Séan Brady, Stephen Carroll, Cáitlín Higgins Ní Chinnéide, Leah Hunnewell, Conor McCann, Felim McGrath, Léan Ní Chléirigh, Séan O'Reilly, and Ciarán Wallace for their friendship. I especially thank Tomás Irish and Sarah Frank for helping me settle into a doctoral program in a foreign country and Alex Dowdall for reading and commenting on an early draft of a chapter. I am also indebted to Ryan Huey, a friend from long before my time at Trinity, for reading and providing comments on a number of chapters.

Thanks must also be given to the staff at the University of Massachusetts Press. Editor in chief Matt Becker has been a constant source of encouragement and helped me think about this book from broader perspectives. Matt also helped me navigate the challenges of being a first-time book author and offered valuable feedback. Managing editor Rachael DeShano provided vital support, while EDP manager Sally Nichols ensured that the book and its cover packed visual pizzazz. The text benefited immensely from copyediting by Amanda Heller.

Finally, I am deeply grateful to my family for all their support. My father, Roger Kamen, encouraged and supported my study of history despite his initial—and understandable—misgivings about my decision to pursue a field of study with difficult employment prospects. My mother, Marcy Parry, has been a pillar of support and copyedited drafts of multiple chapters. Though they cannot read this, my dog, Gwen, and my cat, Quesadilla, have been a source of companionship and much-needed distraction. My wife, Caitlin Wells, cannot be thanked enough for her contributions to this book and everything she has done to enrich my life. She copyedited drafts of this project from its earliest days to the submission of the final draft. Her unwavering confidence and belief made the completion of this book possible. It is to her, and to the love and balance that she brings to my life, that this book is dedicated.

ABBREVIATIONS

ABM	anti-ballistic missile
ADA	Americans for Democratic Action
AFL-CIO	American Federation of Labor–Congress of Industrial Organizations
CAP	Community Action Program
CDM	Coalition for a Democratic Majority
CEA	Council of Economic Advisers
CORE	Congress of Racial Equality
DAC	Democratic Advisory Council
DLC	Democratic Leadership Council
ERA	Equal Rights Amendment
FAP	Family Assistance Plan
FEAC	Full Employment Action Council
ILGWU	International Ladies Garment Workers Union
MFDP	Mississippi Freedom Democratic Party
NAACP	National Association for the Advancement of Colored People
NAFTA	North American Free Trade Agreement
NCC	National Coordinating Committee to End the War in Vietnam
NDC	New Democratic Coalition
NLF	National Liberation Front
NOW	National Organization for Women
NSC-68	National Security Council Report 68
SANE	National Committee for a Sane Nuclear Policy
SDS	Students for a Democratic Society
SNCC	Student Nonviolent Coordinating Committee
SPA	Socialist Party of America
UAW	United Auto Workers
UDA	Union for Democratic Action
UFT	United Federation of Teachers
VMC	Vietnam Moratorium Committee
WSP	Women Strike for Peace

FROM UNION HALLS
TO THE SUBURBS

INTRODUCTION

FROM UNION HALLS TO THE SUBURBS VIA THE NEW POLITICS MOVEMENT

Like many of his fellow political commentators, Todd Purdum was taken by surprise as the contest between Hillary Clinton and Bernie Sanders in the 2016 Democratic primaries brought to light a growing division within the Democratic Party. This was the party, Purdum quipped, "with a well-financed, brand-name candidate who suddenly finds her coronation interrupted by a 74-year-old socialist with a Brooklyn accent as thick as Junior's Cheesecake."[1] The media's frequent fixation on Sanders's age, his accent, and his embrace of the "democratic socialist" label rendered his politics and the divide in the Democratic Party produced by his campaign's challenge to Clinton inexplicable and seemingly unprecedented in liberal politics. With the unexpectedly strong showing of Sanders during the primaries, political commentators began to report on the tensions in liberal politics between economic progressivism and what many termed neoliberal "identity politics."[2] These tensions did not, however, begin with the contest between Sanders and Clinton in 2016. When the Americans for Democratic Action (ADA) helped launch the New Politics movement that emerged alongside Eugene McCarthy's 1968 presidential campaign and later coalesced around the presidential campaign of George McGovern in 1972, those tensions were already palpable. The politics of the ADA—the most prominent liberal organization in the United States for more than a quarter century after World War II—and the New Politics movement it helped to shape contained the seeds for both the economic progressivism associated with the Sanders wing of the Democratic Party and the so-called neoliberal "identity politics" that previously had a near total grip on liberal and Democratic politics.

From Union Halls to the Suburbs illuminates the role of the New Politics movement in shaping the contours of contemporary liberalism and the tensions that run through it by examining the lasting intellectual and political contributions to the movement made by the ADA and its leading figures. The New Politics movement emerged in 1968 out of a focused desire to mount a challenge to the Vietnam War through the existing two-party political system, but it ultimately came to encompass a diverse array of causes and issues that included a sweeping challenge to the Cold War national security state and interventionist foreign policy, a call for a more participatory system of party politics, social democratic approaches to poverty, and a far-reaching politics of race, gender, and sexuality. Too often ignored or given little more than a passing mention, the New Politics movement is a vital thread that connects liberals from the years immediately after World War II to those who have assumed the mantle of a vastly transformed liberalism in recent decades. In the early postwar years, most American liberals focused their attention on the unfinished "bread-and-butter" economic agenda of the New Deal and sought to demonstrate that they were second to none in their commitment to confronting communist expansion on the world stage. By the late twentieth century, liberals typically opposed militaristic US foreign policy and displayed more concern with social and cultural issues than with Franklin D. Roosevelt's "forgotten man at the bottom of the economic pyramid."[3]

This transformation of what American liberalism stood for was both a contributor to and a product of changes in the electoral base that sustained the ideology at the polls. During the 1970s and 1980s, socially liberal white-collar professionals who had little familiarity with or interest in labor unions displaced economically populist, unionized blue-collar workers as the intended—and often the actual—social base of liberalism. With the shift in liberal and Democratic politics from union halls to the suburbs, liberalism increasingly spoke for suburban professionals and to their concerns. Those included not only a variety of social and cultural issues but also a frequently intense desire to protect their home values and limit their taxes. The combination of social liberalism and economic conservatism produced by these concerns makes clear that the politics of seemingly comfortable suburban professionals with liberal inclinations have long been shaped by their economic anxieties as much as their social consciences. John Kenneth Galbraith, Arthur Schlesinger Jr., and other influential ADA intellectuals had mistakenly assumed that the suburban professionals they looked to as the future of liberalism would be as liberal on economic matters as they were on social and cultural issues. The contributions of the ADA and its influential public intellectuals to the transformation of liberalism ushered in by the New Politics movement—including their misguided assumptions—are central to understanding why liberals deprioritized the redistributive bread-and-butter economics of the New Deal and postwar eras in favor of social and cultural issues that do not put home values at risk and require little sacrifice from taxpayers.

By probing the changes in political thought among influential ADA intellectuals who played a pivotal role in shaping the New Politics movement, this book also counters a declension narrative pervasive in studies of postwar liberalism which has led to a narrow focus on factors that brought about a seemingly inevitable liberal demise and conservative ascendency. Taking the 1980 election and the conservative Reagan Revolution that followed as a narrative end point, these studies display far more interest in assigning blame for liberalism's decline than in trying to understand why liberalism changed or how those changes continue to impact the American political landscape.[4] While American liberalism undoubtedly experienced a distinct decline in its intellectual and political currency in the late twentieth century compared to its heights during the New Deal and early postwar eras, it did not simply disappear or cease to be a vital force in the nation's politics. Democrats controlled Congress for most of the 1980s and the White House for most of the 1990s. Whether they explicitly identified as liberals or not, the majority of those Democrats practiced or felt pressure from some form of liberalism that had roots in the New Politics. This is because the prevailing understanding of liberalism has been largely defined by the legacy of the New Politics movement since the mid-1970s.

When Barack Obama extolled avoidance of unnecessary military intervention as a sign of courage and emphasized gay rights, equal pay for women, and the dangers of climate change during his second inaugural address in 2013, the media widely deemed his speech to be a forthright expression of modern American liberalism.[5] The media's assumption that Obama's critical perspective on interventionist foreign policy represented a liberal position indicated a conception of liberalism that has far more in common with the New Politics than with the Cold War militarism that suffused liberalism during the early postwar years. Similarly, when media outlets cited Obama's call for marriage equality and action to fight climate change as evidence that his address represented a clear expression of modern liberalism, they drew on an understanding of liberalism rooted in the insistence of the New Politics that quality-of-life issues and a politics of race, gender, and sexuality should be regarded as crucial components of the liberal agenda.

With an understanding of social and cultural issues largely divorced from economic ones, the liberalism expressed in Obama's second inaugural address reflected the concerns of suburban professionals far more than the bread-and-butter interests of the working class. This is not because social and cultural issues or "identity politics" are inherently unrelated to the economic pressures faced by the working class. Marriage equality, for example, has a significant impact on access to medical insurance in a country that lacks universal health care. Instead, the form of "identity politics" that can be found in Obama's address and throughout Democratic politics during his presidency held limited potential for addressing the concerns of the working class—too often imagined as monolithically straight, white, and male—because it prioritized discourse and symbolic representation at the expense of material concerns.[6] This conception of "identity politics" and Obama's politics more generally owed much to the neoliberal turn of many New Politics liberals during the 1980s. Since then, "neoliberal" has become a catchall term used to describe a diverse array of figures, policies, and institutions that prioritize market solutions to economic and social problems. Before it took on this more capacious meaning, the "neoliberal" label was primarily used in the US context to describe young Democrats such as Gary Hart and Paul Tsongas who cut their teeth on the New Politics movement before urging liberals to rethink their uncritical support for labor unions and government social programs. .[7]

The New Politics had long exhibited a tension between costly social democratic approaches to problems such as the entrenched economic inequality that underpinned racial inequality and an emphasis on social and cultural issues that required far less public spending. Still, during the late 1960s and early 1970s, opposition to the Vietnam War provided a unifying force within the New Politics movement that enabled its participants to paper over many of their differences. After the end of the Vietnam War in the mid-1970s, the differences among New Politics liberals became far more visible. As the Reagan Revolution took hold during the 1980s, Hart, Tsongas, and other neoliberals who would come to be dubbed "Atari Democrats" after the pioneering video game and home computer company appeared to win this struggle for the legacy of the New Politics. The rise of the Atari Democrats also seemed to resolve long-standing tensions in the New Politics by forgoing expensive initiatives such as a guaranteed annual income and full employment in favor of a concentration on social and cultural issues such as de jure gay rights and legal protections for abortion which entailed little in the way of taxpayer money.

The ascendency of neoliberalism in the Democratic Party was not, however, inevitable or absolute. In much the same way that the Reagan Revolution was not preordained and conservatism never fully eclipsed liberalism, the neoliberalism of the Atari Democrats was not simply the natural evolution of the New Politics movement or its sole surviving legacy. From Ted Kennedy's 1980 presidential campaign to Jesse Jackson's bids for the presidency in 1984 and 1988, an alternative legacy of the New Politics movement continued to surface. When Sanders challenged a Clinton campaign that positioned itself as Obama's third term, the unexpected strength of his campaign brought this alternative legacy into focus again. Sanders's campaign did this by demonstrating that the wide array of social issues that had entered the liberal agenda through the New Politics movement need not be divorced from the broader goals of economic and social justice that were central to the movement and its understanding of those issues. By bringing the ADA and its influential public intellectuals into the story of the New Politics movement, *From Union Halls to the Suburbs* allows us to understand why American liberalism shifted toward social and cultural issues conceived of in essentially non-material terms and why the return of economic progressivism in the twenty-first century has been an ongoing source of tension and division in liberal politics.

WHY THE AMERICANS FOR DEMOCRATIC ACTION?

The ADA is perhaps best known for popularizing the scoring of congressional voting records according to ideological criteria. A high ADA score has been prized by many liberal members of Congress, while a low ADA score has been touted by many conservative members. In the years since the ADA began publishing its scores of congressional voting records in 1947, organizations as ideologically diverse as the National Rifle Association and the National Abortion Rights Action League have graded the voting records of members of Congress according to their own criteria. As ubiquitous as these ratings have become, the impact of the ADA on American politics since World War II goes far beyond the popularization of legislative scorecards. By drawing on a desire to continue the social democratic project initiated by the New Deal along with the purpose and energy of the Cold War, the ADA quickly emerged after its founding in 1947 as the foremost architect and representative of postwar liberalism. Members of the nascent organization looked to the New Deal and anticommunism as the twin pillars of American liberalism. In the realm of domestic politics, the anticommunist commitment of ADA liberals entailed a rejection of the broad antifascist coalition of the Popular Front and its emphasis on collaboration with communists as a means of achieving liberal goals. In the formulation of foreign policy, the organization's anticommunism took the form of support for global containment of communism by means of aggressive policies against what appeared to be a monolithic communist bloc beholden to the Soviet Union. Though an independent and nominally nonpartisan political organization committed to advancing liberal politics, the ADA continually found itself acting as a lobbying group seeking to push the Democratic Party toward more liberal positions. At the time of its founding, the ADA assembled a cast of some of the most distinguished liberal intellectuals and political figures in the country, featuring Chester Bowles, Hubert Humphrey, John Kenneth Galbraith, Leon Henderson, James Loeb, Reinhold Niebuhr, Joseph Rauh, Walter Reuther, Eleanor Roosevelt, Arthur Schlesinger Jr., and James Wechsler, among others.[8]

The stature of those figures quickly helped to establish the ADA as a leading voice for American liberalism, but assessing the organization's precise influence on politics and political thought during the postwar era is complicated by the agendas that frequently animated characterizations of it in the press. The most thorough press attention received by the ADA tended to come from writers who were either members of the organization or staunch critics of it. Each of these groups had its own respective reasons for exaggerating the ADA's clout. Seeking to bolster the newly formed group, prominent journalist and ADA member Arthur D. Morse gave his organization credit for Harry Truman's unexpected presidential election victory and the recapture of Congress by Democrats in 1948. Morse asserted a year after the election that "when the election returns were in, ADA's significance as a national force was established." As evidence, he noted that "more than one third of the liberals elected to Congress and governorships were active ADA members, as had been many of their ward and precinct workers."[9]

Conservative writers—albeit for different reasons than with ADA members like Morse—also tended to exaggerate the influence of the group. Writing in the *National Review* in 1963, influential conservative intellectual and former Trotskyist James Burnham portrayed the ADA as a devious organization with power and influence far greater than its size would suggest. Burnham provocatively asked if the ADA was running John F. Kennedy's New Frontier behind the scenes and largely answered his own question in the affirmative. For conservative writers like Burnham, embellishing the power of the organization helped them tar Democrats with the "left-wing" politics of the ADA and make the group into an ominous threat that required determined opposition.[10] Still, while the ADA neither singlehandedly decided the 1948 election nor secretly ran the Kennedy administration, it did exert a diffuse effect on the development of liberal politics and liberal ideas that impacted the political landscape in ways big and small. In doing so, the ADA came to wield an influence on American liberalism unmatched by any comparable multi-issue organization during the postwar era.

No written work better encapsulated the tenets of the ADA's liberalism during the years in which it developed that influence than Schlesinger's seminal liberal treatise *The Vital Center*. Published in 1949, *The Vital Center* offered a playbook for American liberals—both within and outside the ADA—who insisted on engaging the Cold War on political terms that combined a commitment to domestic social progress with firm anticommunism. In distinguishing the "vital center" of liberalism from the dangers he saw on the right and the left, Schlesinger provided a compelling intellectual framework for the ADA's opposition to conservative Republicans and to Progressives who rallied to the presidential campaign of Henry Wallace. *The Vital Center* called on liberals to take a stand against both Republicans who sought to restore the power of the business community and Progressives whose misguided faith in the essential goodness of humanity led them to solicit communist support and adopt naïve approaches to foreign policy. Drawing on the work of Niebuhr, and with Wallace's Progressives firmly in mind, Schlesinger looked to the formation of the ADA in 1947 as "the watershed at which American liberalism began to base itself once again on a solid conception of man and of history."[11]

The Vital Center offers a quintessential articulation of the particular current of liberalism embraced by a significant number of prominent American liberals during the early postwar years, but the variety of diverse and often conflicting meanings attached to the term ensures that defining "liberalism" is never a straightforward task. Much of the difficulty can be found in the fact that the meaning of the term varies substantially depending on the national context in which it is employed. In European politics, the "liberal" label generally refers to an insistence on individual liberty with an accompanying commitment to laissez-faire economics. Although "liberal" in American politics implies a similar dedication to individual liberty, American liberals since the New Deal have usually viewed activist government intervention in the economy and the welfare state as fundamental to the protection of individual liberty.[12] As a result, the left wing of American liberalism has acted as a surrogate for what would be called social democracy in Europe. The economic progressivism that reentered American politics in the wake of Bernie Sanders's 2016 presidential campaign is a case in point. While Sanders self-identified as a "democratic socialist," his politics had far more in common with the social democratic project than with calls for public ownership of the means of production and other positions typically associated with socialism. When Sanders laid out his vision for the United States, it was not the democratically elected socialist government of Chile under Salvador Allende that took center stage but the social democratic legacy of the New Deal and the social democratic achievements of Denmark.

In Europe, the social democratic project has generally consisted of the effort to expand the principles of freedom and equality valued by democrats in the legal and political spheres into the economic sphere through democratic collective action. Typically, this has involved addressing the inequalities produced by capitalism through support for powerful labor unions, progressive taxation, and economic intervention by the state to provide rights to material resources and social services for its citizens.[13] In the United States, the concept of "industrial democracy" that emerged during the New Deal era shared much in common with the basic aims of European social democracy.[14]

Still, there were distinct limits to the scope of what the nascent social democratic project initiated by the New Deal sought to do. As numerous historians have shown, Franklin D. Roosevelt and the New Dealers saw their reforms as a way of saving capitalism from itself, not as a foundation for American socialism.[15] While New Deal liberals and their descendants in the

ADA and the broader American polity were prepared, and sometimes eager, to make significant changes to the way American capitalism worked, they were not willing to abandon capitalism in favor of alternative economic systems. For example, the push of ADA liberals during the 1960s and 1970s for full employment initiatives that called on the federal government to act as an employer of last resort rested on a belief that the private labor market could not be depended on to eliminate unemployment and poverty. This skepticism toward private labor markets represented perhaps the height of American liberalism's embrace of the social democratic project during the postwar era. Even so, it never entailed an outright rejection of capitalism as a means to liberal ends. Despite their challenge to the existing structure of American capitalism, liberal full employment initiatives were still primarily based on using tax revenue raised from privately owned industries and their employees to fund public works rather than on nationalization of those industries. This meant that when the phenomenon of stagflation in the late 1970s produced a widely agreed-upon trade-off between addressing unemployment and tackling inflation, ADA liberals either attacked the validity of that trade-off or pursued politically unrealistic compromises. They did not call into question the basic ability of capitalism to achieve their twin goals of reduced unemployment and lower inflation. This type of outlook was never limited to liberals in the ADA. American liberals have urged and enacted significant reforms to American capitalism, but—unlike socialists—have insisted that the aims of freedom and equality sought by most on the left side of the political spectrum can be realized within a reformed capitalist system.

With a firm belief in the far-reaching potential for social progress to be found in a reformed capitalism, ADA liberals played a leading role in defining and redefining American liberalism in the decades after World War II. On this basis, they established the ADA as the quintessential representative of postwar American liberalism. This is why *From Union Halls to the Suburbs* makes use of the ADA as a vehicle through which to understand the transformation of American liberalism during the second half of the twentieth century. That means that this book is not an institutional history narrowly focused on the ADA as an organization. Still, its exploration of the ADA challenges the prevailing depiction of the group that has endured since the publication of Steven Gillon's *Politics and Vision* in 1987. In what remained at this writing the most recent book-length study on the ADA, Gillon rightly frames the history of the organization as resting on an ongoing struggle to balance political expediency with liberal principles. He largely concentrates, however, on the earlier years of the ADA and depicts its endorsement of Eugene McCarthy's long shot presidential campaign in 1968 as a decision which shattered that balance and led the organization down the path to the political irrelevance that it has suffered since the 1980s.[16]

By contrast, this book focuses much of its attention on the ADA during a later period and gives serious consideration to the rationale behind its leaders' decision to endorse McCarthy and establish the organization as a launching pad for the New Politics movement. Doing so changes our understanding of the ADA in two important ways. First, scrutinizing the ADA after its oft-supposed heyday during the years of John F. Kennedy's "Camelot" makes clear that its leading figures were not the out-of-touch has-beens they are frequently assumed to have become by the late 1960s. In fact, they remained influential political actors and a vital source of liberal ideas throughout the 1960s and into the 1970s. Second, a close examination of how and why those figures contributed to the New Politics movement reveals the political potential they saw in the growing ranks of college students and middle-class white-collar professionals who composed what came to be known as a "New Class."[17] The willingness of Galbraith, Schlesinger, and other veteran ADA leaders to part ways with organized labor in order to endorse McCarthy was not based on idealistic opposition to the Vietnam War winning out over the demands of political pragmatism. They were willing to let the ADA take on the political, financial, and institutional risks involved in backing McCarthy because they believed that the New Class voters drawn to the Minnesota senator's campaign were central to the future of the liberal coalition.

A different understanding of the ADA and its leading figures forces us to rethink the American liberal tradition that they so visibly embodied. The veteran leaders of the ADA avoided becoming relics and retained their intellectual and political influence by adapting the liberal tradition to changing socioeconomic conditions, new geopolitical realities, and the demands of civil rights leaders. Contrary to assumptions that abound in the declension narrative of postwar liberalism, the continued relevance of these figures demonstrates that the American liberal tradition could provide a compelling intellectual and political foundation for addressing the challenges faced by the United States during the civil rights and Vietnam War era. The success of John Kenneth Galbraith, Richard Goodwin, Joseph Rauh, Arthur

Schlesinger Jr., Leon Shull, and other longtime ADA leaders in adapting American liberalism to new conditions and demands helped to establish the New Class in which they invested so much hope during this period as the primary social base for American liberalism. While the term "New Class" came to be used primarily as a pejorative and eventually fell out of regular use altogether, the concerns of middle-class professionals—later referred to by labels such as the "professional-managerial class," "knowledge workers," or "suburban liberals"—continued to grow in importance as the twentieth century drew to a close.[18] The "New Politics" label shared a similar fate, largely vanishing from political discourse by the 1980s. Nevertheless, the story of how social and cultural issues displaced bread-and-butter economic concerns at the center of American liberalism by the turn of the twenty-first century is intimately tied up with the rise of the New Class, the coming of the New Politics movement, and the contributions of veteran ADAers to both of those developments.

BEYOND MCCARTHY AND MCGOVERN

The presidential campaigns of Eugene McCarthy and George McGovern have dominated the relatively limited scholarship on the New Politics movement. As important as McCarthy and McGovern are to the history of the New Politics, a myopic focus on these two presidential campaigns has led to a limited and distorted understanding of the movement and its legacy. With McCarthy and McGovern in the foreground, historians have illuminated many aspects of the politicians and constituencies of the New Politics but have displayed comparatively little interest in the ideas and principles that guided the movement. Inadequate attention to its intellectual foundation has led many of these historians to portray the New Politics movement as a watered-down version of the New Left refashioned for entry into the mainstream of electoral politics.[19] These depictions owe much to the assumption—found all too often in the declension narrative of postwar liberalism—that American liberalism was incapable of facing the social, cultural, economic, and political challenges of the 1960s. This assumption has invited historians to assume that the impetus for the New Politics must have come from outside the liberal tradition. From the perspective of these historians, the inability of liberalism to effect the change necessary to meet the increasingly pressing circumstances of the 1960s has meant that the source of liberal transformation is to be found not within the confines of liberalism but in the pressure and influence of a New Left that emerged just prior to the New Politics movement.[20] When this movement is rendered not as an adaptation of liberalism to new circumstances and challenges but as an effort to transpose the energy of the New Left into the existing party structure and electoral system, little room is left for the involvement of the ADA and its public intellectuals. In other words, if we imagine the New Politics movement primarily as one of young radicals who shaved their beards and cut their hair in order to go "clean for Gene" and canvass for McCarthy in the 1968 Democratic primaries, it becomes difficult to see how the likes of John Kenneth Galbraith or Arthur Schlesinger Jr. would have had much to do with it.

The contributions of Galbraith, Schlesinger, and other veteran ADA leaders to the New Politics movement have been further obscured by static characterizations of them as stodgy representatives of the postwar liberal order. Presuming that the politics and positions of these figures changed little between the early 1950s and the late 1960s, these characterizations have frequently led historians to emphasize younger figures not previously associated with the ADA as the driving force behind the organization's close relationship with the movement.[21] *From Union Halls to the Suburbs* counters these portrayals by showing how some of the ADA's longest-serving and most visible leaders consistently adapted their political thought and outlook to meet new circumstances and in so doing developed an intellectual framework that could and would be drawn on by the New Politics.

Images of older ADA leaders as unbending representatives of Cold War liberalism are often based on the early Cold War period, when they and the broader liberal community—despite differences over desired approaches—joined with conservatives in a consensus on the overriding goals of expanding the economy and containing international communism wherever it might rear its head. Yet some of the ADA's most influential figures had already begun to depart from this consensus by the early 1950s. That is why this book begins by locating in chapter 1 the origins of the New Politics movement in the "qualitative liberalism" advanced by Galbraith and Schlesinger in the 1950s. When they began to sketch the contours of a qualitative liberalism that brought into question the transcendent importance of economic growth and insisted that a broad array of cultural, moral, and social issues were legitimate subjects of concern for liberals, they touched off debates with fellow ADAers, such as Leon Keyserling, who were committed to the "quantitative liberalism" of the New Deal. The substance of those debates would later define the tensions that ran through the New Politics movement. Chapter 2 shows how influential ADA leaders further contributed to the foundation for the New Politics when their early and committed opposition to the Vietnam War led them to reject the policy of global anticommunist containment which had been a pillar of American postwar liberalism alongside an insistence on the imperative of economic growth.

Chapters 3 and 4 explore how and why opposition to the Vietnam War became a transcendent issue in liberal politics and the spark for the New Politics movement. Chapter 3 examines how the civil rights movement impacted the thinking and priorities of liberals within and outside the ADA. When the increasing momentum of the civil rights movement in the early 1960s brought a new level of visibility to the entrenched economic inequality that underpinned racial inequality, the commitment of leading ADA liberals to the fight for civil rights expanded to include the struggle against poverty. While differences rooted in the debates over qualitative liberalism in the 1950s led to disagreement in the organization on how best to approach the complex problem of poverty, a growing number of ADA liberals came to recognize US involvement in the Vietnam War as the first hurdle to implementing a meaningful antipoverty program regardless of the particulars of their desired approach. The pressing need felt by many ADAers to mount opposition to the war in order to tackle poverty and advance civil rights is taken up in chapter 4 with attention to why the ADA became the first non-issue-specific organization with a national reach to endorse McCarthy's uphill challenge to President Lyndon Johnson in the 1968 Democratic primaries. The ADA's decision to part ways with organized labor and endorse the McCarthy campaign, thus launching the New Politics movement, has often been seen as a quixotic choice that put the organization on the path to political irrelevance. This decision was not, however, a hasty act of visionary miscalculation. The decision was a culmination of ADA leaders' repudiation of anticommunist containment as a basis for US foreign policy, their realization that little progress toward racial equality would be made so long as the United States remained involved in the Vietnam War, and their belief that New Class voters represented an essential component of the new liberal coalition taking shape. Instead of heralding the group's effective demise, the endorsement of McCarthy in 1968 enabled leading figures in the ADA to play an instrumental role in shaping an emerging New Politics movement that saw them wield as much influence on the direction of American politics as at any other point in the history of the organization.

Together, chapter 5, chapter 6, and the epilogue follow the substantial evolution of the New Politics movement after 1968 and the lasting impact of those changes on American liberalism. In the years between McCarthy's 1968 presidential campaign and McGovern's run for the White House in 1972, the concerns that animated the New Politics movement came to include not only the antiwar activism that had initially put the movement into motion but also a broadly critical perspective on the Cold War national security state and a diverse array of domestic issues such as affirmative action, women's rights, gay and lesbian rights, party reform, and guaranteed income. Chapter 5 probes the ways in which this evolution of the New Politics movement shaped the critical response and opposition mounted against it by a neoconservative movement that has too often been depicted primarily as a response to the New Left, not the New Politics. This chapter also shows how the evolution of the New Politics movement after 1968 confirmed and acted on a number of ideas with deep roots in the political thought of longtime ADA leaders. In doing so, it demonstrates how unresolved contradictions in the relationship between a qualitative liberalism shaped by the conditions of presumed widespread postwar affluence and a social democratic outlook that gained greater currency in the ADA in the wake of the civil rights movement could readily be found in the New Politics movement. Throughout the late 1960s and early 1970s, the movement often adopted social democratic positions but effectively sought to purge organized labor—which was perhaps the country's strongest political force with any dedication to social democracy—from the liberal coalition on the basis of labor leaders' support for the Vietnam War.

Chapter 6 follows these tensions into the late 1970s and 1980s, when the "New Politics" largely disappeared from political discourse, but the legacy of its basic outlook continued to define liberal politics. Focused on a period when the ADA began its descent into irrelevance as an organization, this chapter partially shifts the spotlight away from the ADA itself and toward the ways in which its ideas and politics played out amid deteriorating economic conditions and the Reagan Revolution. By examining the politics of New Politics liberals who became neoliberal Atari Democrats in the 1980s, chapter 6 highlights the misguided assumptions of Galbraith, Schlesinger, and other influential ADA intellectuals about the New Class. When these leading ADA figures looked to the New Class as the future social base for American liberalism, they mistakenly assumed that New Class voters would be as liberal on economic issues as on social issues. The Atari Democrats who gave the lie to that assumption were not, however, the only legacy left behind by the New Politics movement. As this chapter and the epilogue show, the renewed liberal–labor coalition that emerged after the Vietnam War, and the presidential campaigns of Ted Kennedy, Jesse Jackson, and Bernie Sanders, pointed toward a legacy of the New Politics that did not discard economic progressivism as a necessary means of achieving social justice. The epilogue brings us to the tensions in contemporary liberalism by placing those developments alongside the Democratic Leadership Council, Barrack Obama, and Hillary Clinton as examples of the neoliberal legacy of the New Politics movement.

By following the New Politics movement from its intellectual origins in the 1950s to the dual legacies it left behind after the 1980s, we find that the division in Democratic and liberal politics produced by Sanders's challenge to Clinton in the 2016 Democratic primaries appears neither inexplicable nor unprecedented. When Sanders launched his seemingly unlikely presidential campaign in a rushed ten-minute appearance on the grounds of the US Capitol before a small ensemble of reporters on April 30, 2015, he was able to tap into a legacy of the New Politics movement that had largely lain dormant for years.[22] While the growing crisis of economic inequality and the attention brought to that crisis by the Occupy Wall Street movement were pivotal to making the unexpectedly strong showing of his campaign possible, Sanders's politics owed far more to the social democratic legacy of the New Politics movement than to the anarchist orientation and drum circles of Occupy. From his decision to run in the Democratic primaries rather than mount a third-party campaign to his synthesis of social democratic initiatives and social liberalism, Sanders drew on a strain of the New Politics that sought far-reaching social and economic change through the existing two-party system. The resurfacing of this legacy in the wake of Sanders's 2016 campaign made economic progressivism once again a meaningful current in liberal politics and shattered what had appeared to be the monopoly of so-called neoliberal "identity politics" on American liberalism. Far from being unprecedented, the ensuing debates over the future of the

Democratic Party and American liberalism harked back to the politics of the ADA and its involvement in the New Politics movement during the civil rights and Vietnam War era.

To put it in its simplest terms, the story of American liberalism since World War II can be seen as one in which the social and cultural concerns of the New Class largely displaced redistributive economics and the bread-and-butter interests of the working class before the latter reemerged in a meaningful way in the twenty-first century. The contributions of the ADA and its public intellectuals to the New Politics movement are central to this story. The trajectory of American liberalism has made clear that while the New Politics movement did not develop along the precise lines that ADA intellectuals had hoped for and never achieved the lasting legislative and electoral successes tallied by the New Deal coalition that preceded it, the movement did not usher in the presumed demise of liberalism that abounds in studies of postwar liberal thinking. The contested nature of American liberalism in the twenty-first century speaks to the ongoing vitality of the ideology. If American liberalism had met its demise amid the Reagan Revolution, there would be little reason for politicians, political commentators, and activists to fight over its future direction. By exploring the roots and continuing impact of the New Politics movement, this book demonstrates that liberalism did not simply wither away—as historians have too often assumed—but instead has taken on new forms, enabling it to remain a vital force in the nation's politics.

CHAPTER 1

THE ORIGINS OF A LIBERAL DIVIDE
Debating the Politics of Growth and Qualitative Liberalism in the Affluent Society

When John Kenneth Galbraith and Arthur Schlesinger Jr. sketched the contours of what came to be called "qualitative liberalism" during the Eisenhower and Kennedy years, they left behind powerful images that shaped how many American liberals both inside and outside the ADA saw the social and economic changes taking place in their midst. From Schlesinger they had the image of the typical American as a suburbanite who, thanks to the achievements of the New Deal, had "a job, a square meal, a suit of clothes, and a roof" over their head.[1] Galbraith left them with the image of the shiny, feature-packed car—typically with extravagant tailfins—alongside an appallingly maintained public park.[2] Together those images painted a powerful picture of the United States as a society that had achieved tremendous private prosperity but suffered from a public squalor that constrained the quality of American life. Galbraith and Schlesinger drew on this understanding of social imbalance as they sought to establish the array of quality-of-life issues produced by widespread prosperity as legitimate objects of liberal concern.

Still, while many liberals drew on the basic framework of social imbalance established in the writings of Galbraith and Schlesinger to make sense of widespread changes during the postwar era, the far-reaching implications of their vision for qualitative liberalism became a source of tension in liberal circles that would escalate significantly in the years to come. The insistence running through qualitative liberalism that the cultural, moral, and social issues affecting the quality of American life should be treated as political concerns represented a significant departure from the bread-and-butter orientation of the New Deal and faced criticism and opposition from liberals invested in the "quantitative" approach of Roosevelt and Truman era programs. Foremost among the liberal critics of qualitative liberalism was Leon Keyserling, who served in the Roosevelt administration and chaired the Council of Economic Advisers (CEA) during Harry Truman's presidency before joining the ADA. During the 1950s, Keyserling and other like-minded critics of qualitative liberalism muted some of their concerns and tended to avoid forceful airings of their criticism in public. But as qualitative liberalism's emphasis on seemingly non-material issues became more pervasive during the 1960s, and the Vietnam War pitted liberals against one another, the divide between those who embraced qualitative liberalism and those who remained committed to the quantitative perspective of the New Deal grew and hardened.

From John F. Kennedy's New Frontier and Lyndon B. Johnson's Great Society to the New Left and the New Politics, liberal and radical politics in the 1960s reflected the fundamental conviction of qualitative liberalism that political solutions could and should be found to address the pressing non-material issues faced by an increasingly prosperous nation. Common to the most visible political developments of the 1960s, this expansive vision of politics took shape in response to the political, economic, and social circumstances of the 1950s. The dawn of the age of abundance in the 1950s made it possible to develop a broad liberal vision that went beyond the scope of the bread-and-butter issues that had defined the New Deal and the Fair Deal, while the political circumstances of that decade made it necessary. In a post-scarcity era, in which the productive output of the American economy surpassed the material needs of its people, Galbraith and Schlesinger could urge liberals to turn their attention from economic growth to the matters that determined the quality of American life. Motivated by the growing importance of middle-class voters and the assumption that in the age of abundance, pocketbook issues would no longer draw the votes they once had, Galbraith and Schlesinger looked to quality-of-life issues from education and equal opportunities for minorities to the state of the nation's mass media as the key to Democratic electoral salvation after the devastating defeat in the 1952 elections. Moreover, the demands of the Cold War and the danger of falling behind the Soviet Union not only in technological and military prowess but also as a source of inspiration for the world further persuaded many in the ADA to look beyond economic growth and consumer opulence as they cast about for a greater sense of national purpose. When Galbraith and Schlesinger highlighted the dangers of a society that pursued tailfins at the expense of classrooms, they found the ADA a ready audience for their concerns, if not for the specifics of their policy prescriptions.

The attraction of ADA liberals to a critical perspective on consumerism and social imbalance reflected a growing liberal disillusionment with the values, priorities, and direction of American society during the 1950s. The attention to post-scarcity questions about the "affluent society" spurred by that disillusionment would ultimately take center stage in the policy resolutions of the ADA and establish the organization as a launching pad for the New Politics movement during the late 1960s. Schlesinger did not hesitate to highlight the role that he, Galbraith, and other architects of qualitative liberalism had played in making that movement possible. When he surveyed the American political landscape in 1969, Schlesinger observed that "the combination of the affluent society and the electronic revolution is bringing into existence what has come to be known as the New Politics."[3] Tracing the New Politics movement back to ADA intellectuals' questioning of the transcendent importance of economic growth in the 1950s illuminates the origins of the tensions that ran through the movement and the dual legacies it left behind.

THE PREEMINENT LIBERAL ORGANIZATION IN THE NATION

At first glance, the debates between advocates of qualitative liberalism and quantitative liberalism within the ADA can appear to be a parochial splitting of hairs. This ongoing debate—led by Galbraith and Schlesinger on one side and Keyserling on the other—managed to shape the trajectory of American liberalism and leave behind an enduring legacy because the ADA had become the preeminent liberal organization in the nation by the early 1950s. The organization also came to wield considerable sway over certain segments of the Democratic Party during this period. These circumstances were immensely different from the ones that had surrounded the ADA in the immediate wake of its establishment by members of the small and weak Union for Democratic Action (UDA) several years earlier. The death of Franklin D. Roosevelt and the end of World War II brought about a period of intense crisis for American liberalism. For many adherents, Roosevelt had personally defined and symbolized American liberalism. At the same time, the US alliance with the Soviet Union during the war had muted the issue of communism and cooperation with communists.[4] With Roosevelt no longer available as a unifying symbol for American liberalism and the Cold War beginning to change liberal attitudes toward communists, two new organizations competed for the legacy of the New Deal and the mantle of American liberalism. On December 29, 1946, Roosevelt's former vice president Henry Wallace took charge of the newly formed Progressive Citizens of America (PCA) and sought to establish the organization as the legitimate heir to the legacy of Roosevelt and the New Deal.[5] Less than a week later, on January 4, 1947, members of the UDA and other liberals who rejected the Popular Front convention of collaboration with communists formed the ADA with a desire to claim that legacy for themselves.[6]

Both new organizations had strong claims to the legacy of Roosevelt and the New Deal. Wallace had served as Roosevelt's secretary of agriculture before becoming his vice president in 1941. Roosevelt had wanted to keep Wallace as his running mate in 1944 before giving in to pressure from conservatives in his party who wanted an open vote at the Democratic National Convention, which resulted in Truman taking Wallace's place on the ticket. Despite his resentment at the party machinations that had cost him the vice presidential nomination, Wallace campaigned vigorously for Roosevelt in the 1944 election, and the newly four-times-elected president returned the favor by making him his secretary of commerce.[7] While the PCA's personal connection to Roosevelt rested on Wallace's leadership of the organization, the involvement of Eleanor Roosevelt and Franklin Roosevelt Jr. provided the most visible basis for the ADA's links with the late president. Besides familial ties, the large number of faces associated with the Roosevelt administration present at the founding meeting of the ADA led the columnist Drew Pearson to dub the group a "New Deal in exile."[8]

Although both organizations eagerly sought acceptance as the continuation of Roosevelt's legacy and the New Deal, they diverged sharply on the issue of cooperation with communists and the Communist Party. For its part, the PCA characterized its differences with the ADA as minor and issued calls for unity among liberals. By contrast, ADA members deemed the PCA's acceptance of communist support significant, naïve, and unacceptable. While PCA members sought to maintain the Popular Front framework in order to protect liberal legislation from what they saw as an inevitable postwar turn to conservatism, the ADA charged that liberal ends could never be achieved by means of alliance with totalitarians.[9] The membership of the PCA drew heavily from the ranks of liberals who rejected the ADA's strident anticommunism but also featured members and fellow travelers of the Communist Party. Whether they hailed from solidly liberal backgrounds or operated farther to the left on the political spectrum, members of the PCA stressed the benign intentions of Soviet foreign policy and quickly established the organization as a vehicle for Wallace's 1948 presidential campaign.[10] Despite initially encouraging signs of popular support, Wallace's vision for a united liberal front was soundly rejected by voters, and he came away from the election with just over a million votes and no representation in the Electoral College.[11] Amid the deeply underwhelming performance of Wallace's campaign and the disintegration of his Progressive Party in the years that followed, a Cold War consensus took shape that effectively extinguished any possibilities for Popular Front–type collaboration between liberals and communists. With Popular Front liberalism popularly discredited, the ADA—which had grown out of the minuscule but firmly anticommunist UDA—took advantage of the opening to establish itself as the most influential liberal organization in the nation.

The rapid ascendency of the ADA did not, however, settle fundamental questions about the nature of the organization that had been left largely unanswered since its founding. Throughout its history, the ADA experienced tension between those who saw it as a relatively small but influential organization that emphasized long-term ideological goals—in other words, something like an American version of the British Fabian Society—and those who envisioned the group as a mass political organization geared toward immediate political action. In practice, the ADA became something of an uneasy hybrid of these visions. The resolutions passed by the ADA on a wide variety of issues of importance to liberals tended to be shaped by well-known figures at the higher ranks of the organization. By contrast, endorsements of candidates involved the ADA's sizable national board, and mobilization of resources on behalf of those candidates depended on the work of grassroots members at the chapter level. Despite the importance of its grassroots members, however, the ADA never attracted the broad membership that those who sought to build a mass political organization had desired. Contradictory records make it difficult to pin down precise numbers, but it is unlikely that the membership of the ADA at its peak during the late 1960s and early 1970s ever topped fifty thousand. For the bulk of the organization's history prior to the 1980s, membership hovered somewhere between ten thousand and twenty thousand. Nevertheless, the ADA quickly expanded beyond the small, elite gathering of figures that established the organization at the start of 1947. Within seven months of its founding, the ADA boasted over four thousand members and seventeen chapters across the country.[12]

The relationship of the ADA to the Democratic Party was another fundamental and enduring issue that the organization never fully resolved. Though it was not part of the Democratic Party and was officially nonpartisan, the ADA saw the Democratic Party as the primary means for its mission of advancing "the cause of liberalism in the United States and elsewhere." When the Republican Party still had a meaningful liberal wing, the ADA sometimes threw its weight behind Republican candidates such as Jacob Javits and John Lindsay. As the pool of liberal Republicans dried up, the ADA had a harder time trying to present itself as a nonpartisan organization. With its endorsements of non-Democratic candidates becoming exceedingly rare, the ADA faced the risk of being swallowed up by a behemoth Democratic Party organization whose candidates might be able to take the group's support for granted.[13]

Despite the risks of becoming too entangled in the Democratic Party, ADA involvement in the party provided the readiest means for the organization to pack a political punch far above the weight its relatively small membership would suggest. In the early years of the ADA, the Democrats were hardly a unified political party. Significant differences—on civil rights in particular—divided the northern party from the southern party. As a result, the ADA came to possess significant influence in the Democratic politics of some regions and locales and virtually no presence in others. Given its uneven influence, the ADA focused most of its energy and resources on the northern, liberal elements of the party. At the national level, the Democratic Party was split between its "presidential party" and its "congressional party." The ADA enjoyed greater ties with and influence on the presidential party and what could be called the "quasi-presidential party" during periods when a Republican resided in the White House. Despite early disillusionment with Truman and initial opposition to his election in 1948, ADA leaders met with him in the White House and maintained open channels of communication with his administration throughout the remainder of his presidency.[14] In the years that followed, the ADA devoted considerable resources to Adlai Stevenson's presidential campaigns. Galbraith and Schlesinger established themselves as key speechwriters for the two-time Democratic nominee.[15]

The deep involvement of the ADA and its leading figures at the highest levels of Democratic politics provided the means by which debates in the organization had a tangible and meaningful influence on the national political landscape. This meant that when Galbraith and Schlesinger mounted a debate with Keyserling on the nation's obsessive focus on economic growth, the impact reverberated far beyond the confines of the ADA.

GROWTH CONSENSUS

The early postwar period was a far cry from the period of liberal consensus that many historians once assumed it to be, but a strong consensus could be found along just about the entire political spectrum on at least one issue: the imperative of economic growth.[16] Galbraith observed wryly in 1958 that belief in the transcendent importance of the production of goods and economic growth "is common ground for the general secretary of the Communist Party, the Chairman of the Americans for Democratic Action, the President of the United States Chamber of Commerce, and the President of the National Association of Manufacturers."[17] While liberals moved more quickly to this common ground than their conservative counterparts and established themselves as second to none in the pursuit termed "growthmanship" by commentators in the 1950s, they themselves had only recently converted to the cause of economic growth.[18]

During the Great Depression, many liberals saw the United States as an overdeveloped mature economy that resulted in an economics of scarcity. Liberal doubts about the desirability of growth in an economy that required, above all, basic security would be coupled with uncertainty as to whether or not significant growth was even possible in a highly developed capitalist economy. The doubt and ambivalence displayed by liberals in the years of the Great Depression quickly dissolved when mobilization for World War II and the influence of Keynesian economists in the Truman administration decisively moved the context of liberal economics from the economics of scarcity to the economics of expansion.[19]

Drawing on the economics of expansion but reflecting a fear of return to the economics of scarcity, the Employment Act of 1946 represented both an extension of the economic concerns that defined the Great Depression and a departure from them. Though greatly enfeebled in contrast to original aims for the bill, the Employment Act of 1946 made a formal—albeit nonbinding—declaration of the federal government's responsibility "to promote maximum employment, production, and purchasing power." It also established the Council of Economic Advisers to assist the president in carrying out programs toward those ends. With enactment of the Employment Act, the official aim of the nation's economic policy made the fundamental shift from resurrecting a damaged economy to maintaining and promoting the growth of an increasingly functional one.[20]

Few individuals played a more influential role in the rise of economic growth on the liberal and broader national agenda in the postwar years than Keyserling. He was a highly visible member of the three-person CEA, and his hand in the council's 1949 report ensured that the document amounted to a declaration of the principles that guided his belief in the social and political potential offered by a growing American economy. Reflecting Keyserling's trademark forcefulness, the report framed growth not merely as one fundamental economic goal among others but as an aim that could be seen as the new organizing principle for the American postwar political economy. Keyserling's aggressive, forward-looking economic outlook found a ready audience among liberals. When Edwin Nourse resigned his position as the first chairman of the CEA in October 1949, liberals rallied around Keyserling as their candidate for the post.[21]

With his appointment as chair of the CEA by Truman in the spring of 1950, Keyserling made use of the council as a commanding pulpit from which to press the importance and potential of economic growth on the nation's political thinkers and leaders. During his second term, Truman—the president who had previously been a target of liberal derision and disappointment—increasingly adopted Keyserling's outlook and rhetoric. As mobilization for the Korean War gained steam, the Truman administration embraced Keyserling's expansionary economics and the country produced the rapid economic growth the CEA chair had been advocating. Economic growth greatly buoyed Truman's support among liberals, but its impact would not be confined to the liberal end of the political spectrum. With an increase in the nation's gross national product from $285 billion in 1948 to $350 billion in 1952, the administration demonstrated economic results that firmly established the power and potential of the American economy in the minds of liberals and conservatives alike.[22]

Unlike many conservatives, however, the bulk of liberals looked to economic growth not simply as a source of business profits but as an essential instrument of social progress that provided the foundation for a rising tide of mass material prosperity. Describing the commonly accepted ideas or "conventional wisdom" of the postwar era in his influential 1958 classic *The Affluent Society*, Galbraith noted that the great progress recently experienced in the material well-being of the average American citizen had come not from a redistribution of income but from the tremendous economic growth of the preceding decades. With acute awareness among liberals of that fact, the goal of an expanding economy became fundamental to the conventional wisdom of American liberalism. According to Galbraith, equality, security, and the other, more traditional concerns of economics had given way to a preoccupation with production and the need for its continual increase. Seen as the means to defuse tensions once associated with inequality and the solution to privations previously associated with economic insecurity, concern for production paradoxically grew in tandem with the continued growth of production. As the historian Robert Collins argues, economic growth provided what many in the United States saw as the means for the nation to "square the circle and reconcile its love of liberty with its egalitarian pretensions." With production stimulated by the government's successful application of Keynesian economic principles resulting in reduced unemployment and higher living standards, the aim of economic growth became, in Galbraith's words, the liberal's "program, and it established something akin to a monopoly over his mind."[23]

When Keyserling joined the ADA in 1953 following Dwight D. Eisenhower's election and the economist's departure from the CEA, his influence ensured that the economic perspective of the organization differed from the liberal consensus sketched by Galbraith only in its even more fervent belief in the far-reaching potential of economic growth. From its earliest years, before Keyserling joined the organization, the economic policy resolutions of the ADA stressed the importance of economic growth. Recession under Eisenhower's economic stewardship and the heavy hand of Keyserling in the drafting of the organization's economic policy, however, ushered in a marked shift in emphasis toward the seemingly limitless benefits to be found in growth. Economic policy resolutions passed in the years after the ADA's founding in 1947 reflected a quiet assumption as to the importance of economic growth but expressed more concern with preventing a postwar depression than optimism about the broad potential of what growth could achieve. The organization's 1950 economic policy resolution warned that the continuation of full production and full employment should not be taken for granted and would require vigilant action and cooperation from government, business, and labor. With attention to economic growth as a means of averting depression, the resolution declared: "Depression and mass unemployment bring serious denials of personal freedom. Government action to assure an expanding and fully employed economy . . . is a prerequisite to the preservation of maximum personal freedom."[24]

Within his first year of involvement in the ADA, Keyserling made his mark on the economic policy of the organization with the passage of resolutions reflecting a confident passion for economic growth that would define ADA economic rhetoric well into the 1960s. As the largely stable economic expansion of the postwar years displaced memories of the Great Depression, concerns in the ADA shifted from the return of depression to the potential gains lost during recession. The Eisenhower administration's nominal embrace of government responsibility for fostering economic growth and employment coupled with the post–Korean War recession provided an opening for Keyserling. He took advantage of that opportunity to guide the ADA's economic policy away from the defensive posture of its early years toward a confident assertion of the benefits to be achieved through economic growth and the opportunities to be missed through its absence.

The ADA's 1954 economic policy resolution condemned the complacency of the Eisenhower administration for asserting that the American people should be satisfied if the economy remained at its current level of output or did not fall more than 5 percent below its existing level. Merely maintaining existing levels of production over the coming year, the resolution insisted, would mean millions more unemployed and billions of dollars needlessly added to the federal deficit. Worse yet for the long-term outlook on employment, the federal budget, and the broad array of unmet social needs in the country would be the lost years of potential growth that could never be reclaimed. According to the resolution, "This waste of potential plenty is our great and true national economic deficit."[25]

By contrasting its deep belief in the potential for social progress to be found in economic growth with the conservative budget balancing and complacency of the Eisenhower administration, the ADA gave shape to the perspective that would suffuse its economic policy resolutions over the coming decade. With words that would make their way into the organization's economic policy statements for years to come, the 1954 resolution declared:

"We subscribe to the concept of full employment in an expanding economy as the cornerstone of American economic policy. With continuous full employment, we can year by year gain mightily in domestic strength and world security. Without full employment, we can only lose ground and court disaster." The economic growth sustained by full employment, the resolution estimated, would raise the gross national product from the 1954 level of $365 billion to $500 billion by 1960. Offering an alluring picture of what that growth could mean for liberal objectives, the resolution highlighted as tangible benefits 10 million additional jobs, significant reductions in poverty levels, much-needed expansion of welfare services, and an increase in the American standard of living of at least 25 percent. Furthermore, the resolution claimed that if a level of economic growth clearly within the capabilities of the US economy were maintained, all of these advances could be achieved without increased taxation and with a balanced budget.[26]

For the ADA, economic growth would also be essential to the military outlays deemed necessary to the protection of US interests and security in the Cold War. According to the resolution, the growth of a fully employed US economy would provide "the economic strength to carry forward whatever economic and military programs conform best to our needs at home and to our participation in the joint efforts of the free world." In response to the Eisenhower administration's incipient pivot away from the large military expenditures of the Truman administration, the resolution condemned "any withdrawal from our world responsibilities in the mistaken notion that our economy cannot bear the essential security programs which it has already demonstrated its capacity to support." When the Eisenhower administration put forward its budget-conscious "New Look" foreign policy the following year, the ADA responded with a strong repudiation of its overreliance on nuclear weapons for security. The ADA's 1955 economic policy resolution maintained that military weakness invites aggression and looked to economic growth as a means of maintaining the large-scale conventional military forces necessary for flexible responses to the demands placed on American foreign policy in the Cold War.[27]

In his 1956 "national prosperity budget," Keyserling further developed the confident belief in growth as a means for progress at home and abroad that he had instilled in the ADA's economy policy over the preceding years. Taking great care to distinguish it from the centralized five-year economic plans of the Soviet Union, Keyserling framed his budget as a starting point for a national discussion through which the American people would decide how best to meet the opportunities and responsibilities of a growing economy. In regard to the latter, he saw the strength of the US economy not as a reward or an end but as a challenge and a means by which American society could proceed toward widespread prosperity and justice. Granting that economic growth does not automatically result in progress against deprivation and injustice, Keyserling's budget made abundantly clear that a context of economic stability and growth contributed greatly to solving those ills. Accordingly, he insisted on the vital responsibility of the federal government to maintain growth, arguing that "both our world security and our domestic well-being demand that we build this [economic] strength to the optimum limits of our technology and brains, instead of being content with the 'satisfactory' growth rates of the distant past." Stressing the grave responsibilities but not overlooking the far-reaching opportunities of economic growth, Keyserling boldly declared, "There is almost nothing within reason that the American economy cannot accomplish" with awareness "of the urgency but even more of the promise of our times."[28]

DEMOCRATIC DEFEAT AND THE BIRTH OF QUALITATIVE LIBERALISM

The Eisenhower victory that in 1952 led Keyserling and the ADA to push for more of the same in the form of a more vigorous and comprehensive program for growth liberalism prompted a period of deep introspection among others in the organization. With Eisenhower's landslide win over Adlai Stevenson and the capture of both houses of Congress by Republicans, some in the ADA began to wonder if the economic program of the New Deal and Fair Deal had run dry politically. In the wake of the stinging electoral defeat, Schlesinger wrote an article for *The Reporter* that touched off a far-reaching debate on the implications of the election and helped initiate the crackup of the growth consensus that pervaded the postwar political landscape. In his article, Schlesinger characterized the New Deal and Fair Deal as victims of their own success. According to the Harvard historian, the New Deal reforms that sustained the domestic programs of Roosevelt and Truman had been put in place to respond to the desperate national needs of the time, had largely succeeded in meeting those needs, and had since become such an integral element of the political landscape that Republicans were unable or unwilling to dismantle them. With general Republican acquiescence to New Deal reforms, liberal Democrats faced increasing difficulty in trying to portray those initiatives as live political issues. Liberal leaders, Schlesinger insisted, "expended their energy in summoning the American people to ancient crusades, in sounding the bugle for wars won and forgotten."[29]

For Schlesinger, the revolt of the suburbs and the widespread prosperity that suburbia represented were fundamental to understanding the Democratic defeat. Prosperity, Schlesinger suspected, had cost the Democrats more Catholic votes than Joseph McCarthy. In Schlesinger's estimation, years of full employment and increases in the American standard of living had allowed millions of immigrants and their offspring to move from the cities into the suburbs, abandon tenements for bungalows, and buy new automobiles. Having been enabled by the economic reforms of preceding Democratic administrations to, in Schlesinger's words, "live like Republicans, the new suburbanites ended up by voting like Republicans." In contrast to Democratic leaders who shaped campaign rhetoric around the narrative of prosperity versus depression, he recognized that the suburbs and the new generation of voters increasingly populating them would not be drawn to a Democratic Party bent on reiterating the issues that had won elections in the 1930s. Uncertain as to what new issues and programs might provide liberal Democrats with a road back from the political wilderness, Schlesinger nevertheless remained certain that it was only as liberalism "expresses the possibilities of the future—and not as it revives the memories of the past—that it can once again recover its central place in American life."[30]

Schlesinger may have been unsure as to where the issues that would define the discourse and future possibilities of American politics would come from, but Leon Keyserling remained firmly convinced that they would be found in the realm of economics. Offering his own response to the Democratic defeat of 1952 in a privately circulated memorandum to liberal, labor, and Democratic leaders, Keyserling called not for Democrats to turn their focus away from economic issues but for them to retool the party's economic platform for the challenges and opportunities of American prosperity in the 1950s. Like Schlesinger, Keyserling highlighted the failure of New Deal reforms to inspire votes in the recent election. The New Deal package, he acknowledged, "may contain ingredients which are out of date" and suffered from a "depression 'hangover.'" As he had in his shaping of ADA economic policy, Keyserling urged liberals to turn their attention from the possibility of depression to the prospects for economic growth. According to Keyserling, "the most salient fact of American life today is not that we are in danger of losing what we have, but that we have only commenced to realize the full promise of America." Accordingly, he called on liberals to popularize a program of economic growth in specific quantitative terms that would lift the total output of the American economy by more than $100 billion within the next decade. This expansion, Keyserling contended, would make possible much-needed improvements in Social Security, health services, education, and the American standard of living. From Keyserling's perspective, the American people were prosperous only in contrast to their earlier condition; "they by no means have reached the frontiers of prosperity when measured against what we can achieve."[31]

While Schlesinger and Keyserling differed in their certitude and interpretation of the underlying causes of Democratic failure in the 1952 election, both approached the task of redeveloping the liberal program with a clear sense of political pragmatism. Writing to Keyserling in response to his memorandum, Schlesinger expressed considerable skepticism toward his fundamentally economic approach. Short of a severe recession or outright depression, Schlesinger doubted the potential for prosperity and economic security issues to draw enthusiasm from the American electorate. He suspected that for "people who are already enjoying a full meal," the economic proposals outlined by Keyserling would have a "pie-in-the sky air." Responding to Schlesinger's charge, Keyserling insisted that he was alert to the question whether a prosperous people would be moved by still greater prosperity but would not accept "the proposition that the American people, because they are now well fed, have become contented cows." For Keyserling, the tendency to "think of the people as being well fed, while tending to forget how many are not well fed and how many would like to be better fed," provided evidence of a loss of dynamism in the liberal perspective.[32]

Schlesinger's response to Keyserling confirmed the growing gulf between their political perspectives and indicated the Harvard historian's desire to develop and accentuate a non-material foundation for a liberalism geared to the needs of the age of abundance. With an acute concern for the electoral viability of liberalism, Schlesinger did not discount the continued existence of poverty but considered the poor a shrinking minority in a growing sea of American prosperity. Displaying his belief that the expanding ranks of affluent suburbanites were increasingly replacing the unemployed and the working class as the constituency most essential to Democrats, he remained unconvinced that Keyserling's economic program by itself could meet the political needs of liberals in the 1950s. That was not because the American people were becoming "contented cows" but "because in a state of full employment, they will tend to prefer the most painless route to even greater opportunity—and thus will tend to be seduced by the Republican promises." Schlesinger was not opposed to the further development of liberal economic policies, but he felt that political prospects on that front would be limited and stressed the need to develop a political vision that tapped "some new form of political and moral resources."[33]

The desire to draw on new political and moral resources needed for liberal political viability would lead Schlesinger to sketch the contours of what he and other liberal thinkers termed "qualitative liberalism." Touching off a firestorm of debate, Schlesinger developed the themes of qualitative liberalism in a privately circulated memorandum as he began to provide answers to the probing questions he first posed in the wake of the Democratic defeat in 1952. With an eye to the upcoming 1956 presidential election, Schlesinger further developed the ideas expressed in his memorandum with a widely read and influential article for *The Reporter*. In it he gave shape to qualitative liberalism by distinguishing it from "quantitative liberalism" and its essential concerns of economic recovery, mass living standards, minimum wages, Social Security payments, and the myriad of other material challenges to subsistence and survival. Believing that quantitative liberalism had been, on the whole, a "brilliant success," Schlesinger offered the provocative assessment that "instead of talking as if the necessities of living—a job, a square meal, a suit of clothes, and a roof—where still at stake, we should be able to count that fight won and move on to the more subtle and complicated problem of fighting for individual dignity, identity, and fulfillment in a mass society."[34]

To face those challenges, Schlesinger called for a new liberalism attuned to the miseries produced by the age of abundance. He tempered an otherwise blunt assessment of American material security with recognition of the continued existence of poverty and the firm belief that the new liberalism would not repudiate quantitative liberalism but would rather absorb and build on its achievements in approaching the new qualitative issues of a prosperous mass society. With the old liberalism as its foundation, Schlesinger looked to a new liberalism that addressed the qualitative challenges faced by

American society as the means to liberal and Democratic electoral redemption. Whereas the quantitative liberalism that came of age in the Great Depression concerned itself with the struggle to secure the economic basis of life, the qualitative liberalism of the age of abundance would be dedicated to bettering the quality of life.[35]

Rooted not in the more easily measured and articulated economic concerns that had long been essential to liberals but rather in a slippery and often subjective notion of "quality," qualitative liberalism proved difficult to define in concrete terms. Schlesinger exhibited considerable vagueness in his first article on the topic and others that would follow as he grappled with the difficulties inherent in outlining qualitative liberalism in terms of tangible issues and programs. Still, with an insistence on prioritizing shared quality of life over economic growth as his starting point, he highlighted the need for improved education and medical services, more equal opportunities for minorities, better mass media and popular culture, and more deliberate urban planning as some of the issues the new liberalism would need to address itself to. Evoking a theme that would be developed further by Galbraith in *The Affluent Society*, Schlesinger lamented a nation that was growing ever richer yet devoted a decreasing share of its riches to the public welfare. When the country allowed "the production of consumer goods for the sake of profit [to] achieve a sort of moral priority in our culture," he believed the consequences were visible to all as "our schools become more crowded and dilapidated, our teachers more weary and underpaid . . . our cities dirtier, our roads more teeming and filthy, our national parks more unkempt."[36]

Written in a period defined by general liberal agreement on the transcendent importance of economic growth, Schlesinger's plea for a redefinition of the aims and outlook of liberalism produced seemingly contradictory responses from liberals who professed their general agreement with the Harvard historian despite their fundamental criticisms. The economist Seymour Harris, a fellow member of the ADA, counted himself an avid supporter of his Harvard colleague's new liberal vision but remained skeptical that the age of abundance on which it was based would continue indefinitely.[37] While Keyserling insisted that he agreed with the "general trend" of Schlesinger's outlook, he rejected its fundamental distinction between quantitative and qualitative liberalism as neither "comprehensive [*sic*] to the average citizen or correct in substance." According to Keyserling,

"Effective liberalism, in a free society, does not change its basic characteristics every decade or two." He did not doubt that the quality-of-life issues highlighted by Schlesinger were new and different from the issues that had grabbed liberal attention a generation earlier but maintained that when ultimately discussed in terms of actual programs, they were no less quantitative than those of the New Deal. Improving the quality of education, for instance, would require defining the number of additional schools needed, budgeting the dollars required to build them, and generating the political will needed to allocate the necessary "quantitative" resources. Keyserling took Schlesinger's reliance on citing figures as soon as he began articulating the "new" liberal issues as the clearest evidence of the inherently quantitative basis of "qualitative" liberalism.[38]

Keyserling's insistence on the innately economic nature of qualitative liberalism foreshadowed later developments and debates surrounding the reorientation of liberalism and the Democratic Party in the late twentieth century. Historians such as Lily Geismer have argued against the widespread notion that during the waning decades of the twentieth century, liberals and Democrats turned away from economic matters in order to prioritize "post-economic issues" such as race, gender, foreign policy, and the environment. Instead, liberalism and the Democratic Party came to reflect the material concerns of suburban white-collar workers rather than those of the blue-collar workers who had been the core of the New Deal coalition.[39] Similarly, the qualitative priorities outlined by Schlesinger were not any less economic in terms of how their costs and potential benefits would be calculated than Social Security, the minimum wage, and the other initiatives that defined the "bread-and-butter" orientation of the New Deal. In terms of its economics, Schlesinger's qualitative liberalism reflected the material concerns and interests of the suburbs that were just beginning to challenge the union hall as liberalism's center of gravity. Still—as even Keyserling conceded—it would be a mistake to assume that Schlesinger's vision for a liberalism geared toward the quality-of-life issues of an age of abundance did not represent a significant and new departure in liberal politics. The seemingly permanent economic growth of the postwar era allowed liberals like Schlesinger to take growth for granted and emphasize the need for liberalism to concern itself not only with the pocketbook of the American citizen but also with the potential for cultural, moral, or spiritual development in a society of unrelenting conformity. While it would later become a polarizing source of division among liberals, the Cold War initially proved critical to making room in American liberalism for those far-reaching aims.

QUALITATIVE LIBERALISM AND THE COLD WAR

When Galbraith reflected on *The Affluent Society* in the preface to a later edition of the book, he revealed that prior to publication he had held no high expectations for its reception. He feared that the book would be dismissed by the politically concerned public "as another semi-socialist case for public spending" and by his Keynesian friends as "apostasy." When the Soviet Union launched the first Sputnik in the autumn of 1957, Galbraith no longer harbored such concerns; he knew his book "was home."[40] Demonstrating Soviet scientific and engineering advances as well as military potential, the launch of Sputnik dramatically called into question existing American values, priorities, and sense of national purpose. For many in the ADA and much of the American public, the demands of the Cold War—markedly heightened in the post-Sputnik era—provided the most visible and convincing examples of the consequences that resulted from the country's excessive focus on consumer goods and myopic commitment to economic growth. As they worked to develop a qualitative liberalism rooted in the search for a greater national purpose than economic growth amid tense competition between the world's two superpowers, Galbraith and Schlesinger found the Cold War interests of the United States to be a natural source of inspiration for that search. Still, as much as Galbraith, Schlesinger, and other ADA liberals perceived the Cold War as a valuable means of advancing the public expenditures they desired, they did not see it simply as a matter of political expediency. Their appeals to the importance of strengthening the standing of the United States in its power contest with the Soviet Union also reflected a genuine commitment to waging the Cold War that stood in stark contrast with the foreign policy outlook they would adopt less than a decade later.

While some historians have interpreted the qualitative liberalism of Galbraith and Schlesinger as reflecting the belief that the death of Joseph Stalin meant that the contest for military superiority with the Soviet Union could be given a lower priority, the new liberal vision they developed owed much to a desire to engage the Cold War more vigorously on all fronts, including the balance of military power between the world's superpowers.[41] As they contributed to the search for a new national purpose that gained momentum in the prosperous postwar years, Galbraith and Schlesinger advanced a twofold argument for more dynamic American commitment to the challenges presented by the Cold War. First, as a starting point, they urged greater allocation of resources for the military as they highlighted the dangers of President Eisenhower's "New Look" foreign policy. Providing the necessary resources for the military would require a reorientation in priority from production of consumer goods to production of the military equipment needed to keep parity with—or surpass—the Soviet Union. Second, Galbraith and Schlesinger looked to qualitative liberalism and the search for a new national purpose as the means to once again make the United States an inspiring model for the many nations uncommitted or wavering in a world then seemingly defined by binary Cold War competition. Drawing on Galbraith and Schlesinger, Adlai Stevenson famously asked, "With the supermarket as our temple and the singing commercial as our litany, are we likely to fire the world with an irresistible vision of America's exalted purposes and inspiring way of life?"[42] For the ADA's two leading advocates of qualitative liberalism, the quality-of-life issues produced by the age of abundance would be a guiding light for addressing the concerns raised by Stevenson's probing rhetorical question.

The excessive preoccupation with consumer goods that Galbraith and Schlesinger saw during the Eisenhower era also represented for them a clear detriment to the military demands placed on the United States by the Cold War. Galbraith, Schlesinger, the ADA, and a great many liberals in the 1950s vocally and repeatedly raised their concerns with the dearth of foreign policy options left to the United States as a result of the Eisenhower administration's desire to wage the Cold War on the cheap. Schlesinger believed that military power became a controlling factor in the formulation of foreign policy not when there was too much of it but when there was too little. Highlighting the lack of flexibility produced by Eisenhower's nuclear-reliant "New Look" foreign policy, he remarked that the policy "gives us the choice between making faces at the enemy and blowing up the world."[43] For Schlesinger, it was that tense Cold War context and the failings of the Eisenhower administration that raised the stakes involved in the search for a new national purpose. By making that search a necessary element of the Cold War, Schlesinger's initiative became more readily defensible against charges that his critique of the mass consumption economy simply represented disdain for what he and other elites saw as the crass materialism of the masses. Reflecting both a desire to fend off such charges of elitism and a genuine response to the realities of the Cold War, Schlesinger insisted that the world struggle with the Soviet Union rendered the need for a new conviction of national purpose not a "matter of taste but a matter of desperate necessity."[44]

Galbraith's and Schlesinger's critique of the "New Look" foreign policy shared the insistence of the later-released National Security Council Report 68 (NSC-68) on the vital necessity and economic feasibility of a massive defense establishment to counter Soviet power, but diverged from the outlook of that document by questioning the utility of economic growth for military production. The classified NSC-68 and the policies of the Truman administration both prioritized economic growth as a means of providing the funds required for massive rearmament and a vast expansion of the nation's global security responsibilities.[45] In contrast, Galbraith saw belief in the direct correlation between national military power and economic growth as a pervasive but ultimately dangerous illusion. Putting himself at odds with the "conventional wisdom" that had coalesced in the years since World War II, in *The Affluent Society* Galbraith stressed usable military production rather than gross economic output as the factor that would determine American military might in the Cold War.[46]

Galbraith's criticism of economic growth as a measure of military potential rested not on an opposition to economic growth in its own right but on an objection to the nature of the growth that existed in the United States. The size of the American economy increased, he noted, by increasing the demand for what it produced. Since consumer goods constituted the bulk of the nation's production, economic growth fundamentally depended on increasing the public's desire for those consumer goods. Galbraith saw the widespread belief in the direct relationship between economic growth and actual or potential military power to be founded on a faulty and uncritical assumption. This assumption held that in the event of an emergency, consumer wants could be swiftly suppressed with little trouble, and the production that had fulfilled those desires would be made readily available for the military production demanded by the situation. In Galbraith's estimation, a society that achieves economic growth by expanding consumer wants will never have a significant margin available beyond its seeming needs. He convincingly observed that a society which, during times of peace, ascribes to the satisfaction of consumer wants a transcendent importance and teaches its people that meeting those desires is vital to survival and basic happiness would not be able to "divest itself of those attitudes as simply and naturally as a man removes his nightshirt on arising." With the understanding that needs carefully nurtured through commercial advertising and political pressure would not be easily forgotten, Galbraith saw the nation's economic growth—sustained as it was by the production of consumer goods—not only as offering a poor indicator of potential military power but also as jeopardizing US security interests in the Cold War.[47]

Schlesinger, like Galbraith, highlighted the inherent dangers of the American consumer goods economy to the military position of the United States in the Cold War. Channeling a national anxiety that lingered for some years after the launch of Sputnik, Schlesinger lamented that the Soviet Union, with a gross national product just 45 percent that of the United States, nevertheless maintained parity with American education and defense expenditures. By spending more than twice as large a proportion of its gross national product on education and defense, the Soviet Union trained the physicists and engineers who he believed had allowed it to take the lead in the production of intercontinental ballistic missiles and the contest for space.[48] While the so-called "missile gap" is now known to have been nonexistent, the significance of this seeming failure of the United States to keep up with the Soviet Union in the production of nuclear missiles was a major source of anxiety for Schlesinger.[49] For the historian and his many colleagues in the ADA who shared his concern over the "missile gap," the military demands of the Cold War remained real and pressing. The reason for the supposed gap, he contended, was not that the United States could not afford to keep up with the Soviet Union but rather its detrimental prioritization of private interests over the public interest. Striking a hawkish tone distinctly at odds with the foreign policy outlook he would assume in coming years, Schlesinger maintained that when "the production and consumption of consumers' goods is regarded as the be-all and end-all of existence, the public sector—from schools to missiles—is systematically starved."[50]

While Galbraith and Schlesinger remained fully committed to maintaining the military power they deemed necessary to protect US interests in the Cold War, they did not limit their understanding of the global struggle with the Soviet Union to military matters. As founding members of the Congress for Cultural Freedom (CCF), they were acutely attuned to the dynamics of the "Cultural Cold War" and believed strongly in the importance of the

United States establishing itself as a positive and inspiring model of democratic freedom for intellectuals and nations across the world. The primary mission of the CCF in the years after its founding in 1950 involved organizing non-communist left intellectuals from the United States and Europe with the aim of drawing on their cultural influence to sway the intelligentsia of western Europe away from its lingering sympathies with communism. While it would be revealed in 1967 that the CCF had received the majority of its funding from the Central Intelligence Agency and had undoubtedly been influenced to some degree by the interests of its principal sponsor, the organization nevertheless expressed the genuine belief of many of its participants that American-style democracy and liberalism could be compelling to European intellectuals.[51] The effort to reach out to left-leaning European intellectuals who remained unconvinced by either Soviet communism or American capitalist democracy would not be helped by the materialistic consumer culture that permeated the political and social landscape of the United States. Active involvement in the Paris-based CCF instilled in Galbraith and Schlesinger a sensitivity to how non-Americans perceived American culture and the effect that projections of crass materialism could have on those perceptions.

The Cold War context of the cultural sensibility that Galbraith and Schlesinger brought from the CCF to their critique of American consumer culture and popular culture helped to defend against charges that they were simply expressing subjective snobbery. Galbraith and Schlesinger were not alone among American intellectuals who found the Cold War an effective medium through which to advance cultural and social criticisms that would otherwise have had limited influence. When Vice President Richard Nixon bluntly equated kitchen appliances with freedom during his famous 1959 "Kitchen Debate" with Soviet premier Nikita Khrushchev, many American intellectuals found a ready audience for their probing critiques of the alarmingly narrow vision of American freedom being broadcast to the world.[52] Before the Kitchen Debate put the issues of consumer politics before an international audience, Galbraith found the Cold War a valuable arena for articulating cultural and social criticisms that he would have held to be true regardless of the struggle between the world's superpowers. Still, the context of a Cold War struggle that pitted the American and Soviet ideologies against each other magnified the meaning of those criticisms and demonstrated Galbraith's genuine concern that a shallow and materialistic conception of American democracy would serve as a poor source of inspiration for the world. Projecting his conviction that the United States had more to offer the world than dishwashers and clothes dryers, he charged that those who identified freedom "with the greatest possible range of choice of consumers' goods are only confessing their exceedingly simple-minded and mechanical view of man and his liberties." Galbraith believed that the United States stood its best chance of success in the Cultural Cold War not by adhering to a "supermarket theory of liberty" but through a revitalization of American culture, society, and politics that would reveal the true potential of its system to the world.[53]

Schlesinger, like Galbraith, saw the state of American society as an integral element of US foreign policy. Despite accusations from liberals such as Max Ascoli and Leon Keyserling that his views smacked of isolationism, he remained firm in his insistence on the direct relationship between conditions at home and influence abroad. Burnishing his internationalist credentials in response to such criticism, Schlesinger highlighted the prioritization of private wants as one of the greatest impediments to the projection of American power—both hard and soft—in the Cold War. While Americans "overstuffed" themselves as individuals, Schlesinger opined, the public sector needs that were so vital in the context of the Cold War were going unmet. Schlesinger firmly believed that the existing prioritization of private wants over public needs would have to be corrected if the United States were to compete with communism. He maintained that Americans "cannot convincingly champion free opportunity and civilized values abroad when too many of our own people linger at home in economic want and cultural mediocrity." Advances in American society and culture would, in his opinion, generate an enthusiasm across the world with untold benefits for the position of the United States in the Cold War. Indeed, "nothing would go farther to restore world confidence in American leadership and purpose than a resumption of forward motion in our own society."[54]

The search urged by Galbraith and Schlesinger for a national purpose greater than economic growth proved highly responsive to the times. In the 1950s and early 1960s, the Cold War provided a ready justification and vital source of energy for that search. Their pursuit of a higher national purpose, however, was not intrinsically limited to the Cold War and would later find outlets in other fields of American life. As Galbraith and Schlesinger, along with their political descendants in the New Politics movement, continued the search for a greater national purpose in the latter half of the 1960s, the civil rights movement, opposition to the Vietnam War, and the development of a more participatory political system sustained the pursuit in much the same way that the Cold War had a decade earlier. Just as the Cold War had provided Galbraith and Schlesinger with a compelling defense against charges that their critique of consumer culture reflected a desire to impose their elite views on American society, the major goals of the New Politics movement allowed its advocates to imbue their quest for a higher national purpose with a broad sense of meaning and necessity. While the search for a new American purpose in the post-scarcity era would later lead New Politics activists and the bulk of ADA liberals to reject many of the dogmas of the Cold War, the origins of that search owed much to the concerns that defined the global power struggle between the United States and the Soviet Union.

SPIRITUAL UNEMPLOYMENT

Reflecting on the pervasive conformity and dwindling idealism that accompanied growing prosperity in the 1950s, Schlesinger declared at the close of the decade that "spiritual unemployment can be as powerful a motive for change as economic unemployment."[55] Schlesinger's secular perspective meant that his notion of "spiritual unemployment" entailed no specifically religious or theological concerns but did express his understanding of the failure of consumer abundance to alleviate the mounting non-material discontents of American society. He saw the growing "homogenization" of society as a major source of the cultural, moral, and psychological anxieties that increasingly plagued the nation. Foreshadowing the New Left, which would come to prominence during the following decade, Schlesinger dreaded the growing reality of a society in which people watched the same television shows, listened to the same singing commercials, and bought the same consumer products. Yet he also saw the development as a challenge that could serve as a source of revitalization for liberalism. Diverging from the class- and labor-based traditions that had long sustained liberalism, he called on liberals to see "that the present enemy is not a conspiracy of wealth seeking to grind the faces of the poor, but a conspiracy of blandness, seeking to bury all tension and conflict in American life under a mess of platitude and piety—not the hard-faced men, but the faceless men." The most urgent task for liberalism, according to Schlesinger, would be to develop the social and political means to provide the nation with "the benefits of a mass economy without the cost of a mass culture."[56]

Engagement with the threat of totalitarianism profoundly shaped how Galbraith and Schlesinger viewed the consequences of mass popular culture for the autonomy of individual Americans and the vitality of American society. The rise of totalitarian regimes in Europe during the 1930s and 1940s provided them and many other liberal intellectuals of their generation with a distinct awareness of the dangerous potential for mass media and culture to isolate individuals from one another, mold them into a uniform audience, and manipulate that audience through propaganda.[57] The active involvement of Galbraith and Schlesinger in the CCF during the 1950s further heightened their sensitivity to totalitarian manipulation of the masses. Created to repudiate and oppose totalitarianism of both the left and the right, the CCF provided an institutional outlet for European intellectuals who had directly experienced repression under communist rule and fascism. The experience of working with prominent European intellectuals such as Raymond Aron and Ignazio Silone under the auspices of the CCF instilled in Galbraith and Schlesinger a vivid appreciation for intellectual freedom and autonomy.[58]

While the perspective of Galbraith and Schlesinger on the dangers of mass culture grew out of their secondhand experiences with totalitarianism, neither thought American society faced a genuine internal totalitarian threat. They believed that the primary danger was to be found not in the prospect of America's becoming totalitarian but rather in a consumer culture that developed and encouraged conformity. Schlesinger saw in "the pursuit of spiritual cure-alls, in the obsession with gadgets, in apathy and in boredom" a threat to the national instincts that sustained individual autonomy in American society. The danger to individual autonomy would not be addressed simply by maintaining legal protections for intellectual and cultural freedom. The real challenge, he maintained, was not just to bring about a society in which people can speak their minds but to bring about a society in which they want to speak their minds and have something to say. Schlesinger believed that McCarthyism had confused the nation about the real threat to intellectual freedom. For Schlesinger, conformity was "the greater danger not when it is coerced but when it is sought—when any deviation from what sociologists call the peer-group fills the individual with anxiety and guilt."[59] In his estimation, the potential for this willful drive toward conformity would become more acute if the American people in an age of growing opportunity for leisure sought distraction through a mass media that rendered them increasingly indistinguishable from one another.[60]

Expressing similar concerns with the harmful potential of conformity, Galbraith saw the dangers of mass culture as deeply intertwined with the incessant demand for ever-increasing production. In *The Affluent Society*, he advanced a probing critique of the ways in which businesses manufactured consumer demand for their goods and services to sustain otherwise seemingly unnecessary increases in production. In an age of abundance, he contended, desire for the fruits of increased production did not arise from spontaneous consumer need. Rather, consumer wants had become a servant to the process of production. Galbraith made clear his considerable misgivings with an arrangement in which a near universal insistence on continued increases in production demanded that consumer wants "be effectively contrived" through "the forces of modern salesmanship" wielding the power of mass culture.[61]

Although Galbraith and Schlesinger often articulated their criticism of a mass culture defined by commercial interests as a detriment to the US position in the Cultural Cold War, they strongly believed that this trend represented a source of concern in its own right. When detached from the imperatives of advancing American Cold War interests, however, criticism of mass consumer culture in the United States faced a much higher level of scrutiny and required far greater efforts of justification. For Schlesinger there was the heightened difficulty of justifying his critical perspective on consumerism apart from the demands of the Cold War by planting the seemingly new social and cultural concerns of qualitative liberalism firmly within the liberal tradition. He looked to the deeper roots of an expansive liberal tradition that stretched far beyond the bread-and-butter perspective that sustained the New Deal and Fair Deal to demonstrate the historical basis for treating the quality of American culture and society as a decidedly political issue and a legitimate object of liberal concern. Putting forward his understanding that American liberalism had sprung from two main sources, Schlesinger insisted that the "vindication of the individual against moral and spiritual frustration" represented a traditional wellspring of liberalism just as much as the "vindication of the individual against economic privation and despair."[62]

Schlesinger sought to further establish the liberal legitimacy of the social and cultural issues that he believed would define liberalism in the age of abundance by insisting that the predominantly economic outlook of the New Deal and Fair Deal represented a greater aberration from the main current of the liberal tradition than the perspective of qualitative liberalism. In the series of articles in which he sketched the contours of qualitative liberalism, Schlesinger reminded his readers that despite the immediacy of the Great Depression and the New Deal, the struggle against economic depression had not long been the central issue of traditional American liberalism. Illustrating the point, he contended that while economic depression had produced the New Deal, it was not the impetus for "the ages of Jefferson or Jackson or Lincoln or Theodore Roosevelt or Wilson." Rather, the central concern of liberalism throughout American history had been the status and development of individual freedom and autonomy in a mass society. With the understanding that this concern was not only political and economic but also moral and cultural, Schlesinger insisted that Walt Whitman, Ralph Waldo Emerson, Henry David Thoreau, and Herman Melville be seen as embodiments of the liberal tradition just as much as Thomas Jefferson and Andrew Jackson.[63] Schlesinger hoped that through highlighting the historical roots of liberal concern with non-material issues, qualitative liberalism would be seen not as a departure from the liberal tradition but as a return to its deeper essence.

Schlesinger's call for a liberalism attuned to the less tangible needs of the post-scarcity era sparked significant debate and attracted considerable criticism from fellow liberals who took issue with what they rightly saw as the Harvard historian's complacency about economic deprivation. The criticism drawn by Schlesinger's assertion of the pressing importance of the moral, social, and cultural dimensions of liberalism in an age of abundance conveys the significant difficulties to be found in justifying the non-material concerns of liberalism in isolation from the demands of the Cold War. As the leading voice of such criticism, Keyserling expressed little patience with Schlesinger's claim that "the economic problem at home seems to be fixed up for the moment." For Keyserling, the urgent and essential task for liberals continued to be improvement of the material well-being necessary to sustain the genuine freedom of individuals. In contrast to Schlesinger, he saw this economic task as having been the central concern of the American liberal tradition. While Schlesinger maintained that economic circumstances had not been the driving factor behind Jeffersonian democracy, Jacksonian democracy, the antislavery movement, or the Progressive movement, Keyserling believed that these movements "were directed toward the improvement of the relative and absolute economic and social status of the common man; they were not interested in what he read." By making light of the elitist and subjective overtones he sensed in Schlesinger's political perspective, Keyserling sought to place cultural matters beyond the remit of liberal politics. Unlike Schlesinger, Keyserling "would let each citizen decide for himself whether he prefers Melville to Mary Roberts Rinehart, or whether he would rather listen to the Fifth Symphony than Elvis Presley."[64]

The relative complacency of Schlesinger on economic issues in contrast to his pressing concern with mass culture as a political issue, however, ran fully in line with the central intellectual currents of the time. Sales of over fifty thousand hardcover copies of *The Affluent Society*, hundreds of thousands of copies of David Riesman's *The Lonely Crowd* and William Whyte's *The Organization Man* in paperback, *Dr. Zhivago*'s place atop the best-seller list, the boom in popularity of religious figures such as Billy Graham, and the rise of the Beat Generation all represented for Schlesinger "the desire for reappraisal, the groping for something better." These examples of discontent, he believed, marked a turn from the stagnation of the Eisenhower era that would provide a much-needed source for liberal Democratic electoral redemption and a renewed sense of national purpose.[65]

Schlesinger also came to the conviction that the lethargy of the Eisenhower years was drawing to a close through what he understood to be an inherent cyclical rhythm in national affairs which he had inherited from his father, the influential Harvard historian Arthur Schlesinger Sr. Adapting his father's historical perspective, the younger Schlesinger saw the Eisenhower era as the result of national fatigue after two decades under activist presidents who had called for the intense political commitment of the American people in response to a nearly perpetual torrent of crises. The "Eisenhower lull," he contended, represented a natural and predictable example of the way in which change in the United States had "always taken pace by fits and starts, with the nation rushing ahead until stopped by exhaustion and then standing still until boredom plus the piling up of new problems induce forward motion." Schlesinger cited the 1920s as a compelling example of what was to come. From his vantage point, spiritual and psychological discontent had characterized the 1920s just as much as material prosperity.

Schlesinger saw the defection of writers such as Charles Beard, Sinclair Lewis, H. L. Mencken, and Walter Lippmann from the "official creed" of the existing social order of the time as highly symptomatic of the period's mounting non-material discontents. From his perspective, the 1920s had become "a decade of billowing ferment and criticism and agitation and hope" that would likely have soon produced a new political dynamism and Democratic electoral renaissance even without the disruptive impact of the Great Depression. Although, he conceded, "it may seem odd to ask working politicians to pay attention to cultural matters," the 1920s gave strong evidence that "a period of acute intellectual discontent is likely to foreshadow a period of political revolt."[66]

The revolt against the complacent consensus of the Eisenhower era which Schlesinger expected to emerge out of the period's intellectual and cultural discontents represented for him a means of providing the American people with a sense of dedication and purpose that had been lost in the age of abundance. The emerging political epoch that he anticipated would be defined by a search for the dynamism and resolve that had once been inspired by events such as the Great Depression and World War II. Schlesinger opined that although the threat of communism and the prospect of nuclear annihilation ought to offer a similar source of inspiration, they did not seem to do so. If the Cold War failed to provide such answers to questions of national purpose, he believed that the existing goal of adding to material comforts would certainly do no better.[67] Historians have doubted whether any political initiative would have been able to address the myriad of intangible discontents that Schlesinger and Galbraith took to be indications that the country lacked a compelling and meaningful sense of national purpose. The historian and social critic Christopher Lasch maintained that liberals and radicals had long called for the betterment of American culture but had seldom believed so clearly that the answers could be found in a purely political approach.[68] Given the contention of Galbraith and Schlesinger that the central issues in the age of abundance were cultural, moral, and psychological, the historian Richard Pells expressed skepticism as to how a political solution could achieve the improvement in the *quality* of life they desired.[69] While these and other similar interpretations raise important skepticism about the potential for their means to achieve their aims, Galbraith and Schlesinger did not believe that politics would provide all of the answers to the problems of prosperity that they detailed. They did, however, consider a shift in the social balance away from private wants to the needs of the public interest to be an effective starting point.

Whether or not politics held the potential to address the types of issues highlighted by Galbraith and Schlesinger, political developments in the following years suggested that many shared their conviction that it could. During the 1960s, the belief that a wide range of cultural and moral concerns were integral to politics came to sustain some of the decade's most visible political developments. Liberal politics from the New Frontier to the New Politics as well as the radicalism of the New Left all reflected a clear belief that politics held both the potential and the responsibility to address the array of new non-material issues that defined the post-scarcity era. Though Galbraith would find a growing number of intellectuals, activists, and politicians in the 1960s who shared his understanding of the urgency of facing these new problems, he was under no illusion that the task would be a straightforward one. Whereas the older economic and material aims were clear and direct, the challenge of improving the quality of American life would be anything but. That this initiative would require a willingness to pay for it, however, Galbraith was certain. As he put it, "Most of the things we must do to reveal the quality of our society will cost money—public money."[70]

SOCIAL BALANCE IN AN AFFLUENT SOCIETY

Often vague and abstract, the ideas that underpinned the qualitative liberalism of Galbraith and Schlesinger would be put into their most concrete terms over the course of a far-reaching debate on social balance. As it rose to second place on the *New York Times* best-seller list—an unlikely place for a book written by an academic economist—*The Affluent Society* focused national attention on the issue of social balance.[71] In one of the most memorable and oft-quoted passages of the book, Galbraith painted a stark picture of the consequences of social imbalance:

> The family which takes its mauve and cerise, air-conditioned, power-steered, and power-braked automobile out for a tour passes though cities that are badly paved, made hideous by litter, blighted buildings, billboards, and posts for wires that should have long since been put underground. They pass on into a countryside that has been rendered largely invisible by commercial art.... They picnic on exquisitely packaged food from a portable icebox by a polluted stream and go on to spend the night

at a park which is a menace to public health and morals. Just before dozing off on an air mattress, beneath a nylon tent, amid the stench of decaying refuse, they may reflect vaguely on the curious unevenness of their blessings. Is this, indeed, the American genius?[72]

Although the passage clearly demonstrated Galbraith's aesthetic aversion to what had become of the American landscape, it also reflected his more pressing concern with the "private opulence and public squalor" that he believed defined the postwar era.

In the book, Galbraith traced the roots of the pervasive preoccupation with private production at the expense of public services back to an era of scarcity that had only recently come to a close. In the world into which the study of economics was born, the four most urgent requirements of human life were food, clothing, shelter, and physical security. As the first three lent themselves to private production, public services came to be seen at best as a necessary evil. Galbraith saw the prevailing economic attitudes of the postwar era as anachronistically rooted in the material scarcity of that earlier time. From his perspective, the failure to adjust genuinely to a world of affluence in which private production no longer needed to be endowed with transcendent importance contributed to the highly uneven relationship between the supply of privately produced goods and services and those of the state—or what he termed the "social balance." For Galbraith, scenes such as the feature-loaded family car in a repugnant public park would be commonplace so long as private wants continued to be seen as inherently superior to public desires.[73]

As it challenged the "conventional wisdom" of the postwar era and stirred an ongoing national debate on social balance, Galbraith's influential 1958 book found a highly receptive audience in the ADA. Unsurprisingly, Schlesinger celebrated a book that confirmed his views on the failure of the richest country in the history of the world to allocate the necessary public resources to build an effective educational system, maintain its roads and parks, keep up with the Soviet Union, or even to run a decent postal system.[74] When Senator Paul Douglas of Illinois—a founding member of the ADA and former professor of economics at the University of Chicago—presented the Tamiment Institute Annual Book of the Year Award to Galbraith for *The Affluent Society*, he praised the book and agreed with the premise that the next advance in American society should be the satisfaction of pressing public needs and wants.[75] In a glowing review of the book, Carl

Auerbach, also a founding member of the ADA, declared that "to read it is to acquire an understanding of the realities of American economic society, and a new vision of its possibilities."[76] Even Leon Keyserling, unquestionably the organization's leading partisan of economic growth, hailed the book as a "ringing declaration of the primacy of our neglected public needs" and gave copies of it to his friends with the insistence that "everyone should read the book."[77] Years after its publication, the influence of *The Affluent Society* still ran high in the ADA. Speaking before an audience of ADA members in 1964, Edward Hollander, chairman of the ADA national executive committee, drew on Galbraith's understanding of the revolutionary implications of postwar affluence with repeated references to the age of abundance, private opulence and public squalor, poverty in the midst of plenty, and other major themes from the book to explain the economic and social circumstances faced by the country.[78]

The primary point of contention between Galbraith and other ADA liberals was not to be found in his insistence on greater expenditures for public services. Few liberals at the time would have taken issue with a call for greater public spending. Rather, Galbraith ran afoul of the leading economic policy makers in the ADA with the specifics of how he believed improved public services and other shared liberal goals could and should be met. Galbraith pushed up against deeply entrenched assumptions of liberal economic thinking when he highlighted the inflationary dangers inherent in the ever greater push for economic growth. In contrast to many of his ADA colleagues who displayed an unwavering confidence in economic growth as the foundation for social progress, he did not see the threat of inflation as a bogeyman created by conservatives to justify opposition to public spending. According to Galbraith, not only did increased production fail to offer a solution for inflation, but also growth itself, and the consumer purchasing power that resulted from it, represented one of the most significant inflationary factors in the American economy. Furthermore, he contended, the need to provide the jobs that sustained such growth necessitated an unhappy choice between an economy under the constant inflationary strain of the wages paid by those jobs or the consignment of some part of the labor force to unemployment. Citing the general inability of wages for public employees to keep up with rising prices and the resulting deterioration of public services during past periods of inflation, Galbraith characterized inflation as one of the first enemies of social balance.[79] When Galbraith addressed the ADA's annual

Roosevelt Day Dinner in 1959, he further underscored the danger of rising prices as he gently chided his fellow liberals for undue complacency toward the "highly reactionary phenomenon" of inflation.[80]

Even more than the issue of inflation—a concern that Galbraith and growth advocates in the ADA shared, if to varying degrees—support in *The Affluent Society* for sales taxes as a means of redressing social imbalance proved to be an unavoidable sticking point for many of the book's liberal readers. As the burden of sales taxes fall disproportionately on those with lower incomes who can least afford them, the ADA and American liberals more broadly have long opposed such taxes and championed the merits of the progressive federal income tax. Opposition to sales taxes, Galbraith lamented, "made the liberal the effective enemy of social balance." He looked to an expanded use of sales taxes not as a substitute for the progressive income tax but as a complementary source of revenue that would provide the necessary resources for public services that income taxes had continually failed to provide. All too often, Galbraith maintained, revenue from income taxes was preempted for military purposes or compromised when the debate steered toward issues of economic inequality, which inevitably resulted in a liberal-conservative truce for lower taxes at all income levels and thus no hope of an improvement to social balance. Holding the view that American society was affluent in privately produced goods but poor in public services, he believed the most obvious solution to be the taxation of the former to provide for the latter. Though Galbraith conceded that expanded sales taxes would present some hardship for the poor, who would have to procure the essentials of life at a higher cost, he insisted that improving social balance represented both the nation's most pressing challenge and one of the first prerequisites to raising the poor out of poverty.[81]

Many in the ADA embraced and celebrated *The Affluent Society*'s call for an improved social balance in principle but rejected Galbraith's prescriptions for achieving that balance and remained essentially unmoved in their commitment to economic growth. While Senator Douglas praised Galbraith's call for improved public services, he believed the book exaggerated the reach of affluence and underestimated the scale of poverty that continued to exist. In a provocation not taken kindly in liberal circles, Douglas charged Galbraith with "carrying on an antiphonal chorus with the National Association of Manufacturers and urging the adoption of the sales tax."[82] ADA national chairman Robert Nathan challenged Galbraith's preoccupation with the danger of inflation when he maintained that over the past century there had been almost no inflation except that associated with war and declared that he did not consider the prospect of inflation to be a major problem.[83]

Keyserling echoed these criticisms and advanced others as he became the most outspoken liberal critic of *The Affluent Society* and the strongest voice of opposition to its key principles within the ADA. Though he praised the book for bringing attention to the nation's neglected public services, he diverged from Galbraith in viewing a concerted effort for greater economic growth not as an impediment to improving public services but as the only viable means of producing the resources necessary for that improvement. The former CEA chairman maintained that Galbraith's desired expansion of public expenditures would entail such an increase in spending that it could not be achieved solely by a shift from private expenditures. High levels of economic growth would be needed.[84] Keyserling saw Galbraith's "curious" insistence that improved public services could be achieved only through the sacrifice of equally important economic growth and private consumption not as "new" but as a "reversion to earlier 'equalitarian' thinking, based upon the economic and political impracticability of suppressing one valid interest in order to serve another." Like Galbraith, Keyserling believed that material progress in the postwar years had fundamentally rewritten the rules of the American economy, but differed strongly with the Harvard economist on the meaning and implications of that economic revolution. For Keyserling, the "promise of the new technology" that had vastly enlarged the country's productive capacity meant that the choice between public and private affluence that Galbraith sought to foist on liberals was wholly unnecessary. With a continually growing economy, America could have both tailfins and better parks.[85]

Differing understandings of the reach of poverty and affluence in the United States provided the fundamental basis of the differences between Galbraith and Keyserling on the issue of social balance. Keyserling convincingly insisted that the living standards of the more than 40 million Americans who lived in some form of poverty would not be improved simply by a greater prioritization of public services. Galbraith's belief in an improved social balance as a remedy for poverty, Keyserling charged, amounted to a writing off of those who currently subsisted in poverty on the basis of a distant hope that better education and other public services would eventually allow their children or grandchildren to escape such conditions. According to Keyserling, ameliorating poverty was essentially a matter of raising the income of individuals through advances in production, which would provide work for more people at better pay, expanding Social Security, improving minimum wage laws, and other measures directed at increasing private income. With the understanding of poverty as having insufficient income to consume enough clothing, housing, food, and other necessities, he found it odd that those like Galbraith "who disparage the expansion of private consumption stress the liquidation of poverty." Accordingly, Keyserling had little patience for what he saw as the "fashionable" call made by Galbraith and other liberals to cut back on the private consumption of both luxuries and necessities through expanded sales taxes in order to make resources available for public needs.[86]

The critiques leveled by leading voices in the ADA at the call for a prioritization of public needs over private incomes advanced by Galbraith and Schlesinger underscored the essentially middle-class orientation of the qualitative liberalism they espoused. Galbraith and Schlesinger were not blind to the continued existence of poverty in the 1950s but did not generally see material insecurity and economic inequality as pressing issues until the civil rights movement focused national attention on the enduring scale and depth of poverty in the 1960s. Initially developed in response to Democratic losses in the 1952 election, the qualitative liberalism of Galbraith and Schlesinger rested more on a desire to reach out to the growing ranks of middle-class voters and define the quality-of-life issues that concerned them than on an impulse to address the plight of those who had yet to benefit from the nation's growing affluence.

As much as liberals were drawn to the vision of a post-scarcity society painted by Galbraith and Schlesinger, the desire to appeal to an electorate broader than the middle class and the unappealing nature of their specific policy recommendations ensured that Keyserling's views on the vital importance of economic growth continued to define liberal politics both inside and outside the ADA. The debate carried on between Galbraith and Keyserling in the pages of *The New Republic* and in the ADA also came to the fore in the Democratic Advisory Council (DAC). A policy group created after the losses of the 1956 election to develop ideas for bringing Democrats back to power, the DAC featured Keyserling on its advisory committee on economic policy and Galbraith as the committee's chairman. Keyserling effectively won the debate in the DAC, with the group in 1958 committing to an annual economic growth rate of 5 percent that would later be enshrined in the 1960 Democratic Party platform.[87]

Keyserling's growth perspective enjoyed similar success in the ADA. A widely distributed ADA pamphlet on inflation bore the mark of Keyserling's influence in presenting rising prices not as a possible consequence of economic growth and full employment but as an empty specter utilized by the Eisenhower administration to justify opposition to federal spending that it would have opposed regardless of inflationary dangers.[88] Even more than the publication of that pamphlet and other publications similarly suffused with Keyserling's perspective, the policy resolutions passed by the ADA during the Eisenhower and Kennedy years served to identify the organization with the former CEA chairman's far-reaching belief in economic growth. Without Galbraith's presence on the ADA national board or the domestic policy commissions that developed and revised the organization's policy resolutions, Keyserling ensured that his position was displayed, in his own words, "on all fours with the ADA platform."[89] As the vice chairman charged with economic policy, Keyserling secured an ADA resolution in 1959 calling for a commitment to a 5 percent growth rate that differed little from the one he had recently pressed through the DAC. That same year—less than a year after the publication of *The Affluent Society*—the ADA rejected one of the book's primary policy recommendations when it advanced a newly explicit denunciation of sales taxes with the insistence that they were a fundamental element of the nation's "economically wrong and socially unjust tax policies."[90]

The early 1960s saw little change in Keyserling's heavy influence on the ADA's economic perspective. In 1960 the ADA went further in its rejection of sales taxes, insisting that they were wrong in principle and should be replaced by a sufficiently progressive income tax. Expressing little affinity with Galbraith's concerns about growth as a source of inflationary pressure, the economic policy resolution passed that year plainly declared, "We reject categorically the view that inflation is the nation's most serious problem, or even the nation's most serious economic problem." The answer to inflationary pressures, the resolution insisted, was to be found in still greater levels of production, employment, and growth.[91] The far-reaching belief in growth that underpinned that economic resolution and others like it would be put on display for all to see when the ADA selected "Growth for the Future" as the theme for its 1962 convention.[92]

As the American economy gained steam under the Kennedy administration, belief in the far-reaching potential of economic growth and the demands of political pragmatism combined to ensure that the ADA's economic outlook would continue to be shaped by Keyserling. Robert Lekachman—a professor of economics at Columbia University, occasional participant in ADA conferences, and close associate of many in the organization—clearly saw the political difficulty to be found in following Galbraith's recommendations. The "Galbraithian liberal," he observed, would face the "painful necessity of gritting his teeth and seeking to reallocate demand from private to public purposes via higher taxes."[93] Keyserling, by contrast, called on developers of liberal policy and the American taxpayers to make no such sacrifices. As long as leading liberals continued to believe that economic growth could remedy poverty and improve the nation's social balance without any substantial tax increases, Galbraith's proposals would struggle to find widespread acceptance.

Nevertheless, the celebration of Galbraith's insights into the economy and society of postwar America by liberals in and outside the ADA—despite the political difficulty of acting on them—reflected a widespread liberal disillusionment with the values and direction of American society and politics that would significantly shape liberal political thinking in the years to come. Many liberal observers shared Galbraith's concern with a society that pursued cars with extravagant tailfins and other unnecessary consumer goods at the expense of the parks, roads, schools, and hospitals needed to improve the quality of American life. Although he conceded that Keyserling's proposals were understandably more "ingratiating" than those of Galbraith, Lekachman reflected the sentiment of many liberals when he associated the former with the status quo and lamented that "no sensitive person can rejoice at the image we present to others and the image we present to ourselves."[94] When liberals came to accept the limitations of economic growth for achieving their goals in the 1960s, the ideas developed by Galbraith and Schlesinger in the 1950s would no longer be limited to attracting intellectual sympathy. They would have a profound political impact.

QUALITATIVE LIBERALISM AS A SOURCE OF DIVERGENCE

At the onset of the 1960s, with the Vietnam War and other divisive developments that would emerge during the decade yet to appear visibly on the horizon, the significance of divergent liberal understandings of the post-scarcity era developed over the past decade remained indistinct. With few concrete issues apart from inflation and sales taxes to separate them, Galbraith, Schlesinger, and Keyserling continued to see and articulate their differences as differences of emphasis rather than substance. Their desire to emphasize consensus was, in fact, well grounded by their positions at the time. Galbraith and Schlesinger harbored no opposition to economic growth per se, just as Keyserling offered no disagreement with the need for improved public services. The differences between them seemed to center not on goals but on the means for achieving them and their relative priority. The significant consensus between Galbraith, Keyserling, and Schlesinger, however, and their frequently displayed desire to accentuate that consensus, masked the degree to which qualitative liberalism represented a substantial divergence from the liberalism that had initially taken shape in the postwar years.

The impulse of ADAers to present a united front against conservatives and other genuine opponents of shared liberal goals, coupled with the political difficulty of acting on the policies that underpinned qualitative liberalism, obscured much of the meaning and significance of the political vision developed by Galbraith and Schlesinger. Consequently, many historians have overlooked both the substantive departure of qualitative liberalism and the meaning of its critical socioeconomic perspective in their portrayals of liberal thought in the 1950s and early 1960s. Allen Matusow and Doug Rossinow characterize postwar liberals as displaying no inclination to challenge the economic power of corporations, redistribute wealth, or restructure existing political, economic, and social institutions. In other words, they, and other historians who share their assessment of postwar liberalism, charge postwar liberals with lacking the fundamental criticism of the capitalist system that had driven their liberal and progressive predecessors. According to this narrative of liberal affinity with the promise of the American capitalist economy, postwar liberals dispensed with all ideological commitments apart from anticommunism.[95]

Such notions of postwar liberalism as standing for little other than opposing communism are complicated by the attraction of ADA liberals to the understanding of the post-scarcity era advanced by Galbraith and Schlesinger. The sympathy among ADAers for a political perspective attuned to the direction of socioeconomic changes they increasingly saw taking shape around them demonstrates that even if they were not yet able or ready to act, influential liberal intellectuals harbored significant concerns with American capitalism. By insisting on a shift in national priorities from the satisfaction of private wants to the fulfillment of public needs which fundamentally challenged consumerism, the call for an improved social balance represented a penetrating critique of the foundation of American capitalism, even if the measures proposed—such as increased sales taxes—were far from radical. That critique, though it differed from the class-based perspective of socialists and many liberals during the New Deal era, nevertheless brought into question the transcendent importance of the consumer goods production that accounted for the preponderance of the American economy and drove the bulk of its growth.

Frequently obscured by their desire to present a united front and stress common goals, occasional outbursts between Galbraith, Schlesinger, and Keyserling exposed the substantive divergence from existing liberal consensus entailed by this critical perspective on consumerism. Writing to Galbraith, Schlesinger relayed an encounter with Keyserling after giving a speech on the issue of social balance at the 1960 Midwestern Democratic Conference in Detroit. According to Schlesinger, Keyserling "got very indignant and attacked me bitterly in a press conference." Schlesinger believed that Keyserling's outburst was the result of his regarding him as a "Galbraith stooge" and expressed his regret at the former CEA chairman's "compulsion to transform all differences of emphasis into differences of principle."[96] Like Schlesinger, Keyserling also insisted that the differences between them were only a matter of emphasis and heaped blame on the other side for needlessly magnifying issues of emphasis into issues of substance. The private correspondence between Galbraith, Schlesinger, and Keyserling, however, demonstrates that despite insistences to the contrary by all parties, there were more than issues of emphasis at stake. Their correspondence reveals a far sharper edge to the debate than was typically seen in its public airing in the pages of *The New Republic* or the boardrooms of the ADA as it raised fundamental questions of what it meant to be liberal in the age of abundance.

The significant disagreement that emerged when Galbraith and Keyserling collaborated on a policy pamphlet for the DAC in 1960 exemplified the ways in which their differences in emphasis on the issue of social balance were rooted in liberal perspectives that had genuinely diverged in response to the changes ushered in by the post-scarcity era. As they traded drafts of the pamphlet back and forth, an unusually bitter debate developed that centered on the urgency of improving public services as compared to bettering private incomes. In response to a draft of the pamphlet, Galbraith objected to a passage that he believed effectively equated his views on the nation's social imbalance with support for the "repression of private economic progress."[97] Keyserling agreed to drop the offending section but not without letting Galbraith know that he believed there to be "altogether too much talk about private affluence and public poverty." Keyserling saw the public and private sectors as equally in need of attention and remarked that he was "deeply disturbed" by the extent to which Galbraith and others prioritized the improvement of public services at the expense of expanding private incomes and private consumption. Pointing out that "the number of well-known people all over the country who have interpreted your book to contrast private affluence with public poverty are legion," Keyserling stressed the need to express his own differing viewpoint "firmly and without equivocation."[98]

The ensuing exchange illustrates the fundamental gulf that had emerged from Galbraith and Keyserling's respective efforts to define the meaning of liberalism in the post-scarcity era. Although they had already reached an agreement to cut the passage that had sparked their confrontation, Galbraith interpreted Keyserling's assertion of his desire to express his own contrasting view as indicating that the former CEA chairman wanted to incorporate those views into the pamphlet. Accordingly, Galbraith expressed his belief to Keyserling that the pamphlet in that form would be directly contrary not only to his own position but also to what he took "to be sound liberal policy." Galbraith asserted that he could neither accept nor "be in any way identified with" such a pamphlet and furthermore could not imagine that the "[Democratic Advisory] Council would sponsor what critics would deem an attack on those who have been arguing for a larger allocation for public services."[99] Keyserling responded by accusing Galbraith of displaying "considerable pigheadedness" about his views and expressing resentment that Galbraith had resorted to "veiled threats" as to whether the DAC would approve his positions. Most of all, Keyserling took exception to Galbraith's calling into question the liberal merits of his position and insisted that he had won at least as much of a right as the Harvard economist to assert his views through the Democratic Party machinery. The postscript that concluded Keyserling's lengthy and frank letter to Galbraith ended with a declaration that the DAC "did not intend to set anybody up as an arbitrator or to erect the theory of the affluent society into an untouchable Party principle."[100]

Ultimately, they stuck to their original agreement to exclude the section of the pamphlet that Galbraith believed attacked his views on social balance, but the fundamental nature of their disagreement meant that the two never came to an accord on the deeper issue of liberalism's primary mission in the age of abundance.[101] Keyserling continued to define liberalism in quantitative terms and to find the pressing and necessary purpose of liberalism in the challenge of raising individuals and families out of poverty through increased levels of private income. Galbraith, along with Schlesinger and a contingent of ADAers that would grow in the years ahead, had come to find liberalism's new challenge in improving the public services that would disproportionately benefit those living in poverty while simultaneously improving the quality of life of all Americans. Leading them as it did to fundamentally divergent answers, the question of whether public services or private incomes were in more urgent need of improvement represented a matter of emphasis but also the basis for the fundamental question of what it meant to be liberal in the post-scarcity era. By finding a core component of the liberal agenda in the improvement of public services needed to lift the quality of American life, Galbraith and Schlesinger broadened the mission of liberalism to include a wide array of non-material issues. Still, as long as the differences between qualitative liberalism and growth-centric quantitative liberalism on matters of concrete policy remained limited to inflationary concerns and sales taxes, Galbraith, Schlesinger, and Keyserling could continue to project the consensus of their respective political perspectives. During those years of minimal disagreement on policy, they would also remain close personal friends.[102]

The united liberal front and close friendship maintained by Galbraith, Schlesinger, and Keyserling during these years would seem a distant memory by the latter half of the 1960s. Tensions that had been simmering under the surface in the ADA for years became increasingly unavoidable and unbridgeable as the political implications of what had once appeared to be only differences in emphasis on public spending versus private incomes clearly came to be seen as fundamental questions about what it meant to be an American liberal. By 1968 Keyserling would characterize the prevalence of ideas in the ADA drawn from qualitative liberalism as "destructive trends" that had pushed the organization toward what he considered a dangerous and futile effort to "dump" President Johnson over the Vietnam War.[103] With no doubts that the American economy had the resources for both "guns and butter," Keyserling willfully disregarded the impact of the war on domestic social programs. As he doubled down on his belief in economic growth as an almost limitless engine for social progress and his distinctly quantitative understanding of liberalism, Keyserling increasingly found himself out of step with the ADA as it came to emphasize qualitative issues and focus ever more of its energy and resources on opposition to the Vietnam War.

As qualitative liberalism took shape in the ADA at the expense of figures like Keyserling who stridently emphasized bread-and-butter issues, this marked an important first step in the reorientation of liberalism toward the interests of the middle class. The increasingly middle-class orientation of American liberalism later become far more visible with the rise of the New Politics movement. When New Politics activists sought a political means of ending the Vietnam War, they drew not on the radicalism of the New Left but on a qualitative liberalism rooted in the outlook of the middle class and the desire for a politics that did not limit itself to the bread-and-butter issues that had preoccupied New Deal and Fair Deal liberals. The ADA began moving on the path toward what would become the New Politics movement when questioning of the transcendent importance of economic growth by several of its leading figures established a broad new array of issues as legitimate subjects of concern for liberals. The ADA would continue farther down that path when many of those same figures emerged as early critics of the growing US military intervention in Vietnam and came to question a doctrine of anticommunist containment that had once stood alongside the promise of economic growth as a pillar of postwar liberalism.

CHAPTER 2

RETHINKING THE COLD WAR
The Vital Center and the Vietnam War

In the early 1960s, well before the Vietnam War registered as a pressing issue in American society, a contingent of leading figures in the ADA became some of the earliest critics of the growing commitment of US military forces to the conflict. The ADA went on the record in 1962 in opposition to American military intervention in what it saw as a civil war in a country of marginal strategic importance to the United States, while John Kenneth Galbraith, then the US ambassador to India, wrote to President Kennedy more often about the dangers of committing additional forces to Vietnam than he did about his ambassadorial post.[1] Still, Galbraith, other critics of the Vietnam War in the ADA, and the organization itself have often been seen as less than genuine opponents of US military intervention in Southeast Asia. In 1967 the prominent linguist and radical social critic Noam Chomsky famously assailed Arthur Schlesinger Jr. and other "academic apologists" of the US government for insisting on circumstances for negotiations that could only lead to a continuation of the conflict and the American military presence in the country.[2] In the decades that followed the Vietnam War, historians have continued to cast doubt on the commitment of the ADA and its leaders to opposing it.[3]

Despite the ongoing prevalence of historical accounts that question the nature and degree of their commitment, these ADA leaders were far from the half-hearted opponents of the conflict they have frequently been made out to be. Historians have rightly highlighted the ineffectiveness of their resistance to the war and its failure to make an immediate impact on the course of the conflict. That general ineffectiveness owed much to the tendency of the ADA and its members to see themselves as a "vital center" surrounded by irrational extremes on both the right and the left. Drawing on Schlesinger's seminal 1949 book of the same name, the ADA's continued adherence to a "vital center" framework precluded involvement in mass antiwar demonstrations, where radical activists could always be expected to have a presence.[4] Unable to work with the emerging antiwar protest movement as a means of putting pressure on the Johnson administration, the ADA had to settle on an ultimately unsuccessful petition-gathering initiative as the focus of its antiwar efforts.[5] In spite of the failure of its efforts, the committed opposition to the war mounted by the ADA and many of its veteran leaders contributed to the intellectual and political foundation that would later be drawn on by the New Politics movement.

The widespread view among historians that the ADA's opposition to the Vietnam War should be seen as suspect owes much to a static image of the organization based on its formative years in the late 1940s and the reflexive anticommunism that had been among its most central tenets. During the early years of the Cold War, the ADA played an influential role in building consensus among liberals around the need to contain the spread of communism. The support displayed by some of the ADA's leading figures during the earliest stage of US escalation in Vietnam, and the involvement into the mid-1960s of Cold Warriors who still seemed to embody that consensus, further cemented an image of the organization rooted in the early Cold War. Yet many of the leaders who had initially signaled support for US policy in Vietnam quickly changed their tune, and the Cold Warriors who sought to soft-pedal the ADA position on the Vietnam War found themselves marginalized by the organization's antiwar turn.[6] The conflict that played out in the ADA between vocal critics of the war and organized labor representatives such as Gus Tyler, advisers to the Johnson administration such as John Roche, and prominent liberals such as Leon Keyserling reflected the earnestness of those critics. It also hinted at bigger struggles that would emerge in the years to come between doves and hawks in the broader world of liberal and Democratic politics.

The tendency to assume that critics of the war in the ADA were tepid in their opposition has been reinforced by historians who portray mid-century liberals as having been pushed leftward toward a more negative position on the war by an ascendant New Left and who evaluate the foreign policy posture of those liberals against the straightforward call for unilateral withdrawal demanded by radical antiwar activists.[7] In contrast to the political trajectory depicted in those accounts, the foreign policy outlook and position on the war developed by these ADA leaders during the 1960s owed little to direct pressure from radicals. The revival of leftist politics with the emergence of the New Left had an indirect impact on the ADA in that it allowed the organization to frame its opposition to the war as a responsible "vital center" position, but that very positioning sustained the unyielding divide the ADA leadership insisted on placing between themselves and radicals. As a result, ADA liberals had limited interaction with the New Left and even less interest in its ideas. Whereas radical antiwar activists frequently emphasized corporate interests and imperialism in their opposition to the Vietnam War, ADA liberals highlighted the growth of polycentric communism and the rise of nationalism as developments that rendered the political composition of the South Vietnamese government an issue of limited strategic importance to the United States.

Evaluated on its own merits, the opposition to the Vietnam War advanced by veteran ADA leaders appears not as a less "pure" version of the dissent against the conflict mounted by the New Left but as a dedicated, if less than effective, opposition to US military intervention in a distant civil war. Despite pursuing limited and ineffectual means of opposition to the Vietnam War, the ADA and its leading critics of the war developed a dissent against reflexive anticommunist containment as a pillar of US foreign policy that joined with the ideas of qualitative liberalism to form an important element in the intellectual and political underpinnings of the New Politics movement. When opposition to the Vietnam War later entered the realm of electoral politics through the New Politics movement, the tensions that shaped and circumscribed the dissent against the conflict developed by ADA leaders and like-minded liberals did much to define the contours of that movement.

THE DEVELOPMENT OF DISSENT

When the ADA first came out in opposition to US military intervention in Vietnam in 1962, the conflict in Southeast Asia was not yet on the radar of most Americans. US involvement—which began in 1950 as economic assistance to France in support of its war effort against the Viet Minh to regain control of its colonial territory in Indochina—had transformed into economic and military aid to the new state of South Vietnam, which would see the involvement of over eleven thousand American military personal by the end of 1962. Still, as long as the US military presence in Vietnam remained officially confined to advising the South Vietnamese forces, the media and policy makers devoted little attention to the mounting American involvement.[8] ADA leaders began to develop their dissent against US policy in Vietnam during the early 1960s as they expressed concern about the very real prospect of the United States being drawn into direct conflict with China and the Soviet Union in order to support a repressive regime in a country of minimal importance to American strategic interests. Development of that line of dissent put ADA leaders on a path that would ultimately lead them and their organization to a broader rejection of the principles that had sustained US foreign policy since the earliest days of the Cold War.

It would be some years before he became outspoken in his dissent, but John Kenneth Galbraith demonstrated an early awareness of the stakes involved in Southeast Asia when, as US ambassador to India, he repeatedly wrote President Kennedy to voice his concerns about the American military presence in Vietnam.[9] Writing to Kennedy on March 2, 1962, Galbraith expressed his belief that he continued to be "sadly out of step with the Establishment." His letter made clear that he saw Ngo Dinh Diem's government in South Vietnam as making no real effort toward political or social reform and believed that the United States was increasingly replacing the French as the colonial military force. In a series of dissents against administration policy, Galbraith questioned the strategic value of Vietnam and puzzled over what benefit the United States could gain from alliance with an "incompetent government and a people who are so largely indifferent to their own salvation." Offering advice that would prove to be all too true, Galbraith urged Kennedy to maintain the threshold against the commitment of US combat forces because "a few will mean more and more and more. And then the South Vietnamese boys will go back to the farms. We will do the fighting."[10]

In the months that followed Galbraith's prescient warning to Kennedy, the ADA echoed the Harvard economist's criticism of administration policy in Vietnam with a foreign policy resolution that registered the organization's objection to the growing US military commitment to the conflict. Before the publication of the Port Huron Statement by Students for a Democratic Society (SDS) or the emergence of visible antiwar activism on American college campuses, the ADA became one of the first political organizations with a national presence to go on the record in opposition to

US policy in Vietnam. The foreign policy resolution passed at the ADA's 1962 national convention dissented against administration policy on several grounds. It took issue with the unilateral American military intervention in South Vietnam that had been undertaken without the approval of the United Nations, in contravention of the Geneva Accords of 1954, and with no clear justification to Congress or the public. The resolution also refuted the administration's claims that the communist insurgency was the result of foreign intervention and expressed vigorous opposition to "the unilateral commitment of America's own military power and prestige to sustain governments in Asia or elsewhere against the resistance of their own people." The greatest concern expressed by the resolution, however, would be reserved for the inherent danger of intervening in a country of limited strategic importance, which threatened to bring the United States into a conflict with China or the Soviet Union with the potential to "imperil the whole future of America."[11]

Toward the end of Kennedy's presidency and the early years of the Johnson administration, the ADA's dissent against American policy and actions in Vietnam developed apace with the escalation of the US war effort. As the scale of opposition to Diem's regime in South Vietnam became abundantly clear, the ADA stepped up its dissent with a resolution in 1963 that specifically called on the United States to halt its escalation policy and the commitment of American personnel to combat operations in South Vietnam. The more explicit language of the 1963 resolution also called into question the practice of unconditional support for the South Vietnamese government with the insistence that future American aid to Diem be contingent on basic political, social, and economic reforms to be undertaken by his regime.[12] The American calculus in the Vietnam War then changed dramatically with a swift coup d'état against the Diem regime followed shortly by the assassination of Kennedy. What had been a creeping escalation of the American military commitment to Vietnam took on stark new dimensions after the US Navy made the second of two reports of dubious reliability detailing torpedo attacks by North Vietnamese forces on American destroyers in the Gulf of Tonkin on August 4, 1964. In response to the supposed attack on US naval ships, Johnson sought and won prompt and overwhelming approval from Congress for a resolution on Southeast Asia "to take all necessary measures to repel any armed attack against the forces of the United States and to prevent further aggression." Popularly known as the Gulf of Tonkin Resolution, this seemingly limited congressional action provided the legal basis for

Johnson's later shift of US military personnel from an advisory to a combat role.[13]

By the fall of 1964 the Johnson administration's policies in Vietnam had for some time been attracting growing concern from ADA liberals and a smattering of critics on the left of the political spectrum but still did not register as a major issue or source of controversy. The American public expressed overwhelming support for Johnson's response to the Gulf of Tonkin crisis with public approval of the president's handling of the Vietnam conflict surging in the wake of the resolution. Having demonstrated a firm response to apparent North Vietnamese aggression, Johnson assured the American public that he intended neither to widen the conflict in Vietnam nor to abandon South Vietnam to communist aggression. With the Vietnam War not yet more than a peripheral concern and the prospect of the right-wing Republican presidential nominee Barry Goldwater taking the country "back to the 19th century," the ADA did not hesitate to put aside its objections to the administration's policy in Vietnam and endorse Johnson for president in 1964. The overwhelming majority of American voters harbored no such nagging concerns to brush aside. The American electorate decisively opted for Johnson's professed moderation on the conflict, delivering the incumbent president a landslide victory over the hawkish Goldwater.[14]

Despite campaign rhetoric that contrasted his moderation with Goldwater's call for the bombing of North Vietnam, Johnson responded to an attack by the Vietcong on US forces at Pleiku on February 6, 1965, by ordering an immediate retaliatory air strike on North Vietnam. The air force followed up its initial response with regular bombing raids on industrial and military targets in the North as part of a policy of "sustained reprisal" called Rolling Thunder.[15] While later escalation of the war would lead to increasingly divergent views on the wisdom of the administration's policy among the ADA leadership, virtually all leading members came together in opposition to the continued bombing of North Vietnam. The ADA quickly responded to Rolling Thunder by issuing a public statement calling for the United States to halt the bombing of North Vietnam immediately and announce its willingness to negotiate a settlement to the conflict.[16] With an eye to the counterproductive implications of bombing for producing peace talks, Galbraith pointed out that those responsible for air intelligence in World War II learned that in almost every case, bombing not only failed to weaken the will to fight of those under attack but actually hardened their morale. In the case of Vietnam, Galbraith argued that bombing had stiffened the resolve of the North Vietnamese and proved largely ineffective in disrupting the supply routes of the Vietcong, who utilized virtually invulnerable jungle routes and made extensive use of local resources.[17]

While continuing the bombing campaign in North Vietnam and further escalating the deployment of US ground troops, Johnson sought to reach out to doves by announcing for the first time in a speech at Johns Hopkins University his decision to engage in "unconditional discussions" with the relevant governments and to offer a $1 billion program for the economic development of the Mekong River Valley.[18] Though the ADA represented one of the primary audiences that Johnson sought to reach with his April 7 address, leading members expressed mixed reactions to a speech that offered much hope in the way of rhetoric but little in the way of concrete policy changes. An editorial in the April issue of the organization's monthly magazine, *ADA World*, expressed no question about the "sincerity of the President's offer nor the magnitude of the step it represents in achieving peace in Viet-Nam" but pointed out that the prospects for negotiations were dim as long as the United States continued to bomb North Vietnam.[19] Roy Bennett—former editor of the disarmament-focused journal *The Correspondent* and a key figure in the development of ADA foreign policy—contended that so long as the administration continued to believe that the bombing raids were productive in shifting the military balance in favor of the United States, they would be unlikely to accept much less than a settlement based largely on American terms.[20] Bennett remained concerned about the continued military focus of the administration's policy but saw the Johns Hopkins speech as an important first step that justified "some timid optimism."[21]

Over the following year, ADA liberals continued to air skepticism as to whether the president's overtures would be reciprocated by an actual change of course in the war, but they sang a different tune when it came to the domestic politics of the Johnson administration. Though leading figures in the ADA consistently coupled praise for the administration's domestic initiatives with attention to their fundamental limitations, they nevertheless stressed the historical significance of Johnson's Great Society programs.[22] Schlesinger expressed his appreciation for the president's accomplishments when he told the 1965 ADA convention, "This is the greatest opportunity for constructive liberalism in a generation."²³ When Galbraith delivered the keynote address at the ADA National Convention the following year, he told his audience that the "antique doctrines and humorless achievements of the unimaginative men who got us into the jungle of Viet Nam must not be allowed to obscure the merits of far more liberal and astute achievements at home." Though still advancing criticism of American policy in Vietnam that had begun during his years as ambassador to India, Galbraith asked for perspective from his fellow liberals and reasoned that the gains of the Johnson administration on civil rights far outweighed American losses in support of the South Vietnamese government.²⁴ Together the expressions of appreciation for the domestic achievements of the Johnson administration offered by ADA liberals and the muted nature of their dissent on US policy in Vietnam masked the full implications of an emerging outlook that would reject the Cold War dogmas at the heart of American foreign policy.

A COLD WAR MYSTIQUE AT ODDS WITH REALITY

As the Johnson administration expanded the US military presence in Vietnam from what had been officially limited to an advisory role into a massive bombing campaign and large-scale ground war, ADA liberals began to stress more overtly the profound changes to the international geopolitical landscape seen during the preceding two decades. Speaking before an ADA audience at a Roosevelt Day Dinner in early 1965, Galbraith considered the changes that had befallen the globe during the postwar period and declared the existence of a "Cold War mystique" increasingly at odds with reality. The Cold War mystique, Galbraith insisted, required the world to be organized against the power of monolithic communism, and for all military, political, diplomatic, and economic decisions to be made in accordance with the needs of that struggle. The worldview perpetuated by that mystique could be credible only if communism remained monolithic and united in its hostility toward capitalist nations.²⁵

The ADA had started to distance itself from the Cold War mystique described by Galbraith some years earlier with its criticism of US policy in Vietnam during the early 1960s. When ADA leaders first began to criticize military intervention in a country they repeatedly described as having no clear strategic importance to the United States, they drew on an understanding of the far-reaching implications of splintering among communist states in what they had once believed to be a unified communist bloc. In a world of polycentric communism, where the establishment of a new communist regime did not entail an automatic expansion of Chinese or Soviet power, many in the ADA came to see the US military intervention in Vietnam as far more than a one-off strategic error. For an increasing number of ADA liberals, the growing presence of the US military in Southeast Asia and the hopelessness of its goals provided clear evidence of the need to reject the reflexive anticommunism that had underpinned the foreign policy of American liberals and the US government since the beginning of the Cold War. Ironically, the ADA had played no small part in shaping and establishing that foreign policy consensus during the late 1940s. With the escalation of the US military commitment in Vietnam, however, the ADA turned against the consensus it had helped to create in the first place as it sharpened its critical perspective on anticommunist containment policy. The implicit criticism of that policy which had run through earlier expressions of the ADA's position on the war would become increasingly explicit as more American ground troops arrived in Vietnam.

The earliest ADA criticism of US military intervention in Vietnam frequently drew on and expressed an underlying recognition of the ways in which the emergence of polycentric communism necessitated fundamental changes in American foreign policy. When Galbraith stressed the minimal strategic importance of Vietnam in his 1962 letter to President Kennedy, he was not simply offering his assessment of the country's geographical distance or its limited commercial, economic, and military value to the United States. More fundamentally, he was making the case that a communist government in Vietnam would not necessarily bolster the strength of China or the Soviet Union.[26] The foreign policy resolution passed by the ADA later that year demonstrated a similar consideration of polycentric communism and its implications for the Cold War when it characterized the conflict in South Vietnam as a civil war and consequently deemed the stakes involved to be of relatively little importance to the strategic interests of the United States.[27]

Hinted at in earlier ADA dissents against US policy in Vietnam, rejection of the Cold War dogmas that had sustained American foreign policy for almost two decades became far more overt after 1965 as the organization and its veteran leaders responded to the rapid escalation of the US military presence in the country. Written over the course of 1966 and published in early 1967, Schlesinger's critique *The Bitter Heritage* approached US policy in Vietnam primarily in terms of the need to advance a "middle course" out of the country that recognized and acted upon the ways in which the Cold War had changed since the early postwar years. In his widely read booklet, Schlesinger noted that in the mid-1960s, after half a dozen years of vocal quarreling between China and the Soviet Union, the State Department still referred to "instruments of Sino-Soviet power" and frequently framed the Cold War in terms of "the Communists" and "their world Revolution." Schlesinger acknowledged that even though the State Department and the Johnson administration seemed to have belatedly come to accept the reality of the Sino-Soviet split, they still failed to grasp the greater implications of polycentric communism.[28]

Like many in the ADA, Schlesinger saw the Sino-Soviet split as not simply a conflict between two communist powers but a rewriting of the rules of the Cold War. The schism between China and the Soviet Union, he contended, had set communist states free to pursue their own national policies.[29] Though it has since become clear that some degree of tension and disunity had always existed in the communist bloc, Schlesinger and the bulk of ADA liberals nonetheless believed that, despite later fractures, the communist movement had in fact been monolithic and unified in the early postwar period. Expressing a view shared by many of his ADA colleagues, Schlesinger maintained that during those years the seizure of power by communists in a country meant an extension of Soviet power and an inherent threat to the security of all democratic nations. In contrast, the expansion of communism in the 1960s did not inevitably extend the reach of Chinese or Soviet power. While he clearly believed the establishment of new communist regimes to be neither desirable nor without consequence, Schlesinger saw the issue as involving far lower stakes than had once been the case. Communist expansion would mean that countries had "succumbed to a dismal and dogmatic creed," but in Schlesinger's eyes it did not necessarily represent a serious threat to the security of the democratic world.[30] Schlesinger further encouraged a reassessment of the threat posed by communist expansion when he observed that communism had largely failed as a revolutionary movement. From the historian's vantage point, he noted that despite the explosion of new states in the years since World War II, communists had come to power in only three developing nations.[31]

The growing attentiveness to the transformative implications of polycentric communism displayed by the ADA and many of its longtime leaders in the 1960s owed much to the increasing sway of nationalism and the diminishing hold of ideology that had become ever more apparent in Vietnam with the escalation of the US military presence there. Galbraith revisited the theme of a harmful Cold War mystique over the course of 1967 in a series of influential articles that examined the Vietnam War in terms of the relationship between communism and nationalism. For Galbraith, a fundamental flaw of that mystique could be found in its insistence that communism could never successfully identify with nationalism. He conceded that while communism and nationalism were generally incompatible in Europe, postwar history had plainly demonstrated that such was not the case in Asia. In China, the communists stressed their nationalist credentials in their rise to power. In Vietnam, both North and South, communists staked a far stronger claim to nationalism than a Saigon government indebted to colonial bureaucracy and propped up by American support.[32]

Galbraith's writings in 1967 emphasized the nationalist ambitions of the North Vietnamese government and the National Liberation Front (NLF) in order to frame the conflict as one in which the United States faced not a centrally directed communist threat but a nationalist uprising.[33] Galbraith's interpretation of the conflict, and much of his language, found expression in a resolution on the Vietnam War adopted by the ADA national board in September 1967 that characterized the United States as contending with forces that, if irrefutably communist, had nevertheless seized the "banners of nationalism and social reform." The resolution cited the history of the decolonization movement and stressed that "western powers cannot defeat by military means the forces of indigenous nationalism and if they are wise they do not try."[34] Schlesinger had earlier come to a similar conclusion when he argued in *The Bitter Heritage* that US efforts to oppose nationalism in Vietnam not only might be unwise but also, if successful, could even be counterproductive. For Schlesinger, the most effective bulwark against an aggressive communist state could sometimes be found in neighboring communist states driven by a nationalist agenda. Schlesinger maintained that if the ultimate aim of the United States in the Vietnam War rested on a desire to contain China, "a communist Vietnam under Ho might be a better instrument of containment than a shaky Saigon regime led by right-wing mandarins or air force generals."[35]

Even as they advanced criticism of US policy in Vietnam during the mid-1960s which brought attention to the fallacies of what Galbraith had termed a Cold War mystique, the most vocal critics of the war in the ADA continued to exclude President Johnson from those they believed to be under the spell of that mystique. Moreover, many of those critics also believed that Johnson was executing the Vietnam War with no particular relish and sought nothing more than an opportunity to return to his domestic legislative priorities. One such figure, former Johnson speechwriter Richard Goodwin, was convinced that a show of popular opposition to the escalation of the Vietnam War could help to create that opportunity by providing a counter-pressure against hawks both within and outside the administration.[36] In his eyes, and those of like-minded ADA leaders such as Galbraith and Schlesinger, Johnson's instincts on the Vietnam War did not necessarily correspond with the more hawkish views of those who surrounded him in the White House. With that assumption, hope remained that the president could be pressured to change the course of the war. Still, the question persisted as to how ADA liberals would put pressure on a president they continued to celebrate publicly and on whom they depended for political influence.

THE BOUNDARIES OF THE VITAL CENTER

As ADA liberals faced a US policy in Vietnam that failed to live up to the hopeful rhetoric of President Johnson's 1965 Johns Hopkins speech and appeared to be moving no closer toward a negotiated settlement, a growing antiwar movement emerged alongside the continued escalation of the war effort. On March 24, 1965, the nation's first "teach-in" at the University of Michigan in Ann Arbor drew over three thousand people, who debated the issues surrounding the Vietnam War into the early hours of the morning. Teach-ins quickly became a major source of debate and dissent on administration policy in Vietnam, with over a hundred taking place at colleges and universities across the country in the months following the Ann Arbor event.[37] A protest organized by SDS on April 17, 1965, became the single largest antiwar demonstration ever organized at that point in the nation's history when it attracted some twenty thousand people to Washington, DC. That fall's International Days of Protest, organized by the National Coordinating Committee to End the War in Vietnam (NCC), saw nearly 100,000 people in eighty cities across several countries protest the war, resulting in cases of civil disobedience and arrests in a number of locales.[38] As antiwar demonstrations attracted national attention over the course of 1965, the ADA continued to maintain a "vital center" posture with deep roots in the organization's ideological history. Adherence to that posture—which called for opposition to both the conservative right and the radical left—ensured that the ADA kept its distance from the earliest antiwar protests organized by radical groups. Consequently, the ADA found itself unable to take part in or shape the demonstrations that drove the antiwar movement in its early stages.

The term "vital center" had entered into regular usage with the publication of a widely read article by Schlesinger in the run-up to the 1948 election, but the notion that responsible liberals needed to be on guard against the extremes of both the right and the left had defined the political outlook of the ADA since its founding in 1947.[39] Galbraith later reflected that when the leaders of the ADA became the foremost architects of liberalism during the early years of the Cold War, Henry Wallace's legacy had required them to shirk no opportunity to show they were just as "hard-boiled" as conservatives on issues of foreign policy.[40] For his part, Schlesinger believed that responsible liberalism rested on firm adherence to anticommunism in domestic politics and support for aggressive communist containment on the world stage. In his highly influential book *The Vital Center*, he distinguished liberals from conservatives not in terms of their degree of opposition to communism but by their insistence that a tough anticommunist stand had to be accompanied by efforts to address the unfinished reforms of the New Deal. Schlesinger, like Galbraith, drew on the lessons of the 1948 presidential election to interpret the form that liberalism was to take in the postwar years. When he surveyed the political circumstances of Democrat Harry Truman's victory in the 1948 presidential election, Schlesinger saw an electorate that had repudiated both Wallace's cooperation with communists and the Republican Party's effort to restore the power of the business community.[41]

Throughout the pages of his book, Schlesinger defined the "vital center" he believed had been emboldened by the 1948 election in contrast to the irrationality that he saw on both the right and the left but, like many liberal thinkers of the period, focused his attention primarily on positions to the left of the political center. Writing one year after the publication of *The Vital Center*, the leading literary critic Lionel Trilling famously declared,

"In the United States at this time liberalism is not only the dominant but even the sole intellectual tradition." Trilling maintained that while impulses toward conservatism or reaction certainly existed, and could in fact be quite strong, one would try in vain to find genuine conservative or reactionary ideas in general circulation among intellectuals. For Trilling, the conservative impulse expressed itself not as ideas but "only in action or in irritable mental gestures which seek to resemble ideas."[42] Drawing on a similar, if less blunt, assessment of conservative intellectual contributions to political discourse, Schlesinger saw liberals as defining the terms of intellectual debate and setting the general climate of political opinion. Accordingly, he devoted far more attention to distinguishing the "vital center" from Wallace's Progressives than from conservative Republicans.

The sustained attack mounted by Schlesinger in *The Vital Center* on the Progressives who rallied to Wallace's campaign provided a fundamental component of the intellectual and political framework that animated the ADA and its leading figures during the postwar era. Schlesinger centered much of his indictment of Progressives on what he saw as their sentimental belief in progress. Progressives, he contended, drew on a misguided faith in the essential goodness of mankind that led them to believe that all individual or social shortcomings would eventually be redeemed "by the benevolent unfolding of history." With what Schlesinger characterized as an irrational faith in progress, Progressives saw no need to safeguard against potential tyranny and thus saw no danger in allying with communists to achieve progressive aims. In contrast, Schlesinger's "vital center" drew on the lessons of fellow ADAer and influential Protestant theologian Reinhold Niebuhr to stress the inherent flaws of human nature and reject the Progressive acquiescence to communist support in the dangerous drive to establish utopia. Niebuhr had been the leading figure of the Union for Democratic Action before helping to transform the organization into the ADA in 1947. Written during the era of the UDA, Niebuhr's 1944 book *The Children of Light and the Children of Darkness* crystallized his years of thought and work on the ramifications for politics of the Christian doctrine of original sin. In the volume, Niebuhr attacked Progressives—the "children of light"—on the basis of their unfounded optimism, which led them to believe that the power of human reason can enable societies to transcend self-interest. Niebuhr's political realism, if not his theology, profoundly shaped Schlesinger's political outlook. Channeling Niebuhr, Schlesinger framed his "vital center" as an expression of "the great tradition of liberalism" based on "a reasonable responsibility about politics and a moderate pessimism about man."[43]

With Wallace's Progressives firmly in mind, Schlesinger looked to the formation of the ADA in 1947 as "the watershed at which American liberalism began to base itself once again on a solid conception of man and of history."[44] Schlesinger's colleagues in the ADA may not have shared in all of the specifics of his intellectual assessment of the Progressives, but the notion of the ADA as a "vital center" tasked with facing the irrationality of both the right and left quickly became the predominant framework through which members viewed the organization and determined its potential political allies. The rejection of reflexive anticommunism as a basis for American foreign policy by large numbers of ADA liberals in the mid-1960s represented a significant recasting of the "vital center" that had guided the organization during the early postwar years. A change in the specific positions of the "vital center" did not mean, however, that ADA liberals discarded the political framework that had long surrounded it. The growing number of figures in the ADA who insisted on a US foreign policy attuned to the new geopolitical realities of the world continued to see themselves and the organization as representing a "vital center" in the political landscape.

The acute sensitivity that Schlesinger conveyed in the late 1940s toward the dangers that he saw on the left laid the groundwork for the hypervigilance that he and other ADA liberals would later bring to their perspective on the radical activists of the antiwar movement. This hypervigilance and the continued insistence of ADA liberals that their political position represented a "vital center" flanked by irrationality on both the right and the left meant that the organization's leadership never entertained the prospect of involvement in an emerging antiwar movement shaped by SDS, NCC, and other radical organizations. In the context of the polarized political environment produced by the escalation of the US war effort in Vietnam and the corresponding growth in antiwar demonstrations, the trend toward conspiratorial thinking that ADA liberals saw on both the right and the left provided the basis for a framework that stressed the fundamental irrationality that existed on either side of the organization's "vital center." That framework held that while those on the right saw a communist conspiracy that fomented antiwar demonstrations in the United States and those on the left saw US Vietnam policy as dictated by a capitalist conspiracy to secure markets and expand profits, the ADA and those within the confines of what Schlesinger had termed a "vital center" accepted the complex subtleties of the situation.⁴⁵ The ADA's persistence in delegitimizing positions to its left and right ensured that the radicals who staged the earliest antiwar demonstrations were seen by ADA liberals as unquestionably beyond the pale. Still, this commitment to the "vital center" and the hypervigilance that ADA liberals displayed toward the left did not merely impact their relationship, or lack thereof, with radical antiwar activists. It also greatly hindered their relationship with liberal antiwar activists when liberals began to stake a claim to their own territory in the antiwar movement.

THE PERILS OF MASS DEMONSTRATION

Given the sizable public backlash that protests against the Vietnam War had engendered in early 1965, activists from the National Committee for a Sane Nuclear Policy (SANE) and other liberal organizations took great care to contrast their plans for a November 27 March on Washington with the demonstrations organized earlier by SDS and the NCC.⁴⁶ Many of the participants at those earlier events had called for the unilateral withdrawal of American troops from Vietnam. Although relatively few in number, participants who coupled their demand for unilateral withdrawal with civil disobedience and displays of the Vietcong flag invariably ended up on the front page of newspapers and on the evening news. In contrast, organizers of the November march stressed that their orderly event would be free of civil disobedience and based on a call for the US government to stop bombing North Vietnam, halt escalation of the war, push for a cease-fire, and engage in negotiations with all concerned parties, including the Vietcong. Along with presenting a host of measures familiar to ADA ears and similar in content and tenor to recent ADA resolutions on the Vietnam War, organizers insisted that even if the United States could not negotiate an end to the war by itself, there were a number of initiatives the American government could take that might greatly increase the possibility of a negotiated settlement.⁴⁷ Still, despite their general agreement with the outlook of the march organizers, ADA leaders continued to adhere to the notion of a "vital center" that precluded cooperation with radical antiwar activists and greatly complicated their relationship with demonstrations, where it was inherently impossible to control the composition of participants or the message they projected. This relationship would be further imperiled by the basic resistance of ADA leaders such as Arthur Schlesinger Jr. to mass demonstrations as a means of bringing pressure to bear on complex foreign policy decisions.

Throughout their preparations, organizers of the November march expended considerable energy trying to facilitate the involvement of liberal opponents of the Vietnam War from organizations like the ADA. In a series of memorandums to local organizers, the march coordinator, SANE's Sanford Gottlieb, took great pains to ensure a respectable and moderate image for the demonstration. To safeguard against the presence of Vietcong flags, the memorandum stressed that only the US and United Nations flags would be permitted at the march. It also emphasized the need for neat dress and provided detailed instructions outlining ways of navigating the "delicate problem" of "young people who cherish their informality." In order to control the message and overall perception of the demonstration, all signs would carry wording from a list of preapproved slogans and would be supplied by organizers in Washington, DC. Participants would be allowed to bring signs indicating only their city, state, or school.[48] The issue of permitted flags and sign slogans presented a particularly difficult problem for organizers as confusion surrounded the question of what to do with participants who insisted on joining the demonstration with Vietcong flags, signs calling for unilateral American withdrawal from Vietnam, or other unpermitted items. Despite reports in the *New York Times* that organizers would appeal to police for assistance with groups who joined the demonstration with unauthorized signs, Gottlieb insisted that police intervention would not be sought and expressed the hope that those who refused monitors' requests to discard forbidden signs would simply become "lost in the sea of humanity around them."[49]

Still, despite such efforts to distinguish the November march from earlier antiwar events, Gottlieb nervously complained that the press tended to "blur any distinctions between the November 27 event and previous actions" and "merge all critical activities in one unified movement."[50] The lack of subtlety in the press coverage of the November march further aggravated the already divisive question of the ADA's participation in antiwar demonstrations. Since the march was to be sponsored not by organizations, however, but by individuals, the issue of the ADA's relationship to the event never came up for formal debate or a vote by the national board.[51] Technically adhering to the neutrality necessitated by the lack of a vote on the matter, national director Leon Shull—with the support of national chairman Don Edwards—sent a memorandum to the national board and local chapters informing them that while the ADA was not endorsing the event, members were free to participate as individuals. Shull's memorandum echoed Gottlieb on the need to distinguish the November march from earlier antiwar demonstrations and emphasized both the moderate nature of the planned event and its position on the Vietnam War, which it shared with the ADA. He informed the ADA board and chapters that march organizers would be cooperating closely with local police to ensure order and sought to allay potential concerns with the erroneous assurance, likely based on the *New York Times* coverage of plans for the event, that police assistance would be sought in order to prevent unauthorized signs from being displayed during the march.[52]

Regardless of its ostensibly neutral stance on the November march, the memorandum from Shull fanned the flames of growing tension in the ADA over the question of participation in the demonstration. The misinformation Shull passed along on the planned use of police assistance to separate individuals with unauthorized signs from the bulk of the demonstrators might have served to ease the concerns of those in the ADA who wanted to participate but feared being associated with hecklers waving Vietcong flags. Still, significant elements of the ADA leadership remained troubled about any prospect of ADA association with the event regardless of whether or not police assistance would be sought to control the demonstration. With some already seeing Shull's memorandum as an implicit endorsement of the march, the placement of an advertisement for the November 27 march in *ADA World* alongside two editorials defending the rights of antiwar demonstrators and an article providing additional details about the event offered further evidence for ADA members who feared that the organization had effectively endorsed the demonstration.[53]

The ADA's seeming endorsement unleashed a flurry of critical responses that illuminated the fraught nature of the organization's relationship to the antiwar movement. In response to Shull's memorandum, Henry Meigs, a national board member and leading figure in the southeastern Pennsylvania chapter of the ADA, wrote an angry letter urging the national director to disassociate himself from those who were supporting the march. Meigs also took Shull to task for eschewing an official endorsement in order to avoid bringing attention to the significant discord in the ADA surrounding participation in an antiwar demonstration. Though he clearly missed the fact that the event was to be sponsored by individuals—not organizations—Meigs's belief that the ADA leadership had decided to "fudge the issue by merely encouraging others to participate" indicated the depth of the difficulties that the ADA would have faced had it needed to seek broader support on the national board for an endorsement.[54] ADA national board members Samuel Beer and Paul Seabury earlier expressed similar disapproval of the organization's apparent support for the November march when they wrote to Edwards to state their "grave reservations about lending ADA's support to a very problematical enterprise."[55]

In an effort to distinguish the November 27 march from the general focus on American responsibility for the conflict displayed at earlier antiwar demonstrations, march organizers tactfully sent a telegram to North Vietnamese leader Ho Chi Minh insisting that North Vietnam come to the negotiation table. The telegram also warned Ho that while demonstrations would continue, they would not lead to the withdrawal of US forces.[56] Such gestures made little impact on Beer and Seabury, who condemned the "moralistic unilateralism which sees only the violence of one side" and contended that "literate Americans who read newspapers" would have no respect for any organization that lent itself to the "deception" they believed the march would perpetuate. Unconvinced by the claim made by march organizers to Ho that the demonstration alone would not damage the American will to fight, Beer and Seabury voiced their concern that the more "visible" protests against the war became, the more Hanoi would begin to doubt American commitment to the war and the less likely it would be to negotiate. The wealth of evidence pointing to plans for an event painstakingly focused on maintaining order and a moderate image had no impact on Beer and Seabury. They insisted that by joining those who "roam the streets," the ADA would become associated with "extremist clamor, every bit as dishonest as that of the John Birch Society," and would do little "to prepare the mood of the American public" for negotiations. More to the point, Beer and Seabury stressed that the leadership of certain protest groups that would turn up at the November march were not at all interested in peace as such but rather wanted a Vietcong victory. In their view, ADA members should not lose their nerve or feel that they were risking their "liberal masculinity by refusing to join the fashionable protestors."[57]

As the November 27 march approached, opposition to the ADA's cooperation with the demonstration gained greater currency within the organization when Schlesinger sent a letter to Edwards expressing his desire to "very strongly associate" himself with the earlier letter from Beer and Seabury. Schlesinger concurred with the two that the march's ostensible goal of a negotiated settlement in Vietnam would only be damaged by signaling to the Vietcong and Hanoi that domestic protest in the United States would lead to a de-escalation of the US military effort or even the outright withdrawal of American forces. Revealing a disdain toward popular participation in the formulation of foreign policy, Schlesinger further challenged the merits of the event on the grounds that a mass demonstration did not represent a legitimate way to advance the discussion of foreign policy and made no "serious intellectual contribution to the debate." Schlesinger conveyed even greater doubts as to the motivations and honesty of the march organizers than did Beer and Seabury. With little explanation and no evidence, Schlesinger suggested that the ostensible goal of a negotiated settlement would really be "a mask behind which to organize pressure for an American withdrawal and even perhaps to begin a reconstitution of the popular front of the thirties." He urged the ADA to reverse its decision to cooperate with a "half-baked, un-thought-through demonstration" that would only "place a weapon in the hands of every enemy of the ADA in the country."[58]

The emphatic protests of Beer, Meigs, Schlesinger, and Seabury highlighted the significant opposition within the ADA to any prospect of the organization's cooperation with antiwar demonstrations but did little to change the group's connection to an event with which it had no official relationship. ADA members who responded to the organization's publicity by stating a desire to attend the march joined individuals from other groups such as SANE and Women Strike for Peace (WSP), clergy, and thousands of other Americans from largely liberal middle-class backgrounds in preparing for the event.[59] In the weeks preceding the march, the NCC decided to hold its annual meeting in Washington, DC, the same weekend as the November 27 March on Washington. Organizers of the march had little sympathy for the NCC's efforts to establish a radical alignment for peace that was both anti-imperialist and antiwar.[60] Though the NCC maintained that it simply sought to lend support to the demonstration through the likely presence of its roughly 1,500 delegates and members, many of those in the ADA who planned to participate in the march were unhappy with the development.[61] National board member Louis Braun did not look kindly upon the NCC's offer of support. He wrote to other individual sponsors of the event in the ADA to express his concern that the participation of individuals from the NCC and its constituent groups such as the May 2nd Movement and W. E. B. Du Bois Clubs would cloud both the original purpose of the march and its moderate image. Still, he recognized that the NCC had every right both to hold its annual convention the same weekend as the November march and to encourage its members to participate in the event.[62] By spelling out the basic right of individual members of society to take part in actions such as the November march, Braun revealed the crux of the ADA's difficulty with antiwar demonstrations: the essential inability to control the participation in and message of mass protests.

Among the roughly 25,000 people who assembled around the Washington Monument on November 27—the largest antiwar demonstration ever seen at that point in the nation's capital—a smattering of activists from the NCC, SDS, and other radical organizations could be seen, but the overwhelming majority of demonstrators were middle-aged, middle-class, neatly dressed, and decidedly non-radical.[63] The lineup of speakers on the stage displayed a political composition that mirrored the thousands packed onto the National Mall. The march organizers tasked with lining up the speakers for the event had to avoid alienating liberals from organizations such as the ADA with concerns about the demonstration taking on a radical tenor while also reaching out to the student antiwar movement, which insisted on a strong stance against the war. Compromises were reached in a lineup that included mainstream political figures such as civil rights leader Coretta Scott King, renowned pediatrician and peace activist Dr. Benjamin Spock, former Socialist presidential candidate and pacifist Norman Thomas, and future ADA national chairman Joseph Duffey but excluded radical antiwar activists such as David Dellinger and Staughton Lynd; SDS president Carl Oglesby was the lone radical to take the podium.[64]

The presence, though negligible, of radicals on the stage and in the crowd did not stand in the way of overwhelmingly positive responses to the event in the press but continued to be a major sticking point for many of the ADA's leaders. Reflecting on reactions to the march, Gottlieb wrote that the media expected "a crowd of beatniks and found middle-class America."[65] The *New York Times* approvingly characterized most of the marchers as "middle-class whites in a holiday mood" who "far outnumbered the student groups and the radical left." Though acknowledging a sprinkling of

Vietcong flags in the crowd, the *Times* noted that authorized signs carried by members of organizations such as the ADA, SANE, Women's International League, and WSP predominated throughout the demonstration.[66] *Christian Century* echoed the *Times*' characterization, describing the crowd as "conservatively dressed" and "orderly," and even contended that the event might in retrospect "be viewed as one of the few sane events in an insane age."[67] Still, for many in the ranks of leadership in the ADA, the display of Vietcong flags—however limited in number—and the introduction of the chant "Hey, hey, LBJ, how many kids did you kill today?" into the vernacular of the antiwar movement discredited the entire event. Leading figures in the ADA also likely found a source of anxiety in the message from the president of the National Liberation Front expressing his best wishes for the "brilliant success" of the march and announcing that the NLF had released two American prisoners of war to demonstrate their solidarity with the demonstration.[68]

Despite widespread celebrations of the November 27 march in the press, the event would be the last instance of ADA cooperation—official or otherwise—with an antiwar demonstration until 1969. Positive press reactions had little impact on those who had opposed participation in the event since its announcement. Many of the ADA liberals harbored an aversion to antiwar demonstrations for reasons that went beyond the inability to control such events. Schlesinger expressed a view shared by many of his colleagues on the ADA national board when he insisted that while activists had every right to organize protests, mass demonstrations—even orderly ones—lowered the level of debate and ultimately undermined the greater potential for making real changes to policy offered by political opposition. Months after the March on Washington, at a panel discussion featuring prominent New York–based scholars, writers, and artists, Schlesinger drew a clear distinction between the effective and reasoned opposition of Senate doves and members of the intellectual community on one hand and the counterproductive and often hysterical efforts of antiwar demonstrators on the other. Schlesinger, now a professor at the City University of New York, recalled a conversation with an unnamed Senate dove who told him that if the demonstrations kept up, the only result would be the silencing of senatorial opposition to the war. Facing a chorus of boos and gasps from the audience, Schlesinger insisted that opposition to the war would be best served by advancing arguments through political and electoral means rather than engaging in demonstrations, which served only to provide an "emotional orgasm" for participants. Offering a blunt assessment of the November 27 march, he declared: "I think the speeches of senators Church, McGovern, Fulbright, Robert Kennedy and so on, have had more influence in changing policy than the March on Washington. If the point is to be effective, you don't carry Vietcong banners."[69]

Schlesinger's highly critical stance on the November march revealed more than his objection to events that included the participation of radicals. While the presence of even a limited number of Vietcong flags irked Schlesinger and led him to question the effectiveness of the march, much of his opposition to the event rested on a general rejection of mass demonstrations as a means of influencing complex foreign policy. Schlesinger further developed his position later that year when he wrote that while mass demonstrations could certainly be useful in instances such as civil rights, where the intellectual and moral issues were clear and self-evident, they did not serve the cause of rational debate when the issues were complex and ambiguous, as with the Vietnam War. In his estimation, any initiatives that would diminish the rationality of the debate represented a self-defeating tactic for intellectuals, who, he maintained, would always lose to reactionary anti-intellectuals in a "competition in demagoguery and hysteria."[70]

Schlesinger's unease with a moral and emotional approach to political issues—particularly those that he saw as complex and requiring nuance—stretched back to his days working on *The Vital Center* in the late 1940s. With the supporters of Henry Wallace in mind, Schlesinger derided Progressives for trying to avoid the hard work of developing "wise policies in an imperfect world" by devoting themselves to the "subtle sensations of the perfect syllogism" and "the lost cause." Those Progressives, he contended, saw politics "not as a means of getting things done, but an outlet for private grievances and frustrations."[71] Schlesinger and his fellow ADA liberals had acceded to the moral perspective of the civil rights movement in its struggle against a clearly unjust Jim Crow system which pitted dignified, nonviolent civil rights protesters against violent, racist white authorities and crowds in the South. But when ADA liberals approached the complexities of the Vietnam War, they reverted to their general unease with a moral perspective on politics and cast a critical eye on forms of opposition to the war that they viewed as ineffective moral crusades. Consequently, they bristled at the prospect of joining mass demonstrations. In their eyes, the Vietnam War was a grave mistake of policy, not the sin that most activists who participated in those demonstrations believed it to be. It does not necessarily follow, however, that rejection of a moral perspective on the war made ADA liberals less sincere in their opposition to it.

Even for those in the ADA who did not share Schlesinger's disapproval of mass demonstrations as a means of influencing foreign policy or the specifics of his unease with moral and emotional approaches to politics, the tendency of ADA liberals to see themselves and the organization as a "vital center" surrounded by irrationality on all sides made participation in mass demonstrations virtually impossible. The general conviction that any position to the left or right of the ADA was too irrational to address a complex issue like the Vietnam War perpetuated an intolerance of alternate views and strategies. This in turn ensured that joining mass protests remained off the table as an option for expressing the mounting opposition to the war found in the organization. Edwards, Galbraith, and other important voices in the ADA offered their approval of the November march, but their support for the demonstration proved far less vigorous than the opposition of those in the organization categorically or strategically opposed to cooperating with antiwar demonstrations.[72] With strident opposition to participation in antiwar demonstrations expressed by enough members of the national board to block cooperation even with antiwar demonstrations organized by liberals, the ADA deprived itself of what could have been a valuable form of pressure on the Johnson administration to change the course of the Vietnam War. Unwilling to take part in the demonstrations that drove the growing antiwar movement, the ADA found itself with limited alternatives as it sought to translate its opposition to the Vietnam War into tangible and effective action.

A VITAL CENTER ANTIWAR INITIATIVE

As the antiwar movement continued to grow in scale and momentum, ADA vice chairman Joseph Rauh joined Martin Luther King Jr. on April 24, 1967, in announcing an initiative aimed at putting pressure on the Johnson administration to take steps that they believed would make the realization of a negotiated settlement to the Vietnam War possible.[73] Negotiation Now! sought to collect 1 million signatures on a petition that supported the call by United Nations secretary general U Thant for an unconditional cessation of the bombing of North Vietnam, a de-escalation of the fighting in South

Vietnam, and negotiations between Washington, Hanoi, Saigon, and the NLF on the establishment of a cease-fire.[74] With Galbraith, Schlesinger, and a host of other ADA leaders among its list of prominent sponsors, the campaign launched with high hopes and garnered significant media attention in the spring of 1967. Despite its hopeful start, Negotiation Now! ultimately ended in failure and left behind a complicated legacy. Historians have sometimes portrayed Negotiation Now! as an effort to co-opt the antiwar movement by socialists and liberals who harbored no genuine opposition to the Vietnam War but wished to be seen as doing something to bring the conflict to an end.[75] While such characterizations undoubtedly describe the motivation of some of the individuals involved in Negotiation Now!, they do not accurately depict the aims of the bulk of the campaign's sponsors, who looked to the initiative as the best available prospect for bringing the war to an end. The ADA and its leaders did not place their hopes on Negotiation Now! because they were insincere or uncommitted in their opposition to the war. Rather, they prioritized the petition-gathering campaign because their decision not to participate in antiwar demonstrations left them with little choice but to focus their efforts on an initially promising but ultimately limited and unsuccessful initiative seen by many of its supporters as a "vital center" in a polarized Vietnam War debate.

Negotiation Now! represented just one of several new antiwar campaigns launched during the spring and summer months of 1967 that demonstrate the political diversity to be found in the antiwar movement. In early 1967 the Spring Mobilization Committee emerged as a powerful force in the movement, with its predominantly radical leadership and non-exclusion of any groups or individuals as its driving principle.[76] The Spring Mobilization protest on April 15 in San Francisco represented a record turnout for an antiwar demonstration on the West Coast, attracting some 75,000 people to a rally in Kezar Stadium at the edge of Golden Gate Park. The corresponding demonstration in New York City saw a crowd that some observers placed at 400,000 march from Central Park to the United Nations plaza. The policy of non-exclusion was readily apparent at the New York march, with a crowd that included Blacks and whites, children and grandparents, Vietcong sympathizers and military veterans, hippies and church members, student radicals and white-collar professionals. Many of the individuals who participated in the bicoastal event had never before protested against the Vietnam War.[77]

Despite the impressive numbers and diversity of participants at the Spring Mobilization demonstrations, the radical orientation of the Mobilization leadership and the provocative nature of the demonstrations themselves precluded the participation of many liberal antiwar activists and organizations. Eight days after the Spring Mobilization, Martin Luther King Jr., Carl Oglesby, and Benjamin Spock announced an antiwar project more specifically aimed at promoting liberal-radical cooperation. Modeled after the 1964 Mississippi Summer project of the civil rights movement, Vietnam Summer represented an ambitious effort to bring liberals and radicals together in grassroots antiwar organizing.[78] With the aim of attracting youths who had become interested in the antiwar movement in the wake of the April 15 demonstrations, Vietnam Summer encouraged students to go door-to-door in their own communities to organize existing opposition to the Vietnam War into an electoral base for upcoming local elections and presidential primaries.[79]

In contrast to the confrontational nature of the Spring Mobilization and the radical-liberal cooperation actively sought by the Vietnam Summer initiative, Negotiation Now! organizers set their sights on moderates and the political mainstream. The Negotiation Now! program grew out of the belief that the mass collection of signatures would encourage President Johnson to change the course of the war by bolstering congressional doves and critics of the prevailing policy within the administration.[80] Campaign organizers stressed that the Negotiation Now! program would be minimal enough to appeal to the widest possible range of Americans yet effective enough to help bring the war to an end on "honorable terms."[81]

The narrowly targeted approach of Negotiation Now! held considerable appeal for ADA liberals. Shortly after the announcement of the petition campaign, the ADA threw its weight behind the program, which quickly became the primary focus of its antiwar efforts. Leon Shull called Negotiation Now! "the best vehicle that has yet been created to provide the American people with a coalition program that can bring the war to an end." Hopes for the campaign ran high in its early days. With the participation of local ADA chapters, the campaign filled requests for over 700,000 petitions in the first month of the effort.[82] When delegates of the Negotiation Now! campaign met in Washington, DC, on June 29 to kick off their petition drive and lobby members of Congress, Galbraith addressed the luncheon assembly at the Mayflower Hotel with a detailed proposal for establishing the conditions necessary for peace negotiations. He outlined a plan whereby the United States would cease bombing North Vietnam and abandon the objective of reconquering all of South Vietnam in favor of securing selected urban areas to establish a "holding operation" for negotiations. Expressing considerable confidence in the viability of his plan, he declared, "Rarely in foreign policy is the path of wisdom so clearly etched."[83] Backed by the cheering audience at the luncheon, Galbraith's proposal also resonated with the broader liberal community. In the weeks that followed, the ADA received an unprecedented volume of mail—most of it supportive—in response to Galbraith's influential speech.[84]

Many in the leadership ranks of the ADA shared Galbraith's recognition of the political realities of opposition to the Vietnam War and viewed the Negotiation Now! campaign as a valuable alternative to the antiwar demonstrations that were driving the antiwar movement. One month prior to the April 15 Spring Mobilization, *ADA World* editor Curtis Gans, assessing the planned bicoastal event, expressed concern that the Mobilization's call for unilateral withdrawal and its branding of the Vietnam conflict as a "racist war" would alienate the vast majority of Americans. Gans concluded that the ADA ought to remain entirely out of the Mobilization and work on an alternative program that held some hope of attracting mass support.[85] The actions and tenor of the Spring Mobilization justified a number of Gans's concerns. While the Mobilization march in New York had seen a large number of Americans from all walks of life and respectable political figures such as Martin Luther King Jr. and Benjamin Spock take a stand against the war, the demonstration also included the widespread burning of draft cards, the flying of Vietcong flags from a forty-foot-tall makeshift tower, and other actions deemed irresponsible and extremist by the ADA.[86]

The grassroots organizing undertaken by the liberals and radicals who cooperated in the Vietnam Summer effort represented a far more appealing program for the ADA to cooperate with than the Spring Mobilization but still presented the political risks to be found in associating with unpredictable radicals. The significant autonomy provided to local groups in the loose coalition that made up Vietnam Summer represented a significant hurdle to the ADA's cooperation with the program. Gans noted that Vietnam Summer in some places would take the form of door-to-door organizing and in other places would offer the promise of mass demonstrations and civil disobedience. The proposed plan of the national Vietnam Summer campaign to channel riots in the ghettos into antiwar riots represented a particularly alarming prospect for Gans. Though acknowledging that Vietnam Summer would be a multifaceted campaign—with the bulk of activity taking on less radical forms than ghetto riots—Gans worried about how it would be represented in the media. In light of press coverage of the Spring Mobilization and other demonstrations, he warned that the national image of Vietnam Summer would likely be determined by the campaign's most extreme and headline-grabbing actions.[87]

From the perspective of ADA liberals, Negotiation Now! offered a number of important advantages over Mobilization demonstrations and Vietnam Summer's program for opposing the Vietnam policies of the Johnson administration. Unlike the Spring Mobilization Committee and its successor, the National Mobilization Committee, known informally as the Mobe, Negotiation Now! avoided the pitfalls for the ADA of engaging in mass demonstrations that remained beyond the organization's control. In fact, in the case of the Mobilization events, the policy of non-exclusion meant that control was not just infeasible but explicitly rejected. The Vietnam Summer's campaign of door-to-door organizing with an eye toward building a political base for doves in the 1968 election had more in common with the ADA's general orientation toward political and electoral opposition to the Vietnam War. Vietnam Summer's plan to draw its door-to-door canvassing staff from student populations, however, was a source of worry for Gans, who noted that the majority of recruits would come from the "most radical and activist fringe on the campus." Gans readily conceded that radical students might be the most highly motivated, but to they were unlikely to win acceptance with moderates who answered the door.[88]

In contrast to the mass demonstrations organized by the National Mobilization Committee and the autonomous local efforts of Vietnam Summer, Negotiation Now! presented a well-defined program with a controllable message based on seeking signatures for a petition presenting a narrow statement designed to appeal to the widest possible range of Americans. The campaign would give the broader public a sense of participating in the antiwar movement while ensuring that the message continued to be determined by the Negotiation Now! leadership, not by the radical minority on whom the press could be expected to lavish attention at mass antiwar demonstrations. Unlike the antics of demonstrators who waved Vietcong flags at Mobilization demonstrations and Vietnam Summer activists who knocked on doors and heaped blame for the Vietnam War on the United States, Negotiation Now! would be, in Shull's words, "an effective peace effort" that included "no moral condemnation of America."[89]

Outside the confines of the ADA, however, Negotiation Now!—and the proposals for bringing the Vietnam War to an end that accompanied the campaign—received a far less favorable response than anticipated. When Negotiation Now! efforts kicked off in the summer of 1967, the campaign faced a deeply polarized nation. In June, when Rauh, former ADA national chairman Don Edwards, and two dozen other individuals stood in downtown Washington, DC, with clipboards and pens to collect signatures for the petition drive, they found passers-by nearly as forthcoming with insults as with signatures. Rauh's stint began at the corner of Connecticut Avenue and K Street, where he was called a "Communist S.O.B." and "a disgrace to the whole country." Another passer-by recognized Rauh and told him that he had no right to stand on the street and protest Johnson's Vietnam policies when the ADA had so actively supported the president's election in 1964: "You put him [President Johnson] in there. I gave you $1 to do it." The experience led Rauh to remark, "I've never seen such bitterness on both sides of an issue."[90]

Amid the polarization described by Rauh, members of the Negotiation Now! executive committee who organized the campaign and oversaw its day-to-day activities framed their initiative as a "vital center" in a sea of irrationality and futility. While they did not use the specific phrase in the literature they produced, the Negotiation Now! executive committee nevertheless drew on the "vital center" framework long employed by the ADA in rejecting both the anti-Americanism they saw in the call for unilateral withdrawal at antiwar demonstrations and the military escalation urged by hawkish supporters of the war. Just as the ADA had expended substantial energy contrasting its "vital center" with both Henry Wallace's Progressives and conservative Republicans during the early post–World War II years, Negotiation Now! organizers devoted significant attention to distinguishing their proposals from what they viewed as morally suspect and irresponsible positions on both the left and right.[91]

The commitment of Negotiation Now! to positioning itself as a "vital center" surrounded by irresponsibility had been critical to attracting support from the ADA and other liberal organizations but proved to be a major hurdle in the campaign's goal of reaching 1 million signatures. As the summer progressed, Negotiation Now! organizers and the ADA expressed positive assessments of the signature-gathering effort in order to obscure the lackluster response from the public. At the time of its launch, Negotiation Now! printed 700,000 petitions, and campaign organizers boasted that they expected to obtain not merely 1 million but millions of signatures by the end of summer. Getting petitions signed, however, proved to be far more difficult than printing them. By the end of September, the plural millions quietly went missing from campaign rhetoric, and Negotiation Now! instead focused on its initial goal of obtaining a million signatures. The insistence of organizers on excluding individuals and organizations that supported unilateral withdrawal—even if they agreed to mute their position on the issue for the sake of a successful petition drive—deprived the initiative of vital resources and manpower. As a result, Negotiation Now! had to rely largely on a narrow base of moderate religious organizations and community groups, which left its petition-gathering efforts almost certain to fail. When Negotiation Now! made it halfway to its original goal by scraping together 500,000 signatures, organizers met in Washington, DC, to declare the campaign a success, noting that half a million signatures represented the largest number of names ever gathered on a peace petition in the United States.[92]

Consensus among ADA liberals on the efficacy of Negotiation Now! had started to fall apart even before the poor tallies from the petition effort came in. The ability to strictly manage the message of and participation in the campaign had been a key element in the appeal of Negotiation Now! to ADA liberals in the first place. By now the tendency of the Negotiation Now! organizers toward obsessive control and excessive attention to differentiating their proposals from alternative approaches had begun to alienate even the campaign's initial backers in the ADA. The language of the Negotiation Now! petition initially sponsored by Galbraith, Rauh, and Schlesinger had described negotiated settlement as a "more realistic alternative than unilateral withdrawal." Subsequent campaign literature and the *Negotiation Now! Bulletin*, however, specifically rejected unilateral withdrawal and devoted more attention to delegitimizing any consideration of a pullout of American forces than to making the case against escalation of the US war effort.[93] Though he had been an early supporter of the petition-gathering drive, Gans took issue with what he saw as the transformation of Negotiation Now! from an antiwar initiative into what effectively amounted to an anti–unilateral withdrawal campaign.[94]

The preoccupation of Negotiation Now! organizers with delegitimizing unilateral withdrawal has provided the basis for enduring characterizations of the campaign's prominent sponsors as less than sincere in their professed opposition to the Vietnam War. The position developed by Negotiation Now! organizers over the course of 1967 was such that leaders in the Socialist Party of America (SPA)—who tacitly supported the prosecution of the war by the Johnson administration—could endorse the campaign as a way of being able to claim that they were working to bring the conflict to an end while criticizing the broader antiwar movement as extremist and sympathetic to communists.[95] Unlike those SPA leaders, however, Galbraith, Rauh, Schlesinger, and other leading figures from the ADA who helped to launch Negotiation Now! genuinely sought a swift end to the fighting in Vietnam. Still, the insistence of those ADA leaders on adhering to a "vital center" framework that precluded cooperation with mass antiwar demonstrations, if not quite as exacting as the position of the Negotiation Now! organizers, had nevertheless left them with few options but to work with an inherently limited initiative that relied on a narrow base of organizational support.

In part, the Negotiation Now! campaign suffered from the shortcomings of insisting on a negotiated settlement to the Vietnam War, which became increasingly apparent to many of its supporters in the months that followed the launch of the campaign. The notion that the Vietnam War could be brought to an end if all concerned parties were urged to the negotiating table had seemed doubtful from the earliest days of major US involvement. It is difficult to imagine an arrangement concerning the NLF's future that could have compelled the group to lay down its arms while also satisfying both Washington's insistence on a non-communist government in the South and Hanoi's basic aim of reunifying the country. A negotiated settlement that had always been improbable became an ever more distant prospect as the body counts mounted and all sides dug in on their positions.[96]

The fundamental difficulty of negotiating a settlement to the Vietnam War shaped the dilemma faced by ADA liberals in the mid-1960s. The position of the ADA during the first three years of major American military involvement in the conflict included both a desire for South Vietnam to remain free from communist control and a rejection of the escalation of the US war effort that would have been necessary to secure the survival of a non-communist government in the South. Still, even during the period in which the position of the ADA generally corresponded with that of Negotiation Now!, ADA liberals typically differed from those at the helm of the petition-gathering campaign in that their concern over the type of government that ruled South Vietnam arose primarily from domestic political considerations rather than fear of a growing and supposedly monolithic communist bloc. For that reason, the leading critics of the Vietnam War in the ADA never fully embraced the uncompromising refusal of Negotiation Now! organizers to even consider unilateral withdrawal as a legitimate option available to the United States.

Together the early and consistent opposition of the ADA to US escalation and an understanding of polycentric communism held by its leading figures that rendered the form of government in South Vietnam a question of limited geopolitical importance hinted that, if forced to choose between escalation and withdrawal, the organization would choose the latter. The prospect of "losing" Vietnam as President Harry Truman had earlier "lost" China remained a politically dangerous prospect in the eyes of ADA liberals. Even so, the military circumstances of the Vietnam War and the cutbacks to domestic social programs that resulted from protracted US intervention in the conflict pushed the organization and its leadership toward a more decisive position on the war by eroding the middle ground the ADA had long sought to occupy.

With that middle ground largely untenable by the end of 1967, the implications of the position advanced by the ADA and its leading figures became far more apparent. As the war neared its third year of large-scale US troop involvement, Galbraith expressed little of the confidence in the feasibility of a negotiated settlement that had underpinned his Negotiation Now! speech during the summer, and Schlesinger would concede that while unilateral withdrawal "would hardly be America's finest hour," it "would be greatly preferable to a policy of unlimited escalation."[97] Two years after they committed themselves to Negotiation Now! as the focus of their antiwar activities, Galbraith, Schlesinger, and other veteran leaders in the ADA sided with the overwhelming majority of members in the group who voted for a resolution calling for the immediate unilateral withdrawal of American forces from Vietnam.[98]

Before they embraced the call for a unilateral withdrawal, Galbraith, Schlesinger, Rauh, and other ADA leaders insisted on maintaining a "vital center" position that meant keeping their distance from mass antiwar demonstrations and pushing a negotiated settlement to the conflict with limited and diminishing prospects. These positions, and the ineffective signature-gathering initiative they joined to pursue an end to US involvement in the war, obscured the implications of the foreign policy perspective they had developed. The opposition to the Vietnam War advanced by these veteran ADA leaders expressed a rejection of the insistence on communist containment that had defined the foreign policy of both liberals and conservatives since the early postwar years. Though their opposition to the war was unrealistic in its approach and ineffective in achieving its aims, it was not half-hearted. The committed opposition to the war advanced by these figures put them on a collision course with many of their colleagues in the ADA, the labor unions on which the organization had long depended for financial and political support, and the Johnson administration. In the early years of major US military involvement in Vietnam, the differences over the war in the ADA that ultimately led to this collision could, in many cases, be downplayed or avoided. When, however, concerns over civil rights and poverty that had long inspired opposition to the war in the ADA established the conflict as the defining issue of liberal politics, those differences would become unbridgeable.

CHAPTER 3

BEYOND THE WAR ON POVERTY

The Civil Rights Movement, Social Democracy,
and the Struggle for Racial Equality

In the wake of the 1963 March on Washington for Jobs and Freedom, as a Senate filibuster stalled the bill that would become the Civil Rights Act of 1964, ADA national chairman John Roche described how "the civil rights revolution has opened the door into forgotten America . . . it has revealed far more than the injustice that has been done to millions of American citizens by depriving them of their constitutional rights."[1] By putting the national spotlight on the poverty that narrowed the opportunities and restricted the freedom of a significant number of Americans, the civil rights movement fostered an awareness among ADA liberals of the enduring scale and depth of poverty that had previously been lost to presumptions of widespread affluence and excessive confidence in the social benefits of economic growth. While radical antiwar activists and the broader New Left had limited influence on the political trajectory of ADA liberals during the 1960s, the attention focused on the interconnected issues of economic and racial inequality by mainstream civil rights leaders fundamentally reshaped how the predominantly white ADA viewed the relationship between race and poverty.

Some accounts of postwar American liberalism characterize the ideology as rooted in racist assumptions of Black pathology and as unable to deviate from the demands of a racial capitalism that depends on racial classification and stratification as a means of capital accumulation.[2] Other accounts highlight white liberals who either assumed that the enactment of civil rights legislation by itself could achieve racial equality or were unreliable allies of the civil rights movement.[3] While such characterizations undoubtedly capture certain strands of postwar liberalism and the stance of well-known liberals from the period, they do not account for the change seen within the ADA—an organization frequently taken to be the quintessential representative of the postwar liberal tradition—during the 1960s. In contrast to white liberals who often proved to be less than dependable allies of the civil rights movement in the postwar era, key figures in the ADA such as Joseph Rauh displayed a thoroughgoing commitment to the cause of civil rights and reconciled principle and politics on terms that were frequently similar to those of the nation's major civil rights leaders. Similarly, most in the ADA shared the perspective of civil rights leaders that while civil rights legislation was vitally important, it would be only the beginning of a long and far-reaching struggle for meaningful racial equality. When the increasing momentum of the civil rights movement in the early 1960s brought a new level of visibility to the entrenched economic inequality that underpinned racial inequality, the commitment of ADA liberals to the fight for civil rights expanded to include the struggle against poverty. The ideas and initiatives developed by ADA liberals to advance that struggle stand starkly at odds with characterizations of postwar liberals as unable or unwilling to challenge the status quo of American capitalism.

A newfound commitment to tackling poverty among ADA liberals did not, however, generate a corresponding agreement on how best to attack the complex and deep-seated issue of chronic economic deprivation. In the years that followed President Lyndon Johnson's declaration of an "unconditional war on poverty" during his 1964 State of the Union Address, John Kenneth Galbraith and Arthur Schlesinger Jr. saw considerable potential in the services and human capital development approach pursued by the administration, which embodied many of the ideas central to the qualitative liberalism they had been advancing since the 1950s.[4] Still, despite Galbraith's and Schlesinger's broad influence in the ADA, most in the organization's leadership ranks did not share their general agreement with the approach—if not the scale—of Johnson's War on Poverty. Instead, the bulk of ADA leaders believed that the War on Poverty and the basic orientation of the Johnson administration's Great Society initiatives failed to address structural unemployment and the related economic obstacles that would continue to perpetuate racial inequality even if civil rights and voting rights were enshrined into law.

The insistence on a structural response to poverty centered on jobs and income that prevailed over the approaches advocated by Galbraith and

Schlesinger in the ADA's policies on poverty, the economy, and civil rights in the mid-1960s rested on a far more overtly social democratic outlook than the organization had exhibited in its past. While the ADA's predecessor, the Union for Democratic Action, readily struck a social democratic note in its efforts on behalf of full employment policy in the mid-1940s, the ADA from its founding through the early 1960s looked to economic growth and private industry—with proper government planning and regulation—as the answer to the poverty that persisted in what was seen as an increasingly affluent society.[5] Prompted by a growing recognition of the economic roots of racial inequality, the turn of the ADA toward a social democratic perspective that held the federal government directly responsible for providing jobs and incomes to American citizens stood in striking contrast to both the underlying approach of the Great Society and the more indirect role for government envisioned by the organization in its early years. As it diverged from the main currents of postwar liberal economics, the social democratic position adopted by the ADA turned to the politics of the UDA and the New Deal left as a starting point for solutions to the deeply interconnected problems of economic and racial inequality in the 1960s. Through its efforts to tackle racial inequality by borrowing from the liberalism of an earlier era, the ADA demonstrated that a New Deal framework that had been marked by racial exclusion could jettison its accommodations with Jim Crow and offer a stronger foundation for addressing the economic dimensions of racial inequality than the services and human capital development approach of Great Society programs.

Leon Keyserling drew on the push for large-scale public works projects and a guaranteed annual income that had become central to his economic thinking and the increasingly social democratic outlook of ADA policy when he laid the foundation for a bold new antipoverty initiative as the chief architect of the A. Philip Randolph Institute's "Freedom Budget."[6] By offering a systematic proposal for a jobs-and-income approach to poverty that went far beyond the limited-services approach of the Johnson administration's War on Poverty, the Freedom Budget managed to forge a powerful but brief consensus among a significant number of leading liberals and civil rights leaders. The confidence in the far-reaching social potential of economic growth that suffused the Freedom Budget and sustained a supportive consensus among a diverse array of liberals and civil rights leaders faced a fundamental and, ultimately, insurmountable challenge from a substantial escalation of the Vietnam War that revealed the limits of the American economy.

When it became clear that the United States possessed neither the economic resources nor the political will to wage war on communism in Vietnam and on poverty at home, support for a Freedom Budget campaign that rested on the assumption that the country could have both "guns and butter" evaporated just as quickly as it had emerged. With the diminishing influence of Keyserling's assertion that a growing American economy held almost limitless potential as a source for social progress, ADA liberals increasingly came to recognize US involvement in the Vietnam War as the first hurdle to addressing the economic barriers that continued to render racial equality a distant reality. The waning of Keyserling's influence in the ADA led to a wider acceptance of the ideas and policy prescriptions behind the qualitative liberalism Galbraith and Schlesinger had been championing for years. Still, the lingering influence of Keyserling's structural approach to poverty, and the differences that had developed between him and his former friends over the preceding years, ensured that when the New Politics movement drew on these ideas, it did not inherit a cohesive outlook on how best to address poverty and other economic issues.

WHITE LIBERALS, CIVIL RIGHTS, AND THE MISSISSIPPI FREEDOM DEMOCRATIC PARTY

Throughout the 1950s and 1960s, white liberals proved to be politically necessary though often unreliable allies of the civil rights movement. When the Mississippi Freedom Democratic Party (MFDP) sought to be seated in place of the "lily-white" delegation of the state's regular Democratic Party at the 1964 Democratic National Convention in Atlantic City, Hubert Humphrey and United Auto Workers (UAW) leader Walter Reuther intervened on behalf of Lyndon Johnson. The president had charged Humphrey and Reuther with the task of preventing a walkout of southern delegates that would damage the president's electoral prospects in the South in the November election. Both leading members in the ADA at the time of the convention, Humphrey and Reuther displayed a political expediency that fits the mold of white liberals found in many accounts of the civil rights movement. With emphasis on the divergence that developed between white liberals and civil rights leaders, historians have frequently characterized the former as easily susceptible to political pressures and insistent on confining their support for civil rights to the normal channels of established political institutions.[7] While much of the civil rights activity carried out by the predominantly white and northern membership of the ADA exhibited a desire to work through the traditional institutions of the political establishment, the dedicated involvement of organization leaders such as Joseph Rauh in the effort to seat the MFDP in Atlantic City demonstrates a stronger commitment to civil rights than has been assumed in many of those characterizations. In Rauh's case, erroneous reporting on the events that transpired at the convention continues to obscure the depth of his dedication to civil rights in numerous accounts of the movement. Rauh and other veteran leaders of the ADA were uncomfortable with some aspects of the civil disobedience practiced by those in the civil rights movement and the growing influence of Black nationalism in its ranks, but they did not differ substantially from Martin Luther King Jr., Bayard Rustin, Roy Wilkins, and other major civil rights leaders in terms of their willingness to reconcile principled goals with achievable progress.

Stretching back to its founding in 1947, the ADA provided important support for civil rights advances by bringing its influence to bear within the institutions of the nation's political establishment. At the 1948 Democratic National Convention, the ADA spearheaded support for a civil rights plank against the wishes of the Truman administration and southern delegates threatening to walk out. Humphrey's commitment to principle would later waver at the critical crossroads of the 1964 Democratic National Convention once the offer of the vice presidency was on the line, but in 1948, when he was further from the levers of power, he acceded to pressure from his colleagues in the ADA and delivered the most powerful speech of the convention with an address that provided vigorous support for the civil rights plank put together by the organization.[8] In what would become the most celebrated speech of his political career, Humphrey famously declared that it was "time for the Democratic Party to get out of the shadow of states' rights and walk forthrightly in the bright sunshine of human rights."[9] The ADA achieved its first major victory when delegates approved a civil rights plank that put the Democratic Party on the record in support of abolishing poll taxes in federal elections, passing a federal anti-lynching law, creating a permanent fair employment practice commission, and ending racial segregation in the military.[10] From calling on the Eisenhower administration to enforce *Brown v. Board of Education* and other pivotal Supreme Court decisions to pushing the Kennedy administration to act more urgently on its professed civil rights goals, the ADA continued to undertake consistent, if less than bold, actions to support the advancement of civil rights during the 1950s and early 1960s.

As legal counsel to the MFDP in 1964, Rauh became deeply involved in an initiative that operated distinctly outside the confines of the established political institutions to which the ADA had typically restricted its civil rights efforts. An outgrowth of the Freedom Summer campaign and the organizational work of Student Nonviolent Coordinating Committee (SNCC) leader Bob Moses, the MFDP held elections for delegates and established precinct, county, congressional, and state conventions that paralleled the party structure of the regular Mississippi Democratic Party. Concurrently, the predominantly African American membership of the MFDP attempted to attend the precinct meetings of the regular party—meetings that they had no expectation of being admitted to—in an effort to document evidence of systematic racial exclusion. As the leadership of the MFDP organized elections for delegates and joined with leaders from SNCC and other civil rights organizations to determine future aims for the Freedom Democrats, Rauh and his staff assembled the legal briefs that would form the basis of the party's challenge to take the place of the delegates of the state's regular party in Atlantic City. John Lewis, then a young leader in SNCC working on behalf of the initiative, later described how Rauh was "right in the thick of it" from the middle of June through August, when the MFDP sent local representatives to more than 1,900 precinct meetings across the state. According to Lewis, "Joe Rauh believed in the MFDP, and he came to Mississippi to help guide the Freedom Democrats through the maze of precinct, county and state elections that marked the path to the national convention."[11]

Delegates at the ADA National Convention on May 16 demonstrated a similar belief in the MFDP when they voted to endorse the effort to seat its delegates in place of those from the regular Mississippi Democratic Party and directed local chapters to work on behalf of electing delegates to the Democratic National Convention who were supportive of the initiative.[12] In the months that followed the ADA convention, chapters across the country mounted pressure at their respective states' Democratic conventions to support the cause of the MFDP. Members of the Massachusetts ADA secured passage of a resolution at their state's Democratic convention that put its delegation on the record in opposition to the seating of delegations disloyal to the national ticket and platform.[13] With the delegation of Mississippi's regular party expected to vote against Johnson in the November election in response to the president's support for civil rights legislation, loyalty requirements like those supported by the Massachusetts Democratic Party would be tantamount to unseating Mississippi Democratic regulars at the convention. Though unable to get their state's delegation to commit to a position, members of the Cleveland ADA made a strong display of support for the MFDP at the Ohio Democratic Party convention.[14]

When the MFDP took its challenge to the credentials committee of the Democratic National Convention on Saturday, August 22, Rauh built a compelling case for the party by drawing a picture of the oppressive circumstances of African American life in Mississippi and detailing the extensive actions taken by the state's officials to prevent citizens from voting. Led by MFDP chairman Aaron Henry, witnesses described the brutal and terrifying treatment they experienced while trying to register or vote. The most powerful testimony came from Fannie Lou Hamer, a sharecropper and established grassroots organizer, who recounted the savage beatings and arrests she suffered for trying to exercise her basic rights as an American citizen. "Is this America, the land of the free and the home of the brave," she asked the credentials committee, "where we are threatened daily because we want to live as decent human beings?" Bringing attention to the political circumstances involved in the challenge during his closing argument, Rauh predicted that the delegation of the regular Mississippi Democratic Party would come out in support of the Republican presidential candidate, Senator Barry Goldwater, the following month. Rauh concluded his case by putting forward the situation in stark moral and political terms: "Are you going to throw out of here people who want to work for Lyndon Johnson, who are willing to be beaten and shot and thrown in jail to work for Lyndon Johnson? Are we for the oppressor or the oppressed?"[15]

Infuriated by the MFDP's testimony before the credentials committee and intent on avoiding any action that would further jeopardize his electoral support in the South or disrupt a convention expected to nominate him unanimously as the party's presidential candidate, Johnson dispatched Humphrey and Reuther to engineer a compromise that would avoid a bruising floor battle before a national television audience. By dangling the vice presidency in front of the Minnesota senator and employing the considerable political leverage he held with the UAW president, Johnson compelled Humphrey and Reuther to act as liberal emissaries tasked with pressuring Rauh and the MFDP to accept a compromise. Put forward by Johnson backers on the credentials committee, the initial compromise offered only to make the MFDP delegation "honored guests" of the convention before being amended to allot the delegation two seats. When delegates from the MFDP discussed the deal with King, Moses, and Rauh on Sunday evening, all expressed opposition to the compromise and sought to press forward with the effort to bring the challenge to the floor of the convention, where they had high hopes that it would ultimately prevail. With only eleven votes from the 108-member credentials committee needed to send the MFDP's challenge to the convention floor, Rauh remained unswayed by Humphrey's entreaties on behalf of the compromise.[16]

On Tuesday, the fourth and final day of the credential committee's deliberation on the challenge of the MFDP, the hopes of Rauh and other advisers to the Freedom Democrats for a floor fight came up against the political powers at play in Atlantic City. To ensure that no politically damaging floor debate took place, Johnson backers pressured liberal delegates on the credentials committee to drop their support for the MFDP. One delegate on the committee was informed that her support for the Freedom Democrats would cost her husband the judgeship he was seeking, while another delegate was told that he would lose his job in the Panama Canal Zone if he persisted in supporting the MFDP. With the votes needed to take the challenge to the floor dwindling away and the final vote approaching, Congressman Charles Diggs of Michigan handed Rauh—who was serving on the credentials committee as a delegate from the District of Columbia—a note with a phone number instructing him to call Reuther. Upon reaching Reuther, Rauh was told of the final compromise offer from Johnson: two at-large seats for delegates from the MFDP selected by the administration, Aaron Henry, the party's chairman, and Ed King, a white chaplain at the historically Black Tougaloo College; the requirement of a loyalty oath that would effectively toss the delegation of the regular Mississippi Democratic Party out of the convention; and the barring from future conventions of any state delegation that excluded voters and delegates on the basis of race. Unable to secure a postponement that would have allowed him to consult with Henry, Rauh voted against the compromise. When television coverage erroneously reported that the credentials committee had accepted the compromise unanimously, Moses and other MFDP advisers expressed bitter disappointment with Rauh and other white liberals who they believed had abandoned them.[17]

When a floor challenge became impossible, Rauh, like King, Rustin, Wilkins, and other civil rights leaders advising the Freedom Democrats, urged the delegates of the MFDP to accept a far less than ideal compromise. Nearly everyone associated with the MFDP involved in discussions on the compromise was particularly upset that not only did the deal provide just two seats for the party but also the administration had decided who the delegates had to be, leaving sharecroppers like Fannie Lou Hamer unrepresented. Still, Rauh pushed the compromise as better than nothing, while King and Rustin spoke in favor of the deal, stressing the importance of political pragmatism and the need for the civil rights movement to look beyond protest and begin shifting its sights to the political arena. Among the delegates of the MFDP, Aaron Henry and Ed King supported the compromise, but the overwhelming majority of the party's sixty-eight delegates rejected Johnson's offer. Hamer, speaking for the delegation, insisted, "We didn't come all this way for no two votes." John Lewis later lamented that "when the smoke finally cleared, Joe Rauh would be seen as a villain, a traitor, a back stabber." Believing that to be "a shame," Lewis described Rauh as "a good man who worked incredibly hard to bring this moment about. It's ironic that the situation he had worked so hard to create wound up skewering his reputation, at least among the black community."[18]

The failure of the Democratic National Convention to seat the Freedom Democrats' delegation sparked a wholly understandable disillusionment among members of the MFDP, SNCC, and other civil rights organizations with white liberals and the Democratic Party, but that failure does not capture the efforts, motivations, and commitments of individuals like Rauh. Liberals such as Humphrey and Reuther had more to lose in opposing Johnson and quickly conceded to pressure from him. Rauh, however, had both the political independence and the devotion to the cause of the MFDP to tell Humphrey that he would have to relay to the president the news that his efforts to broker a compromise had been unsuccessful because "Joe Rauh is an incorrigible son of a bitch."[19]

Other veteran ADAers did not face the dramatic test of commitment to civil rights confronted by Rauh in Atlantic City but shared with him the belief that civil rights represented the most pressing issue on the liberal agenda in the early 1960s. Speaking before a gathering of students at Spelman College in 1961, Schlesinger insisted that civil rights represented "the overriding domestic issue of our day" and the "moral crux" of the nation.[20] During his time as special assistant to President Kennedy, Schlesinger frequently mustered what meager influence he had in the administration to urge the president to move more decisively on the civil rights front.[21] The day after Kennedy's assassination, Galbraith met with Johnson and stressed to the new president that civil rights should be the number one domestic initiative pursued by his administration.[22] As the civil rights movement illuminated the enduring economic inequality that perpetuated racial inequality, the ADA's longtime leaders came to see poverty as a civil rights issue. When the commitment of the ADA to civil rights expanded to include the struggle against poverty, attention to economic inequality and material deprivation, which had sometimes receded into the background in the organization amid exaggerated estimates of the reach of the affluent society, would be brought to the forefront of the organization's priorities.

POVERTY AS A CIVIL RIGHTS ISSUE

John Kenneth Galbraith reflected in 1964 that ever since he wrote *The Affluent Society* he had "been accused of believing that there are no poor people left in the United States."[23] While the widely read Harvard economist did not believe that everyone in the country had achieved affluence, he and leading figures in the ADA during the 1950s and early 1960s had minimized the significance of poverty as a pressing issue. As the civil rights movement gained momentum and mounted a massive march on Washington that focused national attention not only on the issue of civil rights but also on the deeply connected problems of economic and racial inequality, ADA leaders revisited their earlier tendency to assume that poverty represented only a minor problem in a nation of growing affluence. Historians have frequently associated white postwar liberals with a departure from the class-based approach of the New Deal that led them to naïvely overestimate the impact that enshrining civil rights and voting rights into law would have on the lives of African Americans.[24] The bulk of ADA liberals, however, demonstrated a forthright receptiveness to the ambitious social, economic, and political vision of the civil rights movement and harbored no misunderstanding as to the far-reaching measures that would be needed to achieve full racial equality. By focusing national attention on the millions of Americans whose poverty constrained their lives and inhibited their freedoms, the civil rights movement led ADA liberals to see poverty as a civil rights issue and reinvigorated their commitment to social democratic values, which had wavered at times during a postwar period characterized by seemingly widespread material prosperity. When the commitment of ADA liberals to civil rights expanded to include a commitment to fighting economic inequality, poverty ceased to be a peripheral issue in the organization and became a central and ongoing concern.

In the 1950s, although Galbraith did not see poverty as a major issue or one directly related to civil rights, he nevertheless illuminated distinctive features of poverty in the postwar era that shaped the debates on economic inequality which would capture far greater attention during the following decade. In the lone chapter in *The Affluent Society* devoted to the issue of poverty, he detailed the nature of a modern poverty impervious to the general advancement sustained by economic growth. Galbraith divided the intractable poverty of the United States in the 1950s into two broad categories. In the category of "case poverty" he placed those who, because of some characteristic specific to themselves or their family—such as alcoholism, inadequate education, or intellectual disability—did not and could not benefit from the general increase in material well-being. People who lived in various locales in Appalachia, urban ghettos, or other geographic "islands" of near universal poverty cut off from broader economic progress typified what he termed "insular poverty." Those who fell into either of Galbraith's categories of contemporary poverty had not only received little to no benefit from the postwar economic boom but also become a minority of the population with limited political significance. In contrast to the era when the poverty-stricken represented a significant cross-section of the country with political clout to match its size, Galbraith observed, in the 1950s "any politician who speaks for the very poor is speaking for a small and also inarticulate minority."[25]

Galbraith's insights into the nature of modern poverty—so often obscured by a preoccupation with the book's title—came to wider public attention when Michael Harrington drew on them to frame the problem of poverty in his unexpected 1962 best-seller *The Other America*. Harrington, then serving as editor of *New America*, the newspaper of the Socialist Party of America, had witnessed the devastating effects of urban poverty firsthand when he lived and worked at the Catholic Worker house in New York's Lower East Side during the 1950s. Hoping to find a wider audience for his stark depiction of poverty, he made no effort to obscure his general political perspective but avoided any specific mention of socialism in the book. Though the omission of an explicit avowal of socialist politics troubled his conscience, the decision opened the door to both popular and influential audiences, leading many observers to credit the work with sparking the War on Poverty and Harrington as the man who "discovered poverty." Among its most dedicated readers, socially minded liberals—both within and outside the ADA—devoured the book in large numbers. *The Other America* also found its way into the hands of the most highly placed of audiences, with the book making its way onto reading lists within the Kennedy administration and onto the desk of the president, who read Dwight Macdonald's long-form review of the book in *The New Yorker*.[26]

In his far-reaching and influential exposition of poverty, Harrington departed from Galbraith in substantial ways but also approached the issue from a perspective that owed much to foundations laid by the Harvard economist. Before he joined the ADA national board in 1966, Harrington praised Galbraith as one of the first writers to understand the newness of contemporary poverty and found himself in agreement with the author of *The Affluent Society* that this "new poverty" demonstrated "a certain immunity to progress." Still, he stressed the need to reevaluate the roots and scale of poverty in order to develop a greater awareness of those whose standard of living had fallen ever farther behind a broader prosperity that held nothing for them. Though in agreement with Galbraith that physical and mental disabilities were a major factor in the persistence of poverty among some individuals, he maintained that characteristics such as alcoholism that landed people in the Harvard economist's category of "case poverty" were generally the consequence of a corrosive "environment, not the biographies of unlucky individuals." Yet for Harrington, Galbraith's notion of "insular poverty," and the resulting implication that poverty was only a minor issue, represented an even more "dangerous" idea. While noting that Galbraith rightly identified the poor of modern America as "the first minority poor in history," he took issue with the misleading notion of "insular poverty" in a country where the reach of poverty extended to 40 or 50 million people.[27]

Harrington's departure from Galbraith on the origins and scope of poverty resulted in part from his socialist background but also owed much to his involvement in the civil rights movement. When he wrote *The Affluent Society*, Galbraith harbored an abstract commitment to civil rights but had virtually no direct experience with the civil rights movement, which was then entering a new stage of national visibility. In contrast, Harrington joined the Manhattan branch of the National Association for the Advancement of Colored People (NAACP) in 1954, became deeply involved in the civil rights movement through his contact with Bayard Rustin, and devoted much of his time during the years in which he wrote *The Other America* to civil rights activities. Involvement in the movement heightened Harrington's attention to the issue of race and lent his politics a sense of human empathy and understanding that many liberal social commentators lacked in the 1950s.[28] Harrington, like Galbraith, believed the intractability of modern poverty to be its defining feature but went much further than the Harvard economist had four years earlier in examining the relationship between the "new poverty" and race. Whereas Galbraith had given race only the slightest attention in *The Affluent Society*, Harrington stressed it as one of the most powerful of factors that confined individuals to a life of poverty in the face of broader prosperity. Leaving no question as to his understanding of the limits of what could be achieved by civil rights legislation alone, he insisted that equal rights before the law would not address "the poverty that is the historic and institutionalized consequence of color." For Harrington, so long as this form of poverty continued to be a glaring reality in the nation, "being born a Negro will continue to be the most profound disability that the United States imposes upon a citizen."[29]

As with its impact on Harrington, the civil rights movement pushed leading figures in the ADA to reevaluate their understanding of the relationship between poverty and race. Media coverage at the time and popular history since have focused primarily on the efforts of the civil rights movement to dismantle Jim Crow segregation in the South in the latter half of the 1950s and the first half of the 1960s. The major civil rights organizations of the twentieth century, however, had never limited their agenda simply to the struggle to strike down de jure discrimination. Civil rights leaders explicitly articulated an agenda committed to both the legal protection of civil rights and the advancement of broad social welfare policies aimed at improving the economic standing of all Americans who lived in what Harrington termed "the other America."[30] When the 1963 March on Washington for Jobs and Freedom attracted nearly 250,000 demonstrators to the capital and brought the full agenda of the civil rights movement to the nation's attention, ADA liberals resoundingly embraced its underlying message that the struggle against poverty represented a continuation of the fight for civil rights.[31]

Historians have challenged a sanitized popular memory of the March on Washington that has obscured the economic demands of the demonstration by reminding us that the largest gathering of people ever to protest in the nation's capital at that point marched not only for freedom but also for jobs. When he issued the call for the march, Negro American Labor Council president A. Philip Randolph—a committed socialist—initially envisioned the demonstration developing around the central themes of economic justice and the need for full employment. The longtime president of the predominantly African American Brotherhood of Sleeping Car Porters, Randolph had previously organized a march on Washington set to be held in 1941 that compelled President Franklin D. Roosevelt to issue Executive Order Number 8802, which prohibited racial discrimination in the defense industry and established the Fair Employment Practices Committee to enforce that prohibition. In exchange for the executive order, Randolph agreed to call off the march. The economic demands that Randolph saw as the purpose behind the aborted 1941 march were also integral to how he conceived of the 1963 march that shared the same name.[32] Accordingly, when he addressed the crowd gathered before the Lincoln Memorial on August 28, 1963, Randolph did not limit his speech to the vital importance of passing the civil rights bill then before Congress. He also urged the civil rights movement to organize on behalf of initiatives to address the unemployment and poverty that limited the freedom of millions of Americans of all races. Randolph was not alone in stressing economic demands at the podium during the March on Washington. After endorsing the bill with "grave reservations," SNCC chairman John Lewis stressed in his speech the need for "a bill that will provide for the homeless and starving people of this nation."[33]

The explicit connection made between civil rights and economic justice by Randolph, Lewis, and other speakers before a mass assembly of approximately a quarter of a million Americans—most of whom were Black but a significant number of whom were white—had a profound impact on how ADA liberals viewed the relationship between race and poverty.[34] When Congress later passed and President Johnson signed into law the Civil Rights Act of 1964, ADA liberals joined civil rights leaders in celebrating the landmark legislative achievement while simultaneously insisting that securing legal rights represented only the beginning of the struggle for full racial equality.[35] In contrast to characterizations that have emphasized the excessive confidence displayed by white postwar liberals in the prohibition of racial discrimination as an all-encompassing means of addressing the deep-seated and multifaceted problem of racial inequality, ADA liberals clearly demonstrated their understanding of the essential yet limited reach of civil rights legislation.[36]

Drafted in the months that followed the March on Washington, the ADA's 1964 civil rights resolution reflected the organization's ready embrace of the far-reaching social, economic, and political program advanced by the civil rights movement. The resolution committed the organization for the first time to an agenda rooted in the fundamental relationship between civil rights and economic justice. With no illusions as to the enormity of the challenge entailed by such an expansive definition of equality, the statement insisted that "dignity requires the abolition of poverty; it requires the restoration of full employment; it requires integrated and high quality education at all levels; it requires adequate nutrition; it requires excellent medical care for all ages; it requires a decent, safe, and sanitary house in an integrated neighborhood."[37]

To achieve those ends, the resolution called for a "massive attack upon poverty and an all-out effort to create full employment." Aware of the political challenges to be found in pushing for a vast increase in federal expenditures, the ADA celebrated the achievements of the civil rights movement that had so effectively "dramatized the plight of the poor people in this country" as a turning point in the struggle for full employment. Buoyed by the powerful coalition of civil rights activists, members of religious organizations, labor unionists, and liberals that secured passage of the Civil Rights Act of 1964 and would later propel President Johnson to a landslide election victory, ADA liberals acknowledged the dimensions of the task. Still, they expressed confidence in this "coalition of conscience" to "fight for the social and economic legislation to make the guarantee of rights meaningful." Bold new action to secure full employment and other measures necessary to achieve full racial equality, the resolution made clear, could "be the dawn of a bright new day for all Americans."[38] As ADA liberals joined together in a consensus that held the battle against poverty to be a continuation of the fight for civil rights, they would come up against the complexities of how best to attack the entrenched economic and racial inequalities that plagued American society.

CIVIL RIGHTS, THE WAR ON POVERTY, AND THE ADA'S SOCIAL DEMOCRATIC TURN

During his 1964 State of the Union address, President Lyndon Johnson boldly committed the US federal government to "an unconditional war on poverty."³⁹ In the nineteen months that followed, the country saw, in rapid succession, the passage of the Civil Rights Act of 1964, the Economic Opportunity Act, and the Voting Rights Act. The ADA joined the broader liberal community in celebrating the historic legislative achievements of Johnson's Great Society. Still, many in the ADA believed that the domestic initiatives of the Johnson administration—bold and important as they were—failed to address the structural economic barriers to full racial equality that made realization of a great society more a distant hope than a tangible prospect. As the Johnson administration launched its Great Society programs, most—though not all—from the ranks of leadership in the ADA parted ways with the economic assumptions those programs rested on. Instead, they turned to a social democratic outlook that harkened back to the New Deal left and an earlier era in their organization's past to provide the structural response to poverty that would be needed to achieve meaningful racial equality.

From the moment the Johnson administration announced the War on Poverty, ADA liberals displayed little reluctance to stress the fundamental limitations of the initiative. Rooted in the view that poverty was primarily the result of insufficient human capital development, the initiatives launched by the Economic Opportunity Act of 1964 sought to break the self-perpetuating "culture of poverty" through the provision of counseling, education, job training, and a Community Action Program (CAP) that sought to empower poor individuals.⁴⁰ An editorial in *ADA World* published shortly after Johnson's State of the Union address welcomed the president's message "as a long-awaited first salvo in the war against poverty" but regretted "that this first battle is not to be fought in greater strength." In blunt terms the editorial stated, "The poor are poor because they do not have enough money." While describing CAPs and the broader development of social services launched by the War on Poverty as "solid steps in the right direction," the editorial also recognized that it was "illusory to suppose that they are substitutes for adequate Social Security, unemployment insurance and public assistance to provide income necessary to buy enough to eat, a decent place to live, good medical care, and the amenities of life."⁴¹ Another editorial in *ADA World* placed similar emphasis on the need to raise substandard incomes as it stressed the importance of achieving a full employment economy. Characterizing "social, cultural, and spiritual impoverishment" as a consequence of unemployment, the editorial offered as a solution a full employment economy coupled with a dramatic increase in the "archaic standard of the employment insurance, social security, and public assistance systems."[42]

The organization's 1964 resolution on poverty synthesized the views found in those editorials and in the writings of key arbiters of ADA economic policy such as Leon Keyserling. In doing so, it emphasized that the legislation of the existing War on Poverty represented "good intentions" but "cannot be expected to eliminate poverty; at best, it may palliate some of its more festering sores." The resolution urged a "much more extensive attack" to "adequately deal with the awesome economic and motivational problems raised by the plight of millions of the unemployed, the unemployable, the underemployed, and the underpaid." Stressing an aggressive full employment program as essential to the struggle of those millions, the resolution deemed the manpower ethos of the War on Poverty a "hollow concept."[43] The accompanying civil rights resolution passed by the ADA directly tied the cause of full employment to the struggle for civil rights by making clear that there could be no excuse for discrimination but insisting nevertheless that "equal employment opportunity would be easier to achieve if there were not a desperate struggle for an inadequate number of jobs."[44] To tackle the deeply interconnected issues of racial and economic inequality, the ADA looked to the Employment Act of 1946 as a starting point for action in the mid-1960s.

The push of ADA liberals for full employment policies long predated both the ADA's attention to the economic dimensions of racial equality and the existence of the organization itself. When Congress debated passage of the Full Employment Act in response to fears of a postwar depression in the mid-1940s, the ADA's predecessor, the Union for Democratic Action, devoted virtually all of its resources to leading the charge for the bill initially introduced in the Senate that included a right to employment guaranteed by the federal government.[45] In the years that followed passage of the greatly enfeebled Employment Act of 1946, the ADA centered much of its domestic policy on proposals that sought to make many of the initial aims of the act a reality, but missing from its efforts was the bold dedication to the right of guaranteed employment found in the UDA's earlier lobbying.[46] Rather than the expanding and contracting public works called for by the initial full employment bill to guarantee employment for all able-bodied Americans seeking work, the ADA in the late 1940s and 1950s looked to macroeconomic management of the economy to stimulate economic growth and foster the conditions necessary for private industry to provide full employment.

By bringing the nation's attention to the enduring poverty suffered by many African Americans despite a growing economy and relatively low national unemployment rates, the civil rights movement fundamentally changed how ADA liberals viewed full employment measures and their basic goals. The ADA's calls for full employment in the early postwar years drew heavily on a desire to stimulate the economic growth needed for the high military expenditures deemed necessary in the context of the nascent Cold War. In the wake of the growing visibility of the civil rights movement, the ADA increasingly stressed full employment as a means of eliminating poverty. Displaying a greater awareness of the significant number of individuals who faced limited to nonexistent employment opportunities, the ADA in 1964 called for a $2 billion public works program to create jobs in some of the country's most economically depressed areas.[47] That awareness owed much to a civil rights movement that illuminated the ways in which economic growth and employment in private industry had passed millions of Americans by. Less confident in the ability of economic growth and private industry—even with the aid of economic planning and the fiscal tool kit at the disposal of the federal government—to provide all of the jobs that would be needed to eliminate poverty in the United States, the ADA adopted a more overtly social democratic perspective than at any prior point in its almost two-decade history. With a social democratic outlook that echoed earlier currents in the New Deal left, the ADA called on the federal government to more directly shoulder the responsibility of ensuring that employment opportunities existed for all American citizens. While this social democratic approach to poverty prevailed in the ADA's policy resolutions during the mid-1960s, it was neither without its own contradictions nor the sole perspective on poverty to exert pull in the organization.

QUALITATIVE LIBERALISM AND DIVERGENT PERSPECTIVES ON POVERTY

The complexities involved in tackling a problem as multifaceted and deep-seated as poverty meant that no single approach would be embraced by all of the leading voices in the ADA. In contrast to the consensus on the need for full employment measures found in editorials in *ADA World* and ADA resolutions on poverty and civil rights, Galbraith and Schlesinger displayed an affinity for the general approach, if not the scale, of the Johnson administration's War on Poverty. In the late 1960s, these differences would contribute to the tensions that ran through the economic perspectives found in the New Politics movement. In the mid-1960s, however, ADA leaders were able to reconcile their divergent perspectives on poverty because—whether or not they agreed with the basic approach of Johnson's War on Poverty—they shared the conviction that poverty represented a civil rights issue that needed to be tackled far more aggressively.

Schlesinger, like most ADA liberals, addressed the problem of poverty with a new sense of urgency as the civil rights movement gained momentum in the 1960s. Departing from the prevailing view in the organization, however, he found much to like in the services approach of the War on Poverty, which put into action ideas similar to those he had developed as pillars of qualitative liberalism in the 1950s. Having stressed improved education and medical services, equal opportunities for minorities, and urban renewal as necessary for both the material well-being and quality of life of the American people in the 1950s, Schlesinger displayed confidence in the 1960s that the human capital emphasis of the War on Poverty held great potential to address the nation's enduring poverty.[48]

Similarly, Galbraith gave greater attention to poverty in the 1960s and approached the issue through the lens of the qualitative liberalism that he too had been advancing since the 1950s. As he had during the prior decade, Galbraith continued to see a vast expansion in public services as one of the first prerequisites for tackling intractable poverty. In 1964 Galbraith argued, as he had since writing *The Affluent Society*, that the majority of those suffering the very worst poverty consisted of individuals who were unable to contribute to the economy and were thus unable to receive benefits from it, regardless of how high the overall economic growth rate might be. Reflecting the assumption that jobs would be available for the bulk of individuals who were properly prepared to take them, he believed that substantial improvements in education, training, retraining, medical care, counseling services, public housing, urban recreational facilities, and other public services were essential for enabling individuals to take advantage of a growing American economy.[49] While his emphasis on the need for improved public services largely dovetailed with the approach of the War on Poverty, Galbraith consistently made clear when he addressed the issue throughout the mid-1960s that any such efforts would require "much, much more money" than was being devoted to the task by the Johnson administration.[50]

The prevailing consensus in the ADA differed substantially from the thinking of Galbraith and Schlesinger in offering a far more negative assessment of the state of the labor market and its ability to provide for all poor Americans the jobs needed to rise out of poverty, regardless of their training or qualifications. At the same time, ADA liberals increasingly shared with the organization's leading architects of qualitative liberalism a critical perspective on economic growth as the central answer to poverty. The turn of the ADA to large-scale public works projects as a solution reflected skepticism that economic growth and private industry, however well managed and regulated, could provide employment and material security for all Americans. This skepticism stood in marked contrast to the heady optimism ADA liberals displayed in the 1950s toward the ability of the American economy, with some prodding from the federal government, to secure general prosperity.

An embrace of Galbraith's and Schlesinger's critical perspective on economic growth did not mean, however, that ADA liberals subscribed to the specifics of their antipoverty proposals. In the 1950s, ADA liberals adopted many of the concerns that had animated Galbraith's and Schlesinger's vision for qualitative liberalism while rejecting most of their specific policy prescriptions on taxes and other issues. Similarly, most leading figures in the ADA in the 1960s came to share their critical view as to the supposedly inherent benefits of economic growth while nevertheless pursuing a different approach to the problem of chronic poverty. For their part, Galbraith and Schlesinger embraced the prevailing opinion in the ADA that the struggle against poverty represented a continuation of the fight for civil rights. Under the surface of divergent views, Galbraith, Schlesinger, and the bulk of ADA liberals responded to the civil rights movement with a new passion for eliminating poverty and an insistence on approaches that differed considerably from those advanced by the organization a decade earlier. The perspective of ADA liberals on the American economy and the enduring problem of poverty would undergo still further reevaluation as the growing trend toward automation threatened millions of jobs and challenged the feasibility of full employment as a policy goal.

FULL EMPLOYMENT, AUTOMATION, AND GUARANTEED INCOME

In 1966 the ADA boldly called for the establishment of a guaranteed annual income to provide every family "with a standard of income appropriate to

America's productivity." The ADA pegged that standard at $4,000 per year for a family of four, an amount substantially higher than the average benefit levels then provided by the Aid for Families with Dependent Children program.[51] The guaranteed annual income, an idea deemed "nutty" and "utopian" by the media in early 1964, became the subject of a national commission appointed by the Johnson administration later that year to study it, and by 1968 had gained the backing of more than one thousand prominent economists. Largely lacking in concrete details when they first garnered national attention, guaranteed annual income proposals attracted support from politicians across the political spectrum who attached a variety of divergent meanings and purposes to the concept.[52] A number of historians have depicted liberal versions of the guaranteed annual income that sought to establish the right of all American citizens to a minimum income on the basis of need alone as a radical turn from the "opportunity liberalism" of the New Deal to an "entitlement liberalism" that spurned the American tradition of individualism.[53] Yet the ADA's proposal did not represent a break with the New Deal tradition but rather was an extension of the social democratic currents that had run through it. The ADA built its guaranteed income proposal on the foundation laid by the Employment Act of 1946, the "last gasp" of the New Deal. Looking back to the Employment Act of 1946 and inspired by the spotlight then being put on enduring poverty by the civil rights movement, the ADA framed its proposal as a necessary response to structural economic inequality and the growing trend toward automation that threatened millions of American jobs.

Urban uprisings in the Watts section of Los Angeles and other predominantly African American neighborhoods during the "long hot summers" of the mid-1960s imbued the ADA's push for an expansion in the scale and scope of the War on Poverty with a growing sense of urgency. Yet the most powerful impetus for the organization's call for a guaranteed annual income came from the spread of automation, which was making the already uphill struggle for full employment even more difficult. Michael Harrington, who joined the ADA national board in 1966, did much to draw the attention of liberals to the new challenges created by automation. With his 1962 book *The Other America*, Harrington opened the eyes of many liberals to the plight of individuals with limited education and training who had lost their jobs and had little prospect for future employment as technological advances in industrial automation made their unskilled or semiskilled labor unnecessary.⁵⁴ Speaking from center stage of the civil rights movement, A. Philip Randolph later stressed the human impact of automation when he insisted during his address at the March on Washington that a fair employment practices act, though vital, would do little good "if profit-geared automation destroys the jobs of millions of workers, black and white."⁵⁵

As they grappled with the meaning of automation in the 1960s, ADA liberals echoed leading voices in the civil rights movement that stressed the disproportionate effects automation had on African Americans. Leon Keyserling charged in 1965 that the Johnson administration fundamentally failed to understand the implications of automation for African American employment. For Keyserling, the administration's narrow focus on providing training for the unemployed—a disproportionate number of whom were African American—to prepare them for jobs that required higher-skilled labor represented a futile effort in the face of spreading automation that was eliminating those very jobs.⁵⁶

When the University of Pennsylvania law professor Louis Schwartz presented a guaranteed annual income proposal to his colleagues on the ADA national board in early 1966, he put his plan forward explicitly in terms of racial equality and the devastating consequences of automation on the prospects for African American economic advancement. He clearly linked his guaranteed annual income proposal to the cause of civil rights by characterizing poverty as a "dark badge" that is "worn for life by millions and transmitted to their children—an inherited status like slavery." Further evoking the language of the civil rights movement, he maintained that "poverty is a restriction of freedom" that left poor people with few choices open to them and described the guaranteed annual income as a "Twentieth Century Emancipation Proclamation."⁵⁷

Schwartz drew on what he and many of his ADA colleagues saw as the clear moral imperative of the civil rights movement to make the case for the necessity of more determined action to attack poverty. In the long term, the connections drawn by Schwartz and other liberals—both within and outside the ADA—between the cause of civil rights and the struggle against poverty inadvertently contributed to a politically disabling racialization of poverty discourse in American politics. At the time, however, such connections provided the moral and intellectual foundation for challenging the Johnson administration's War on Poverty from the left and highlighting its weaknesses. Offering an implicit critique of the War on Poverty's training and services approach, Schwartz deemed it "evil nonsense" to withhold rights "until the poor have been 'retrained' for jobs which may or may not materialize."[58]

Morally grounded in the cause of civil rights, the economics and politics of Schwartz's guaranteed annual income proposal rested on the tentative foundation laid by the Employment Act of 1946. Schwartz insisted that the proposal to establish an economic floor for all American families did not represent a "radical innovation" but was rather a natural extension of the social democratic ethos embodied in that act and earlier liberal measures such as compulsory free education, the graduated income tax, minimum wage laws, Social Security, and unemployment insurance. For Schwartz, those important achievements and other similar measures amounted to "fragments of an inarticulate and uncoordinated national incomes policy." The establishment of a guaranteed annual income, he contended, would fully actualize the underlying objectives of the existing "hodge-podge of laws" and offer a "new synthesis to carry us from the liberalism of the thirties to the welfare liberalism of the sixties and the seventies."[59]

Passed by the ADA national board and approved by the ADA national convention in April, the resolution based on Schwartz's proposal for a guaranteed annual income of $4,000 per year for a family of four established the organization as an early advocate of what represented a progressive form of guaranteed annual income.[60] While liberal support for guaranteed annual income proposals has often been depicted as an abandonment of the American work ethic and the "opportunity liberalism" of the New Deal, the resolution crafted by Schwartz and others in the ADA did not reflect an innate desire to detach income from productive employment. Instead, the resolution reflected its authors' critical assessment of the American labor market. Put simply, the resolution insisted that "the way to end poverty is to give poor people more income, preferably derived from productive jobs that pay wages, but more income at all events." Holding the view that the willfully idle suffered from a "psychological condition" that was "itself a consequence of poverty" and constituted, in any case, a small minority of the total number of poor Americans, the ADA believed stepped-up measures that sustained a full employment economy would ensure the ability of individuals to obtain a "decent standard of living" through productive work.[61]

The broader economic policy resolution passed by the ADA in 1966 coupled the proposal for a guaranteed annual income with the call to undertake the "democratic economic planning" and public works projects necessary to establish a growing full employment economy that the architects of the original full employment bill had envisioned in 1946 but still remained unfulfilled two decades later. The resolution stressed economic planning as a crucial tool to maximize economic growth and employment opportunities in the private sector, but, like the ADA's proposal for a $2 billion public works program two years earlier, it expressed the growing conviction in the organization that the private labor market could not be depended on to eliminate poverty. The resolution called for a federally financed five-year program to create at least 5 million sub-professional jobs to be made available to the jobless millions who faced dim employment prospects in a private labor market that already provided an inadequate number of jobs and looked certain to contract still further as a consequence of automation.[62] As automation continued to eliminate jobs and the civil rights movement focused national attention on the disproportionate consequences for African Americans, many in the ADA committed their support and intellectual energy to a new initiative that reflected their views on full employment and guaranteed income.

THE ECONOMICS OF LEON KEYSERLING AND THE FREEDOM BUDGET

A. Philip Randolph launched the November 1965 planning session for the White House Conference on Civil Rights by calling for a "Freedom Budget" that would establish "a nationwide plan for the abolition of ghetto jungles in every city, even at the cost of a hundred billion dollars."[63] While Randolph served as an important figurehead for the Freedom Budget, Leon Keyserling developed the bulk of the budget with assistance from Randolph Institute co-founder and executive director Bayard Rustin. The Freedom Budget quickly became a primary focus of the ADA and a clear expression of its understanding of the need for a national full employment policy coupled with a guaranteed annual income. At a time of growing division in the civil rights movement, the Freedom Budget—a plan that followed the model of Keyserling's growth-based economics and differed little from recent ADA economic policy—also attracted support from the country's five major civil rights organizations. Firmly optimistic about the far-reaching potential of economic growth as a vehicle for social progress, the Freedom Budget both reflected and helped further establish consensus among a notable number of prominent liberals and civil rights leaders on the need for a social democratic response to the entrenched economic inequality that underpinned the nation's enduring racial inequality. For a brief moment before the large-scale escalation of the Vietnam War, a significant grouping of white liberals and civil rights leaders united in support of a systematic antipoverty proposal that drew on the economic perspective of the ADA as the foundation for an initiative that made the Johnson administration's limited poverty initiative look more like a skirmish than a war.

With the goal of liquidating poverty in the United States by 1975, the Freedom Budget stressed the need for a more structural approach to economic deprivation than the services and cultural uplift emphasis that underlay the Economic Opportunity Act of 1964 and the broader War on Poverty. Rather than emphasize training and education for poor Americans to prepare them for jobs that might or might not materialize in the future, the Freedom Budget aimed not just to provide opportunity but to establish—as a fact and as a result—increased economic standing and security for the significant number of Americans who continued to suffer from poverty. Like ADA policy on full employment and guaranteed income being developed at the same time, the Freedom Budget owed more to the social democratic ethos that ran through parts of the New Deal and the Employment Act of 1946 than to the human capital development orientation of the Johnson administration's War on Poverty. Employing the language of Franklin D. Roosevelt's "Four Freedoms," the Freedom Budget articulated the goal of directly ensuring the right of all Americans to "freedom from want" through guaranteed employment for anyone able to work, with the federal government acting as an employer of last resort and a guaranteed income for anyone unable to work.[64]

With Keyserling as the driving force behind its design, the Freedom Budget drew on the ADA's rekindled interest in New Deal era economics and its relatively newfound understanding of full employment as central to addressing the interconnected issues of poverty and racial inequality. When drafts of the Freedom Budget first began circulating in early 1966, the ADA wasted no time in offering public support for a document that largely resembled its own economic platform. Endorsements from twenty-one of its national board members for the final published version would establish the ADA as the institution with the greatest representation among the list of prestigious signatories to the document.[65] The social democratic approach of the Freedom Budget, rooted in the economics of Keyserling and the ADA, also held considerable appeal for the initiative's broad array of major civil rights backers who endorsed the proposal at a time when the civil rights movement faced growing division and polarization. Though he would later remove himself from the list of signatories, Stokely Carmichael, the chairman of SNCC who was instrumental in its shift to Black nationalism, initially joined the leaders of the Congress of Racial Equality (CORE), the NAACP, the National Urban League, and the Southern Christian Leadership Conference in endorsing the Freedom Budget. As the first instance in which the five major civil rights groups agreed to work together publicly on a major national program since the rise of tensions over the issue of Black Power earlier in the year, the Freedom Budget evidenced a striking—and for 1966 otherwise unlikely—point of agreement.[66]

The economic platform that drew support from a collection of civil rights leaders and organizations that were increasingly diverging from one another on a variety of other issues in 1966 largely relied on the earlier efforts of Keyserling and the ADA to adapt the universalistic social democratic framework found in some aspects of the New Deal to address economic, social, and racial inequality in the mid-1960s. Highlighting the singular importance of his own contributions, Keyserling saw the Freedom Budget as the "logical progression" of his earlier "interest and efforts on behalf of translating the Employment Act of 1946 into what it was intended to be ... the uniting of our economic resources with the fulfillment of our social needs."[67] With an emphasis on full employment policy, a higher minimum wage, and other proposals that built on the achievements of the New Deal and the Fair Deal, much of the Freedom Budget represented innovation not so much in its ideas as in the tremendous scale of the initiatives called for. Still, retooling the policy framework of the New Deal into an initiative that sought to address areas of racial and economic inequality which the federal government had either left untouched or actively reinforced during the New Deal era represented a politically difficult and enormously expensive task.

Keyserling approached that task with an emphasis on economic growth as a means of fighting poverty that allowed the Freedom Budget's initial backers to see what might otherwise have appeared to be a prohibitively expensive proposal as both economically feasible and politically palatable. Based on the optimistic expectation that the good times would continue and the United States could maintain an annual rate of economic growth of around 4.5 to 5 percent, the Freedom Budget proposed to eradicate poverty not by redistributing wealth but by making use of only a fraction of the "economic growth dividend" projected to be produced by the growing economy. According to the budget's authors, the productive power of an American economy that provided far more than the resources necessary to establish "freedom from want" by 1975 rendered the issue of poverty neither economic nor financial but moral.[68]

If the strength of the American economy made it possible to frame poverty as a moral issue, the civil rights movement provided the broad moral appeal that the architects of the Freedom Budget looked to as they sought to establish the lofty purpose of their initiative. In the text of the Freedom Budget pamphlet that he was primarily responsible for writing, Keyserling made sure to highlight how the "unique suffering" of African Americans had gone "a long way toward awakening the American conscience with respect to civil rights and liberties." With the assertion that the most significant role to be played by African Americans in the Freedom Budget would be not as beneficiaries but as a "galvanizing force," the text of the budget stressed that the debt owed to African Americans and their allies in the civil rights movement "will be increased many times" as they helped "to win the battle against unemployment and poverty and deprivation."[69] Keyserling further displayed his belief in the moral appeal of the civil rights movement that resounds throughout the text of the Freedom Budget when his urging ensured that the name of the A. Philip Randolph Institute would remain prominently displayed on the cover of the published pamphlet.[70]

For Keyserling and his collaborators on the Freedom Budget, the moral imperative of addressing the economic inequality that could be expected to perpetuate racial inequality despite recent advances in civil rights legislation imbued the task of tackling enduring poverty with a new importance. Despite putting together an initiative that relied on seemingly permanent economic growth, the architects of the Freedom Budget did not frame economic growth and private industry alone—however well managed by the fiscal tools at the disposal of the federal government—as the answer to poverty. The growing skepticism toward the ability of the private labor market to address entrenched unemployment and poverty expressed in recent ADA policy on full employment and guaranteed income also informed the Freedom Budget's approach to structural unemployment and economic inequality. Convinced that the private labor market would never be able to provide all of the jobs needed to eliminate unemployment, Keyserling made sure that the Freedom Budget called on the federal government to make an "unqualified commitment" to create the jobs required to provide employment for all those who sought work. With the view that a guaranteed annual income would be necessary to ensure a decent standard of income for "those who cannot or should not work," the Freedom Budget echoed recent ADA policy in positioning guaranteed income as a supplement to, rather than a replacement for, national full employment policy.[71]

ADA liberals responded with enthusiasm to a Freedom Budget initiative that could count the nation's leading civil rights figures among its supporters and held the potential to advance many of the economic and civil rights policies that the organization had championed. An editorial in the October 1966 issue of *ADA World* declared the Freedom Budget "the only proper approach to poverty." The same month, ADA legislative representative David Cohen joined Keyserling, Rustin, Randolph, and other key backers at a press conference in Harlem to present the finalized Freedom Budget to the public.[72] In December, Rustin's summary of the Freedom Budget reached the entire membership of the ADA through publication in *ADA World*, which had to be reprinted because of widespread demand.[73]

With the Johnson administration refusing to receive the Freedom Budget publicly in any manner that would give the impression that they supported the ambitious proposal, the spirited involvement and response of ADA liberals proved to be especially important in getting the initiative off the ground. Conceding that waiting would do little to further the chances of obtaining the White House's blessing, the Randolph Institute decided to proceed without the administration and sent Keyserling and Rustin on a cross-country speaking tour in support of the budget.[74] Speeches by Keyserling and Rustin before a five-hundred-person rally in Philadelphia organized by the local ADA chapter generated considerable local support and spurred the formation of an ad hoc local Freedom Budget committee featuring 150 prominent Philadelphians.[75] The positive response of ADA liberals and others in Philadelphia to the Freedom Budget was joined by a broad outpouring of support from ADA members across the country. ADA national director Leon Shull expressed satisfaction that "ADA chapters everywhere have been enthusiastic" and that there existed "a good deal of feeling that this should be a very major project for us."[76]

THE FREEDOM BUDGET AND THE VIETNAM WAR

Just as the Freedom Budget began to gain momentum with the ADA, the broader liberal community, and civil rights leaders, the ongoing escalation of the Vietnam War called into question the fundamental principles on which the initiative rested. Over the course of 1966 and 1967, the number of US troops deployed by the Johnson administration to Vietnam soared from 185,000 to just under half a million.[77] As the commitment of American troops continued to grow, the notion that the United States possessed the economic resources and political wherewithal to wage both a ground war in Southeast Asia and a meaningful War on Poverty at home became increasingly suspect to many liberals. Based on an allocation of expected economic growth rather than a redistribution of existing economic resources, the Freedom Budget attracted a powerful but short-lived consensus among leading liberals and civil rights leaders around a social democratic response to poverty that went far beyond the aims of the Johnson administration's effort. When escalation of the Vietnam War fundamentally brought into question the assertion of the Freedom Budget that the United States could have both "guns and butter," that consensus quickly evaporated. Many in the ADA continued to press for full employment, a guaranteed income, and other measures that had been central to the Freedom Budget but diverged from the insistence of its chief architect, Leon Keyserling, that the productive power of the American economy held almost limitless potential as a source of social progress. Others such as Galbraith and Schlesinger called for a scaling up of the approach of the War on Poverty. In either case, as the influence of Keyserling and his belief in economic growth diminished, ADA liberals came to stress opposition to the Vietnam War as integral to the antipoverty measures needed to achieve full racial equality.

The waning of Keyserling's long outsized clout in the development of ADA economic policy came not long after the organization began to commit itself to a Freedom Budget initiative that clearly displayed the hallmarks of his economic thinking. Just as the ADA started to devote significant resources to the campaign for the Freedom Budget, large-scale escalation of the Vietnam War drove a wedge into what had seemed only months before to be a unified movement for social and economic justice. While ADA liberals overwhelmingly responded in favor of the Freedom Budget, and few in the organization took issue with the set of comprehensive domestic initiatives it called for, the insistence of its developers on dodging the "guns and butter" question proved to be a growing source of contention. With a general outlook sustained by confidence in the productive power of the US economy, the Freedom Budget stressed that its revenue and cost projections would not require cutbacks to military spending generally or an end to the Vietnam War in particular. The text of the Freedom Budget made clear that it could "and should be implemented, whether or not an early termination of the Vietnam conflict is achieved, or even were there to be substantial increase in its economic and financial burdens."[78]

From the perspective of a number of key figures in the ADA, the Freedom Budget's projection of and accommodations for future expenditures for the Vietnam War effectively amounted to tacit approval of the US military commitment in Vietnam. Herbert Gans, a major figure in the development of ADA domestic policy and an early contributor to the Freedom Budget, wrote to Rustin to express his displeasure at not having had the opportunity to see the final draft. Gans reported that the appearance of his name on the document had brought him his "share of snipping over the seeming endorsement of the Viet Nam war in the budget." For Gans, language in the budget based on Keyserling's "casual acceptance of the war effort" readily opened up the budget to such charges.[79]

Rustin, writing back to Gans, agreed that it had been a mistake not to clarify sufficiently their position on the war in the Freedom Budget, but the very noncommittal stance of the text served a strategic purpose for him and those most involved in the development of the budget.[80] As Keyserling would point out to detractors, the Freedom Budget specified that it took no position as to the status quo of US military expenditures or policy in Vietnam despite a multitude of figures projecting a continuation or increase of present military spending. In his calculation, not committing to a position on the Vietnam War would allow the Freedom Budget to attract the broad coalition of support necessary to make the proposal a reality. The base for that coalition would be sabotaged, he maintained, if it was "limited to those who, for all practical purposes, act upon the assumption that these domestic purposes are unattainable unless there is a very drastic change in national policies with respect to military and space" expenditures.[81]

With rising tension in the ADA over the escalation of the war in Vietnam, vocal critics of the conflict and those who sought to downplay the war's broader significance increasingly approached the issue from divergent perspectives. While Keyserling and Rustin stressed the need to avoid the question of the Vietnam War and consequently developed the Freedom Budget around a noncommittal position aimed at attracting the broadest possible range of support, significant figures in the leadership of the ADA and other liberal organizations saw no reasonable or even feasible way in which the issue could be avoided. Robert Browne, an influential figure in SANE, wrote to Randolph to express his belief in the irresponsibility of the Freedom Budget's failure to take a position on the Vietnam War. Browne pointed to "burgeoning war spending" as the "first obstacle to the realization of the Budget's goals" and stressed that failing to acknowledge it as such would only serve to raise false hopes.[82] Offering an even more critical assessment when he later reflected on the Freedom Budget, Joseph Rauh bluntly deemed it "a fake" and an "effort to make the Vietnam War look good."[83] While both those who supported and those who criticized the noncommittal position of the Freedom Budget on the Vietnam War shared a belief in the moral cause of the budget, their irreconcilable differences on the issue of the war laid down the lines of a division in the organization that would only grow in significance in the coming years.

The ADA continued to provide nominal support for the Freedom Budget over the course of 1967, but the growing schism over the Vietnam War within the organization quickly dissipated the early enthusiasm for the budget. In the polarized context of an escalating Vietnam War, any rationale that had existed for taking no position on the conflict disappeared. With non-commitment on Vietnam off the table as a viable option, ADA liberals increasingly demonstrated little tolerance for what many took to be implicit support for the war. Keyserling and Rustin had sought to avoid the issue in order to create a broad coalition of support for the Freedom Budget, but in doing so, they ended up losing the wholehearted backing of key ADA figures and other important potential liberal allies. By October, Keyserling had no choice but to concede that the budget's initial "army of supporters" seemed "to be vanishing into thin air."[84] With the Freedom Budget finding little interest in Congress following heavy Democratic losses in the 1966 election, waning liberal support—both within and outside the ADA—proved to be especially damaging to the budget's already meager legislative prospects.

The difficulties encountered by the Freedom Budget with liberal audiences amid the ongoing escalation of the Vietnam War owed much to the inherent limitations of Keyserling's economic and political outlook.

The nearly exclusive preoccupation with economic growth and the tacit approval of the Vietnam War that suffused the Freedom Budget reflected beliefs deeply held by Keyserling, but also bore the stamp of scrutiny that he and his wife, Mary Dublin Keyserling, faced during the 1940s and early 1950s. Self-described socialists in the 1930s, neither Leon nor his wife was ever a member of the Communist Party or a fellow traveler. Nevertheless, in a context of allegations of guilt by association, their left-leaning politics, and Mary's involvement in a number of organizations speciously classified by government authorities as communist fronts, landed the couple in a series of protracted loyalty investigations. Like many who had operated on the left end of the political spectrum in the 1930s, Keyserling moderated his political views during the Second Red Scare. Over years of investigations that consistently failed to find any evidence of communist involvement, Keyserling tried to downplay the socialist currents that had run through his earlier politics by citing his firm belief throughout the postwar years that poverty could be eliminated through economic growth rather than redistribution. In his work for the Conference on Economic Progress and the Freedom Budget, he maintained his long-standing commitment to improving the material and economic standing of the poor and working class, but he parted ways with the redistributionist proposals and scathing criticism of capitalism found in his politics during the 1930s.[85]

The near total reliance of the Freedom Budget on economic growth expressed Keyserling's genuine belief in the social potential of economic expansion but also indicated the unease with redistribution that entered his politics in the wake of harrowing loyalty investigations. Similarly, Keyserling's commitment to Cold War military spending and his uncritical acceptance of the Vietnam War reflected real concerns that he had about the dangers of communist expansion but were also—at least in part—a residual consequence of his efforts to convince authorities of his anticommunist bona fides. With a political and economic outlook appreciably narrowed over the course of the Second Red Scare, Keyserling never entertained the option of thoroughgoing redistribution in the event of poor economic growth or questioned a war that was sapping funds which could be put to use for domestic purposes as he laid the foundation for the Freedom Budget.[86] While ADA liberals had proved themselves capable of discarding the New Deal's racial exclusivism and adapting Roosevelt era reforms to provide a foundation for addressing the economic dimensions of racial inequality in the 1960s, they could not overcome the limitations imposed on liberal reform by the Second Red Scare.

THE KERNER REPORT AND DOUBLING DOWN ON OPPOSITION TO THE WAR

The structural approach to addressing entrenched economic inequality championed by the Freedom Budget with little success received new consideration from the White House and Congress when the National Advisory Committee on Civil Disorders released its report in 1968 on the violent uprisings seen in urban areas across the country the preceding summer. The report, widely referred to as the Kerner Report after committee chairman and Illinois governor Otto Kerner, depicted a startling situation in the nation's inner-city ghettos and called for a federal response that went far beyond any of the Johnson administration's existing programs. Unsurprisingly, ADA liberals responded positively to a presidentially commissioned report that lent weight and urgency to many of the antipoverty measures they had been advocating for years. But while the Kerner Commission diligently avoided taking a position on the Vietnam War in a report that nevertheless ruffled the feathers of the White House on other issues, the ADA was quick to seize on the war as the first and most significant hurdle to realizing the commission's recommendations.

Drafted by the staff of committee vice chairman and liberal New York Republican mayor John Lindsay, the opening summary of the report sought to shock and rouse the nation's conscience by diverging from the more muted tone found in its four-hundred-plus-page body.[87] The summary opened with what would become a famous indictment of American society, declaring, "Our nation is moving toward two societies, one black, one white—separate and unequal." Highlighting white racism and its implications for Black poverty as the fundamental factor in the previous summer's violence, the report stated: "What white Americans have never fully understood—but what the Negro can never forget—is that white society is deeply implicated in the ghetto. White institutions created it, white institutions maintain it, and white society condones it."[88]

The Kerner Report concluded that addressing the crisis of the urban ghetto would require a concerted, expansive, and sustained effort backed by the resources of the world's richest and most powerful nation. It called for the creation of 2 million jobs over the next three years, extensive efforts to eliminate de facto segregation in schools, a program to bring 6 million new and existing homes of decent quality within the reach of low- and moderate-income families, and a guaranteed annual income for all Americans.[89] Very few of the Kerner Report's recommendations were new. The key measures called for by the committee read much like pages from the Freedom Budget or domestic policy resolutions passed by the ADA in the preceding years. As the product, however, of a presidential commission comprising prominent figures from across the political spectrum, the Kerner Report brought those measures a great deal of attention and lent them a significant degree of legitimacy.

Spurned by the administration that had called for its investigation into the causes of urban violence, the Kerner Report found a highly receptive audience in the ADA. In contrast to President Johnson's refusal to endorse or even receive in an official manner a report that illuminated the limitations of his Great Society legislative achievements and called for massive increases in federal expenditures which he saw as politically infeasible, the ADA lauded the Kerner Report and called for swift implementation of its recommendations. Speaking on behalf of the organization as its chairman, Galbraith deemed the recommended measures to be "on a scale coordinate with the problem to be solved" and declared that there "can be no excuse that resources are needed for other purposes." Still, as much as he praised the work and findings of the Kerner Commission, the ADA chairman devoted more of his short statement to the Vietnam War than to the report itself. He asserted that it should not be forgotten that hawks "who talk most unctuously about the more or less imaginary liberties of the [South] Vietnamese are usually those who have given the least practical help to advancing the cause of liberty and social justice for Negroes and other minorities here at home."[90] This direct focus on the link between the Vietnam War and the failures of the struggle for social justice at home marked a turning point for Galbraith and others in the organization. Until the release of the 1968 federal budget, the ADA chairman had, by his own admission, been "strung along with the idea that the Vietnam War was not affecting our domestic programs."[91] By the time the Kerner Commission reported its findings in 1968, the insistence of the Freedom Budget that the wealthiest nation on the planet could have both "guns and butter" held little credibility in the ADA.

The impossibility of avoiding the subject of the Vietnam War or taking a noncommittal position on it meant that the ADA would not be able to accommodate the kinds of differences long aired in the organization on a variety of issues when it came to the conflict in Southeast Asia. The affinity displayed by Galbraith and Schlesinger with the general approach of a War on Poverty that shared much in common with the emphasis on public services found in their vision for qualitative liberalism had long distinguished their views from the prevailing consensus in the ADA on more social democratic solutions to poverty. Galbraith and Schlesinger, however, had no particular aversion to a social democratic approach to poverty and could readily find common ground with their ADA colleagues on the need for increased resources for the struggle against poverty, if not the particulars of how that struggle should be waged. The dividing lines that formed in the ADA during the escalation of the Vietnam War would not be as forgiving. Keyserling, organized labor leaders, and those in the ADA with ties to the Johnson administration who either supported the war or sought to curry favor with the administration by refraining from voicing opposition would find themselves not just out of step with the organization but beyond the pale. With the 1968 presidential election looming on the horizon, the conviction of Galbraith, Schlesinger, and other like-minded ADA leaders that poverty represented a civil rights issue in desperate need of a far greater commitment of resources prompted them to prioritize opposition to the Vietnam War and reevaluate their willingness to support President Johnson's reelection bid. Ultimately, the notion that the Vietnam War represented a transcendent political issue led those ADA liberals to part ways with a variety of longtime allies, look to a new social base for American liberalism, and establish their organization as a launching pad for the New Politics movement.

FIGURE 1. Leon Keyserling speaking before the congressional Joint Economic Committee in 1949. Keyserling served as chairman of the Council of Economic Advisers during Harry Truman's presidency and became one of the most visible and outspoken proponents of economic growth in the ADA or anywhere else during the postwar era. Harris & Ewing courtesy of the Harry S. Truman Library & Museum.

FIGURE 2. Arthur Schlesinger Jr. speaking at the 1954 convention banquet of the ADA's student organization, Students for Democratic Action. A founding member of the ADA and its national co-chairman at the time, Schlesinger was one of the most well-known and influential leaders in the organization in the postwar era. Even during the heyday of the ADA, however, Students for Democratic Action and its successor organization, the Campus Americans for Democratic Action, struggled to gain traction and maintain membership. Courtesy of the Wisconsin Historical Society, WHI-156736.

FIGURE 3. Joseph Rauh (rear center with bow tie) with (from left to right) Cleveland Robinson, Rabbi Joachim Prinz, A. Philip Randolph, and John Lewis at the Lincoln Memorial during the 1963 March on Washington for Jobs and Freedom. A civil rights lawyer and founding member of the ADA, Rauh remained an influential force within the organization until his resignation following its endorsement of Jimmy Carter's reelection in 1980. Stanley Tretick, photographer, LOOK Magazine Photograph Collection, Library of Congress, Prints & Photographs Division.

FIGURE 4. Bayard Rustin at a press conference the day before the 1963 March on Washington for Jobs and Freedom. A longtime civil rights activist and leader, Rustin was the principal organizer of the 1963 march but took the official title of deputy director and stayed somewhat behind the scenes because of concerns that his homosexuality would politically imperil the event. With his appointment to the ADA national board in 1965, he became one of the few non-white figures in the national leadership of the organization during the period and collaborated with Leon Keyserling on the Freedom Budget. Warren K. Leffler, photographer, Library of Congress, Prints & Photographs Division.

FIGURE 5. An undated portrait of Leon Shull. National director of the ADA from 1963 to 1985, Shull was a tireless servant to the organization who was ostensibly supposed to maintain a neutral position on matters of policy but nevertheless left a lasting imprint on the group with his support for the New Politics movement. Courtesy of the Wisconsin Historical Society, WHI- 151090.

FIGURE 6. John Kenneth Galbraith with Eugene McCarthy during the Minnesota senator's 1968 presidential campaign. A founding member of the ADA and its national chairman from 1967 to 1969, Galbraith was among the most visible and influential leaders in the organization for decades after its founding. His strong support for McCarthy's fledgling presidential campaign during his time as national chairman helped to establish the ADA's enduring relationship with the New Politics movement. Courtesy of the John F. Kennedy Presidential Library and Museum.

FIGURE 7. Joe Duffey with actor Paul Newman at a Eugene McCarthy campaign event in 1968. When Duffey succeeded John Kenneth Galbraith in 1969 with the support of the Harvard economist and other veteran ADA leaders, he became the organization's youngest national chairman in its history. His youth and activist background helped the ADA reach out to the students and other young people who had rallied to the presidential campaigns of Eugene McCarthy and Robert Kennedy the year before. Associated Press.

FIGURE 8. Allard Lowenstein with Don Peterson speaking to the press at the Conference for an Open Convention during the 1968 Democratic National Convention in Chicago. ADA Wisconsin chairman Peterson served as chairman of Eugene McCarthy's campaign in Wisconsin, while Lowenstein campaigned for McCarthy and won a seat in the House of Representatives as a New Politics Democrat in Nassau County, New York. Following his reelection loss in 1970, Lowenstein succeeded Joe Duffey as ADA national chairman and continued the organization's deep involvement in the New Politics movement. Photograph by Paul Cannon for the Associated Press.

FIGURE 9. George McGovern (front) with John Kenneth Galbraith (in the center of the group behind him) at a campaign event at the Harvard economist's summer home in Vermont in 1972. McGovern's victory in the Democratic primaries that year brought a New Politics movement shaped in important ways by the ADA and its leading figures to the biggest stage of presidential politics. Photograph by Ray Bates.

FIGURE 10. Representative Paul Tsongas in his office in 1977. One of many "Watergate babies" elected in 1976, Tsongas won election to the US Senate in 1978 and became a key neoliberal "Atari Democrat." He sought to resolve the tension that had existed in the New Politics movement between costly social democratic solutions and an emphasis on social and cultural issues that required less public spending by forgoing the former in favor of the latter. Marion S. Trikosko, photographer, U.S. News & World Report Magazine Photograph Collection, Library of Congress, Prints & Photographs Division.

FIGURE 11. Gary Hart at a campaign event during his 1984 run for president. Having been George McGovern's campaign manager in 1972 before becoming a US senator from Colorado and mounting two bids for the White House as a neoliberal "Atari Democrat," Hart followed a political path that exemplified the transformation of the New Politics into neoliberalism. Bernard Gotfryd, photographer, Library of Congress, Prints & Photographs Division.

FIGURE 12. John Kenneth Galbraith and his wife, Kitty Galbraith, with President Bill Clinton at the Franklin D. Roosevelt Memorial Commission Dinner at the White House in 1996. Confounding Galbraith's expectation that suburban New Class voters would be as liberal on economic matters as they were on social and cultural issues, many middle-class voters from the suburbs supported Clinton and other economically conservative New Democrats in the wake of the early 1990s recession. Courtesy of the William J. Clinton Presidential Library & Museum.

FIGURE 13. An undated photo of Arthur Schlesinger Jr. with President Bill Clinton. Prior to the revival of meaningful economic progressivism in liberal politics with the unexpectedly strong showing of Bernie Sanders's 2016 presidential campaign, the neoliberalism of Clinton and the New Democrats appeared for decades to be the sole surviving legacy of the New Politics. Courtesy of the New York Public Library Manuscript and Archives Division.

CHAPTER 4

THE COMING OF THE NEW POLITICS MOVEMENT

The Vietnam War and the Promise of the New Class

In the months that followed Eugene McCarthy's stunning near defeat of President Lyndon Johnson in the New Hampshire Democratic primary on March 12, 1968, the notion of a "New Politics" took hold among political observers and became a regular feature of political discussion. Contrasting themselves with the "old politics" of party regulars and organized labor, the activists, intellectuals, and politicians who rallied under the banner of the New Politics in 1968 sought to shift the balance of power in the Democratic Party toward grassroots activism in order to mount political opposition to the Vietnam War through the existing two-party system. Before its unexpected showing in the New Hampshire primary, the McCarthy campaign that put the New Politics movement into motion received an invaluable boost on February 10 when the ADA voted to endorse the Minnesota senator's long-shot challenge to the incumbent Democratic president.

The ADA's endorsement of McCarthy has often been seen as a harbinger of its later political eclipse. In his influential history of the ADA, Steven Gillon depicts the decision to endorse McCarthy as an act of principle committed at the expense of political prudence that paved the way to irrelevancy by settling the protracted tension in the organization between politics and vision decisively in favor of the latter.[1] The decision of longtime ADA leaders to break ranks with organized labor and push their organization to endorse McCarthy did not, however, represent a hasty moment of visionary overreach. Rather it reflected a culmination of their growing skepticism toward the principle of anticommunist containment and a long advocacy of the qualitative liberalism that underpinned their belief in the electoral potential of the college students and white-collar workers who made up what many were beginning to term a "New Class." Instead of heralding their effective demise, the endorsement of McCarthy in 1968 enabled leading figures in the ADA to play an instrumental role in shaping an emerging movement that saw them wield as much influence on the direction of American politics as at any other point in the history of the organization. By adapting a postwar liberalism that had been defined by anticommunist foreign policy and the bread-and-butter issues of the New Deal political agenda to the new circumstances and challenges of the 1960s, veteran ADA leaders were able to sustain their political and intellectual sway. Their enduring influence also helped to ensure that the New Politics movement that was taking shape depended on New Class liberals, who demonstrated remarkable unity on the seemingly non-material issue of the Vietnam War but displayed considerably less cohesion in terms of shared economic interests with the other constituencies of the New Politics coalition.

The path to the New Politics and the new liberal coalition on which it depended started in the 1950s, when John Kenneth Galbraith, Arthur Schlesinger Jr., and other longtime ADA leaders began to see the nation's growing affluence as ushering in the end of the liberal coalition forged during the New Deal era. Resigned to their fate, these ADA liberals, who believed that their coalition was in the process of fraying beyond recognition, looked to the growing ranks of the New Class as an essential social base for the future of liberal politics. Hopes for the liberal potential of the New Class took on a new meaning in the 1960s with the escalation of the US war effort in Vietnam and the heightened national visibility of the civil rights movement. The intensification of the Vietnam War sharpened the doubts many ADA liberals harbored about a policy of anticommunist containment and raised the stakes for the criticism they had been advancing since the earliest days of American involvement in the conflict. At the same time, the momentum of the civil rights movement led ADA liberals to a newfound awareness of both the enduring scale and depth of poverty in the country and its direct relationship to deep-seated racial inequality. As they came to see the question of whether South Vietnam was to be ruled by a communist dictatorship or a military one as an issue of diminishing importance in the age of polycentric communism, many in the ADA began to regard American involvement in the war as the primary barrier to undertaking the antipoverty initiatives needed to carry on the struggle for civil rights.

When ADA liberals became convinced that little progress would be made in addressing the economic inequality that underpinned racial inequality so long as the United States was mired in Vietnam War, they insisted that the war could no longer be seen as one issue among many and had to be recognized as a transcendent principle that defined the liberal agenda.

Committed to mounting political opposition to the Vietnam War and emboldened by their belief in the promise of the New Class as a political force, a contingent of veteran ADA leaders led the charge for an endorsement of McCarthy's struggling presidential campaign that would establish the organization as a vehicle for the New Politics movement. Coming at a moment when McCarthy was facing a virtual vacuum of political support as other liberal organizations and politicians opposed to the Vietnam War failed to offer him their backing, the ADA's endorsement of the Minnesota senator proved critical to getting the campaign that would spark the New Politics movement off the ground. As the movement coalesced around the campaigns of McCarthy and Robert Kennedy, the ADA found itself well positioned to play a central role in the development of the New Politics. Comprised of activists steeped not in contemporary radical politics but in a tradition of liberal reform that stretched back to the supporters of Adlai Stevenson in the 1950s and the Progressives of the early twentieth century, the New Politics movement grew out of a political and social milieu that had long included the deep involvement of the ADA and its chapters. After the endorsement of McCarthy, ADA chapters across the country quickly mobilized on behalf of the Minnesota senator and provided the New Politics movement emerging around his campaign with a valuable network of contacts and an existing organizational base to build on. Beyond the furnishing of important organizational resources, the deep, shared conviction of longtime ADA leaders and New Politics activists that the political establishment responsible for the Vietnam War could be—and needed to be—challenged through the accepted channels of American democracy offered a strong basis for the organization's ongoing relationship with the movement.

Still, it was the desire to preserve and foster that relationship which led the aging leadership of the ADA to look to a new generation of leaders whose youth and activist background would enable the organization to reach out to young people who had no sentimental connection to the ADA. The veteran leaders of the ADA who had led the charge for the McCarthy endorsement paved the way to the ranks of leadership in the organization for younger figures such as Joseph Duffey and Allard Lowenstein. While in terms of their political backgrounds and styles this new generation of leaders differed greatly from the likes of Galbraith and Schlesinger, they nevertheless drew from the same intellectual and political wellspring that had sustained the politics of the ADA's founding generation. During the late 1960s and early 1970s, the membership of the ADA became younger and displayed a growing preference for action over rhetoric which stood in marked contrast to the organization's long-established penchant for writing resolutions as a means of advancing political issues. This new-look ADA nurtured the relationship between the organization and the New Politics movement that had begun with its bold endorsement of McCarthy's fledgling campaign. As the New Politics movement evolved into a major force in liberal politics, the strength of that relationship ensured that longtime ADA leaders and their ideas—including the tensions and contradictions that ran through those ideas—remained an integral part of the movement.

THE VIETNAM WAR AS A TRANSCENDENT ISSUE

As the commitment of the ADA to the fight for civil rights expanded to include the struggle against poverty, leading figures in the organization approached the issue of chronic economic deprivation with a newfound urgency and emphasized the severe inadequacies of the War on Poverty and the broader initiatives of the Johnson administration's Great Society. Yet even those already meager efforts saw an appreciable reduction in funding and commitment as the administration continued to escalate the Vietnam conflict. With the war consuming more than $1.5 billion a month, Arthur Schlesinger Jr. lamented in 1966 that the "Great Society is now, except for token gestures, dead." Tallying the consequences, Schlesinger remarked, "The fight for equal opportunity for the Negro, the war on poverty, the struggle to save the cities, the improvement of our schools—all must be starved for the sake of Vietnam."[2] Skeptical of economic growth as a social panacea and the notion that the country could have both "guns and butter," Schlesinger, Galbraith, and other veteran ADA leaders came to see opposition to the war as integral to the antipoverty programs needed to achieve full racial equality. When these ADA liberals began to approach the Vietnam War not simply as one important matter among many but as a transcendent political issue on which the fate of the broader liberal agenda depended, they put their organization on a collision course with organized labor and the Johnson administration that would have lasting consequences for the ADA and the trajectory of liberal politics.

The first signs of the tension that would accompany efforts to prioritize opposition to the Vietnam War in the ADA could be seen at the organization's national convention in 1966. When delegates secured passage of a resolution expressing the hope that "Vietnam will see the end of indiscriminate anti-communism as a pillar of American foreign policy," a clear divergence emerged between those who supported the resolution and the largely labor-based contingent who opposed it.[3] Labor leaders in the ADA, like the bulk of labor leadership in the country, had no desire to jeopardize their relationship with President Johnson and provided staunch support for the administration's Vietnam War policies. This support was not, however, simply a response to immediate political pressures. It was also an expression of labor leaders' hardline Cold War posture with roots in a hypervigilant anti-communism born out of their earlier struggles against communists in the labor movement.[4] Still, despite these deeply held and divergent perspectives in the organization, the absence of any concrete political commitments in the ADA's 1966 resolution on the Vietnam War ultimately dulled the edge of the debate seen at that year's convention.

The dispute became far more heated at the following year's ADA national convention when questions of how critical a stance to take on the Johnson administration's Vietnam War policy and the degree to which American policy in Vietnam should serve as a test of liberal politics came to the fore. In this increasingly tense atmosphere, delegates split along lines similar to those that had developed the previous year.[5] Against the desire of International Ladies Garment Workers Union (ILGWU) assistant president Gus Tyler and other key labor representatives for a milder resolution, the convention passed by an almost two-to-one margin a political resolution expressing "disenchantment and dismay over many aspects of administration policy in Vietnam and a parallel retreat at home." Particularly offensive to labor representatives was the resolution's suggestion that the ADA might not support President Johnson in the 1968 election if he did not correct the failures of a foreign policy that blunted any genuine hope of domestic social progress. The resolution welcomed a serious liberal challenger to the president from the Republican Party—partly to dispel perennial criticism that dependence on the Democratic Party made the ADA politically ineffective, but also to put genuine political pressure on Johnson. Still, the resolution walked a very fine line and reached out to the president's supporters by omitting mention of a challenger to Johnson from within the Democratic Party. The resolution also tempered its position against the president by expressing the hope that a Republican challenge would lead to "a counter attack led by the President himself in the reasoned, dedicated spirit of his 1964 campaign."[6]

The fine line walked by the resolution proved short-lived. At the national board meeting on May 20, with only 44 of 134 board members in attendance, the majority present passed a resolution that expressed the intention of the ADA "to support in the 1968 election that liberal candidate of either major party, who offers a genuine hope for restraint in the conduct of the war in Vietnam and for its peaceful resolution on honorable terms."[7] The May 20 resolution marked a stark divergence from the political resolution passed shortly before at the national convention by welcoming a challenge to President Johnson from either major party—as opposed to the Republican Party alone—and in making Vietnam the critical factor for determining ADA support in 1968.

Passed by a bare minimum quorum of the national board shortly after the more fully attended meeting of the board at the national convention in April, the May 20 resolution, with its more aggressive tone and substance, sparked a bitter conflict in the ADA. The ensuing confrontation pitted those in the organization who saw Vietnam as one issue among many against those who viewed it as the defining question of liberal politics. With the support of David Dubinsky, Leon Keyserling, Robert Nathan, John Roche, Bayard Rustin, Paul Seabury, and some fifty other members of the national board with close ties to organized labor or to the Johnson administration, Gus Tyler initiated a vigorous response to the resolution. In a memorandum to the national board, Tyler expressed the belief of a sizable contingent of ADAers that the May 20 resolution would turn the group into a one-issue organization and remove it from the stage of liberal politics in the United States.[8] Schlesinger quickly countered Tyler's memorandum with a letter of his own to the members of the national board in which he contended that the May 20 resolution created a political opportunity for liberals by sending Johnson the message that he could not expect unconditional support from them regardless of his policies. For Schlesinger, the only way the liberal community could have leverage against the administration was to suggest that liberals did in fact have other options.[9]

Beyond tactical questions of how to press the Johnson administration on its policy in Vietnam, Schlesinger's letter emphasized the break between the increasingly influential bloc within the ADA that saw Vietnam as the organizing principle of liberal politics and a largely labor-based bloc who feared that strident opposition to the war posed a danger to the liberal-intellectual-labor coalition that had long sustained the organization. In response to Tyler's charge that those who supported the May 20 resolution suffered from "monomania" on the issue of Vietnam, Schlesinger answered that supporters of the resolution were motivated by the conviction that "far from being an isolated issue, the Vietnam War is intimately related to the slowdown in the struggle for civil rights" and "the war against poverty." Schlesinger articulated a view held by a prominent contingent of longtime ADA leaders as well as the growing ranks of younger board members when he argued that the direct connection between the war in Vietnam and the lack of social progress at home meant that giving special attention to the issue of Vietnam did not make the ADA a "one-issue" organization.[10]

In the ongoing battle of memorandums, Keyserling followed up Schlesinger's missive with one of his own that lined him up firmly on the side of organized labor representatives and administration supporters in the ADA. In his memorandum Keyserling expressed strong support for Tyler's position and fervent disapproval of both the expedient means by which the May 20 resolution was passed and the substance of that resolution. Keyserling took issue with the failure to inform members of the national board that discussion of a resolution representing a substantial departure from the position adopted at the national convention was to be on the table at the May 20 meeting. He cited this failure and the subsequent passage of the resolution by such a questionable majority—less than one third of the total membership of the board—as evidence that fundamental principles of democratic procedure had been violated. Turning his attention to the substance of the resolution, Keyserling, writing shortly after the outbreak of the Six-Day War between Israel and its Arab neighbors, objected to the way the resolution lifted Vietnam to primacy over all other issues and pointed to the development of hostilities in the Middle East as obvious proof that not all matters of importance to liberals were related to the Vietnam War. Together, those procedural and substantive objections led Keyserling to charge that the powerful minority of board members behind the resolution had compelled the ADA to give "zealous" priority to the divisive issue of Vietnam rather than to the numerous issues that united the organization.[11]

Despite Keyserling's accusation, by 1967 those in the ADA who saw the Vietnam War as a question of transcendent importance for liberals represented not a noisy minority with disproportionate influence but rather the majority of the organization's leadership and rank and file. The series of resolutions passed by the national conventions and the board over the course of 1966 and 1967 on the Vietnam War and related political policy demonstrated that while labor representatives and their supporters remained a sizable minority in the ranks of leadership, they were nonetheless a minority, and a shrinking one at that. Oblivious to many of the sweeping changes taking place in the organization, labor leaders and their supporters struggled to accept that their continued belief in the need for global communist containment had been brushed aside by a new consensus in the ADA based on belief in the transcendent importance of opposing the Vietnam War.

As Galbraith, Schlesinger, and other veteran leaders in the ADA nurtured a consensus that marginalized a significant number of their longtime colleagues, they also began to reevaluate the effectiveness of the principal campaign through which they had mounted their opposition to the war and their belief in the prospects for a negotiated settlement to the conflict. Less than six months after helping launch Negotiation Now! in the hope that a mass collection of signatures by the campaign would pressure the Johnson administration to cease bombing North Vietnam, de-escalate the war in the South, and make a more determined effort toward negotiating a settlement, Galbraith and Schlesinger called into question the basic premise of the initiative. In November 1967, they individually published widely read articles that had much in common, including an emphasis on the difficulties of seeking a negotiated solution to the Vietnam War and the decreasing likelihood that the Johnson administration could or would bring the hostilities to an end. Galbraith's article for the *New York Times Magazine* drew on the general contours of the plan to end the war made in his well-received Negotiation Now! address the previous June, but its emphasis on the difficult path to negotiations left it with little of the confidence that had characterized his earlier speech.[12]

Similarly, in a widely read article for *The New Leader*, Schlesinger warned critics of the Vietnam War to be under no illusions as to the ease of a negotiated solution. For Schlesinger, a strong case against bombing

North Vietnam could be made on the grounds of either its military ineffectiveness or its moral callousness but not on the assumption that ceasing bombing would produce negotiations. Schlesinger found a depressing irony in the fact that if the Johnson administration finally attempted a serious peace effort, no rational government in Hanoi could be expected to do anything but stall until the next administration took over. In his estimation, this meant that with the 1968 presidential election looming, "the negotiation season will draw to a close." The pessimism expressed in his article challenged the link between a cessation in bombing and the path to the negotiating table that most liberal critics of the war had clung to since the beginning of major US military intervention in the conflict. The severing of that link led Schlesinger and a growing number of liberals to look for alternatives to a Negotiation Now! campaign that still saw calling for an end to the bombing of North Vietnam and urging negotiations as a viable means of ending the Vietnam War.[13]

Advancing a more critical perspective on the Vietnam War and negotiations than the Negotiation Now! campaign provided required Schlesinger to grapple with the difficulties of developing an alternative formulation for ending the war and the questioning of support for President Johnson entailed by that effort. While pessimistic about the prospects for negotiations, Schlesinger expressed no particular attraction to calls for the unilateral withdrawal of American military forces from Vietnam. Still, he declared himself open to unilateral withdrawal as a potential—if not desirable—policy alternative with the concession that while withdrawing unilaterally "would hardly be America's finest hour," the option "would be greatly preferable to a policy of unlimited escalation." Seeing the prospects for negotiations as dim, he struggled to define an appealing and tenable alternative to either unilateral withdrawal or escalation but expressed no doubts as to the failure of the Johnson administration's persistent policy of escalation over the past thirty-two months. With the deaths of more than thirteen thousand American soldiers and countless Vietnamese, an expenditure of nearly $90 billion, and an irresponsible and dangerous neglect of the many domestic problems faced by the nation, he saw the United States as no closer than it had ever been to winning the war or even establishing a viable government in South Vietnam. Schlesinger made clear that if the country's leadership did not change its course on the war, the country would have to change its leadership.[14]

Those who shared Schlesinger's conviction that the ADA's support in the 1968 presidential race should hinge on the transcendent issue of the Vietnam War had to face the difficult prospect that a direct move against Johnson's reelection would almost certainly jeopardize the ongoing involvement of labor leaders in the organization. While a majority of the national board had come to believe that opposition to the Vietnam War should be the focus of the ADA's operations and the critical factor in its political strategy, the organization still remained dependent on funding from labor unions and deeply rooted in the liberal-labor-intellectual coalition that had sustained it since its 1947 founding.[15] The entrance of a challenger to Johnson in the Democratic primaries and the prospect of growing numbers of white-collar, middle-class Americans as a base for a new liberal coalition created an opening for Galbraith, Rauh, Schlesinger, and others in an influential contingent of ADA leaders to push for a fundamental reorientation of their organization and of American liberalism. With that opening, these veteran ADA leaders could see breaking ranks with labor to establish the organization as a base for political opposition to the Vietnam conflict not only as a morally necessary response to a misguided war and dire domestic needs but also as an act of political realism.

POLITICAL PRAGMATISM, THE NEW CLASS, AND THE MCCARTHY ENDORSEMENT

When the ADA became the first non-issue-specific organization with a national standing to throw its weight behind Eugene McCarthy's campaign for president on February 10, 1968, many saw the move as an act of unmitigated idealism.[16] Years before being portrayed by the historian Steven Gillon as an act of principle and vision committed at the expense of political pragmatism, the endorsement was characterized in *The New Republic* as a victory for the organization's "moralists" over its pragmatists.[17] Yet those in the ADA who led the charge for an endorsement of the Minnesota senator's seemingly quixotic campaign did not act without regard for the sense of political realism that had long guided them and their hopes for the future of liberal politics. Aware of the challenges ahead and McCarthy's obvious limitations as a candidate, they believed that his challenge to Lyndon Johnson in the Democratic Party primaries on the issue of the Vietnam War would be able to draw on the significant electoral power of the college students and well-educated white-collar workers who filled the ranks of a growing New Class. Similarly, these longtime ADA leaders believed that an endorsement of the McCarthy campaign would put the ADA in touch with the large number of individuals from the New Class who harbored antiwar views and an intense frustration over the difficulty they encountered in trying to bring those views to bear on the political establishment. Despite long-held assumptions to the contrary, the willingness of these ADAers to sacrifice the support of organized labor in order to endorse McCarthy did not represent a rash disavowal of politics in favor of vision. Rather, it was the consequence of their belief in the liberal potential of the New Class that grew out of their thinking on the changing social and political circumstances of the postwar era stretching back to the Republican electoral victories of 1952.

John Kenneth Galbraith, along with Arthur Schlesinger Jr. and other like-minded figures in the ADA, initially became interested in the political potential of what they would frequently call the "New Class" in the 1950s. This was a decade when a sizable bloc of white-collar, middle-class, largely suburban voters produced by growing postwar affluence began to move into the national spotlight. Galbraith first turned his attention to this new category of Americans, which he variably characterized as the "academic and scientific community," the "socially concerned," and later as members of the "technostructure," in his 1958 book *The Affluent Society*. As described by the Harvard economist, these were people who found themselves released from the hard physical toil of manual labor and many of the economic concerns that prevailed among the working class. In order to pursue a career from which they could derive self-fulfillment, members of the New Class required an educational background that served to develop their critical faculties on issues such as foreign policy and racial equality, which Galbraith and other proponents of the New Class believed to be qualitative in nature and unrelated to the material self-interest of those who made up its ranks.[18] Individuals in the New Class derived their status and income not from the ownership of property but on the basis of a professional position largely determined by their educational attainment. The highly educated professionals employed at corporations, government agencies, universities, and other large organizations accounted for most of the adults in the New Class, while its youth could be found in the country's rapidly expanding colleges and universities.[19]

Enduringly difficult to define and label, those who constituted the New Class have found themselves addressed with an even wider variety of terms by scholars and journalists in the years since the publication of *The Affluent Society*. With labels ranging from the "new middle class," "professional-managerial class," "creative class," and "white-collar proletariat" to "knowledge workers" and "suburban liberals," no consensus on terminology has emerged.[20] With complicated intellectual roots in the work of figures as diverse as the progressive sociologist Thorstein Veblen, conservative political theorist James Burnham, and dissident Yugoslav communist Milovan Đilas, the term "New Class" is not without its own difficulties.[21] Still, the term captures the essence of the broad grouping of students and white-collar professionals whose politics appeared to many observers to hinge more on moral concerns than on economic self-interest while avoiding the implication of a specific occupation or living environment carried by other comparable labels.

ADA liberals drawn to the New Class first became interested in the political potential of this burgeoning bloc of white-collar workers and students as they began to recognize the fraying of the New Deal coalition in the early postwar years. Schlesinger articulated variations on the theme that growing postwar affluence had dampened the political appeal of the New Deal program and begun to break apart its political coalition as far back as Adlai Stevenson's loss to Dwight Eisenhower in the 1952 presidential election.[22] With a greater awareness of the continuing presence of poverty in the wake of the civil rights movement, Schlesinger in the 1960s displayed a sharpened attention to those who remained beyond the reach of the "affluent society" but carried with him from the 1950s the conviction that liberals needed to reconcile themselves to the reality that the traditional New Deal coalition had withered away.[23]

The thinking that underpinned that conviction in the 1950s would take on new meaning and relevance in the 1960s as Schlesinger came to see the rise of general—if not universal—affluence in American society as meaning that educational attainment had displaced income as the critical factor in determining an individual's politics. Schlesinger believed that in a society of abundance, where quantitative economic issues were giving way to questions of foreign policy, racial equality, and other qualitative issues, high levels of education rather than low income had become the characteristic most common among those attracted to liberal politics. The presumption that foreign policy matters such as the Vietnam War represented a qualitative issue to be approached on largely abstract and moral terms illustrated the gulf between Schlesinger and working-class families, who faced a far greater likelihood than their middle-class counterparts of seeing their sons drafted to fight in the war. Schlesinger's distance from the experiences of working-class Americans also impacted his formulation of the new dividing lines of politics in the 1960s that rested in no small part on the assumption—widespread in the ADA—that the working class shared the staunch support for the Vietnam War policies of the Johnson administration displayed by organized labor leaders. Thus, even before the media crystallized images of helmeted and unionized construction workers assaulting antiwar protesters in lower Manhattan in May 1970, Schlesinger characterized less-educated, low-income whites as often "the most emotional and primitive champions of conservatism." While the white working-class defenders of the status quo described by Schlesinger wanted to "crack down on the 'niggers,' imprison the long-haired college kids and bomb hell out of the North Vietnamese," the affluent and better educated tended "to care more about rationality, reform and progress."[24]

In the years since Schlesinger and like-minded ADA liberals joined intellectuals from a broad array of ideological backgrounds in casting a media-amplified narrative of reactionary working-class whites opposed to the antiwar activism of the affluent and educated, historians and other writers have discredited many of the assumptions that narrative drew upon. Their scholarship has demonstrated not only that antiwar attitudes prevailed at a slightly higher rate in the working class than in the country at large but also that the greatest support for the war came from the privileged and the educated.[25] By assuming that level of education acted as the dividing line of politics in the 1960s, these ADA liberals made a mistake that would have lasting consequences in effectively writing off the involvement of not just labor leadership but the working class more generally in the new liberal coalition they sought to build on the ashes of the New Deal coalition.

However misguided those assumptions have proven to be, they served to establish the vital importance of the New Class to the post–New Deal coalition envisioned by a number of leading figures in the ADA. Schlesinger could more readily cast doubt on the liberal potential of the working class in light of the 7 million college students and nearly three quarters of a million professors expected to be found in the United States by 1970 offering a potential base for the new liberal coalition.[26] Galbraith expressed a similar optimism toward the growing ranks of the college-educated when, during his acceptance speech as national chairman of the ADA, he highlighted the large capacity of the "academic and scientific community" for influence and leadership. With an explosion in numbers since the turn of the century, Galbraith painted this community in highly favorable colors: "It is literate, has good political memory and a special interest in foreign policy and it presently feels an intense sense of frustration over its difficulty in registering its views."[27]

The importance of reaching out to the growing ranks of the New Class weighed heavily on Schlesinger and Galbraith as they considered the position of the ADA on the Vietnam War. Schlesinger believed that the ADA would have no hope of winning support from the independent-minded individuals of the New Class if it dismissed the Vietnam War "as just one among many issues."[28] Similarly, Galbraith saw the Vietnam War as a central concern around which the ADA could reach out to the nation's vast bloc of college students and the college-educated.[29] Schlesinger, Galbraith, and similarly minded ADA liberals hoped that by establishing itself as a major source of political opposition to the Vietnam War, the organization would become attractive to the significant numbers of white-collar, middle-class Americans who harbored strong feelings of opposition to the war but were unlikely to join the protests of antiwar radicals in the streets. While the New Class would later be brought to wider attention as the target of neoconservative attacks in journals, magazines, and the op-ed pages of the *Wall Street Journal*, influential leaders in the ADA championed the students and workers of the New Class as the key to the future of both the ADA and liberal politics.[30]

Belief in the political potential of the New Class and a desire to bring those who filled its ranks into the ADA fold emboldened these leading figures to push for opposition to the Vietnam War as the critical factor in the organization's political strategy. Still, the constraints of political pragmatism continued to shape their decisions as they navigated the events leading up to the 1968 presidential election. In the summer of 1967, Curtis Gans, the young editor of *ADA World*, and Allard Lowenstein, a recently elected ADA vice chairman, approached Joseph Rauh with the hope of utilizing the ADA as an existing base to organize a challenge to Lyndon Johnson in the Democratic Party primaries. Despite lacking a candidate, Lowenstein believe that as soon as the initiative—known as the "Dump Johnson" campaign—demonstrated the depth and extent of dissatisfaction among Democratic voters with the Johnson administration's Vietnam policy, a viable candidate would emerge. Skeptical of a plan that involved proceeding with a challenge to Johnson without a candidate, Rauh sounded out Senators Frank Church, Robert Kennedy, Eugene McCarthy, and George McGovern to see if any of them would be willing to run. Finding no takers for an uphill challenge to the incumbent Democratic president, Rauh proceeded to develop an alternative plan that would seek to secure passage of a strong "peace plank" at the 1968 Democratic National Convention. Gans and Lowenstein went ahead with preparations for the Dump Johnson campaign. Meanwhile, Rauh made the case to his colleagues in the ADA for a push to elect delegates to the Democratic National Convention pledged to a "peace plank." He insisted that the initiative would provide a far greater opportunity to show the strength of the peace movement than a Dump Johnson effort that would struggle to find support without a candidate and allow hawks to claim that the peace movement had no political strength. Reflecting both Rauh's significant influence and the prevalence of similar political considerations in the organization, the ADA national board soundly rejected Lowenstein's Dump Johnson initiative and instead approved Rauh's "peace caucus" proposal by a vote of 72 to 12 when it met on September 23 to consider the two plans.[31]

Despite developing the plan and selling it to his colleagues in the ADA, Rauh had never been satisfied with the "peace caucus" approach as the basis of the organization's opposition to the Vietnam War. Even while he pushed the plan as the best option politically available to the organization, he conceded to his fellow ADA board members in private that if "Kennedy, McGovern or McCarthy" had decided to challenge Johnson, he would be "working for one of them right now." Rauh and other ADA liberals who had settled for the plan out of political necessity were—despite their public rhetoric—continually skeptical that a plank would be able to inspire mass enthusiasm or support. Galbraith had been sympathetic to Lowenstein's Dump Johnson campaign from the beginning and his desire to mount a more compelling campaign against the Vietnam War than the "peace caucus" plan led him to go as far as exploring the possibility of running against Johnson himself despite the constitutional hurdle of his Canadian birth. Still, in the end, Galbraith's brief consideration of an implausible presidential campaign gave way to political realities when he opted instead to commit himself to establishing the ADA as an organizational base for Rauh's "peace caucus" campaign.[32]

The political calculations that led Galbraith, Rauh, and other veteran ADA figures to support a far less than ideal "peace caucus" approach as the basis of the organization's antiwar efforts changed dramatically on November 30 when Eugene McCarthy announced his intention to challenge Lyndon Johnson in the Democratic primaries on the issue of the Vietnam War. Soon after the announcement, Rauh made a television appearance to stump for McCarthy's nascent campaign.[33] With the ADA National Board not due to meet until after the turn of the year, Galbraith, as the organization's national chairman, maintained an official silence on McCarthy's candidacy but wrote to the Minnesota senator in early December to privately offer his best wishes and support.[34] Not confined to those in the highest ranks of leadership, a majority of the organization's rank and file had come to support McCarthy's candidacy by the beginning of 1968. As most labor representatives in the ADA held positions at the national level, local chapters proved even more receptive to McCarthy's candidacy than the national leadership. When he surveyed the organization's membership in mid-January, Leon Shull estimated that two thirds of all ADA members and a smaller majority of the national board favored an endorsement for McCarthy.[35]

As support for McCarthy's candidacy took hold at all levels of the organization, it quickly became apparent that the cerebral former professor, onetime Benedictine novice monk, and devoted poet did not fit the mold of what many in the ADA would have held to be the ideal challenger to President Johnson. Writing to Galbraith on January 19, Shull sadly reported that McCarthy's campaign in California was in a state of collapse primarily because "he is simply not a good candidate." Echoing the widespread perception of McCarthy as aloof and uninspiring, Shull lamented that fundraising events in California had demonstrated that "he arouses relatively little enthusiasm." Beyond issues of style and presentation, others in the ADA highlighted McCarthy's votes in the Senate in favor of oil and pharmaceutical interests as they began to question his voting record on issues besides the Vietnam War.[36]

Yet in those faults, some ADA leaders also recognized a number of McCarthy's strengths as a candidate with the ability to attract New Class voters. Rauh saw McCarthy's low-key, soft-spoken demeanor not as an impediment to his ability to generate enthusiasm but rather as a key source of his appeal to suburban voters.[37] Similarly, Schlesinger believed that while McCarthy frequently let down his in-person audiences, he sounded "reasonable, thoughtful, reassuring" to the mass television audiences that were playing an ever greater role in the political process.[38] On the issues,

McCarthy's position on the Vietnam War trumped the lapses in his voting record for those in the ADA who had come to see the war as the transcendent issue of liberal politics. As Rauh would later recall, McCarthy "was right on the war, and the war was everything." In any case, Rauh could point critics to the impressive 92 percent ADA rating accumulated by McCarthy over his nineteen years in Congress as evidence that the senator offered more than a forthright position on the Vietnam War.[39]

Whatever misgivings they may have had about McCarthy's personal qualities as a candidate, the contingent of ADA leaders who had been pushing the organization to throw its support behind the Minnesota senator's campaign arrived at the ADA's February 10 national board meeting with high hopes and a clear resolve. The launch of the Tet Offensive in early 1968—which resulted in North Vietnamese and Vietcong attacks in cities across South Vietnam, including a breach of the US Embassy compound in Saigon—gave the lie to Johnson's continual insistence that victory in the war was around the corner and moved many ADAers who had been on the fence toward support for an endorsement of McCarthy.[40] As impactful as it was, however, the Tet Offensive does not explain the initial spearheading of the McCarthy endorsement by veteran ADA leaders or solely account for the eventual outcome of the vote by the ADA board. The leaders who championed McCarthy's candidacy launched their campaign for endorsing him well before the surprise launch of the Tet Offensive on January 31. They did so because they saw the move as both a moral response to a disastrous war that imperiled necessary social progress and a politically prudent action that would enable the ADA to reach out to a growing bloc of New Class activists. Not confined to those who had spearheaded the endorsement, similar concerns and interests led many on the ADA national board to vote for an endorsement of McCarthy.

However hopeful they were about what this could mean for the ADA and the future of liberal politics, the veteran leaders who led the charge for endorsement had no illusions as to the consequences involved. In preparation for the labor exodus likely to result from a McCarthy endorsement, Galbraith, Rauh, and Schlesinger collaborated with longtime ADA colleagues Richard Goodwin and James Wechsler to draft a statement that framed the expected walkout of labor leaders as an event from which the ADA would emerge as a stronger and more united organization.[41] After more than seven hours of intense debate at the best-attended board meeting in the history of the ADA, members of the national board voted on a resolution endorsing McCarthy's candidacy. Written by Galbraith, the resolution would put the ADA on record in support of McCarthy's candidacy and against the Vietnam War not because it was "preoccupied with this one issue important though it is, but also because it is blighting every liberal and progressive program here at home." After the board adopted the resolution by a fairly narrow 65-to-47 vote, Gus Tyler, speaking for the large minority in opposition, charged that the endorsement would "pretty much dissolve the liberal coalition of twenty-one years." Speaking for the majority, Galbraith celebrated the endorsement as a realization of the ADA's enduring commitment to reconciling principled ideals with political realities.[42]

As expected, the move touched off a series of resignations from the organization. Those resignations, however, would not be limited to individuals with direct ties to organized labor. Within minutes of the vote, former national chairman John Roche submitted his resignation and angrily declared, "I'm through."[43] Roche's swift departure would be followed in the coming days and weeks by resignations from Carl Auerbach, Leon Keyserling, Paul Seabury, and others who had long played pivotal roles in the organization.[44] Two days after the vote, I. W. Abel, president of the United Steelworkers of America, Louis Stulberg, president of the ILGWU, and Joseph A. Beirne, president of the Communications Workers of America, turned in their resignations. Among those resignations, the biggest blow to the ADA's bottom line came from the departure of Abel and the resulting loss of the significant funding that his 1.1 million-member union had long provided to the organization.[45] With the Steelworkers far from the only union to pull their financial support in the wake of the McCarthy endorsement, organized labor ceased to be a major source of funding for the ADA.[46]

Despite these setbacks, the upside of the McCarthy endorsement outweighed the downside. The endorsement established the ADA as an appealing base for organizing political opposition to the Vietnam War among the significant number of New Class voters and activists looking for a meaningful way to act on their moral horror over the conflict. Following its McCarthy endorsement, the organization also attracted far greater press coverage than it had seen in years. When Shull reported to the national board at the end of 1968, he described a "manyfold" increase in membership and a fundraising total that nearly doubled the amount taken in during 1967. With funding increasingly based on sizable numbers of modest contributions from

New Class liberals opposed to the war rather than large grants from labor unions, the ADA became more responsive to its grassroots membership and less dependent on the labor representatives who remained in the organization.[47] Beyond the profound impact on its own composition and funding, the ADA's early endorsement of McCarthy provided support that would prove to be crucial to putting the Minnesota senator's struggling campaign, and the New Politics movement that emerged around it, into motion.

THE MCCARTHY CAMPAIGN AND THE NEW POLITICS MOVEMENT

The grassroots organizing that propelled Eugene McCarthy to within a hair of defeating Lyndon Johnson in the New Hampshire Democratic primary marked what Arthur Schlesinger Jr. described as the initial revolt of the New Politics movement. When Johnson withdrew from the presidential contest less than a month later, the New Politics had, in Schlesinger's words, "scored its first triumph."[48] More than being admiring commentators on the New Politics movement, Schlesinger and other ADA leaders were instrumental in producing the circumstances that made the emergence of the movement possible. By pushing the ADA to endorse McCarthy's campaign at a time when support from prominent liberals and Democrats was virtually non-existent, they provided backing that proved to be critical in getting the campaign that sparked the New Politics movement off the ground. Many historical accounts have depicted the movement as a sanitized version of the New Left adapted to the circumstances of mainstream electoral politics. Yet the New Politics movement that coalesced in the wake of McCarthy's campaign took its cues not from radical politics but from a deep tradition of liberal reform in which the ADA and its chapters had long played a central role. With a base drawn from a growing New Class that dwarfed the numbers of middle-class professionals seen during the time of earlier liberal reform movements, and the Vietnam War as an issue around which to organize its political aims, the New Politics movement reshaped the tradition of liberal reform as it took that tradition to new heights in the political arena.

The initial excitement generated by McCarthy's announcement of his candidacy in November 1967 had, by the turn of the year, given way to the bleak reality of a campaign struggling to gain traction. A widely syndicated column published in early January painted a dim picture of the campaign, noting that

McCarthy's fellow critics of the Vietnam War in the Senate such as Robert Kennedy would be giving the Minnesota senator "their moral support—but little else."[49] An editorial sympathetic to McCarthy's campaign published the same day lamented the "failure of the Bobby Kennedys, the William Fulbrights, and the Wayne Morses to come out in support of Sen. Eugene McCarthy in his challenge of President Johnson's Vietnam policies." According to the editorial, "Now that there is the real opportunity to do something about changing US policy—by the election of a new President this year—the loudest critics are suddenly silent when McCarthy needs help." The absence of support from established politicians, the editorial charged, had "stalled" McCarthy's campaign before it had even had a chance to get going.[50]

In that vacuum of political support, the endorsement of the ADA—widely recognized as the leading liberal organization in the country—enhanced McCarthy's standing among liberals and provided a much-needed boost to a campaign that was looking likely to falter before the first elections of the primary season took place. The New Politics movement that would take shape around McCarthy's campaign expressed a desire to shift the balance of politics from professional politicians and establishment figures to grassroots activists, but the backing of an organization and individuals with some political stature was necessary to provide the initial momentum for the campaign that put the New Politics movement in motion. A syndicated column published in the run-up to the ADA's decisive February 10 national board meeting opined that "formal backing from the organization would be a boon to the Minnesota senator, whose campaign has been slow to gain momentum."[51] Following the ADA's endorsement of McCarthy, the *New York Times* surveyed the financial and organizational problems plaguing the senator's campaign and concluded that the endorsement had helped him "pick up a bit of speed" and improved his position as a liberal alternative to Johnson.[52] A front-page article in the *Washington Post* deemed the display of support from the ADA to be "the most prestigious endorsement McCarthy has gotten so far."[53]

Beyond the vital impact of its endorsement, the ADA provided McCarthy's nascent campaign with an organizational network to draw on and much-needed leadership at the grassroots level. Support for McCarthy had been building for some time in many of the ADA's chapters, but the prohibition on local chapters taking or advancing positions at odds with the national organization prevented them from becoming directly involved in the senator's campaign prior to the endorsement. The national board's endorsement of McCarthy freed local ADA chapters to devote their energy and resources to the campaign. Across the country, ADA chapters provided McCarthy campaign groups with valuable contacts that allowed them to build on an existing organizational network. Members of local ADA chapters took on leadership positions in many of those McCarthy campaign organizations. In New Jersey, individuals from the local ADA chapter filled the ranks of leadership in the state's McCarthy campaign. Connecticut ADA chairman Joseph Duffey served as chairman for the McCarthy campaign in Connecticut, while Wisconsin ADA chairman Don Peterson assumed that position in his state's McCarthy campaign organization. In New York City, the New York ADA took over a section of the McCarthy campaign office and set up an "ADA desk" to coordinate the chapter's efforts on behalf of the campaign.[54]

The ADA's endorsement and the widespread involvement of its members in the campaign helped to set the stage for the vast grassroots initiative that propelled McCarthy beyond all predictions for the New Hampshire primary. When the votes were tallied, McCarthy came away only 230 votes behind the incumbent president. McCarthy did in fact lose to the president, but the shockingly narrow result of the March 12 primary demonstrated Johnson's political vulnerability and established McCarthy as a serious presidential challenger.[55] The ADA's endorsement of McCarthy and the organizational efforts of its chapters had helped pave the way for what amounted to a symbolic victory in New Hampshire, but the state's conservative political climate limited the organization's direct impact on the outcome of the first-in-the-nation primary. When the McCarthy campaign sought to carry the momentum from its unexpected performance in New Hampshire to the next primary in Wisconsin, the ADA and its chapters took on a more instrumental role. A deeply rooted liberal tradition in Wisconsin meant that the ADA's endorsement and the campaigning activities of its chapter in the state carried a far greater weight than they had in New Hampshire.[56] The greater influence enjoyed by the ADA and its members would be joined by a new influx of contributions to the campaign, a growing contingent of student volunteers, and improved name recognition to produce favorable prospects for McCarthy in Wisconsin as Election Day approached. With the political winds shifting decidedly against him, two days before the Wisconsin primary Johnson announced to a shocked nation that he was bowing out of the presidential race.[57]

As the "New Politics" entered the nation's political vocabulary following Johnson's departure from the race, Schlesinger deemed the term to be "more uttered than understood."[58] In part the confusion surrounding the New Politics resulted from the different approaches and visions advocated by those associated with the term. Prior to McCarthy's entry into the 1968 presidential election, the notion of a New Politics typically implied working outside the two-party political system. When over three thousand liberals and radicals of various stripes from some 372 organizations gathered for the National Conference for a New Politics in Chicago over Labor Day weekend in 1967, general agreement could be found on the need to mount opposition to the Vietnam War and push for broader participation in the American political process. Beyond those general contours of agreement, however, no coherent plan for action emerged. For some, the New Politics entailed coalition building around a proposed presidential "peace" ticket of Martin Luther King Jr. for president and pediatrician and peace activist Benjamin Spock for vice president. For others more skeptical of the prospects of bringing the war to an end directly through the electoral process, the New Politics meant community organizing and grassroots education efforts. Among the delegates most disillusioned with the American political system, the New Politics implied the politics of immediate revolution.[59]

The immense gathering of leftists seen at the New Politics conference in Chicago represented the culmination of years of work to build a coalition between New Left radicals and liberals who could find common ground on issues such as the Vietnam War, racial equality, and poverty.[60] Displaying as little openness toward cooperation with the radicals of the Chicago conference as they had when similar questions of collaboration with radicals emerged around mass antiwar demonstrations, ADA leaders had no interest in the attempts at coalition-building that animated the event. Following the Labor Day conference, Joseph Rauh expressed his concern that the efforts of radicals at the gathering—even when focused on participation within the electoral system—would ultimately undermine the goals they shared with their potential liberal allies. Rauh saw the election of a reactionary Republican president as the most likely outcome of a King presidential candidacy, which would attract significant but clearly limited support. In his estimation, the Republican Party would benefit from a third-party presidential ticket headed by King, which could be expected to deprive the Democratic Party of a substantial number of African American votes and around a million votes from whites who would cast their vote for King as a protest against the war.[61]

After McCarthy's strong showing in the New Hampshire primary and his victory in the Wisconsin primary, grassroots activists, journalists, politicians, and ADA liberals began to speak of the New Politics in reference not to the Chicago conference but to the political movement that had lifted the Minnesota senator's campaign to unexpected heights and pulled Robert Kennedy into the race.[62] In contrast to those who advanced radical perspectives and third-party politics at the National Conference for a New Politics, the liberal reformers who assumed the label insisted that any effort to end the war in Vietnam or work toward broader social change would have to take place within the existing two-party system. Like those in the ADA who had pushed their organization to endorse McCarthy, the New Politics activists of the 1968 Democratic primaries believed that change could be achieved by opening up the Democratic Party to greater grassroots participation and weaning it from its dependence on organized labor in favor of a post–New Deal coalition that would draw heavily from the ranks of the New Class.

Though the aims of those who carried the New Politics banner in the 1968 Democratic primaries and their allies in the ADA appeared to share much in common with the New Left's demands for an end to the war and greater participation in the political process, their politics owed little to the influence of contemporary radicalism. Those in the ranks of leadership who pushed the ADA to endorse McCarthy and members of local ADA chapters who filled important positions in the senator's campaign developed their position on the Vietnam War during years when they had little direct interaction with New Left radicals and even less interest in their ideas. At both the national and chapter levels, ADA liberals who championed the New Politics did not see the movement as a watered-down version of the New Left's antiwar program. Instead, they saw the New Politics as offering an effective means of opposition to the war that forced vital questions of foreign and domestic policy onto the national agenda by calling on the existing party system to recognize those questions and take steps to address them.

Like many advocates of the New Politics in the ADA, Schlesinger took great pains to distinguish the New Politics from the New Left. He believed that the fundamental difference between the New Politics and the New Left could be found in the former's determination to master the existing political system and use it to bring the war to an end, in contrast to the latter's insistence that the existing system had to be rejected and overthrown in order to meet that same end. For Schlesinger, this distinction owed much to the different ways in which the two movements understood the circumstances that led to the war in the first place. According to him, those associated with the New Politics saw the Vietnam War as the result of particular individuals making a series of errors in a course of events that had not been inevitable. In contrast, those associated with the New Left saw the war as "a predetermined expression of an evil system that would have imposed an imperialistic policy on whatever body of men sat at the councils of state."[63]

The New Politics activists who garnered national attention during the 1968 Democratic primaries came to politics not by way of the New Left but through a deep tradition of liberal reform politics in which the ADA had long played a key role. The myth that McCarthy's campaign was driven by vast numbers of young radicals who went "clean for Gene" has demonstrated considerable staying power in historical accounts of the 1968 election, but the overwhelming majority of individuals who canvassed for McCarthy were not radicals who dispensed with beards and long hair to make a respectable appearance on the doorsteps of voters.[64] Young radicals were not likely to work for a politician they viewed as an establishment figure. Many of McCarthy's young canvassers were students—frequently graduate students—with liberal backgrounds from elite eastern colleges and universities.[65]

Students played an undoubtedly important role in McCarthy's campaign, but a significant number of the Minnesota senator's supporters were upper-middle-class professionals who had supported Adlai Stevenson in the 1950s and been involved in a club politics movement with strong connections to the ADA. Like the largely well-educated, middle-class Progressives of the early twentieth century, the old Stevensonians who rallied to McCarthy in 1968 saw themselves as working for a principled leader who put issues of national interest over party loyalty or career advancement. Many of those old Stevensonians had become involved in politics through the growing club politics movement of the 1950s. The middle-class, intellectually oriented amateurs of the club movement viewed politics not in terms of individual politicians and personal benefit but rather in terms of ideas and principles. Despite their ostensible aversion to personality politics, Stevenson—with his compelling intellect and wit—became a focal point for "amateur Democrats" when his campaigns for president in 1952, 1956, and 1960 swelled the membership of amateur clubs across the country. For many amateur Democrats, Stevenson represented a genuine champion of ideas, issues, and principles in contrast to the undemocratic and unrepresentative world of political machines, party bosses, and patronage that defined the Democratic politics of many metropolitan areas.[66]

Across the country, significant overlap existed between the membership of local amateur Democrat clubs and ADA chapters. In some cases the ADA chapters themselves served as the organizing base for reform-minded amateur Democrats. In Illinois, amateur Democrats established the Independent Voters of Illinois, the ADA affiliate in the state, principally to challenge the hold of the Chicago political machine on Cook County Democratic politics. The New York ADA served a similar purpose in New York City, where it became an important base of opposition to Tammany Hall. Whether they participated in local ADA chapters or established their own organizations, amateur Democrats and ADA liberals alike drew on a liberal reform tradition that stretched back far beyond the galvanizing, though ultimately unsuccessful, Stevenson campaigns.[67]

Despite shared roots and similar constituencies, the New Politics movement differed from earlier reform movements in a number of significant ways. During the Progressive era of the early twentieth century, the number of middle-class professionals in the country was minuscule. Even in comparison to the significantly more numerous white-collar workers of the 1950s, the sizable New Class and the sense of its increasing importance in the 1960s provided the New Politics with a far more powerful base of support than earlier liberal reform movements could lay claim to. Furthermore, the Vietnam War presented the liberal reformers of the New Politics movement with the pressing issue that had been missing from reform politics during the 1950s. Paradoxically, the reformers drawn to Stevenson often spoke of politics in terms of ideas and issues, and have typically been described as issue-driven, but frequently they struggled to articulate clearly defined issues with broad national implications. When a critical mass of individuals from the growing ranks of the New Class—including a soaring population of college students—joined together in opposition to the Vietnam War, they drew on a long tradition of liberal reform movements but projected political power on a much greater scale than had past representatives of that tradition. The New Politics movement would further set itself apart from earlier liberal reform movements with indictments of the Vietnam War and the political establishment far more pointed than the polemics seen from middle-class reformers in the past.

TURNING AGAINST THE ESTABLISHMENT

The New Politics activists of the late 1960s who called attention to the death and destruction suffered by millions in a seemingly endless war in Southeast Asia, and members of the ADA who championed their cause, displayed a far more critical perspective toward the nation's political establishment than any expressed by their predecessors in the liberal reform tradition. Frequently described as a "constituency of conscience," the activists from the New Class who sustained the New Politics movement had a strong tendency to articulate their opposition to the Vietnam War and positions on other political issues in moral terms. Individuals from the "constituency of conscience" and the politicians they were drawn to steered clear of the broad denunciation of American society insisted on by many in the New Left but often emphasized the moral horrors of the Vietnam War as they made their case against US involvement in the conflict.

For their part, older ADA liberals typically eschewed the moral language more common among their younger counterparts and the broader New Politics movement as they challenged the political status quo and took aim at the political establishment they had once unmistakably belonged to. Veteran ADA figures tended to emphasize the ways in which the political establishment and the military-industrial complex harmed the national interest, while New Politics activists tended to hand down moral indictments against the Vietnam War and its far-reaching consequences. The differences in these approaches contributed to tensions that would sometimes flare up in the New Politics movement. Still, underneath these different approaches to challenging the status quo there existed a shared conviction that the political establishment perpetuating the war could—and should—be challenged through the existing channels of American democracy. With this shared conviction as a starting point, a mutually beneficial relationship developed as older ADA liberals advanced searing criticisms of the political establishment and military-industrial complex that helped to legitimize the antiestablishment perspective of younger New Politics activists, who in turn sustained a movement that emboldened their liberal elders to push those criticisms still further.

Older ADA liberals who sought to shed their establishment reputations faced an uphill battle. John Kenneth Galbraith, who had served as the ambassador to India during the Kennedy administration, conceded, "You can't refer to someone as 'the radical Ambassador.'"[68] As special assistant to President Kennedy, Arthur Schlesinger Jr. had enjoyed direct access to the Oval Office and has frequently been referred to as the administration's "court historian."[69] Galbraith and Schlesinger grew increasingly critical of Democratic leadership in the years that followed their service in the Kennedy and Johnson administrations, but doubts continued to linger as to the degree to which they could be considered to have left the establishment. In an in-depth profile of the Harvard economist, journalist David Halberstam described Galbraith as a critic who "denies vehemently any Establishment association" but nonetheless "manages to keep as many lines out as possible." Offering a far more scathing assessment, Noam Chomsky assailed Schlesinger as an establishment intellectual who bore significant responsibility for leading the United States into the Vietnam War in the first place.[70] Despite the continuing traction of such characterizations, the positions staked out during the escalation of the Vietnam War by Galbraith, Schlesinger, and other ADA leaders with past administration links had the tangible effect of putting the organization and its leading figures at a considerable distance from the halls of power. During the early years of Johnson's presidency, ADA leaders worked closely with the president and his administration on civil rights legislation and a variety of other initiatives. By the time the ADA and its leading voices came out decidedly against the Johnson administration's escalation of the war, however, the working relationship between the organization and the president had ceased to exist. Rauh later recalled that when Johnson signed the 1968 Civil Rights Act into law, he was not invited to the signing ceremony even though he "was half-author of the goddamn thing."[71]

The critical perspective on the political establishment developed by these aging ADA liberals during the years of growing distance between the organization and the Johnson administration fell well short of the wholesale condemnation demanded by Chomsky and other radical intellectuals. Nevertheless, it represented some of the most penetrating criticism of the political status quo advanced by liberals during the Cold War. Propelled by years of fruitless effort to bring the Vietnam War to an end through political means, the ADA and its leaders focused much of their criticism of "the

Establishment"—frequently spelled with a capital E—on an unresponsive and unaccountable national security bureaucracy. In the view of many ADA liberals, the national security bureaucracy had wrested the prerogative of shaping foreign policy from the nation's elected leadership and pursued its own ends irrespective of the national interest or the will of the American people. A resolution passed by the ADA in 1969 channeled many of those concerns into a strident demand for the restoration of "the military establishment to its traditional place in our constitutional system, as the servant and not the master of our national purposes."[72]

ADA liberals, however, were clear in their insistence that the motivations of the military establishment and the source of its power were not to be found in the conspiracy theories that often accompanied discussions of the military-industrial complex. Schlesinger deemed the drivers of American foreign policy to be "neither evil men" nor "war criminals" but "professional men trying to do a professional job and making exactly the arguments the nature of their profession requires."[73] Similarly, Galbraith characterized those who constituted the military establishment and the national security bureaucracy as "mostly honest men whose public and private behavior would withstand public scrutiny as well as most." For Galbraith, the military establishment posed a grave problem to the nation not because of any innate maliciousness but because it—like any great bureaucracy—tended "to develop a life and purpose and truth of its own." Bureaucracies, he contended, acted neither on behalf of the greater public interest nor in accord with the reality of the world but in pursuit of organizational interests and in response to the "bureaucratic truths" that served those interests. Thus, the "bureaucratic truth" of the national security establishment, according to Galbraith, transformed "what was essentially a civil war between the Vietnamese" into "an international conflict with rich ideological portent for all mankind."[74]

Fostered by the continuation of the Vietnam War against both reason and popular will, the growing skepticism in the ADA toward a national security bureaucracy ill-equipped to serve the national interest represented a dramatic transformation in the views on technocratic approaches to foreign policy found in the organization. Galbraith and Schlesinger had joined the Kennedy administration as part of a contingent of academic and industry leaders famously dubbed the "best and brightest" by David Halberstam and largely shared the confidence in technocratic solutions displayed by their fellow recruits. Despite frequently finding themselves on the periphery of the Kennedy administration, Galbraith and Schlesinger did not significantly waver in their belief that complex issues such as foreign policy were best addressed by those with the necessary expertise.[75] Schlesinger no longer held an administration post during the early years of major US involvement in the Vietnam War but continued to harbor significant doubt as to the capacity of the public to engage the complex subtleties of the conflict with the reason and sobriety he deemed necessary.[76] By 1968, however, Schlesinger was lambasting Hubert Humphrey for implying that foreign policy should be left to the experts to whom "the mere layman must of course bow."[77] Galbraith, in a similar fashion, denounced that same year the hold of the "bloodless expert" on the determination of foreign policy when he asserted that the nation could never again afford to "have a foreign policy that is a monopoly of the military and experts" who were "divorced from public opinion and political responsibility."[78]

Notwithstanding the rhetorical attention they gave to the built-in flaws of the national security bureaucracy and its technocratic insulation from democratic pressures, the aging liberals at the helm of the ADA saw the ultimate responsibility for the destructive direction of American foreign policy as residing with the nation's political establishment. Schlesinger considered it "foolish" to blame the national security bureaucracy for the nature of the advice it gave and "far more to the point to blame those who take their advice."[79] Despite a more pessimistic estimation of the national security bureaucracy's grip on power, Galbraith too found the political establishment to be at fault for the circumstances that shaped the nation's foreign policy. After US and South Vietnamese troops moved into Cambodia in 1970, Galbraith called on his audience at that year's ADA national convention to recognize that the United States was continuing to expand the war because the political establishment had created a "vast military machine" that "makes policy and makes war on its own." The support of a bipartisan collection of "parliamentary poodles," he contended, had enabled the military bureaucracy to operate outside the political system. With the view that the problem boiled down to far more than simply the president taking or not taking the advice given to him by the national security bureaucracy, he stressed that establishing effective control of military power would be the most pressing issue for liberals in the coming years. If liberals were to "ask the young to remain in the system," Galbraith insisted, they must "also get the generals back in."[80]

The increasingly critical views of the political establishment advanced by Galbraith, Schlesinger, and other older leaders in the ADA developed over the course of frustrating years of opposition to the Vietnam War but also owed much to the rapid rise of the New Class. The substantial growth in the number of politically engaged white-collar liberals which had enabled these ADA leaders to see breaking ranks with organized labor and the Johnson administration as a politically viable option also proved crucial to emboldening the critical views on the political establishment that had begun to take shape in the ADA. Galbraith characterized 1969 as a time when "a strong anti-establishment, anti-institutional, and particularly anti-bureaucratic, anti-military mood" was "sweeping through the country much more rapidly than would have been possible as recently as ten years ago." He believed the enormous influx of young people into colleges and universities to be a critical impetus for the dramatic shift in the national mood that he saw taking place.[81] Like Galbraith, Schlesinger looked to the new generation of college students as a vital force in the struggle against the political establishment. He emphasized the political importance of the growing numbers of college-educated, issue-oriented voters eager for increased participation in the decisions that determined their lives. Schlesinger perceived great promise in the potential political power of what he described as an "aggressive new constituency" of youth and working adults from the New Class that "regards the old political establishment with mistrust."[82] On the basis of similar considerations, many ADA liberals came to see challenging the political establishment as not only a necessary response to circumstances that perpetuated war and impeded social progress but also a politically pragmatic move.

Often referred to as a "constituency of conscience," the New Class activists and voters who bolstered the antiestablishment posture of the ADA and provided the base of the New Politics movement frequently articulated their opposition to the political establishment by interpreting political issues in moral terms. Many of those from the New Class drawn to the New Politics viewed the movement as a moral crusade that drew on the energy and spirit of the civil rights and antiwar movements to challenge the "old politics" of the political establishment.[83] David Halberstam echoed many of the journalistic accounts of the New Politics movement published during the 1968 election season with a characterization of its base as primarily interested in "the moral thrust of America."[84] Lanny Davis, a young campaign staffer for Eugene McCarthy in 1968 and later a member of the ADA national board, offered a similar assessment when he later recalled the sense of self-righteousness and moralism that had animated him and his fellow New Politics activists during that year's Democratic primaries.[85]

The activists of the New Politics movement differed from many older ADA leaders in terms of style and temperament but shared with them a desire to unseat the political establishment responsible for a seemingly endless war. While the ADA's aging leadership generally avoided moral language and focused instead on the ways in which the political establishment and its commitment to the Vietnam War harmed the interests of the United States, the bulk of New Politics activists were animated by the moral issues raised by the war. By articulating his opposition to the Vietnam War in a calm and reasonable but nevertheless morally direct manner, McCarthy attracted significant support among the New Class voters who quickly became the base of the emerging New Politics movement. In a widely read article for *Look* magazine intended to bolster his support among the "constituency of conscience" prior to the New Hampshire primary, McCarthy laid down a forceful challenge to the political establishment by detailing the human cost of the war that its policies prolonged: the physical destruction of a small developing nation by the most powerful military on the planet; 100,000 to 150,000 civilian casualties in South Vietnam alone; the unraveling social order among a South Vietnamese population who counted one fourth to one third of its people as refugees; and combat losses for the United States through December 23, 1967, of 15,944 killed and 99,305 wounded.[86]

Four years later, George McGovern carried on the banner of the New Politics movement and attracted the same New Class voters who had rallied to McCarthy in the previous presidential election with impassioned speeches on the Vietnam War that again drew attention to its tragic moral consequences. Like McCarthy, McGovern frequently employed shocking moral language to challenge the political establishment that had perpetuated the Vietnam War. In the run-up to the 1972 presidential election, McGovern drew rapt attention when he asked an audience in Los Angeles: "What is it that keeps a great and decent county like the United States involved in this cruel killing and destruction? Why is it that we cannot find the wit and the will to escape from this dreadful conflict that has tied us down for so long?"[87]

The moral indictments of the Vietnam War and the political establishment responsible for its continuation made by McCarthy, McGovern, and the New Class activists who propelled their campaigns benefited from the piercing yet well-reasoned criticism of the military-industrial complex and the political establishment advanced by older ADA leaders. Owing both to their status as widely recognized arbiters of liberalism and their careful framing of the issues involved, these ADA liberals helped to legitimize forthright criticism of the military-industrial complex and the broader political establishment. By taking great care to contrast their critical perspective with the conspiracy theories and radical posturing that often surrounded discussion of the military-industrial complex, Galbraith, Schlesinger, and other ADA leaders of their generation helped to bring direct and sometimes shocking charges against the political and foreign policy establishment into mainstream political discussion by distancing the underlying ideas from those of the paranoid fringe and radical politics.

The challenge to the political establishment mounted by both younger New Politics activists and older ADA leaders expressed a basic and enduring confidence in the American democratic tradition as a means of ending the Vietnam War and bringing about other necessary changes. When James Wechsler appraised the outcome of the 1968 elections the following year, he strongly refuted the argument of those who "somewhat triumphantly" insisted that the failure of McCarthy's bid for the Democratic nomination demonstrated the futility of trying to achieve meaningful change through the established political system. In his judgment, the McCarthy campaign and the New Politics movement succeeded in their original objective of toppling the candidacy of an incumbent Democratic president and bringing the escalation of the war to a close. According to Wechsler, they "did so in the face of widespread diagnosis—on the New Left and the Old Right—that neither of these objectives was remotely realizable, and that those who involved themselves in it were captives of their own idiot dreams."[88] The shared conviction of older leaders from the ADA such as Wechsler and the New Politics activists who rallied to McCarthy's and McGovern's campaigns that it was both possible and necessary to challenge the political establishment through the existing two-party system provided a strong starting point for the ongoing relationship of the ADA and the New Politics movement. Still, a desire to reach out to the younger New Class activists needed to breathe new life into the ADA and sustain the organization's relationship with the New Politics movement would lead the aging leadership of the ADA to look to a new generation of leaders with the youth and antiestablishment credentials that they clearly lacked.

A NEW GENERATION OF LEADERSHIP

Joseph Duffey, a thirty-seven-year-old theology professor and activist in the civil rights and antiwar movements, became the youngest ever national chairman of the ADA when he succeeded John Kenneth Galbraith in 1969. On the surface, Duffey's election as national chairman appeared to mark a significant departure from the older generation of leadership that preceded him. His activist background lent him far more easily recognizable antiestablishment credentials than his predecessors could lay claim to and engendered in him a strong preference for concrete political action over the writing of resolutions. Yet the distance between Duffey and those such as Galbraith who preceded him at the helm of the ADA was far less than historians have assumed.[89] Despite unmistakable differences in their respective political backgrounds and demeanor, the older ADA leaders who led the charge for the McCarthy endorsement and new leaders such as Joseph Duffey and Allard Lowenstein had similar intellectual roots and were informed by the same set of fundamental liberal values. Duffey drew from the same well of Niebuhrian thought that had long shaped the political outlook of veteran ADAers, while he and Lowenstein both shared their belief that a liberalism committed to the rational political processes of the democratic system could yield tangible social progress. Duffey and Lowenstein did not come to leadership roles in the ADA in the face of reluctance or opposition from the organization's veteran leaders. Instead, the longtime leaders who remained after the McCarthy endorsement paved the way for a new generation of leadership who shared their basic political outlook and designs for the future of the organization but whose youth and unambiguous antiestablishment background enabled them and the ADA to reach out to a younger generation.

By the late 1960s, the need for the ADA to attract more young people had been apparent to the organization for some time. Its affiliated student organization, Campus Americans for Democratic Action, never developed the mass constituency hoped for by both its own leaders and the leadership of the ADA. Concerns with the lack of young members in the organization emerged in the late 1950s and continued to grow in the 1960s. Boston attorney and ADA national board member Richard Miller reflected the sentiment of many of his ADA colleagues in 1967 when he noted that he was "impressed by the fact that the median age of Americans today is 28; the average age of the group meeting last weekend was closer to 40." Not many in the ADA would have argued with his observation "that there were precious few faces in the room which suggested the well springs of future leadership." As the ADA's founders continued to advance in age and struggled to bring new blood into the organization, the ADA risked becoming, in the words of James Wechsler, "an alumni association of aging liberals."[90]

Though the bulk of the ADA's established leadership eventually came around to seeing the importance of cultivating a new generation of leaders who would enable the organization to reach out to young people, the prospect of passing the reins of leadership to younger, less eminent figures with political backgrounds different from their own initially raised many a skeptical eyebrow. At the forefront of the charge to bring a new generation into leadership positions, Galbraith encountered much of that skepticism when he recommended Duffey, a political newcomer, to be his successor as ADA national chairman. Duffey had been a leading figure in McCarthy's campaign in Connecticut and accumulated a significant activist pedigree through dedicated involvement in the civil rights movement. He organized student civil rights groups at Hartford Seminary, where he served on the faculty, and nearby Trinity College. In 1963 Duffey was arrested during a protest against discriminatory hiring practices at a construction site in the Bedford-Stuyvesant area of Brooklyn. Two years later, he took part in Martin Luther King Jr.'s historic march from Selma to Montgomery in Alabama.[91]

Duffey's activist, antiestablishment background was central to Galbraith's understanding of what he could bring to the ADA and his appeal to the younger generation but did little to assuage the unease of those in the organization's leadership with concerns that he lacked the nationwide prominence of past ADA national chairmen. Although he later became one of Duffey's most vocal advocates, Leon Shull had initially been stunned when Galbraith recommended Duffey as his successor. Schlesinger was skeptical of Duffey's religious background and had reservations with the prospect of a young, relatively unknown theology professor from West Virginia as Galbraith's heir. Against the uncertainty of Schlesinger and other leaders, Galbraith continued to stress Duffey's ability to put the ADA in touch with the new generation as he lobbied on behalf of his young protégé's candidacy. Galbraith's ongoing support proved decisive. When delegates gathered for the 1969 ADA National Convention, Duffey won the election to succeed the sixty-year-old Harvard economist as ADA national chairman.[92]

Just as Galbraith's influence had been key to Duffey's election to the top post in the ADA, the support and background maneuvering of other longtime leaders in the organization made Lowenstein's 1971 election as national chairman possible. Like Duffey, Lowenstein had an extensive antiestablishment background steeped in activism but little national stature when he first joined the ADA in the mid-1960s. An early and outspoken opponent of the apartheid regime in South Africa, Lowenstein became deeply involved in the Freedom Summer campaign to register African American voters in Mississippi in 1964. By the time Rauh, Schlesinger, and Wechsler approached Lowenstein about running for the post of ADA chairman after Republican gerrymandering in 1970 cost him the congressional seat he had won two years earlier, he had gained both national prominence and a powerful reputation as a polarizing figure. Initially reluctant to take a position that he felt might limit the range and depth of his involvement in outside political activities, Lowenstein eventually decided to put himself forward for the post after weeks of lobbying from the trio of veteran ADA figures.[93]

When a stop-Lowenstein initiative that sought to draft Duffey to run for an unprecedented third term as national chairman began to pick up momentum, Rauh, Schlesinger, and Wechsler moved to bring the initiative to a quick halt by persuading the sitting chairman to make it clear that he would not be running again. Those who sought to block Lowenstein's election as national chairman, Wechsler later reflected, seemed to be "oblivious" to the reality that the organization "badly needed the stimulus of a chairman who would reach out to a fresh constituency . . . and refurbish its reputation among a younger generation to whom it had little sentimental appeal." With the staunch support of longtime ADA leaders who continued to wield significant influence in the organization, Lowenstein prevailed in a divided election at the 1971 ADA national convention.[94]

The activist backgrounds of Duffey and Lowenstein had done little to impress those who opposed their rise to the ranks of the leadership, but it led the young chairmen to a preference for action over rhetoric that held considerable appeal to a new generation of activists often inclined to see the ADA as little more than a tired organization concerned with writing resolutions.[95] During his acceptance speech as ADA national chairman in 1969, Duffey declared, "It is not only the impatience of a new generation but also a new experience of the urgency for action and a certain disenchantment with the easy rhetoric of resolution which I must ask some of you to accept with patience," for these were "the marks not only of my personal temperament but of the mood of thousands of persons who today represent the ADA's only viable constituency."[96] With a similar commitment to deed over word, Lowenstein devoted much of his energy and the ADA's resources to a large-scale youth voter registration drive shortly after becoming national chairman in 1971. Putting the need for the registration drive in blunt terms, Lowenstein explained, "We are working for a country where 18-year olds won't be forced to choose exile or jail as alternatives to dying in an unjust war."[97]

As national chairmen, Duffey and Lowenstein appeared to represent a stark departure from the founding generation of ADA leaders, who had devoted years to polishing the language of resolutions passed by the organization and whose muted style often obscured the antiestablishment substance of their politics. While their demonstrated desire for action over rhetoric and an outspoken approach to pressing political issues did stand in marked contrast with the approach of the founding generation, Duffey and Lowenstein nevertheless had grown from similar intellectual roots and drew from the same wellspring of liberal values as their predecessors. Historians have sometimes assumed that the younger generation of liberal reformers associated with the New Politics movement abandoned the Niebuhrian pessimism that had guided many postwar liberals as they advanced what has been depicted in their historical accounts as passionate but simplistic opposition to the Vietnam War.[98] Yet Duffey, like many older ADA leaders, looked to Niebuhr as a foundational influence on his own intellectual and political outlook. In the late 1950s, Duffey took charge of a parish outside Boston principally so that he could go to the weekly lectures that Niebuhr was giving in the city at the time. A proponent of Niebuhr's views on the inherent flaws of human nature and the need for realism in the formulation of foreign policy, Duffey wrote articles that attracted the attention of the eminent theologian and was published in his influential journal, *Christianity and Crisis*.[99] Combining his Niebuhrian sense of realism and pessimism with a basic commitment to the rational processes of the democratic system, Duffey identified himself during his acceptance speech as ADA national chairman in 1969 with those who viewed the political system "with skepticism, yet who continue with a cautious will to persist, with great longings for a new America, and with a sober, chastened hope for a meaningful change."[100]

With an intellectual worldview shaped more by political than intellectual figures, Lowenstein received guidance from older ADA liberals such as Frank Porter Graham and Eleanor Roosevelt as he developed an unbending confidence in the democratic process. Put to the test by the loss of his congressional seat to gerrymandering in 1970 and a defeat by the slimmest of margins in a 1972 congressional election in Brooklyn riddled with voting irregularities, Lowenstein never wavered from his belief in the ability to effect meaningful change through the democratic system. Having worked alongside Lowenstein, Lanny Davis described him as having a "liberal-political process oriented liberal ideology that he carried around as almost a matter of religious faith." Shull deemed Lowenstein's commitment to the democratic process to be "the defining belief of his life" and particularly important to his success at operating in an organization like the ADA. He later recalled being pleasantly surprised when he began to work with Lowenstein after his election as national chairman. During those years, Shull had become "used to dealing with people who were against the war, the radical youth" who did not seem to him to "give a damn about democratic norms." While he admittedly "didn't know how to deal with" those radical activists, Shull forged a strong working relationship with Lowenstein on the basis of a shared belief in the potential to achieve tangible progress through the accepted channels of democracy.[101]

Much like the seemingly divergent politics of Duffey and Lowenstein, the bold new positions adopted by the ADA as the 1960s drew to a close represented not a fundamental departure for the organization but instead a continuation of trends that Galbraith, Schlesinger, and other older ADA liberals had been instrumental in initiating. Foremost among the striking policy changes undertaken by the ADA during those years was the organization's emphatic reversal of its long-held opposition to the unilateral withdrawal of American forces from Vietnam. When delegates gathered for the ADA's twenty-second annual national convention in 1969, they faced a choice between two resolutions representing dramatically different scales and tenors of opposition to US policy in Vietnam. The majority report of the foreign policy commission advocated a staggered drawdown of troop levels leading to a withdrawal of around 200,000 of the 540,000 troops in Vietnam and an immediate cessation of offensive military operations. The commission's minority report instead issued a straightforward call for the Nixon administration to "withdraw unilaterally all U.S. Armed Forces . . . from Vietnam immediately." Hans Morgenthau, chairman of the ADA's foreign policy commission, and other veteran ADA leaders on the commission such as Robert Nathan and Victor Reuther, remained steadfast in their opposition to unilateral withdrawal as they helped to pass the majority resolution through the commission.[102]

The continued resistance of veteran figures on the foreign policy commission to unilateral withdrawal did not, however, reflect the views of all longtime leaders in the ADA. Galbraith, Schlesinger, and others aligned with the New Politics movement had been casting doubt on the feasibility of a negotiated settlement to the Vietnam War and advancing a line of opposition to the conflict with logic that increasingly pointed toward unilateral withdrawal for almost two years. When, after two hours of sometimes bitter debate, delegates on the floor voted by a two-to-one margin in favor of the minority report, they established the ADA as the first mainstream political organization with a national standing to call for the immediate unilateral withdrawal of American forces from Vietnam.[103] The convention's overwhelming vote in favor of unilateral withdrawal demonstrated the marginalization of veteran figures in the ADA who sought to soft-pedal the organization's position on the war but offered general agreement with the logic that had been animating the position of Galbraith, Schlesinger, and other older leaders on the conflict for some time.[104]

By pushing the turn to a new generation of leadership and pointing the way toward positions such as unilateral withdrawal from Vietnam that advanced the frontier of liberal politics, Galbraith, Rauh, Schlesinger, and other veteran ADAers ensured that the changes in composition and funding sources that had been touched off by the organization's endorsement of McCarthy in early 1968 gained still more momentum. With new leadership, a growing commitment to direct involvement in grassroots politics, and a forthright position on the Vietnam War, the ADA carried the excitement it generated during the 1968 election into the following year. The organization enjoyed continued growth in its membership and established chapters in Beaumont, Texas; Charleston, South Carolina; Knoxville, Tennessee; and a number of other cities in regions not known for their liberal politics. The ADA's membership growth in 1969 maintained the organization's trend toward getting its funding from rank-and-file members and enabled it to improve on its unprecedented fundraising total from the previous year despite receiving no contributions from labor unions. Much to the pleasure of those who had long bemoaned the advancing age of the average ADA member, the organization's membership growth skewed young. The national conventions of the ADA at the close of the 1960s and the dawn of the 1970s saw less gray hair and noticeably more longhaired youths in jeans.[105]

Increasingly young and drawn from the growing ranks of activists who hailed from the New Class, this new-look ADA enjoyed a degree of political influence equal to the highest points in the organization's history. The rejuvenation of the ADA's political sway ensured that the contributions of its older leaders to the New Politics movement did not end with the endorsement of McCarthy, which had been so critical to getting the movement off the ground. The new-look ADA of the late 1960s and early 1970s was also a portent of American liberalism's future. Forged by the willingness of Galbraith, Rauh, Schlesinger, and other older leaders to part ways with organized labor leaders and other longtime allies in order to endorse McCarthy, this revitalized ADA displayed a far-reaching consensus on the seemingly non-material issue of the Vietnam War. Yet the organization struggled to find similar unity on economic questions and other issues when its members approached those matters outside the context of the war. Similarly, the New Politics movement the ADA helped to shape demonstrated vigorous agreement on the need to oppose the Vietnam War but considerably less cohesion in the way of shared economic interests. As the New Politics movement came to encompass far more than the antiwar activism that had initially inspired its challenge to the political establishment, the tensions and contradictions that ran through the movement would be brought into clearer focus.

CHAPTER 5

THE EVOLUTION OF THE NEW POLITICS
A Broader Movement, Neoconservatives, and the
Struggle for the Mantle of Liberalism

The New Politics movement underwent a profound evolution in the time between the two political campaigns most commonly associated with it. Norman Podhoretz later reflected, "In the four years since I had first committed myself to Eugene McCarthy, I had grown so hostile to the New Politics that I offered my help to Muskie."[1] Podhoretz, an early opponent of the Vietnam War, could readily sympathize with the activists who sparked the New Politics movement to life when they rallied to McCarthy's campaign in opposition to the conflict in 1968. During the 1972 Democratic primaries, however, he threw his support behind Edmund Muskie's establishment-backed bid for the presidency and opposed an insurgent campaign mounted by George McGovern that drew on the ideas, activists, and voters of the New Politics movement. Podhoretz's decision to support Muskie over McGovern reflected both his growing conservatism and the far-reaching changes seen in the New Politics over the four preceding years.

The New Politics activists of the 1968 Democratic primaries regularly insisted that their prioritization of opposition to the Vietnam War represented not a myopic obsession with a single issue but rather dedication to a transcendent challenge that imperiled American society in a wide variety of ways. Still, the immediate aims and energy of the New Politics movement that came into being in opposition to the Johnson administration's policies in Vietnam never strayed far from the particulars of that war. By the time of the McGovern campaign in 1972, the concerns that animated the New Politics movement included not only opposition to the Vietnam War but also a broadly critical perspective on the Cold War national security state and a diverse array of domestic issues such as affirmative action, women's rights, gay and lesbian rights, party reform, and guaranteed income. When Podhoretz and others who would similarly find themselves pegged as neoconservatives formed the Coalition for a Democratic Majority (CDM) in late 1972, they contended for control of the Democratic Party with a New Politics movement that had been shaped in important ways by ADA liberals as it came to encompass far more than the antiwar activism that had initially set it in motion.

The evolution of the New Politics movement in the years after the McCarthy campaign of 1968 confirmed and acted on a number of ideas with deep roots in the political thought of longtime ADA leaders in ways that brought out the tensions and contradictions that ran through that thinking. The social base of the movement visibly demonstrated the shift in liberal and Democratic politics from the union hall to the suburbs, first forecast by John Kenneth Galbraith and Arthur Schlesinger Jr. when they sketched the contours of qualitative liberalism more than a decade earlier. By reproducing the assumptions of working-class conservatism and middle-class liberal potential found in the qualitative liberalism of Galbraith and Schlesinger, the individuals and organizations most involved in the New Politics movement at the grassroots level further reinforced the existing middle-class orientation of the movement.

The ideas articulated by ADA intellectuals also influenced the New Politics in a variety of specific policy areas. In the realm of foreign policy, the movement displayed an understanding of the far-reaching implications of polycentric communism with roots in criticisms long advanced by ADA leaders as they mounted a searing indictment of the bloated defense budgets and interventionist foreign policy that movement activists believed would continue to distort the nation's priorities regardless of the future direction of US policy in Vietnam. On matters of domestic policy, the New Politics movement—and, ultimately, the Democratic Party—expressed many of the same ambiguities and tensions that had developed through debates in the ADA over the preceding decade. Unresolved contradictions in the relationship between a qualitative liberalism shaped by the conditions of presumed widespread postwar affluence and a social democratic outlook that gained greater currency in the ADA in the wake of the civil rights movement could be readily observed in the New Politics movement. Those contradictions became magnified in a New Politics that often struck social democratic notes but had intentionally distanced itself from the labor unions that were among the strongest political forces with any kind of commitment to social democracy. As the movement expanded its immediate focus beyond the Vietnam War after 1968, the competing emphasis between "bread-and-butter" material issues and issues understood as social or cultural became an ever greater source of tension.

From an institutional standpoint, the organizational work of ADA liberals proved crucial to carrying the momentum of the New Politics movement past the 1968 presidential election and played an instrumental role in bringing the influence of its leaders—both old and young—to bear on the future direction of the movement. Extensive ADA involvement from the ranks of leadership down to the grass roots helped to establish the newly formed New Democratic Coalition (NDC) as the leading representative of the New Politics in party politics by bringing together former supporters of Robert Kennedy and Eugene McCarthy. The ADA and its increasingly multigenerational membership also sustained the New Politics movement by making use of the relationships between its members and key figures outside the organization to facilitate a range of efforts from the Vietnam Moratorium Committee (VMC) to the Coalition on National Priorities and Military Policy. These initiatives regularly put young New Politics activists in contact with an older generation of liberals from the ADA. When sweeping reforms to the process of delegate selection in the Democratic Party produced a dramatic increase in the influence of white-collar, middle-class Democrats, the McGovern campaign reaped the benefits and brought a movement that bore the stamp of ideas and policies with deep histories in the ADA to the biggest stage in presidential politics.

The neoconservatives of the CDM who sought to roll back the New Politics ascendency in the Democratic Party faced a political movement with a far broader set of aims than the one that had existed in 1968. Many of the changes in the New Politics movement in the years between the McCarthy and McGovern campaigns can be traced back to the political thought previously developed by ADA leaders such as Galbraith and Schlesinger and the ongoing involvement of their organization in the movement. For critics of the Vietnam War in the CDM such as Podhoretz, it was those changes and the resulting agenda—which encompassed a wide variety of issues ranging from multiculturalism to the broader role of the United States in the world—that motivated their response and determined the course that it took. Older ADA liberals like Galbraith and Schlesinger did not agree with all of the directions in which those changes took the New Politics movement, and the movement never developed a consensus around domestic political priorities or a coalition with shared economic interests. Still, the New Politics movement prevailed over the CDM in the struggle for the mantle of the liberal tradition and the future of American liberalism. Despite their best efforts, the stalwarts of the CDM found themselves definitively placed under the neoconservative banner by political observers and historians alike, while the terms "New Politics" and "liberal" would become increasingly synonymous.

THE NEW DEMOCRATIC COALITION AND THE NEW POLITICS AFTER 1968

On the night Hubert Humphrey secured the presidential nomination of the 1968 Democratic National Convention, a number of ADA liberals and several dozen other dissident Democrats met to discuss the future of their party. Out of those discussions came a commitment to establish a new organization through which to unite the Democratic Party around the participatory, issue-oriented politics that had proved highly successful for New Politics activists during that year's Democratic primaries.[2] By bringing together the activists and political leaders who had rallied behind the McCarthy and Kennedy campaigns, the resulting New Democratic Coalition provided an organizational framework that carried the energy and ideas of the New Politics movement beyond the November election. With a number of rising stars from the ADA among its ranks, the overwhelmingly youthful leadership of the NDC involved in building that framework acted on an understanding of politics with roots in the qualitative liberalism advanced by Galbraith and Schlesinger beginning in the 1950s. In doing so, the young leaders of the NDC brought the influence of older leaders from the ADA to bear on the direction of the New Politics in a way that ensured the middle-class orientation of the movement would continue.

As the NDC took shape, the organization became something of an institutional alternative to the Democratic National Committee and a counterweight to state party establishments with extensive ADA engagement at both the grassroots and leadership levels. The involvement of Julian Bond, Sam Brown, Curtis Gans, Michael Harrington, Allard Lowenstein, and others from the ADA on the NDC steering committee provided a strong representation of ADA views and facilitated close collaboration between the two groups. Don Peterson, chairman of the Wisconsin ADA, and ADA national board member Paul Schrade served as co-chairmen of the nascent political organization. At the grassroots level, a significant percentage of the hundreds of thousands of individuals who participated in the thirty-four state NDC organizations across the country hailed from local chapters of the ADA.[3]

Although the notable ADA presence at all levels of the NDC meant that the two organizations shared a distinctly similar political perspective, ADA liberals did not join the NDC in order to create another ADA. The two organizations differed in important ways in their institutional purpose and the focus of their political activity. Unlike the ADA, the NDC was part of the Democratic Party and primarily sought to use its role within the party to win power for New Politics Democrats. Whereas the more issue-oriented ADA concentrated its efforts at the national level, the NDC focused much of its attention on specific candidates and heavily involved itself in political organization at the state and local level.[4]

In practical aims and outlook, however, both the ADA and the NDC sought to push Democratic politics to the left and believed that the liberal–labor coalition that had once served that goal had been fractured beyond viability by the hawkish foreign policy positions of labor leadership. As West Coast regional director for the United Auto Workers, co-chairman Schrade was one of a very small number of labor representatives of any consequence in the organization. With a foreign policy perspective decidedly at odds with that of the established labor leadership, Schrade became one of the most outspoken critics of the Vietnam War in the UAW as the union's leadership crept toward an antiwar position that contributed to its disaffiliation from the staunchly pro-war American Federation of Labor–Congress of Industrial Organizations (AFL-CIO) in the summer of 1968. Having grown up in a middle-class family in New York and attended Yale University before dropping out to head west in search of factory work as a means of becoming involved in union politics, Schrade had a social and academic background closer to that of his largely white-collar colleagues in the NDC than to most organized labor leaders.[5] For an organization virtually devoid of labor involvement apart from the less-than-representative Schrade, the "new" in the New Democratic Coalition largely meant the inclusion of college students and college graduates at the expense of an organized labor movement considered to be beyond the pale on a variety of foreign policy issues.

With no place for organized labor in its plans, the NDC believed that college-educated liberals of the New Class, envisioned as a "constituency of conscience," together with the minorities and poor who constituted a "constituency of the oppressed," could provide the mass base for a new liberal coalition. Peterson and Schrade saw the growing ranks of the "constituency of conscience" as consisting mainly of relatively affluent people in the professions, business, academia, and "especially the new breed of militant students who by 1976 will constitute a very large part of the 40 percent of the voting public that will have been college educated." According to the NDC co-chairmen, the "constituency of the oppressed" would be comprised of African Americans, Native Americans, poor whites, Spanish-speaking Americans, and "other groups within our society that have traditionally been pacified with tokens when they clamored for justice." The organizational approach of the NDC rested on the belief that a strong coalition could be forged by joining together those oppressed by social injustice and material insecurity with individuals from largely well-educated and materially secure backgrounds morally driven to champion the cause of the oppressed. Describing the NDC as "in the business to affect the course of the Democratic Party, not to be an elliptical memorandum writing group," Peterson stressed the potential political power of "a coalition of those who are most badly treated by the society and also of people who want to see politics become a moral enterprise."[6]

Making that coalition a reality, however, required an NDC leadership drawn almost exclusively from the "constituency of conscience" to recruit individuals and leaders from the "constituency of the oppressed." Although the participation of civil rights leaders Julian Bond and Channing Phillips alongside Bert Corona of the Mexican American Political Association on the NDC's initial steering committee provided some smattering of diversity, the organization that took shape was overwhelmingly white and middle class from its leadership down to the grass roots.[7] This lack of diversity became readily apparent as early as the NDC's first national convention in February 1970.

Stephen Schlesinger, son of Arthur Schlesinger Jr. and an up-and-coming figure in his own right within the ADA, expressed worried disappointment with the composition of the delegation that he saw at that convention. Reporting on the gathering as editor in chief of *The New Democrat*, which he had recently launched with Grier Raggio as a mouthpiece for the New Politics movement, Stephen Schlesinger lamented "a make-up of the NDC that was quite different from its theoretical one." The young editor described the lack of minorities among the five hundred delegates at the convention as "painfully apparent," noting that George Wiley, head of the predominantly Black National Welfare Rights Organization, was the only Black leader present. Even then, Wiley had attended, according to Schlesinger, only "to tongue-lash the NDC for its lack of commitment to his campaign for a $6500 guaranteed income for a family of four." Despite all of its hopes and efforts, the NDC became and remained what Peterson and Schrade had feared it might become: "a band of white liberals lacking significant ties to those for whose rights we propose to fight."[8]

The NDC's genuine and concerted efforts to attract greater minority participation, however unsuccessful, stood in contrast with efforts to reach out to white working-class Democrats that were limited at best. While the overwhelming majority of those who made up the "constituency of the oppressed" were from working-class backgrounds, NDC organizers—like many contemporary political commentators—typically saw working-class minorities in racial rather than class terms and read the working class as implicitly white. The NDC effectively wrote off the white working class with the same brushstroke that had excluded the leaders of organized labor from their coalition-building plans. The dynamic between NDC caucuses and party regulars at state Democratic conventions vividly illustrated the organization's general lack of interest in engaging the concerns of white working-class voters or in any other way striving to overcome the social chasm that separated it from blue-collar Democrats and their representatives. Despite an institutional presence in well over half the states in the country, many state NDCs wielded limited political influence. However, the NDC organizations in Connecticut, New York, Wisconsin, and other northern industrial states constituted a powerful political force.[9] Of the states where the NDC exercised substantial political power, few better embodied the social and cultural gulf between the organization and party regulars who represented working-class constituencies than Wisconsin.

At the 1969 Wisconsin Democratic convention, an NDC majority easily steered through a resolution calling for the immediate withdrawal of

American troops from Vietnam but encountered a chorus of vocal opposition when they tried to pass a resolution calling for a tripling of the state's tax on beer. Displaying little appreciation for the importance of the beer tax as either a symbolic or bread-and-butter issue, NDC delegates pushed the tax increase as a straightforward measure to balance the state's 1969–1971 budget. Party regulars, however, saw the proposed tax hike as an example of the NDC delegates' inability to relate to matters of importance to the state's blue-collar voters. They urged the convention not to "deny the working man a good glass of beer for 15 or 20 cents" and declared that "the Democratic party is the working man's party and beer is the working man's drink." Having displayed little inclination to reach out to or understand the party regulars or their working-class constituents, the NDC failed to obtain the two-thirds majority necessary to pass the resolution calling for the beer tax increase.[10]

The absence of working-class support and the general failure of the NDC to reach beyond a narrow middle-class base alarmed some with ties to the ADA who were associated with the organization. Michael Harrington, an early leader in the NDC who had become increasingly involved in the ADA in the run-up to the 1968 presidential election, insisted that the NDC had to draw support from the unionists, minorities, and poor people who would be essential to the construction of a liberal majority in the Democratic Party. In his view, it was "just as possible for middle and upper class liberals and radicals to be an isolated, self-righteous minority within the Democratic Party as well as outside of it." Speaking before an NDC conference shortly after his election as ADA national chairman, Joe Duffey, the son of a West Virginia coalminer, worried aloud that "liberalism has become an activity of the affluent for whom the concerns" of the working class and the very poor "emerge primarily in abstract terms and categories."[11]

The bulk of the NDC's leadership, however, saw little wrong with the organization's largely middle-class orientation and its lack of white working-class support. The very notion of forging a coalition between the "constituency of conscience" and the "constituency of the oppressed" that guided the organizational efforts of the NDC drew on an understanding of politics with roots in the qualitative liberalism of Galbraith and Schlesinger that led them to effectively write the working class out of their plans.[12] Just as Schlesinger had presumed working-class conservatism on the Vietnam War as he did on other issues that he considered to be qualitative in nature,

Peterson and the other largely middle-class leaders of the NDC took for granted white working-class support for a war that they approached on moral and abstract rather than concrete terms. The presumption that only poor and minority Americans who suffered from the domestic spending cuts that resulted from the Vietnam War, and members of the New Class whose affluence afforded them the freedom to see politics as a moral endeavor, could be expected to oppose the war blinded NDC leaders to the widespread antiwar sentiments found in the working class. Studies have shown that blue-collar families—white and minority alike—bore much of the brunt of the fighting and opposed the war at higher rates than their college-educated counterparts.[13] The tendency of NDC leaders to conflate the views of labor leaders with those of the working class at large further reinforced their mistaken belief in strong support for the war among working-class whites. With the conviction that the Vietnam War represented the defining issue of liberal politics and that the working class shared the benighted foreign policy perspective of labor leaders, the middle-class activists of the NDC could see no place for the white working class in the new liberal coalition they were seeking to build.

The NDC leaders who assumed that working-class whites had become fundamentally conservative and placed their hopes for the future of liberal politics on the "constituency of conscience" and the "constituency of the oppressed" ensured that when their efforts to reach out to the latter failed, the new liberal coalition they envisioned would be comprised almost exclusively of the former. Consequently, the political formation that emerged from the efforts of the NDC represented less a coalition than what Representative Bella Abzug once described as "an ethnic bloc—of white, middle-class, educated liberals."[14] Despite the limited reach of its base, the NDC became a powerful political force, thus establishing the middle-class orientation of the qualitative liberalism advanced by Galbraith and Schlesinger as an enduring characteristic of the New Politics. As the most visible and influential organized force working on behalf of the New Politics in the years following the 1968 election, the NDC provided a vehicle through which ideas developed earlier by Galbraith, Schlesinger, and other longtime ADA leaders continued to play an instrumental role in shaping the New Politics. The influence of these ADA liberals on the evolution of the New Politics movement would extend well beyond their contributions to its middle-class orientation as the call to reorder the nation's priorities became a rallying cry for the movement's activists.

REORDERING NATIONAL PRIORITIES

As the 1960s drew to a close, Arthur Schlesinger Jr. declared, "Nothing has distorted United States foreign policy more in recent years than the military insistence that every other interest be subordinated to their own."[15] The following month, at the opening session of the Congressional Conference on the Military Budget and National Priorities, John Kenneth Galbraith cautioned, "We shall have accomplished very little if we get out of Vietnam and leave unchecked and uncontrolled the influences that were responsible for this disaster . . . and these bloated military budgets."[16] The sentiment behind those declarations drew on and contributed to what became a rallying cry for liberals in the late 1960s and early 1970s: the call to reorder national priorities. Galbraith, Schlesinger, and many of their colleagues in the ADA would demand a reordering of national priorities from military purposes to domestic needs by taking their understanding of the implications of polycentric communism to its logical conclusion. As they constructed the intellectual foundation of the call to reorder the nation's priorities, these ADA liberals also established themselves among the leading champions of the call and its far-reaching political agenda. Through their ideas, advocacy, and organizational work, leading figures in the ADA mounted a vigorous challenge to the Cold War national security state that compelled elements of the New Politics movement to broaden their aims beyond the more narrow focus on the Vietnam War that had initially provided the impetus for the movement.

From the earliest days of the New Politics movement that emerged around Eugene McCarthy's 1968 challenge to President Johnson, leading voices in the ADA and among the volunteers who drove the campaign insisted that their opposition to the Vietnam War represented not a preoccupation with a single issue but rather a commitment to a transcendent issue with profound implications for American society. When declaring his intention to challenge Johnson in the Democratic primaries, McCarthy had stressed the central role of the Vietnam War in "the failure to appropriate adequate funds for the poverty program here, for housing, for education and to meet other national needs."[17] Still, McCarthy's rhetoric, like that of the New Politics activists who flocked to his campaign, remained largely focused on the Vietnam War as the primary hurdle to domestic social progress. The call to reorder national priorities that gained momentum in the ADA and on the national stage after the 1968 election provided the New Politics with a powerful vocabulary with which to highlight, analyze, and challenge factors beyond the particulars of the Vietnam War which had preempted the resources that could otherwise be made available for domestic social programs.

Historians have often looked to the New Left as the source of growing liberal attention to the harmful consequences of the military-industrial complex that sustained the Cold War national security state. Doug Rossinow highlights as a representative case Texas liberals, who, he argues, criticized the military-industrial complex only as long as the New Left was there to prod them into doing so.[18] Leading figures in the ADA, however, came to their critical perspective on the military-industrial complex not as a rearguard response to the New Left but out of their understanding of what polycentric communism meant for US national security. The unmistakable dissolution of what had once appeared to be a monolithic communist bloc, which had led many ADA leaders to reject the insistence of the Johnson administration that communism needed to be reflexively contained on a global scale, ultimately prompted them to question the need for the massive military establishment and budgets deemed necessary to protect the United States from a supposedly unified communist threat.

When leading figures in the ADA mounted an indictment of the military-industrial complex in their call to reorder national priorities, they drew on concerns over a national security state seen as beholden to mistaken assumptions of an earlier period that they had been voicing for much of the decade. Speaking before the Congressional Conference on the Military Budget and National Priorities, Galbraith laid down a challenge to the military-industrial complex that echoed the grounds on which he and other ADA liberals had long advanced their opposition to the Vietnam War. The reach and scale of the military-industrial complex, he contended, could be traced to the period in the 1950s and early 1960s when a pervasive fear of a united communist threat compelled the nation to devote a substantial proportion of its resources to military purposes. In striking contrast with the unity that had seemed to describe the communist world a decade earlier, Galbraith now saw "a collage of bickering states living principally in fear of one another."[19]

A column published in the *ADA World* later that year offered a similar line of thinking with the characterization of the nation's security apparatus and military-industrial complex as "implicitly based upon the assumption that there is a Communist monolith, stretching from the middle of Europe to the western shores of the Pacific Ocean." Conceding that the Soviet Union remained a great power and that China held the potential to become one, the column nevertheless stressed that the dangers then faced by the country were not the dangers that had seemed so threatening two decades earlier.[20]

By the late 1960s, the ADA no longer saw the Cold War national security state as a necessary bulwark of freedom against a unified and expansionistic communist threat but, rather, perceived it as a "Frankenstein monster" that undermined the nation's security and distorted its priorities.[21] A resolution passed by the organization in 1969 charged the military-industrial complex with continually exaggerating the capabilities of the communist nations and accelerating an arms race with the Soviet Union that imperiled the future of humanity. Bringing the implications of polycentric communism to bear not only on the Vietnam War but also on a broader security establishment that consumed half of the federal budget, the resolution stressed that projected outlays for defense would soon climb to over $100 billion even if US involvement in the Vietnam War could be quickly terminated.[22]

The 1969 resolution on the military-industrial complex passed by the ADA also indicated the ways in which the organization's recognition of changes in the international landscape had transformed its approach to domestic social progress. Whereas the ADA and its major initiatives such as the Freedom Budget had once looked to economic growth as a social panacea, the organization's searing resolution on the military-industrial complex urged a reordering of national priorities to address "the festering bitterness of poverty and discrimination, the growing alienation of our youth and black population, and the resulting spread of the cult of violence."[23] The resolution reflected the notion that in a country with national priorities grossly distorted by an expansive military-industrial complex, the reflexive anticommunism that underpinned the policy of containment and sustained the national security state represented a greater danger than the communist nations themselves. Putting that view in practical terms at the Congressional Conference on the Military Budget and National Priorities, Galbraith succinctly noted that twenty years earlier his fellow conferees were principally concerned with the advance of "Communist imperium," but that everyone now sitting at the conference table with him seemed "far more alarmed about the crisis of our cities."[24]

ADA leaders acted on their understanding of the dangers to be found in the nation's distorted priorities as they came to the forefront of efforts to focus liberal attention on the excesses of the Cold War national security state through their work in the Coalition on National Priorities and Military Policy. Recently out of office as a US senator from Pennsylvania, in May 1969 Joseph S. Clark, a former ADA chapter chairman and longtime national board member, became chairman of the newly formed organization that also saw extensive involvement from Edward Lippert and Leon Shull on behalf of the ADA. A coordinating body for several dozen peace, liberal, religious, and scientific organizations such as SANE, ADA, the Southern Christian Leadership Conference, and the Federation of American Scientists, the coalition sought to reverse what it described as the "militarization" of US policies and resources. In its efforts to mount a broad and sustained challenge to the myriad of politicians and organizations with a vested interest in protecting the status quo of the national-security state, the coalition exerted considerable influence on the New Politics movement by working across organizational lines.[25]

The institutional and personal links of ADA liberals were crucial to establishing the bridge between two generations of liberal activists that made the coalition's inter-organizational work possible. The strong ADA presence among both the older establishment-type figures of the coalition and the younger New Politics activists of the Vietnam Moratorium Committee proved crucial to facilitating collaboration between the two organizations. Founded by Sam Brown of the ADA and other young veterans of the McCarthy and Kennedy campaigns, the VMC initially developed its mission around the aim of building broad-based support for the political position in favor of immediate unilateral withdrawal of American forces from Vietnam.[26] To achieve that aim, the liberal leadership of the VMC organized a recurring "moratorium on business as usual" that would allow individuals to spend a day taking part in antiwar programs in their local community. The VMC scheduled the first day of the moratorium for October 15 and indicated that the moratorium would expand one additional day each month until the United States fully ended its military involvement in the Vietnam War.[27] Some 3 million people took part in antiwar activities in hundreds of locales, making the October moratorium the largest coordinated protest of any kind in the nation's history. The VMC built on that success with a two-day moratorium the following month that drew tremendous crowds and demonstrated the extent to which antiwar activism had entered the mainstream but also tapped the energy of activists and the commitment of politicians who had provided vital support. With interest for its planned three-day December moratorium waning, the VMC looked to cooperation with the Coalition on National Priorities as a key source of revitalization for its antiwar effort.[28]

Collaboration between the coalition and the VMC took the form of organizing town hall meetings in some forty cities that visibly widened the aims of the Moratorium beyond the cause of unilateral US withdrawal from the Vietnam War which had initially brought the effort into being. At the meetings, both the young activists who had participated in the Moratorium's earlier antiwar demonstrations and the more established figures of the coalition spoke of their fear that, if left unchecked, the military-industrial complex would continue to distort national priorities regardless of the outcome of the war. The lively discussion at the meetings stretched far beyond the Vietnam War to highlight local needs, the military budget, and federal taxes.[29]

The success of the combined effort demonstrated the appeal that the far-reaching and critical perspective on the Cold War national security state espoused by longtime ADA leaders held for the young leaders of the VMC. With the Nixon administration's policy of Vietnamization beginning to defuse the war as a political issue, the demand for unilateral withdrawal that had recently brought antiwar liberals together now ceased to provide an effective rallying point.[30] Finding that their own more narrowly antiwar focus yielded diminishing enthusiasm, VMC leaders readily embraced the broader agenda that their more distinguished allies articulated with the call to reorder national priorities. While the new life breathed into the VMC by the town hall meetings could not make up for the endemic financial and organizational problems that resulted in the closure of its national office months later, the call to reorder national priorities which had attracted its young leaders and activists remained an enduring fixture of the New Politics movement. After the national office closed its doors, many of those who had been involved in the VMC joined other young activists and notable ADA figures such as John Kenneth Galbraith and Richard Goodwin to support congressional candidates committed to a reordering of national priorities as part of the Referendum '70 campaign. As they focused their efforts on the 1970 congressional elections, the campaign's cross-generational assemblage of activists secured the place of a variety of issues relating to the broader military and foreign policy establishment alongside the Vietnam War on the agenda of the New Politics movement.[31]

Among those issues, none better dramatized the concern of ADA liberals and their New Politics allies over distorted national priorities than the anti-ballistic missile (ABM) system in the process of development and deployment at the turn of the decade. Described by Schlesinger as a "test case of the military's ability to continue to shake down Congress and the public," the proposed ABM system combined the prospect of limited protection from enemy missiles with a very real danger of escalating the arms race with the Soviet Union and unparalleled military expenditures for a new weapons system. With the view that the ABM issue represented the most important political struggle of 1970, the ADA devoted considerable resources to channeling criticism of the Nixon administration's support for the system into a broad-based campaign against excessive, wasteful, and often counterproductive military expenditures. Defeat of the ABM could, in the words of ADA national director Leon Shull, "mark a tuning point, a new awareness in Congress that the defense budget is not sacrosanct."[32]

The large number of local ADA chapters that undertook the grassroots organizing necessary to make that goal possible found the ABM controversy to be a powerful issue for attracting the support of New Class activists, who became the base of mass support for the effort. Many who were involved in the anti-ABM effort worried about the effects that proposed ABM sites would have on their property values, tax rates, television reception, or other local concerns expressed by the outcry against "bombs in the backyard." Some based their opposition on the tremendous amount of funding required by the system which might otherwise be put to use for domestic social purposes, while others cast the issue in moral terms that stressed the increased dangers of nuclear warfare. Whatever their reason for joining the struggle against the ABM system, New Class activists sustained the anti-ABM efforts of the ADA and similar campaigns directed by a variety of peace and scientific organizations that were instrumental in prompting substantial opposition in the US Senate to a major weapons system for the first time in twenty years. Although the vote to halt funding and deployment of the ABM system fell short by one vote, the opposition of fully half the Senate to the system legitimized searching questions concerning the nature of the military-industrial complex and the size of the total defense budget.[33] Reflecting concerns that ADA leaders had been raising since the early 1960s, those questions provided an intellectual foundation for the call to reorder national priorities and initiated a broadening in the outlook of the New Politics movement that would ultimately encompass far more than the foreign policy issues that had once defined it.

SOCIAL DEMOCRACY, QUALITATIVE LIBERALISM, AND IDENTITY POLITICS

Arthur Schlesinger Jr. famously and provocatively declared in 1956 that the quantitative liberalism of the New Deal had secured the necessities of living—"a job, a square meal, a suit of clothes, and a roof"—for such a great many people that liberals should be able "to count that fight won and move on to the more subtle and complicated problem of fighting for individual dignity, identity, and fulfillment in a mass society."[34] The confidence in the reach of material prosperity expressed in that statement and Schlesinger's broader articulation of qualitative liberalism would later seem misplaced after the civil rights movement vividly awakened him and his ADA colleagues to just how many Americans lacked the basic material necessities of life. The civil rights movement also led ADA liberals to see the struggle for individual dignity, identity, and fulfillment not as the prerogative of middle-class whites but as something to which all Americans should be enabled to aspire. In the wake of the civil rights movement, many ADA liberals increasingly recognized that the marginalization of a variety of social groups greatly impeded the search for personal identity and dignity among the individuals who made up those groups.

This perspective informed a series of policy resolutions passed by the ADA in the late 1960s and early 1970s on issues of race, gender, and sexual orientation that demonstrated the organization's growing commitment to what would later be termed "identity politics." Schlesinger and the older figures in the ADA who had steered the organization toward the McCarthy endorsement and helped to broaden the New Politics movement beyond the Vietnam War had little to nothing to do with the drafting of these resolutions. Decades later, Schlesinger even wrote a wrote a book-length condemnation of what he called "militant" multiculturalism.[35] Older straight white male leaders of the ADA like Schlesinger may have kept their distance from the politics of race, gender, and sexuality, but they nevertheless made important contributions to the intellectual foundation of identity politics. They did so by helping to make room for it in liberal politics through their years of advocacy for a liberalism that did not limit itself to material and economic concerns. The politics of race, gender, and sexuality advanced by the ADA in the late 1960s and early 1970s drew on a synthesis of the social democratic values of the New Deal that addressed material well-being with the aims of individual identity and dignity called for by the qualitative liberalism developed by Schlesinger and his colleagues. This form of identity politics demanded the extension of an expansive social citizenship to a variety of marginalized social groups. The notion of social citizenship on which the ADA's identity politics rested insisted that as members of the American polity, African Americans, homosexuals, Latinos, women, and other social groups that had been long excluded from full participation in the social, political, and economic life of the nation had a right to their own distinctive culture, lifestyle, or identity as well an adequate level of material and economic security.

Identity politics has frequently been used as a pejorative label and is often associated with trends in the New Left. But the politics of race, gender, and sexuality that became an integral component of the New Politics and entered mainstream Democratic politics in the 1970s had far more in common with the synthesis of social democratic values and qualitative liberalism seen in the ADA than with developments on the radical left. Important figures from the early 1960s period of the New Left such as Todd Gitlin have located the origins of identity politics in what they describe as the descent of the New Left from the universalist aims of its early years to the dispersion and separatism that characterized the movement after the late 1960s.[36] While those tendencies in the New Left encouraged a form of identity politics that would have long-term impacts on American society and politics—particularly in the academy—the politics of race, gender, and sexuality that proved so controversial for the Democratic Party in the early 1970s drew far more heavily on the social democratic outlook and perspective of qualitative liberalism cultivated by the ADA than on the separatist ethos of the New Left in its later years.[37]

With their long but frequently wavering commitment to social democratic values reawakened by the civil rights movement, many ADA liberals sought the extension of a comprehensive social citizenship that would provide material security for individuals from marginalized social groups as a first step toward facilitating the social inclusion of all Americans. The historian Jonathan Bell has shown that the idea of state-sponsored economic and social citizenship that gained ascendency in California in the postwar period led the way to what has come to be termed identity politics as it coalesced with the "rights revolution" ushered in by the civil rights movement.[38] The politics of race, gender, and sexuality advanced by ADA liberals rooted in the New Deal tradition and focused on national politics makes clear that the path from the New Deal to identity politics via the civil rights movement identified by Bell was not unique to California.

The impact of the civil rights movement on the ADA went far beyond the pressing concerns of material insecurity and economic inequality. The civil rights movement also transformed how the ADA articulated the struggle for individual identity and dignity that became an important part of the organization's political outlook with its embrace of qualitative liberalism in the late 1950s and early 1960s. In the wake of the civil rights movement, many ADA liberals—if not its older and most well-known figures—came to believe that the ability of individuals from marginalized social groups to establish their own identity and dignity often depended on the status and recognition of the social groups to which they belonged. Drafted by a variety of lesser-known ADAers from state chapters, the policy resolutions passed by the ADA in the late 1960s and early 1970s on issues of race, gender, and sexual orientation demonstrated the clear trajectory of the organization toward identification with an inclusive social citizenship that would recognize and encourage the diverse identities of long-marginalized social groups. The far-reaching resolutions also indicated a newfound awareness among ADA liberals of the unique hurdles that prevented individuals from those social groups from enjoying the full rights of social citizenship.

One of those resolutions, a statement on Mexican Americans passed in 1970, registered the ADA's growing recognition that civil rights in the United States was not an issue that involved only Blacks and whites. In a lengthy resolution that highlighted the high rates of unemployment and poverty in the Chicano population, the ADA called for reform of public education to make it more responsive to the needs of Mexican Americans and emphasized the particular importance of developing effective bilingual and bicultural education programs.[39] With implications that stretched far beyond the confines of education policy, the ADA's support for bilingual and bicultural education reflected a wider commitment in the organization to the rights of

Chicanos to both their own distinctive culture and the entitlements that came with American social citizenship. That dual right would be articulated more fully three years later with a resolution that stressed the inequities faced not only by Chicanos but also by the broader Latino population. In unequivocal terms the ADA insisted that Latinos had the right to unfettered access to public education, social services, and other benefits of social citizenship on terms that would not hinder them from "asserting their cultural identity both as a composite group and as separate ethnic groups."[40]

With few Latino members and a limited understanding of the issues that most impacted the Latino community, the ADA largely took its cues from the Southwest Council of La Raza when developing its resolutions on Mexican Americans and Latinos. Not to be confused with the more radical independent political party La Raza Unida, the Southwest Council of La Raza was established in 1968 with a sizable grant from the Ford Foundation and the primary aim of improving social conditions in the barrios of Arizona, California, Colorado, New Mexico, and Texas. In 1970 the ADA formally endorsed the council and offered it both financial and logistical support.[41] The similarities between the policies of the Southwest Council of La Raza and the ADA's resolutions on Mexican Americans and Latinos mean that while the ADA was hardly blazing a new trail in its positions on these issues, its status as a multi-issue organization with a national presence helped to establish these issues as core elements of the liberal agenda. More fundamentally, these resolutions were one part of a broader liberal shift toward recognition of difference as a means of social inclusion.

Resolutions passed by the ADA on the rights of gay men and lesbians in the late 1960s and early 1970s demonstrated a similar, albeit ultimately more limited, commitment to encouraging social diversity through recognition of marginalized groups and affirming the rights of the individuals who constituted them to the full benefits of social citizenship. Passed the year before the Stonewall uprising, which is often seen as launching the modern gay rights movement, the ADA's first resolution pertaining to the rights of homosexuals in 1968 simply established their right not to be arrested by declaring that the private sexual activity of consenting adults was not an appropriate matter for criminal or legal sanctions. Three years later the organization began to call for state action to protect the rights of gay men and lesbians with the insistence that all antidiscrimination laws on the books be extended to include discrimination against homosexuals. In 1973 the ADA passed a resolution that expressed a more inclusive notion of social citizenship as it spelled out the rights of gay men and lesbians with greater specificity. Although the resolution failed to mention marriage for same-sex couples and other important civil rights that would be needed to establish full social citizenship, it put forward what represented an advanced position on the rights of gay people in the context of liberal politics in the early 1970s. During those years, liberal feminist organizations such as the National Organization for Women (NOW) sought to distance themselves from gay rights out of concern that they and the broader feminist movement would be attacked by critics as lesbian-inspired. The predominantly male ADA did not face these kinds of pressures and did not have to adopt homophobic positions to gain greater social acceptance. Reflecting this comparative freedom, the ADA's 1973 resolution insisted that discriminatory notions of normative social behavior that excluded homosexuals should not determine the scope of social citizenship. The resolution affirmed "the right of gay Americans to their lifestyle and support measures to extend to them unobstructed opportunity to achieve their full potential as human beings."[42]

Far more approachable on the national political stage than gay and lesbian rights—though still highly contentious itself—the struggle for women's rights offered the ADA an avenue to more fully and forcefully champion its vision for inclusive and comprehensive social citizenship through vigorous state action. In 1970 the ADA passed its first resolution that specifically addressed women's rights with a statement recognizing that women in the United States had been "relegated to second class citizenship" and calling for "political, economic, and social equality between the sexes." In order to extend the full benefits of social citizenship to women, the resolution demanded the establishment of a range of positive rights to be made possible by robust state action. From creating free child care centers and nursery schools available to all parents regardless of marital status to ensuring the right of a woman to return to her job after childbirth without loss of disability credits or seniority, the ADA sought state action in a variety of new areas to begin the process of leveling the playing field between women and men. The 1970 resolution did not explicitly express support for abortion rights, but the resolution passed the following year clearly stated the belief of the ADA "that the basic right of every woman to freedom of action and expression includes the right to have an abortion."[43]

Taken together, the policy positions of the ADA on gay rights and women's rights were not out of line with the liberal feminist politics of NOW. Compared to the positions of NOW during the period, the ADA was somewhat ahead of the liberal feminist reform group on gay rights, in line with them on child care, and somewhat behind on abortion rights. Like its resolutions on Mexican Americans and Latinos, the ADA's resolutions on gay rights and women's rights were not necessarily groundbreaking, even within the realm of liberal politics. Nevertheless, the attention given to these issues by the preeminent liberal organization in the country helped to shake the foundations of a liberal tradition rooted in the New Deal and its focus on providing economic security for white male breadwinners and their families.[44]

Resolutions on women's rights passed in the following years articulated a view of positive rights that reflected the ADA's growing belief in the need for affirmative action programs to ensure not only equal opportunities but also greater participation and achievement for women and other marginalized social groups. In 1972 the ADA urged political parties to take affirmative action to include women throughout party hierarchies in proportion to their numbers in the general population. The following year, the organization called on colleges and universities to develop and implement affirmative action programs to provide equal opportunity and representation for women among students and faculty.[45]

While most of these initiatives were led by younger and less well-known individuals, some were spearheaded by older, more established figures in the ADA. For example, the Minority Advancement Plan developed by Galbraith with MIT economics professors Edwin Kuh and Lester Thurow would require the federal government and any company employing two thousand people or more to bring the distribution of women and minorities within its salary hierarchy into reasonable conformity with the representation of such groups in the labor force of the surrounding area. The Minority Advancement Plan found a largely receptive audience in the ADA. The organization quickly endorsed it and devoted significant resources to getting a bill based on its policies introduced in Congress.[46] Although the plan ultimately failed to receive a hearing in Congress, it indicated that many ADA liberals—including some of its older stars—had come to see affirmative action as an important means of fostering social inclusion by addressing enduring social, political, and economic inequalities.

Despite prevailing in the ADA's policy resolutions and major proposals, affirmative action and the broader politics of race, gender, and sexuality remained a point of contention among many older members. During initial discussions, longtime national board member David Cohen deemed the plan exclusionary and proposed that it be made to apply to all ethnic groups.[47] Schlesinger gave some indication of where he stood on the politics of sexuality in 1971 when, as a member of a "Usage Panel" for the *American Heritage Dictionary*, he asserted that "'gay' used to be one of the most agreeable words in the language. Its appropriation by a notably morose group is an act of piracy." In 1994 he expressed regret for his earlier "flippancy" and saluted "the new acceptance of homosexuality and the pride that accompanies it."[48]

Still, Schlesinger's later recantation came on the heels of his influential 1991 book on the dangers of identity politics. In *The Disuniting of America*, Schlesinger tried to carve out a "vital center" between conservative opponents of multiculturalism and the "cult of ethnicity" that he saw as threatening to a common purpose that could bind Americans together. Elaborating on the dissenting opinion he had written as a consultant to the New York State Social Studies Review and Development Committee, the book devoted significant attention to the debates surrounding public school curriculums that raged during the late 1980s and early 1990s. Throughout its pages, Schlesinger expressed a concern with history curriculums that forgo history as an "intellectual discipline" in favor of history as a "social and psychological therapy whose primary purpose is to raise the self-esteem of children from minority groups." In place of ADA support for bilingual and bicultural education that stretched back to the early 1970s, his book offered the blunt pronouncement that "bilingualism shuts doors. It nourishes self-ghettoization, and ghettoization nourishes racial antagonism." During the promotional tour for the book, Schlesinger opined that the politics of gender, race, and sexuality—or what he termed "the political correctness movement"—was not a product of liberalism but rather a "movement of disillusioned radicals left over from the 1960s."[49]

In spite of Schlesinger's insistence that identity politics had little to do with the liberal tradition and fueled separatist tendencies, the politics of race, gender, and sexuality that took shape in the ADA, pervaded the New Politics movement, and entered the Democratic Party in the early 1970s was rooted in a liberal desire to foster social inclusion. For many liberals in the ADA and the broader New Politics movement, support for social diversity and recognition of the unique challenges faced by various social groups was not an expression of separatism or balkanized politics but a necessary means of fully including those groups in American society. During this period the most visible expression of this perspective could be found in the 1972 Democratic Party platform. A sizable contingent of ADA liberals serving as delegates at the 1972 Democratic National Convention played some role in the inclusion of a plank in the party platform on "the right to be different, to maintain a cultural or ethnic heritage or lifestyle, without being forced into a compelled homogeneity." Still, the striking similarities between the resolutions passed by the ADA in the preceding years and the articulation of the rights of African Americans, Latinos, Native Americans, women, the elderly, the young, and other marginalized social groups in the Democratic platform was not simply the product of the direct influence wielded by ADAers at the convention. More broadly, it reflected the degree to which the perspective that suffused those resolutions had also come to define the political outlook of New Politics liberals across the country.[50] Ultimately, the clear presence in the platform of the idea that social inclusion required recognition of difference owed as much to sweeping party reforms as to its hold on the minds of liberal activists. Through their intellectual and organizational contributions, ADA liberals—young and old alike—involved themselves in a process of party reform that would bring the views they had brought to bear on the New Politics movement to a new and more prominent stage.

PARTY REFORM, NEW CLASS ASCENDENCY, AND THE MCGOVERN CAMPAIGN

When the overwhelming majority of the seven hundred delegates at the 1972 ADA national convention voted by a show of hands to endorse George McGovern for the Democratic presidential nomination, they could relish the rising prospects of a major party candidate whose politics were closer to the priorities and political outlook of their organization than at any other point in its history. The ADA's endorsement hailed McGovern "as one of the first men in American public life to warn against escalation in Vietnam" but also made clear that he was not a one-issue candidate. McGovern, the endorsement stressed, had "been at the forefront of campaigns for welfare reform and a guaranteed annual income, for racial justice, for civil liberties, for women's rights, for amnesty, for environmental protection, for adequate benefits to Vietnam veterans, for helping the cities."[51] Less than three months later, McGovern overcame the long odds his campaign had initially faced when he secured the Democratic presidential nomination at the party's national convention in Miami. Made possible by far-reaching reforms in the Democratic Party that greatly increased the influence of New Class voters and activists in party politics, McGovern's rapid rise breathed new life into the New Politics movement which had rallied to his long shot campaign. By leading the way in the effort to enforce those reforms and helping to legitimize the New Class ascendency expected to result from them, the ADA and its most influential figures provided valuable support for a party reform process that enabled the McGovern campaign to bring a New Politics movement they had been instrumental in shaping into the spotlight of presidential politics.

The process of party reform that paved the way for the successes achieved by the McGovern campaign began when ADA liberals and their New Politics allies managed to push through a motion at the 1968 Democratic National Convention to establish a party reform commission. Those reformers had failed in their efforts to derail Hubert Humphrey's nomination and pass a "peace plank" that dissented from the Johnson administration's policy on the Vietnam War. They did succeed, however, in committing the Democratic Party to a process of reform with far greater implications for the future of the party and American politics than many of the Democratic regulars who had gone along with the plan realized at the time. Chaired initially by McGovern and later by Donald Fraser, the commission acted on a mandate from the 1968 convention to open up the party to broader participation. Among the myriad policies adopted by the McGovern–Fraser commission to carry out that mandate, two new requirements fundamentally transformed the procedures and composition of the Democratic Party. First, African Americans, women, and youth would have to be represented among a state's delegates at the 1972 convention in "reasonable relationship" to their numbers in the demographic makeup of the state. Second, state central committees would be able to appoint no more than 10 percent of convention delegates, making primary elections or open party caucuses a necessity for many states.[52]

The ADA quickly became a major source of support for the sweeping reforms mandated by the McGovern–Fraser commission. Acting on its commitment to an inclusive politics of race and gender, the ADA established a task force that became one of the most significant bodies outside the Democratic Party in the effort to ensure that state parties complied with the new demographic requirements for delegate representation.[53] Though encouraged by the demographic requirements mandated by the McGovern–Fraser commission, the ADA remained concerned about their implementation and formed the 1972 Convention Task Force in the spring of 1971 to oversee delegate selection procedures. Nominally charged with acting as a watchdog for both major parties, the task force, in practice, concentrated its efforts on the Democratic Party, which had made a much stronger commitment to fundamental reform. With the 1972 election year looming and numerous states failing to comply with the commission's requirements—particularly those concerning the demographic representation of delegates—the ADA charged the task force with compelling adherence to the reform measures through all available means. By taking legal action in the courts, working with official party reform commissions, and mounting credentials challenges at the 1972 Democratic National Convention, the ADA hoped to ensure compliance among state parties with the McGovern–Fraser reforms.[54]

The new demographic requirements stipulated by the commission and the ADA's efforts to ensure that they became reality profoundly altered the demographic composition of the delegates at the 1972 Democratic National Convention, but the more lasting impact on the direction of Democratic and liberal politics came from reforms that expanded the influence of the well-educated middle-class liberals who constituted the New Class.[55] Foremost among these were the far-reaching changes to the delegate selection process mandated by the McGovern–Fraser commission. The political scientist Byron Shafer has shown that the implementation of a participatory model that required more states to use primaries and open caucuses for the selection of delegates created opportunities for mass participation that shifted the balance of power from the party's blue-collar constituency to its white-collar voters. According to Shafer, the *opportunity* for direct participation also amounted to a *requirement* of participation if individuals sought to wield influence. Since levels of participation in primary elections, caucuses, and party conventions have always varied according to social background—with those of higher education and income far more likely to take part—the influence of white-collar New Class Democrats was amplified by the implementation of an extensively participatory process of delegate selection. The number of New Class Democrats had grown significantly over the preceding decades, but they nevertheless still constituted a minority in the party. With organized labor, urban machines, and other institutions traditionally seen as representing the working class no longer able to exercise uncontested power, the opportunity arose for highly motivated New Class activists to direct the party toward their own concerns and interests.[56]

Unlike the declared goal of increasing female, minority, and youth representation, the expanded New Class influence was never a stated aim of party reformers but was clearly recognized by those following the reform process as the likely outcome. In the spring of 1969, some months before the McGovern–Fraser commission announced its major reforms, Schlesinger convened a conference at the City University of New York that brought together other ADA liberals, historians, political scientists, and politicians to discuss the issues of party reform. Over the course of a wide-ranging discussion, Schlesinger let slip an unusually candid assessment of party reform. While he was generally careful to avoid portraying the reforms as specifically benefiting New Class representation, he suggested at one point that the growing demand for participation could be seen as "a push by a certain group, namely, certain educated middle-class suburbanites who want to have a position of influence in party politics." A few months after attending Schlesinger's conference, former ADA national chairman Samuel Beer reflected on what he had seen at the regional hearings of the McGovern–Fraser commission in large cities across the country. The virtual absence of party regulars, organized labor, and other traditional components of the Democratic Party at the hearings made clear to Beer that party reform was "really a suburban, white, middle-class movement" with clear indications as to what direction the reforms would take and who would be most likely to benefit from them.[57]

The prospect that the McGovern–Fraser reforms would align the Democratic Party with the interests of its New Class minority worried Beer and others who had receded into the background of or parted ways with the ADA in the preceding years, but it represented a positive development from the perspective of those then at the helm of the organization. ADA leaders who sought greater influence for white-collar, middle-class liberals in Democratic Party politics took great pains to legitimize the expanded political influence the New Class stood to gain from party reform by stressing the moral qualities of those who filled its ranks. By the late 1960s, many of those ADA leaders had come to see the New Class as the primary base for a "constituency of conscience," with concerns derived less from their own material self-interest than from moral opposition to the Vietnam War, the military-industrial complex, entrenched gender and racial inequality, and other sources of social injustice. A leading proponent of the "constituency of conscience" in the ADA, Schlesinger consistently depicted the well-educated individuals of the New Class from which it drew its strength as better attuned to the pressing moral problems of American society than their working-class counterparts.[58]

Even Michael Harrington, an avowed socialist long committed to class politics, became a vocal champion of the "constituency of conscience" both within the ADA and in the broader political world. Drawing on the recent work of David Bazelon, Daniel Bell, and John Kenneth Galbraith on the New Class, Harrington extolled the potential of the "constituency of conscience" in his influential 1968 book *Toward a Democratic Left*. The "constituency of conscience," according to Harrington, drew from a New Class that was composed not of the typically conservative "old middle class of small-property owners and entrepreneurs" but of the growing number of "scientists, technicians, teachers and professionals in the public sector," who were inclined toward a liberal political outlook. In an increasingly postindustrial society, Harrington believed, it was possible that the economy would create a social structure that vastly enlarged a "constituency of conscience" driven by a "non-material interest in basic change."[59]

ADA liberals who shared Harrington's enthusiasm for the "constituency of conscience" sought to further legitimize party reforms expected to increase New Class influence by framing those reforms not as the means for a power grab by an unrepresentative minority but as a legitimate response to ostensibly inevitable forces. Despite the remark he had let slip that the growing demand for participation in the Democratic Party should be seen as "a push by a certain group," Schlesinger's comments at the conference he convened on party reform portrayed reforms likely to disproportionately benefit New Class Democrats as the culmination of seemingly inexorable trends toward participation in presidential primaries that had been growing since World War II. According to Schlesinger, the moral cause of greater intraparty democracy which had set that trend in motion was being reinforced and accelerated by rapid technological progress. From television coverage that put politicians in the homes of voters to sophisticated and widely publicized opinion polls that greatly reduced the ability of political bosses to control the party, he highlighted the effect of technology on politics as transformative in its democratizing impact. In the face of a legitimate and popular demand for greater responsiveness in party politics made all the more inevitable by advances in technology, Schlesinger declared it futile to "think that anyone in any place can very long resist the forces tending to democratize party procedures."[60]

Galbraith imbued the push for party reform with a similar sense of inevitability in his depictions of the circumstances that had given rise to the initiative. According to Galbraith, the New Politics movement, and its collision with the traditional brokers of political power at the 1968 Democratic National Convention in Chicago, had brought to light the concerns of individuals who felt that "ineluctably and without recourse, their lives are being made subordinate to organization." Such tension, Galbraith maintained, was inescapable in an advanced industrial economy dependent on the contributions of the New Class. On the one hand, he noted, the successful operation of an advanced economy required organization and discipline. On the other hand, the functioning of such economies called for a large New Class with an educational and intellectual background that stirred critical thought and skepticism. For Galbraith, the continuation of US involvement in a war in Vietnam that few Americans had had the opportunity to weigh in on illuminated the tension between the individual and organization, and transformed the conflict from an abstract academic concern into a pressing political issue.[61] Whether they emphasized a natural desire for greater democracy in party politics, ongoing technological progress, or the tensions inherent in all advanced industrial societies, Galbraith, Schlesinger, and other leading figures in the ADA were keen for the forces that drove party reform to be seen as both legitimate and inevitable.

The reforms ultimately adopted by the McGovern–Fraser commission resulted in a composition of delegations at the 1972 Democratic National Convention that confirmed widely held presumptions that party reform would enable a far more instrumental role for New Class liberals in the party. A survey conducted by the *Washington Post* showed that 39 percent of the delegates at the convention held postgraduate degrees, in contrast to the fewer than 4 percent of people in the United States who had undertaken any form of postgraduate work. The survey also demonstrated the impressive advances in making the Democratic Party more open and inclusive since its 1968 convention: twice as many African Americans, four times as many women, far more young delegates, and fully 80 percent of the delegates attending a political convention for the first time. Still, the survey also made clear that those newcomers tended to have far more education and income than most in their respective demographic groups.[62]

Before its prominent display at the 1972 Democratic National Convention, the New Class ascendency enabled by party reform sustained McGovern's campaign throughout the primary season and established the South Dakota senator as the leading candidate for the Democratic presidential nomination.[63] Confirming political trends that Galbraith and Schlesinger had begun to identify in the 1950s, McGovern's success in the primaries unmistakably signaled the shift of the Democratic Party toward a new center in the suburbs and among the white-collar voters of the New Class. By connecting opposition to the Vietnam War and the military-industrial complex to the economy, poverty, racial inequality, and a variety of social and quality-of-life concerns, McGovern attracted widespread support from the growing ranks of the New Class. The overwhelmingly white-collar, middle-class New Democratic Coalition played a critical role in transforming McGovern from an outsider with little hope of winning the nomination into a genuine contender. The NDC's organization of pre-primary conventions that endorsed and then worked for McGovern's candidacy unified liberal support behind his campaign and proved decisive to his primary victories in a number of key states. Strong support for McGovern from the NDC in New York, Pennsylvania, Massachusetts, and elsewhere convinced Schlesinger that McGovern was the clear "heir of the Kennedy and McCarthy efforts, the New Politics of 1968."[64]

McGovern's success in securing the Democratic presidential nomination ensured the lasting impact of the New Politics movement that had coalesced around his campaign by taking that movement beyond the Democratic primaries and into the high-stakes politics of the general election. The New Politics movement owed much to the ideas of veteran ADA intellectuals and the organizational work they and their younger colleagues had taken on over the preceding years. By 1972, the movement frequently expressed a penetrating criticism of the Cold War national security state and support for a politics of race, gender, and sexuality that recognized difference to facilitate social inclusion. This evolution led the movement to encompass a far broader set of aims than had animated it when it emerged in opposition to the Vietnam War policies of Lyndon Johnson in the 1968 Democratic primaries. The rapid ascent and devastating defeat of the

McGovern campaign in 1972 prompted an organized response with a political impact every bit as far-reaching and long-lasting as that of the New Politics movement's evolution.

THE NEOCONSERVATIVES' RESPONSE

Exactly one month after George McGovern's landslide loss to Richard Nixon, the newly formed Coalition for a Democratic Majority launched itself with a full-page advertisement in the *New York Times* and the *Washington Post* containing the plea "Come Home, Democrats." Turning the "Come Home, America" theme from McGovern's acceptance speech at the Democratic National Convention in Miami on its head, the CDM manifesto marked a new era in neoconservative politics. The manifesto urged Democrats to return the party "to the great tradition through which it had come to represent the wishes and hopes of a majority of the American people." Spurned by McGovern, the "great tradition" celebrated by the CDM rested on commitment to a vigorous and internationalist foreign policy posture, economic growth, law and order, equal opportunity, and bread-and-butter economic issues.[65]

The disaffected Democrats who formed the CDM were neither the first neoconservatives nor the sole representatives of neoconservatism in the 1970s. They were, however, the first to move neoconservatism from the pages of intellectual journals such as *The Public Interest* into the thick of major party politics and quickly became the most visible and consequential of its representatives during the period. Neoconservatism has been characterized primarily as a response to the New Left by both neoconservatives themselves and many of the historians who have examined its origins.[66] While the neoconservatism that animated the CDM arose in reaction to a diverse range of developments, including the New Left, it was prompted far less by the politics of the radical left than the transformation of liberal politics ushered in by the New Politics movement. This meant that despite their frequent insistence to the contrary, the neoconservatives of the CDM were primarily responding to a political movement that owed much to the ideas advanced and actions taken by the ADA and its leading figures over the preceding decades.

In its efforts to reverse the ascendency of the New Politics in the Democratic Party, the CDM assembled an impressive array of high-profile figures. The appointment of Hubert Humphrey, a founding member and former national chairman of the ADA, alongside the ardent liberal Cold Warrior Henry "Scoop" Jackson as honorary co-chairmen provided the nascent organization with valuable name recognition. Max Kampelman, Penn Kemble, Jeane Kirkpatrick, Richard Schifter, Ben Wattenberg, and others with close ties to the presidential campaigns of those two standard-bearers of Cold War liberalism carried out the bulk of the initial organizing work for the CDM. The list of signatories to the CDM's manifesto included many prominent intellectuals such as Daniel Bell, Nathan Glazer, Seymour Martin Lipset, Michael Novak, and Norman Podhoretz; political advisers such as Zbigniew Brzezinski, and Midge Decter; and union leaders such as United Federation of Teachers (UFT) president Albert Shanker and ILGWU president Louis Stulberg. With the bulk of the cost for publishing the full-page manifesto paid for by union contributions, the involvement of labor leaders proved especially crucial to getting the CDM off the ground.[67]

The CDM also represented a natural destination for those who had become disillusioned with the ADA when the organization became a leading force in the New Politics movement following its endorsement of Eugene McCarthy in 1968. The membership of the CDM featured a striking number of individuals formerly or still nominally associated with the ADA. In its earliest days, Bayard Rustin and former ADA national chairman John Roche served on the organizing committee that brought the CDM together and charted its future. By the mid-1970s, the CDM had attracted Hyman Bookbinder, Leon Keyserling, Daniel Patrick Moynihan, Paul Seabury, and others who could lay claim to long histories with the ADA.[68]

Whether or not they came to the CDM by way of the ADA, many in the nascent organization looked to the ADA as a model for an effective political organization despite significant differences between the nature and purpose of the two organizations. Unlike the ADA, the CDM exhibited no ambivalence as to whether it should develop into a small, elite organization along the lines of the Fabian Society or into a mass political organization. Decidedly choosing the former, the CDM never attempted to organize local chapters and relied instead on the influence wielded by its small number of well-connected members. The steadfast commitment of the early ADA to global communist containment and the organization's success in influencing Democratic and liberal politics, however, served as an important source of inspiration for the CDM. When Kampelman, Kemble, Schifter,

Wattenberg, and others met at the 1972 Democratic National Convention to discuss the formation of the CDM—a conversation that would be kept secret until after the election so as to avoid accusations of undermining the McGovern campaign—they envisioned the CDM as waging an ideological battle along the lines of the one once carried out by the ADA. Wattenberg described the initial idea for the CDM as stemming from a conversation with Richard Scammon in which his collaborator on *The Real Majority* suggested the need for "a new ADA" to counter the growing influence of New Politics. Scammon and Wattenberg believed that the ADA had come to espouse many of the same tendencies in liberal politics that the organization had derided in its formative years, when it came into existence in opposition to Henry Wallace's supporters in the Progressive Party. From their perspective, "the ADA had bought into far too much of the countercultural, pro-Vietnamese, and neoisolationist ideas of the New Politics."[69]

Scammon's and Wattenberg's characterization of the ADA and the New Politics as on the side of the counterculture and Vietnamese communists was typical of neoconservative attempts to intentionally conflate the New Politics and the New Left. Beginning with the declaration in its manifesto that "the voices of common-sense liberals have been barely audible in the blare of the New Politics," the CDM frequently identified the New Politics as its primary target. While the CDM often attached the New Politics label to the positions it stood in opposition to, much of the rhetoric from the organization and its leading voices exhibited a determined effort to elide the differences between the New Politics and the New Left. When Podhoretz and Wattenberg detailed their respective paths from liberalism to neoconservatism in their political memoirs, they rarely mentioned the New Politics without an accompanying assertion of its connections to the New Left and consistently used the terms almost interchangeably.[70] Deliberate conflation of the New Politics and the New Left served an important political aim for Podhoretz, Wattenberg, and other CDM members who sought to tar the New Politics with the brush of radicalism and establish themselves as the legitimate claimants to the liberal tradition. The broad brushstrokes initially produced by neoconservatives have been uncritically reproduced by historians who harbor no such political aims but nevertheless have echoed neoconservatives in depicting the New Politics as a watered-down version of the New Left and inadequately distinguishing between the two political movements.[71]

When the neoconservatives of the CDM sought to retake the Democratic Party from a New Politics movement with origins, aims, and a political perspective distinct from those of the New Left, foreign policy concerns played a newly important—though not exclusive—role in motivating them. Foreign policy issues had not always been a primary focus for neoconservatives. The foremost concerns of the first neoconservatives who coalesced around journals such as *Commentary* and *The Public Interest* in the latter half of the 1960s were primarily domestic in nature and were expressed in terms of a growing skepticism toward the ability of social welfare programs, and government action more broadly, to achieve their stated aims.[72] With the advance of the New Politics movement, opposition to the Vietnam War and a critical perspective on the Cold War national security state were transformed, in the words of Galbraith, from "dissent into organized and legitimate political opposition."[73] Consequently, fundamental questions over the nature of the Cold War and the role of the United States in the world entered the arena of electoral politics and became an integral aspect of the neoconservative's critical response to the direction then being taken by liberal politics. While unequivocal expressions of alarm with what they saw as the drift of liberalism toward a position of isolationism clearly distinguished the concerns of the neoconservatives of the CDM from those of neoconservatives during the prior decade, the neoconservatism of the CDM represented a broad response to the multifaceted New Politics movement which had taken shape by the early 1970s. The neoconservatives who joined together to create the CDM sought to oppose the growing influence of a movement whose belief in the liberal potential of the New Class, critical perspective on the Cold War national security state, and insistence that social inclusion required recognition of difference could—in many cases—be traced back to the actions and ideas of ADA liberals.

The very name Coalition for a Democratic Majority represented the conviction of the organization's members that an unrepresentative minority of New Class liberals had captured the Democratic Party. The CDM manifesto declared that "in the turbulence and confusion of the past few years, the national Democratic Party has come to be unduly influenced by forces and ideas unrepresentative of traditional Democratic principles." Despite the insistence that the developments it opposed were of recent origin, the CDM's attack on the New Politics took aim at assumptions about working-class conservatism and New Class liberal potential that Galbraith and Schlesinger had been visibly advancing for years. According to the manifesto, the "new" in the New Politics could be found in its "contempt" for the labor unions and working-class Americans who had long been the foundation of the Democratic Party's electoral strength. The desertion by the New Politics of traditional Democratic pillars of popular support, the manifesto charged, had "allowed the Republican Party—a party so long and so accurately known as the party of privilege—to represent itself for the first time as the champion" of the "values and daily concerns of tens of millions of ordinary people."[74] From the perspective of the CDM, the Democratic Party had ceased to represent a mass constituency and become instead the vehicle of a New Class described by Penn Kemble and Josh Muravchik as constituting "an interest group which differs from the 'old' interest groups chiefly in its refusal to acknowledge the degree to which it hungers for political power and patronage."[75]

Criticism of the New Class articulated by the CDM and its leading voices frequently drew on a line of argument that held the moralism exhibited by New Class liberals to be a pretense that obscured ultimately self-serving aims. Michael Novak maintained that the support of New Class liberals for ostensibly moral causes such as the elimination of poverty owed less to a genuine concern for the poor than a desire for expanded government social programs to create the jobs and opportunities that would make meaningful use of their extensive skills and education.[76] Similarly, Irving Kristol argued that the efforts of the New Class to represent itself as driven by concerns for marginalized social groups and the greater good of society served primarily to mask the "simple truth" that it was "engaged in a class struggle with the business community for status and power." Although Kristol never joined the CDM, his influential criticisms stood alongside those of Novak as core elements of the organization's critical perspective on the New Class.[77]

The CDM coupled its fundamental questioning of New Class political motivations with a strong challenge to the goals of the New Politics movement's campaign against the Cold War national security state. Frequently articulated as the call to reorder national priorities, New Politics opposition to the excesses of the security state found its most visible expression through the McGovern campaign's slogan "Come Home, America." An explicit rejection of McGovern's slogan, the CDM's call to "Come Home, Democrats" implied that "the belief that the security of the United States depends upon a stable and progressive world community has been challenged by the idea that the United States must withdraw from its international responsibilities and effect a serious diminution of its own power."[78]

If the widening of the foreign policy aims of the New Politics movement from a near singular focus on opposition to the Vietnam War to a broadly critical perspective on the national security state was what prompted the CDM's plea to Democrats to "come home," it also proved to be a critical factor in determining the nature of the CDM's opposition to the trajectory of Democratic and liberal politics. Zbigniew Brzezinski, Nathan Glazer, Norman Podhoretz, and a considerable number of other signatories to the CDM's manifesto favored the withdrawal of US troops from Vietnam but saw the sweeping opposition of the New Politics movement to interventionist foreign policy and the national security state as an alarming overreaction to the Vietnam War, however misguided those CDM members believed that particular war to be.[79] Making clear that the CDM did not intend to limit its membership to proponents of the Vietnam War, the organization's manifesto reached out "to all who believe that, regardless of past miscalculations or failures of policy, United States involvement in international affairs continues to be necessary to the establishment of a stable and viable international order." Shaped in part by Galbraith's and Schlesinger's call to "reorder national priorities," the New Politics movement's attacks on the Cold War national security state prompted Podhoretz to take what he saw as a necessary "stand against the dangers of an . . . indiscriminate American withdrawal from the fight against Communism." Like many in the CDM, Podhoretz envisioned the organization as a vital force for taking that stand.[80]

In the realm of domestic politics, the CDM focused much of its energy on the effort to roll back the demographic requirements for delegate representation mandated by the McGovern–Fraser reforms. Implicitly attacking those requirements, the CDM's manifesto asserted that "the principle of individual merit without regard to inherited status has been challenged by the idea of proportionalism in accordance with birth and group origin."[81] CDM opposition to the demographic requirements reflected its members' broader rejection of the politics of race, gender, and sexuality that had come to the fore in liberal and Democratic politics by the 1970s. Most ADA liberals, virtually the whole of the New Politics movement, and the 1972 Democratic Party platform insisted on recognition of difference as a vital means of furthering social inclusion. Even those ADA liberals who, like Schlesinger, harbored significant concerns with identity politics and would later become more vocal in expressing those concerns did not stand in the way of the organization's embrace of the politics of race, gender, and sexuality during the early 1970s.

By contrast, UFT president Albert Shanker—who attracted national attention and faced accusations of racism during the New York City teachers' strikes of the late 1960s—denounced affirmative action—which he saw as tantamount to racial quotas—long-term bilingual education, and other state-supported efforts to recognize and encourage difference. He considered such measures politically harmful and feared that they would foster separatism and balkanize Democratic politics.[82] When Shanker and his colleagues in the CDM attacked the growing influence of the politics of race, gender, and sexuality in the Democratic Party, they were responding neither to the New Left nor to what Podhoretz described as a version of the New Left that had been "cleaned up" to work within the electoral system. Rather, the source of their concerns can be traced back to long-term trends in liberal politics that drew on the social democratic values of the New Deal, the "qualitative liberalism" of Galbraith and Schlesinger, and the impact of the civil rights movement.

From the politics of race and gender expressed in the 1972 Democratic Party platform to McGovern's call to "Come Home, America," CDM members sought to render the various aspects of the New Politics movement as analogous to or the offspring of the New Left in order to establish themselves as the true representatives of the liberal tradition. Midge Decter complained in 1976 that she had been pressed to relinquish the "liberal" label "by everyone from Lester Maddox to the *Village Voice*." Still, she insisted that she "had no choice but to be a liberal" and could never be relieved of her obligation "to do battle" with those seeking to undo the achievements of the liberal tradition and "abscond with its good name."[83] Regardless of their determination to wage that battle, Decter and her fellow CDM members faced steep and, ultimately, insurmountable challenges to their aspiration of laying claim to the mantle of the liberal tradition.

THE STRUGGLE FOR THE MANTLE OF LIBERALISM

Michael Harrington first brought the term "neoconservative" into common usage in 1973 with the publication of a widely read and influential article in *Dissent*. Harrington's article focused on Daniel Bell, Nathan Glazer,

Daniel Patrick Moynihan, and other liberal critics of 1960s social welfare programs, but the presence of those three individuals in the CDM and the organization's general agreement with their political outlook meant that its members quickly found themselves pegged with the neoconservative label.[84] Initially termed "Scoop Jackson Democrats" by the press, members of the CDM became known as neoconservatives, but many persisted nevertheless in insisting that they were liberals. Those in the CDM who continued to see themselves as liberals conceived of the organization as a force vying with the New Politics not only for control of the Democratic Party but also for the legacy of the "vital center" and the broader liberal tradition. Ultimately, the visible and ongoing commitment of the ADA to the New Politics movement frustrated the CDM in its aspirations to lay claim to the mantle of the "vital center," while the general acceptance among political observers of the New Politics as the new standard-bearer of liberalism consigned the CDM and its members to carrying the banner of conservatism in one form or another.

The roots of the New Politics in "vital center" liberalism and the continued involvement of the individuals and organization most identified with that political tradition in the New Politics movement greatly complicated the efforts of CDM members to present themselves as the heirs of the "vital center" tradition. No individual bore a stronger personal association with the "vital center" than Schlesinger—who coined the term in what became a playbook for liberal intellectuals in the early postwar years. Throughout its history, the ADA regularly cast itself as a "vital center" and became the most readily accepted embodiment of the political tradition that it spawned. With the escalation of the Vietnam War, Schlesinger and other leading figures pushed the ADA to formulate a new "vital center" that maintained a determined position against both the New Left and conservatism but shed the reflexive anticommunism that had been so integral to its original incarnation. The ADA's formulation of and continued commitment to a reshaped "vital center" demonstrated that the substance of that political tradition could and should change to meet new circumstances. While the CDM stressed the continuity of its political perspective with the specific policy positions of the "vital center" outlined by Schlesinger in 1949, the ADA established the New Politics as a living and breathing embodiment of the "vital center." The ADA's new "vital center" stood in vigorous opposition to the political extremes of an increasingly polarized political landscape while facing the realities of a world that had changed dramatically since the early years of the Cold War. In the context of the 1970s, the political outlook of the CDM looked less like the dynamic "vital center" once described by Schlesinger than a rigid set of dated policy prescriptions. No matter how closely the CDM hewed to the particular policies that once defined the "vital center," it would be unable to stake a claim to the political tradition in a way that held any genuine meaning in the waning years of the Vietnam War era.

CDM members faced similarly difficult prospects in their struggle to be accepted as liberals of any stripe, "vital center" or otherwise. As insurgents who sought to challenge the status quo of Democratic politics, New Politics activists—first in their opposition to the Johnson administration and the campaign of Hubert Humphrey and then as advocates of party reform in the years after 1968—were consistently labeled liberals by journalists, while those who stood in their way were regularly named as or implied to be conservative. David Halberstam offered a characterization typical of the period when the opposition of organized labor to the New Politics movement prompted him to describe labor unions as "fast becoming a conservative force in America."[85] Similarly, an article in the *New York Times* reflected the consensus of the media when it reported that "moderate and conservative spokesmen" seeking to roll back various aspects of party reform were "brushed aside by liberal backers of Senator George McGovern."[86] When the CDM entered the political scene in late 1972, it quickly inherited the conservative label that had been pinned to earlier opponents of the New Politics. According to the *Wall Street Journal*, the charges against the New Politics in the CDM's manifesto differed little from those "made several years earlier by the Republican Party."[87]

The CDM and its members lost the battle with the New Politics for the liberal label on a variety of fronts, from social and culture issues to affirmative action, but none more conclusively and with more far-reaching impact than in the area of foreign policy. Elliot Abrams, a member of the CDM and special counsel to Jackson during his 1976 presidential campaign, insisted that the opposition of the New Politics movement to an interventionist foreign policy of communist containment amounted to a rejection of "the absolute primacy of liberty as a political value" which put it distinctly outside the bounds of the liberal tradition. In his estimation, "the sole tie between the New Politics view and traditional American liberalism is the fact that most New Politics enthusiasts are former liberals ... if they are old enough to be former anythings." Still, Abrams conceded that those who did not share the "new 'liberal' views" of the New Politics had come to be deemed conservatives by the "cadres of the media, who either share the New Politics outlook or are entirely ignorant of the historical meaning of liberalism in America."[88] Gus Tyler never joined the CDM but maintained a political perspective nearly indistinguishable from the organization's in most regards and shared Abrams's critical assessment of the state of political labels in the 1970s. From the vantage point of the mid-1970s, Tyler lamented the way in which liberalism had been "redefined during the Vietnam conflict. By a new test, doves were liberals and hawks were conservatives. This put a huge chunk of the old Rooseveltians in the right-wing camp, since many of them in their continuing war against Communism and isolationism were principled cold warriors."[89]

To a significant degree, the widespread adoption of the New Politics definition of liberalism described by Abrams and Tyler rested on the broader acceptance of ascribing a specific foreign policy outlook to notions of what defined the boundaries of liberalism. In the 1950s, Schlesinger argued that the quantitative material concerns of the New Deal were increasingly giving way to non-material qualitative issues such as foreign policy. When Schlesinger first outlined the qualitative issues that he believed would rise on the nation's agenda during the tense period of the early Cold War, conservatives and liberals harbored few fundamental differences in their perspectives on foreign policy. During those years of bipartisan consensus on communist containment, various developments—such as the dispute over the so-called "missile gap" that raged during the 1960 presidential election—brought foreign policy issues to the forefront of national politics. The commitment of liberals and conservatives alike to waging the Cold War, however, meant that the distinction between hawkish and dovish foreign policy postures had little direct bearing on ideological and partisan identification.

When the McCarthy campaign and the New Politics movement that coalesced around it brought opposition to the Vietnam War into electoral politics, a once unshakable bipartisan commitment to global anticommunist containment began to crack. As a result, foreign policy became an ideological and partisan issue in a way and to a degree formerly unseen during the postwar era. Whereas liberalism previously had no inherent relationship to a distinct set of foreign policy positions, the growth of liberal opposition to the Vietnam War in electoral politics in the face of conservative support for the conflict meant that critics of the war came to be termed liberals while supporters were seen as conservatives. When liberal opposition to the Vietnam War widened to include a critical perspective on the Cold War national security state, opposition not just to that particular conflict but to vigorously interventionist foreign policy in general became a critical requirement for entry into what had come to be accepted as liberal politics. As long as that requirement remained, the CDM's call to Democrats to "come home" to an aggressively interventionist foreign policy would leave them with little hope of passing the liberal litmus test.[90]

The respective directions of liberal and conservative politics during the 1970s and 1980s have ensured that the legacies of neoconservatism and the New Politics remain as divergent as they have been consequential. Finding little success in laying claim to the liberal tradition, many of the neoconservatives from the CDM abandoned any pretense of representing themselves as liberals and gravitated toward the Republican Party, where they rose to the top in formulating foreign policy in the administrations of Ronald Reagan and George W. Bush.[91] With neoconservatives largely out of the picture, the outlook of the New Politics became pervasive in American liberalism. From the insistence that social and cultural issues such as environmentalism, gay rights, and women's rights are central to the liberal agenda to the rejection of the bipartisan militarism that prevailed throughout much of the Cold War era, liberals in the late twentieth century practiced a variety of politics much closer to the New Politics than to the New Deal or the liberalism of the early postwar years. While the New Politics all but disappeared as a term of political discussion by the late 1970s, it secured a powerful legacy, as much of what had once been known as the New Politics could, in many respects, simply be called liberalism. In the decades that followed, however, the unresolved tensions between "bread-and-butter" material issues and issues understood as social or cultural that had run through the New Politics movement produced a split in American liberalism that ensured the movement's legacy would be plural.

CHAPTER 6

FROM NEW POLITICS TO NEOLIBERALISM

Atari Democrats and the Dual Legacies of the New Politics Movement

When Massachusetts senator Paul Tsongas gave the keynote address at the 1980 ADA national convention, he warned his audience that "liberalism is at a crossroads. It will either evolve to meet the issues of the 1980s or it will be reduced to an interesting topic for Ph.D.-writing historians." In a speech that championed the imperative of economic productivity and challenged some of the most deeply held principles of those gathered at the convention, Tsongas urged liberals to try to understand and reach out to a new generation critical of unions and government social programs in order to forestall conservative dominance.[1] He was not, however, the only Massachusetts senator to speak before the convention. Addressing the assembly during the latter stages of his insurgent campaign against the incumbent president, Jimmy Carter, in that year's Democratic primaries, Ted Kennedy stressed the vital role played by the federal government in helping American citizens during hard times and railed against a proposed federal budget that would be balanced on the backs of the working poor, the jobless, and minorities.[2] The ADA delegates gathered at the convention responded to Tsongas's speech with polite indifference and to Kennedy's with an outpouring of cheers.[3]

The speeches given by Tsongas and Kennedy before the ADA represented starkly different visions for the future of American liberalism. They also reflected the two political trajectories that developed out of the New Politics movement. Tsongas and a number of the other influential young Democrats who came to be called neoliberals during the 1980s had roots in the New Politics movement and resolved the tension within the New Politics between costly social democratic solutions and an emphasis on social and cultural issues that required less public spending by forgoing the former in favor of the latter. In contrast to neoliberal Democrats, Kennedy remained committed to the social democratic outlook of the New Politics movement and sought to build bridges between those who had been drawn to that movement and other elements of the traditional liberal coalition—such as organized labor—that had become largely estranged from it.

In recent years, the terms "neoliberal" and "neoliberalism" have been used with varying degrees of precision in a wide variety of contexts to describe individuals and ideologies that prioritize market solutions to economic and social problems.[4] The terms have been associated with figures as varied as Chilean dictator Augusto Pinochet, British prime minister Margaret Thatcher, and US president Bill Clinton, and imply no necessary connection with any form of liberalism other than its classic late-nineteenth-century laissez-faire variety. Before it took on this more capacious meaning and came to describe the general nature and dominant political paradigm of late-stage capitalism, the "neoliberal" label was primarily used to distinguish young Democrats like Tsongas and Senator Gary Hart—who moved to the right on economic issues while maintaining a commitment to liberal social and cultural values—from more economically progressive New Deal–oriented liberals. On the basis of their support for high-technology industries and entrepreneurship as means of rebuilding the American economy, young neoliberal Democrats came to be dubbed "Atari Democrats" in the early 1980s in reference to the Atari company's rapid growth and success in the video game and computer industry.

Less than five months after Tsongas and Kennedy offered competing visions for liberalism at the 1980 ADA national convention, Ronald Reagan defeated Jimmy Carter in a landslide presidential election and Republicans regained control of the US Senate for the first time since 1952. The scale of Republican victories and Democratic losses in 1980 made the Democratic Party highly receptive to the seemingly new ideas advanced by neoliberal Democrats like Tsongas and Hart and neoliberal writers like *Washington Monthly* editor Charles Peters. Most in the ADA were far less keen than Democratic functionaries on the ideas and outlook of neoliberal Democrats. Arthur Schlesinger Jr. gave some sense of what separated him and other ADAers from the neoliberal perspective when he opined in 1983 that neoliberal Democrats "saw 1980 as an ideological repudiation of the whole concept of affirmative government. Reagan, they concluded, had a secret, and, if they could only master the secret too, they might succeed as Reagan had done."[5]

But the politics of neoliberal Atari Democrats did not—as Schlesinger suggested—suddenly take shape in response to Reagan's electoral victory in 1980. The historian Lily Geismer has demonstrated that the basic political outlook of the Atari Democrats and their New Democrat successors predated the 1980 election and that their rise should not be seen simply as a rearguard reaction to the Reagan Revolution. Geismer offers a far more nuanced accounting of the Atari Democrats than can be found in Schlesinger's polemical characterizations of them, but she similarly neglects to trace the roots of neoliberal Democrats back to the New Politics movement.[6] Unearthing those roots illuminates the origins of the synthesis of economic conservatism with liberal social and cultural values produced by neoliberal Democrats in the thought of ADA intellectuals like Schlesinger, despite the contempt they displayed for Democratic neoliberalism.

If the 1980 election did not create Democratic neoliberalism, it did create a political opening for its advocates and exert a significant influence on their politics. While Schlesinger's charge that Democratic neoliberalism represented little more than "Me-Too Reaganism" distorts the origins of the politics embraced by neoliberal Democrats, Atari Democrats did embrace elements of Reagan's economic agenda, if not his social and cultural conservatism.[7] They may not have had the same reasons for favoring market mechanisms over government programs as the Reagan administration and often had different ideas about how those mechanisms should work or whose interests they should serve, but they nevertheless joined Republicans in beating the drum for business-friendly policies and privatization. By the late 1980s, Atari's business fortunes had declined and the "Atari" prefix fell out of favor as a way of describing neoliberal Democrats. Still, despite these changes in nomenclature, the political outlook of the Atari Democrats—whose politics both preceded the Reagan Revolution and were fundamentally shaped by it—increasingly came to define liberal and Democratic politics. As the neoliberal perspective tightened its grip on liberalism and the Democratic Party in the 1990s, the "bread-and-butter" economic progressivism of the New Deal era gave way to an emphasis on social and cultural issues that required limited public spending.

The overwhelming influence gained by neoliberals in the Democratic Party by the end of the twentieth century can make the rise of Democratic neoliberalism seem almost inevitable. It can also make neoliberal Democrats seem like the sole surviving legacy of the New Politics movement. Yet the renewed liberal–labor coalition that drew on the support of unions and New Politics constituencies in the mid-1970s to push for meaningful full employment legislation and propel Kennedy to within touching distance of denying an incumbent president his party's nomination in 1980 makes clear that the rise of neoliberalism in the Democratic Party was neither inevitable nor total. Through their work on behalf of the Humphrey–Hawkins Full Employment Act and their early support for Kennedy's insurgent 1980 presidential campaign, the ADA and its leading figures helped to maintain a version of the New Politics with its social democratic impulses intact. Just as conservatism did not entirely prevail over liberalism during the 1980s, neoliberalism did not fully displace more economically progressive manifestations of the New Politics in liberal and Democratic politics. This meant that when the New Politics—and American liberalism more broadly—survived the Reagan Revolution, they survived with dual legacies.

THE NEW POLITICS AND THE WATERGATE BABIES

Before there were neoliberals or Atari Democrats, there were Watergate babies. Fresh on the heels of Richard Nixon's resignation in August 1974 and the unpopular pardon granted to him by his successor, Gerald Ford, the following month, a Democratic wave in that year's midterm elections brought seventy-five new Democrats to the House of Representatives. Widespread voter disgust with the Republican Party in the wake of the Watergate scandal also helped to bring new Democratic faces to the Senate and governors' mansions across the country. The largest infusion of new Democratic officeholders in decades skewed young, with an average age of forty. Dubbed "Watergate babies" by the press, many of the young Democrats elected in 1974 hailed from suburban districts that had long been Republican electoral strongholds and emphasized their New Politics credentials while distancing themselves from the "old politics" of the New Deal and "interest-group liberalism."[8] With many inspired by the causes that had animated the New Politics movement and winning office through the support of white-collar suburban voters morally repulsed by the corruption of the Nixon White

House, the Watergate babies appeared to be the clearest vindication to date of the hopes that Arthur Schlesinger Jr., John Kenneth Galbraith, and other ADA intellectuals placed in the New Class as the key social base for liberal politics. At the same time, the economic conservatism displayed by many of these young Democrats and their ambivalence toward traditional liberal constituencies such as organized labor called into question the nature of their liberalism and the faith that ADA intellectuals had placed in the New Class voters who had helped them to win office.

The desire of the Watergate babies to distance themselves from the liberalism of previous generations and tread a new political path became apparent shortly after the 1974 elections, when Gary Hart famously pronounced that that he and his cohort of young, newly elected Democrats were "not a bunch of little Hubert Humphreys." Hart had served as campaign manager for George McGovern's New Politics–driven 1972 presidential campaign and looked to the same growing ranks of New Class voters who had sustained that insurgent effort when he embarked on his own successful campaign for the US Senate in 1974. Hart later apologized to Humphrey for the remark, but his desire to take on the tenets of New Deal–Great Society liberalism and his firebrand style quickly became his calling card and that of many of his fellow Watergate babies. Bob Edgar, elected to the House of Representatives from Pennsylvania, described himself and the other members of the "Class of '74" as "the sixties generation that didn't drop out." Before running for Congress, Edgar was an activist in Philadelphia committed to work on issues surrounding racial discrimination, gangs, and housing.[9] Future "Atari Democrat" Paul Tsongas served in the Peace Corps before winning election in 1974 to represent a suburban Boston congressional district. Prior to winning a House seat in southwestern Michigan, Democrat Bob Carr made a name for himself in campus activist circles.[10]

Yet as much as the Watergate babies brandished their activist backgrounds and railed against the corruption of the Nixon years in moral terms, they portrayed themselves first and foremost as non-ideological problem solvers. For the Watergate babies, the bulk of political issues were technical problems that had right answers rather than competing interests that needed to be reconciled or issues that could be understood from an ideological perspective. Raised on John F. Kennedy, these young Democrats embraced Kennedy's insistence that "the central domestic problems of our time do not relate to basic clashes of philosophy and ideology, but to ways and means. . . . Technical answers—not political answers—must be provided."[11] Channeling the sociologist Daniel Bell's influential "end of ideology" thesis by way of Kennedy, the Watergate babies sought to balance the moral energy they brought from their activist backgrounds with a cool and detached technocratic approach to politics.[12]

The desire of the Watergate babies to present themselves as free from the shackles of ideological dogma and independent of the Democratic establishment also owed much to the particular constituencies they represented. With his 1974 win, Edgar flipped a district that had not elected a Democrat since 1858. Tsongas's win made him the first Democrat elected to the House from his district in the twentieth century. Carr's district had sent a Democrat to Congress only three times in four decades prior to his 1974 election.[13] Representing districts that had typically elected Republicans, these young Democrats were keen to downplay their ideological and partisan commitments. In the years to come, some of the leading figures that emerged from the "Class of '74"—such as Tsongas—would insist that they were trying to redefine liberalism, not abandon it. Once they were newly in office, however, as a result of an election that they were desperate to prove was not a fluke, many of the Watergate babies preferred to avoid any association with liberalism. Sam Fields, an ADA staff member, reported that in early 1976 he received calls from several freshman Democrats begging not to be included in the organization's annual rating of liberal votes. According to Fields, "a lot of freshmen are nervous about the ADA ratings. They see that as a cross to bear this year, particularly if they won in a normally conservative Republican district. They read the Harris polls that say the country is going conservative and they think the ADA rating can be used against them to identify them as a big liberal spender."[14]

Despite the hesitancy many of the Watergate babies felt toward being publicly identified as liberals, they entered office with two primary goals that were shared by the bulk of liberal congressional Democrats during the mid-1970s: reforming Congress and definitively ending US intervention in Southeast Asia. The votes of the seventy-five new Democrats elected to the House brought about the culmination of efforts to reform the chamber's procedures that had been brewing for years. The year before the election of the Watergate babies, Democrats decided that their full caucus would vote on the appointment of committee chairmen, rather than the chairmanship automatically going to a committee's most senior Democrat.

Less than a month into their terms, the "Class of '74" Democrats joined forces with more senior Democrats to topple three aging "Southern power barons" from their committee chairmanships in what the press termed the "freshman revolt."[15] Many of the Watergate babies acted similarly swiftly to help bring an end to what remained of US involvement in Vietnam in 1975. As North Vietnamese and Vietcong troops advanced toward Saigon and Congress debated a $150 million package of humanitarian aid, Watergate babies were among the most skeptical and critical of additional aid for the imperiled South Vietnamese government. Edgar and other newly elected Democrats in the House offered amendments to the humanitarian package intended to ensure that the money would not be used for military purposes and US troops would not be called upon to fight. While those amendments were defeated, the strong stand taken by many Watergate babies helped to cement the sense that the writing was on the wall for US aid to the South Vietnamese government and the likelihood of its survival.[16]

In contrast to the solid backing most Watergate babies gave to the well-established liberal issues of congressional reform and opposition to the Vietnam War, they displayed far more hesitancy toward issues that mattered to the traditional liberal constituency of organized labor. While the ADA and New Politics liberals had broken with labor leaders over their support for the Vietnam War in the late 1960s, they continued to support labor rights legislation and remained committed to the broad economic policy priorities of organized labor. But even with the Vietnam War and foreign policy no longer the polarizing issue it had been in the 1960s, many of the Watergate babies kept their distance from labor. Several newly elected Democrats supported amendments to weaken a bill that would allow unions to picket an entire construction site over a dispute with one of the contractors on the site, a key legislative priority of the AFL-CIO in 1975. Similarly, the votes of Watergate babies that year against an AFL-CIO-backed $9 billion economic recovery program helped to doom the legislation. When Kenneth Young, the assistant director of the AFL-CIO's legislative department, assessed the votes of the "Class of '74" Democrats, he noted that "the freshman Democrat today is likely to be an upper-income type and that causes some problems with economic issues. . . . I think a lot of them are more concerned with inflation than unemployment. They aren't emotionally involved in unemployment. It's a political issue, and they come down on the side that unemployment is bad, but inflation is more important to their constituents."[17] As the economy deteriorated further in the late 1970s and the widely presumed economic trade-off between inflation and unemployment took center stage in American politics, the economic priorities of the Watergate babies whom New Class voters had helped to bring into office would further upend the political hopes that ADA intellectuals had long placed in the New Class.

THE STRUGGLE FOR FULL EMPLOYMENT

In the mid-1970s, Americans became wearily familiar with the term "stagflation" and the reality of an economy that paradoxically combined stagnation and inflation. Conventional economic theory struggled to account for the simultaneous rise in unemployment and consumer prices experienced during the 1970s—two developments believed by most economists to be at odds with each other. As the recession deepened and unemployment rolls climbed, Hubert Humphrey, back in the Senate after his failed presidential bid, and Augustus Hawkins, a Democratic congressman from southern California, picked up the pieces of a recent bill and introduced the Full Employment and Balanced Growth Act of 1976. Aiming to achieve many of the unfulfilled aims of the hollowed-out Employment Act of 1946, the Humphrey–Hawkins bill sought to establish the right of every American to employment "at fair rates of compensation" and reduce unemployment to 3 percent or less by 1980. Like the original 1946 act, Humphrey–Hawkins looked to the federal government as an employer of last resort to ensure that those goals would not be derailed by shortfalls in private employment.[18] Given that unemployment rates among African Americans and other minority groups were typically double that of whites, the sponsors of the bill and most of its supporters also saw Humphrey–Hawkins as a civil rights measure. With a Democrat back in the White House following Jimmy Carter's win in the 1976 presidential election, passage of Humphrey–Hawkins became a central priority for the renewed liberal–labor coalition which bridged many of the divides that had developed during the Vietnam War era. By bringing together the ADA and elements of the New Politics movement with organized labor and the Democratic establishment, the struggle for Humphrey–Hawkins signaled that the Watergate babies who had been inspired by the New Politics movement were not the movement's sole surviving legacy in the late 1970s. Despite its ultimate failure to win passage of meaningful full employment legislation, the broad coalition that formed around Humphrey–Hawkins offered the possibility of an enduring New Politics movement that—unlike the Watergate babies—did not discard its social democratic elements.

In the case of the ADA, its rapprochement with organized labor began before the push for Humphrey–Hawkins brought an array of New Politics groups into coalition with labor unions. The ADA's endorsement of Eugene McCarthy in the 1968 Democratic primaries had led to an exodus from the organization of labor leaders, who continued to support Lyndon Johnson and his Vietnam War policies. More importantly, from a financial perspective, the break between the ADA and labor leaders over the Vietnam War ended what had been one of the organization's most significant and reliable sources of funding. Despite the acrimony surrounding the break, the rift between the ADA and organized labor did not last long. With the departure of US troops from Vietnam in 1973, foreign policy differences between the ADA and a labor leadership that favored containment policy diminished in significance. Additionally, by the mid-1970s the issue of party reform no longer pitted the ADA and organized labor against each other. While most labor unions had initially stood in staunch opposition to the McGovern–Fraser reforms, organized labor became more adept at bending the rules of the reformed delegate selection process to their benefit in the years following the 1972 Democratic National Convention and came to embrace or at least live with many aspects of the post-1968 reforms.[19] This receding of divergent positions and interests led to sizable increases in financial contributions from unions to the ADA. Funding from organized labor went from being negligible in the early 1970s to becoming one of the key sources of money for the ADA in the years and decades that followed. Alongside their increased financial contributions, unions came to wield more direct influence in the organization as the number of labor officials serving on the ADA national board grew during the latter half of the 1970s.[20]

Warming relations between the ADA and organized labor also owed much to changing views among labor leaders during the 1970s. Aging union bosses who had long been known for espousing liberal positions on economic matters and conservative positions on social and cultural issues started to become more accepting of the cultural changes of the preceding decade. Some of the changes among labor leaders occurred in more superficial areas. The long hair and beards associated in the popular imagination with the counterculture and antiwar movements during the 1960s ceased to draw the same kind of ire from labor leaders in the 1970s. Other changes involved matters of greater substance. Although the AFL-CIO had long had difficult relations with feminist organizations and causes, the federation endorsed the Equal Rights Amendment (ERA) in 1973 and quickly became one of its most influential champions. This turnabout resulted from feminists organizing within labor unions, sharing ideas across networks of labor-oriented feminists, and building points of common interest outside of the specific concerns of feminists. The organizing and activism of feminist unionists compelled the virtually all-male upper echelons of labor leadership to take their concerns seriously. Moreover, labor leaders calculated that in the increasingly conservative political climate of the 1970s, organized labor needed feminists as much as feminists might need labor.[21]

These new circumstances also made possible the coalition that came together under the umbrella of the Full Employment Action Council (FEAC). Founded in 1974 by Coretta Scott King, Dr. Martin Luther King Jr.'s widow and an influential civil rights leader in her own right, and Murray Finley, president of the Amalgamated Clothing Workers of America, the FEAC initially worked for the full employment legislation introduced by Humphrey and liberal New York Republican senator Jacob Javits before throwing its weight behind the revamped legislation sponsored by Humphrey and Hawkins. With funding from labor unions and political influence through the Congressional Black Caucus, the FEAC devoted much of its resources to coordinating grassroots efforts on behalf of Humphrey-Hawkins.[22] The council organized rallies, provided organizational and media training for local groups, and solicited letters to the editor.[23] On its sprawling board of directors, the FEAC could count the names of representatives from many of the nation's largest labor unions and leading civil rights, religious, and public interest groups. A significant contingent of representatives on the board came from organizations in the orbit of the New Politics movement. The "good government" watchdog group Common Cause—a quintessential New Politics organization, which had intimately involved itself in the work of the McGovern–Fraser commission—maintained a continual presence on the FEAC board. So too did Dolores Huerta, who was the vice president of the United Farm Workers and had stood beside Robert Kennedy as he delivered his victory speech for the California Democratic primary at the Ambassador Hotel in Los Angeles before being fatally shot in the hotel's kitchen. The presence of Eleanor Smeal, president of the National

Organization for Women, and Gloria Steinem, an influential feminist activist who had recently launched *Ms.* magazine, offered evidence of the growing collaboration between liberal feminists and organized labor. ADA national director Leon Shull played an active role on the board and ensured that an organization which had championed full employment policy since the 1940s maintained a strong presence in the coalition.[24]

No longer associated with the ADA, Leon Keyserling served on the FEAC's board of directors and became the leading voice on its Special Task Force of Economists. He also worked directly with the bill's principal sponsors and was instrumental in shaping its basic premises. While Keyserling was not involved in drafting the original version of Humphrey–Hawkins, the bill unmistakably bore the trademarks of his economic thinking, and he became deeply involved in the numerous revisions it underwent in subsequent years. *The New Republic* went so far as to characterize him as the "father" of Humphrey–Hawkins.[25] Like the Freedom Budget that he had been the chief architect of a decade earlier, Humphrey–Hawkins was rooted in Keyserling's pro-growth economic framework and sought to mitigate economic inequality as a means of addressing racial inequality. Moreover, the central premises that provided the theoretical foundation for Humphrey–Hawkins clearly reflected both Keyserling's direct and indirect intellectual influence. The bill rested on the assumption, very much shared by Keyserling, that stagflation was far more a problem of stagnation than of inflation. Accordingly, Humphrey–Hawkins was predicated on the insistence that the American economy needed significant stimulus to bolster demand and that such actions could be initiated with limited concern for their inflationary prospects.[26]

Whereas support for the Freedom Budget and Keyserling's work on behalf of the initiative had been derailed by the Vietnam War, inflation became the divisive center of the debate that surrounded Humphrey–Hawkins. The dynamics of the debate around full employment and inflation were baked in early when the bill's sponsors struck an agreement with the AFL-CIO not to include federal controls on wages and prices. Humphrey and Hawkins were stuck in a difficult position from the beginning. Their bill stood no chance of proceeding legislatively without the support of organized labor, but labor leaders would never support mandatory controls on wages and prices that would restrict a central function of unions: negotiating for higher wages. The necessity of excluding wage and price controls from the bill, however, opened it up to charges that economic stimulus without mandatory controls would throw more fuel on the economy's already roaring inflationary fire.[27]

Without mandatory wage and price controls, Humphrey–Hawkins faced difficult prospects in becoming law despite widespread support for full employment legislation amid the worst economic downturn since the Great Depression. The opposition of the many Republicans and southern Democrats who lined up against the bill had little impact on the political calculus surrounding Humphrey–Hawkins since there had never been much hope of the bill's winning support from the traditional voices of fiscal conservatism in Congress. Yet the position of the Watergate babies—the bulk of whom hailed from northern, midwestern, or western districts—greatly imperiled the legislation. Worried that voting against Humphrey–Hawkins would splinter the Democratic caucus and that voting for it would hurt their reelection bids, Democratic freshman voted 65 to 10 in the summer of 1976 to ask House leaders not to put the bill to a vote.[28]

Paul Tsongas expressed a viewpoint shared by many of his fellow Watergate babies when he offered support for the general goal of full employment sought by Humphrey–Hawkins but lobbed criticism at its means and particulars. Confirming the earlier assessment from AFL-CIO assistant legislative director Kenneth Young that the Watergate babies and their constituents were more concerned about inflation than about unemployment, Tsongas expressed "serious reservations about the potential inflationary impact involved in the implementation" of Humphrey–Hawkins. In particular, Tsongas took issue with the bill's requirement that wages in public employment programs must be competitive with those in private industry. Expressing a fealty to free market principles that would increasingly characterize the Watergate babies, Tsongas charged that the "prevailing wage" provision of Humphrey–Hawkins "threatens to drive wages upward across the board and eliminates the employee's incentive to ultimately secure work in the private sector." Even without the "prevailing wage" provision, Tsongas remained concerned—on the basis of Congressional Budget Office analysis—that the bill's primary goal of reducing unemployment to 3 percent or less by 1980 would inevitably increase inflation.[29]

The inflationary red flags raised by economists at the Congressional Budget Office made it difficult for many Democratic members of Congress who were sympathetic to the general goal of full employment to get behind the legislation in its existing form. The concerns expressed by well-known and influential Keynesian economists further imperiled Humphrey–Hawkins. Critical testimony offered by Carter's Council of Economic Advisers chairman Charles Schultze proved to be particularly damaging to Humphrey–Hawkins's prospects. A former member of the Budget Bureau during the Johnson administration and no fiscal conservative, Schultze offered testimony on the inflationary impact he believed Humphrey–Hawkins would have, which provided substantial intellectual and institutional support for some of the central criticisms advanced by opponents of the bill.[30] In his testimony before the Senate Committee on Banking, Housing, and Urban Affairs, John Kenneth Galbraith endorsed the aims of Humphrey–Hawkins but echoed the concerns expressed by Schultze and other economists on the inflationary impact that the bill would have in its present form. Stressing that aggressive government action to address unemployment without wage and price controls would undoubtedly lead to inflation, Galbraith called on the bill's stakeholders to "not imagine that God is a liberal gentleman who will work miracles for liberals merely because He loves His own." Galbraith had served as deputy head of the Office of Price Administration during World War II—or in his words as "price tsar"—and had long displayed considerable confidence in the ability of mandatory wage and price controls to successfully control inflation. On that basis, he insisted on the necessity of adding wage and price controls to the bill. Galbraith clearly understood the political difficulty of doing that: wage controls would endanger union support for Humphrey–Hawkins, while price controls would end any possibility of business support. Still, Galbraith insisted that the greatest danger to Humphrey–Hawkins was the prospect of "losing the support of those who fear inflation." Moreover, Galbraith contended that the loss of union backing was not inevitable, because "[AFL-CIO president] George Meany has said many times that labor will accept an incomes policy if it applies to all incomes" and "does not single out the union man for special attention."[31]

Galbraith was right to fear losing the backing of inflation-minded voters and politicians but overly optimistic on the prospects for an income policy that could garner enough support to become law and satisfy the concerns of organized labor. In direct response to the concerns raised by prominent economists and members of Congress whose endorsement would be necessary for passage of Humphrey–Hawkins, the House Education and Labor Committee voted late in the summer of 1976 to make several key changes to the bill to address the issue of inflation. Those changes, however, bore little resemblance to what Galbraith had urged. Rather than instituting wage and price controls, the substitute bill weakened its unemployment measures by excluding teenage workers from the calculation of its 3 percent unemployment goal and stipulating that "last resort" jobs funded by the federal government would be primarily low-paying.[32]

Early the following year, testifying before the Employment Opportunities Subcommittee on behalf of the ADA, Shull urged the committee to scrap the recent changes to the bill on youth employment and public jobs. In his lengthy testimony, he avoided the divisive issue of inflation altogether and called for a full employment bill that largely resembled the original version introduced by Humphrey and Hawkins. More willing to wade into the debate over inflation in private, Shull followed up his testimony with a letter to Humphrey in which he shared the ADA's disapproval of an approach that scaled back full employment measures to guard against the threat of inflation. Shull's letter made clear that he and the ADA were not oblivious to the danger and hardships of inflation, but their proposed solution of including standby wage and price controls in the bill showed that they did not have an answer that was achievable in the existing political context.[33]

As the ADA pushed for a politically unlikely return to the original measures of the bill, the Carter administration moved ahead with plans for passage of legislation that would be little more than Humphrey–Hawkins in name only. Like all of the other major candidates in the 1976 Democratic primaries, Carter had offered vague support for the goals of Humphrey–Hawkins. Once in the White House, the former Georgia governor found that he could not afford to alienate the broad coalition assembled by the FEAC. Carter, however, was an instinctual fiscal conservative and shared the prevailing view among his middle-class voters that inflation posed a greater threat to the nation's economy than unemployment. With the Carter administration cynically co-opting Humphrey–Hawkins, congressional committees and individual members of Congress introduced myriad amendments intended to hollow out the bill's original goal of guaranteeing the right of every American to a decently paid job.[34]

Still, the ADA and the broader FEAC coalition had little choice but to continue to push for the legislation they had been championing for years. When the FEAC launched a nationwide grassroots mobilization for the bill called Full Employment Week during the week of Labor Day in 1977, the ADA encouraged its chapters to make the initiative their highest priority. Later that year, the ADA executive committee feebly took the position that the legislation was worthy of support but that it should be substantially strengthened. The following summer, the FEAC insisted that the final push was "on to pass Humphrey–Hawkins without gutting amendments," despite the evisceration of the bill that had already occurred.[35]

Unsurprisingly, the bill that Carter signed into law on October 27, 1978, bore little resemblance to the legislation initially introduced by Humphrey and Hawkins. Instead of establishing a right to employment and compelling the federal government to act as an employer of last resort to make up for shortfalls in private employment, the Full Employment and Balanced Growth Act of 1978 established an unenforceable goal of reducing unemployment to 4 percent by 1983 rather than 1980 and did little more than require the president to recommend policies toward that end. Further disappointing the ADA and other liberal backers of Humphrey–Hawkins, the law established a goal of reducing inflation to 3 percent by 1983 that largely derailed the original purpose for the legislation by institutionalizing the widely presumed trade-off between full employment and inflation. At the muted signing ceremony for a piece of legislation that he had never genuinely supported, Carter focused most of his attention on inflation.[36] In the weeks and months that followed, the ADA remained virtually silent on what had been its central legislative priority for years. Still, despite its failure to win substantive full employment legislation, the revived liberal–labor coalition that took shape amid the struggle for Humphrey–Hawkins would come to play a central role in the 1980 presidential election as Carter's popular support plummeted.

TED KENNEDY AND THE NEW POLITICS IN 1980

When delegates gathered at the Mayflower Hotel in Washington, DC, for the 1979 ADA national convention, there was little chance they would be voting to support Jimmy Carter's reelection. The key questions were how far they would go in their rhetoric against the increasingly unpopular president and whether they would join the nascent effort to call on Massachusetts senator Ted Kennedy to challenge Carter for the Democratic nomination for president in 1980. On its final day, the convention overwhelmingly passed a resolution that condemned the "broken promises and abandoned principles" of the Carter administration and committed the organization to trying to "create an irresistible national mandate" for Kennedy to seek the presidency. As the largest and most influential organization to formally endorse the "Draft Kennedy" drive, the ADA played a key role in convincing Kennedy that he should run and helped to make possible a campaign that drew much of its energy and support from the renewed liberal–labor coalition that had coalesced around the push for Humphrey–Hawkins.[37] After an unsuccessful start aimed more at independent voters in the general election than Democratic voters in the primaries, Kennedy pivoted to the left and began to pose a serious challenge. Although it did not prevail in the uphill battle to deny an incumbent president his party's nomination, the Kennedy campaign revealed that an embrace of the New Politics which maintained its social democratic impulses could garner a significant degree of popular support.[38]

Incumbent US presidents seeking reelection rarely face significant challenges in winning their party's nomination, but few presidents have alienated their political base as severely as Carter had by the late 1970s. The year after eviscerating Humphrey–Hawkins in 1978, Carter nominated Paul Volcker for the chairmanship of the Federal Reserve. Once at the helm of the Fed, Volcker prioritized the struggle against inflation above all other concerns and sought to rein in consumer prices through radically aggressive interest rate hikes and management of the money supply. For his part, Carter spurned even the pretense of the full employment policy called for in the version of Humphrey–Hawkins he signed into law and sought to tackle inflation through fiscal austerity and balanced budgets. Outraged liberals charged Carter with deploying the conservative Republican playbook to address the nation's economic woes.[39]

Leading the liberal charge against the conservative direction of the Carter administration, the ADA began mounting critiques of the former Georgia governor early in his tenure in the White House. In May 1977, Joseph Rauh, Leon Shull, and other ADA leaders met with Vice President Walter Mondale in the White House to warn him that liberals would not hold back against the president if he kept failing to live up to his campaign promises. The day after the White House meeting, George McGovern—who became ADA president in 1976 after the position of national chairman had been renamed—took aim at the fiscal conservatism of the Carter administration at the ADA's national convention. Reflecting on Carter's election victory over

Republican president Gerald Ford, McGovern remarked that "it sometimes seems difficult to remember who won last fall" and slammed the administration's efforts to "balance the federal budget on the backs of the poor, the hungry, and the jobless."[40] By the following spring, Schlesinger privately declared that Carter was "beyond redemption," lamenting: "People do not change at Carter's age, and I don't think we can count on his being thrice-born. I think we must begin to think about some alternative in 1980."[41]

Liberals and union leaders became more serious about and focused in their desire for a Democratic challenger to Carter following the 1978 midterm Democratic convention in Memphis. Among the reforms produced by the McGovern–Fraser commission in the early 1970s, the midterm Democratic "mini-conventions" were intended, in part, to provide a forum for holding a Democratic president accountable to the platform passed at the last national convention. Kennedy sought both to fulfill that aim for the midterm convention and to boost his own political stock when he took the podium in Memphis. In a fiery speech, he insisted, "We cannot accept a policy that cuts spending to the bone in areas like jobs and health, but allows billions of dollars in wasteful spending for tax subsidies to continue and adds even greater fat and waste through inflationary spending for defense."[42] The day after Kennedy's rousing speech, Carter's surrogates at the convention narrowly defeated a resolution calling for significant increases in social spending. The dissent at the convention and the close margins by which the sitting Democratic president managed to head it off signaled to several activists the weakness of the president and the opportunity that existed to challenge his renomination. Among those activists, William Winpisinger, president of the International Association of Machinists; Michael Harrington, still a member of the ADA national board and chairman of the recently established Democratic Socialist Organizing Committee; and Leon Shull were further heartened by the growing opposition to Carter in the party. Winpisinger, Harrington, and Shull believed that a split with the president over bread-and-butter spending issues rather than issues they saw as social and cultural such as abortion, affirmative action, or mandatory busing provided a strong basis for building on the recently renewed liberal–labor coalition. Following the Memphis midterm convention, they worked together informally for a Kennedy candidacy.[43]

When the ADA gathered for its national convention the following June, the Carter administration deemed the situation serious enough and the

ADA significant enough that it dispatched an envoy to the gathering. Carter's chief domestic adviser, Stuart Eizenstat, warned the delegates that "a few of the people, perhaps in this room, felt Hubert Humphrey was not pure enough. And they fought him every step of the way ... and they elected Richard Nixon."[44] Eizenstat's warning had little impact on Arthur Schlesinger Jr. When his turn at the podium came, he quipped: "The Democratic national chairman tells us that if we oppose Carter's renomination we will elect a Republican president. That is no great threat. The fact is that we elected a Republican president in 1976."[45] In the end, ADA delegates voted overwhelmingly to join the Draft Kennedy movement but left the door open for supporting Carter should he win the Democratic nomination by striking from the resolution the inflammatory assertion that he was a "one-way ticket to defeat and a trip to a party bankrupt of principles and devoid of officeholders in 1980." While ADA liberals clearly wanted Kennedy to be the Democratic nominee, they did not necessarily want to leave Carter so politically damaged in the process that they could not endorse him later as the lesser of two evils.[46]

In the months that followed the ADA national convention, support for a Kennedy candidacy grew rapidly with the establishment of Draft Kennedy committees in thirty states. With polls giving Kennedy a two-to-one advantage over Carter among Democratic voters during the summer and early fall of 1979, the Massachusetts senator set his sights on the general election and stressed the need for stronger leadership in the White House rather than citing specific issues when he formally announced his candidacy in November. Still, despite Kennedy's efforts to downplay ideology and his liberal voting record as a senator, the campaign team that he put together drew heavily from the New Politics movement in general and the presidential campaign of George McGovern in particular. Kennedy campaign co-chair Gerard Doherty had strong links to the venerable New Politics group the New Democratic Coalition. McGovern speechwriter Robert Shrum and Rick Stearnes, who had been the McGovern campaign's expert on delegate reform, filled key positions in the Kennedy campaign.[47]

The rollout of the campaign did not go as Kennedy and his staffers had hoped. Three days before Kennedy formally declared his candidacy at Faneuil Hall in Boston, Iranian students in Tehran took fifty-two American diplomats hostage at the US Embassy. The day before Christmas, the Soviet Union invaded Afghanistan. Amid twin foreign policy crises, huge numbers of Americans rallied behind the president, and Kennedy found his opportunities to attack Carter on foreign policy greatly limited. In the wake of a two-to-one defeat in the Iowa caucuses, the first contest of the primaries, Kennedy pivoted to the left in an effort to provide a rationale for his candidacy and reverse his fortunes. Before a cheering crowd at Georgetown University, Kennedy effectively re-launched his campaign with a speech that positioned him as the liberal alternative to Carter. Summoning an energy that he had thus far failed to display on the campaign trail, Kennedy criticized Carter's "helter-skelter militarism" and passionately called for federal action to tackle unemployment, the immediate establishment of gasoline rationing, and wage and price controls to address inflation.[48]

As the Massachusetts senator found his footing in the campaign after the re-launch of his bid for the presidency at Georgetown, the youngest and last surviving of the Kennedy brothers assembled an impressive coalition that drew from both organized labor and the New Politics. While charisma, personality, and the legacy of the Kennedy family helped him appeal to seemingly disparate constituencies, the success of his campaign in bridging the once significant gulf between organized labor and the New Politics owed much to the renewed liberal–labor coalition that had taken shape around the fight for Humphrey–Hawkins during the preceding years.[49] Winpisinger and the International Association of Machinists had been at the forefront of the effort to draft Kennedy and devoted substantial resources to his campaign after he declared. Taking considerable risk in bucking a sitting Democratic president, the United Auto Workers and fourteen other unions also threw their weight behind Kennedy.[50] On the New Politics front, Kennedy won support from gay rights activists and environmentalists. Despite scrambling his initial campaign plans, the Soviet invasion of Afghanistan and Carter's decision to reactivate the Selective Service System enabled Kennedy to cultivate the peace constituency that had been central to the New Politics movement in the late 1960s and early 1970s. By voicing his opposition to the resumption of draft registration, Kennedy was able to win sizable support on college campuses.[51] The last time an incumbent Democratic president faced an insurgent challenge in the primaries in 1968, the unions and student activists had been on distinctly opposing sides. In 1980, significant numbers of unionized workers and students joined together on behalf of Kennedy's campaign.

The coalition that Kennedy forged during the primaries momentarily pushed Carter toward the edge of defeat but ultimately fell short in the daunting task of denying an incumbent president the party's nomination for reelection. Drawing on the votes of the financially vulnerable and disaffected, Kennedy gained momentum in the later stages of the primaries, closing them out with big wins in California and New Jersey. When all the votes were counted, Kennedy came away with around 37 percent of the delegates up for grabs and finished within two points of depriving Carter of the majority he needed to secure the nomination before the convention. Stressing the enduring shadow of the Chappaquiddick incident and the boosts that Carter gained from events in Iran and Afghanistan, the historian Timothy Stanley argues that historical accident played a significant role in denying Kennedy the Democratic nomination and that his loss should not be seen as evidence that by 1980, liberalism no longer brought voters out to the ballot box.[52]

Still, the mitigating factors for Kennedy's loss against Carter did not change the predicament the ADA found itself in as the November election approached. In September, Rauh and Schlesinger wrote to their fellow ADA national board members and implored them not to endorse Carter. Citing his record and the scathing criticism the organization had launched at him for years, they insisted that endorsing the president would "demonstrate that we never really meant what we said about him these past four years and give final validation to the public perception of ADA as part and parcel of the Democratic Party ready to endorse anyone running on the Democratic ticket."[53] After an acrimonious debate, the ADA national board rejected the advice of its two veteran members and voted 72 to 54 to endorse Carter. The tepid resolution passed by the board had relatively little to say in praise of Carter and focused primarily on the dangers of electing Republican Ronald Reagan.[54] It also led Rauh to resign angrily from the organization he had helped to found in 1947.[55]

DEBATING THE "REAGAN REVOLUTION"

No one could deny the scale of Republican victory and Democratic defeat in the 1980 election. Ronald Reagan prevailed over Jimmy Carter to win the White House with a landslide margin of nearly ten points in the popular vote and 489–49 in the Electoral College. Republicans won control of the Senate for the first time since 1952 and defeated an array of venerable liberal senators that included Frank Church, Warren Magnuson, George McGovern, and Gaylord Nelson. What those results meant, however, was very much up for debate. Offering a blunt assessment of the electoral wreckage the day after the vote, Paul Tsongas told reporters, "The New Deal died yesterday." Gary Hart opined that "traditional liberalism" was no longer "marketable."[56] In contrast, Arthur Schlesinger Jr. saw the election not as a rejection of liberalism but as a repudiation of Carter's failed presidency and "the miserable result of the conservative economic policies of the last half dozen years."[57]

Journalists and historians have frequently labeled the 1980 election and the conservative turn in American politics ushered in by Reagan's presidency the "Reagan Revolution."[58] Still, in the immediate aftermath of the election it was not at all certain that a political realignment had occurred or was taking place. The ways in which liberals of different stripes interpreted the Republican wins and Democratic losses of 1980 played a central role in reinforcing their existing political tendencies and determining the course they believed liberalism needed to take to remain a viable ideology in the 1980s. Despite devoting more attention to pressing issues like the energy crisis and international economic competition, Schlesinger and other ADA liberals largely stayed the course in pushing an unrepentant liberalism in the wake of the election. For the Watergate babies and other Democrats who had been distancing themselves from economic progressivism since the mid-1970s, the election underscored the need to rethink liberalism fundamentally in order to adapt the ideology to the realities and circumstances of the 1980s.

Many of the liberals who understood the 1980 election as a rejection of Carter and his failed economic policies had seen the contest between Carter and Reagan as a choice between two conservatives. Some of those liberals chose not to make that choice and backed John Anderson's independent bid for the presidency. As a Republican congressman from Illinois, Anderson remained fiscally conservative but became more socially liberal over the course of the 1970s. After determining that he could not win the presidential nomination of an increasingly conservative Republican Party, he dropped out of the Republican primaries and launched an independent campaign that drew support from almost one quarter of the electorate in the summer of 1980. Aiming to win over Kennedy's supporters after Carter clinched the Democratic nomination, Anderson further embraced liberal positions with vocal endorsements of abortion rights and the Equal Rights Amendment as well as opposition to nuclear power and the draft. Anderson's pick of former

Wisconsin governor Patrick Lucey—a liberal Democrat in the New Politics mold—as his running mate rounded out his campaign's bid for liberal backing.[59] Even before he quit the Republican primaries and declared as an independent, Anderson discerned that suburban liberals and college students would be the core of his campaign and his main base of support. Tellingly, he made a pitch to those very constituencies with a speech to the Brookline, Massachusetts, chapter of the ADA not long before launching his independent campaign.[60]

While considerable hostility to Anderson could be found in the ADA, and its national board voted to endorse Carter in the run-up to the November election, Arthur Schlesinger Jr. and Joseph Rauh threw their weight behind Anderson's independent candidacy. Both lifelong Democrats, Schlesinger and Rauh felt a pressing need to justify their support for the former Republican congressman. In his regular column in the *Wall Street Journal*, Schlesinger explained that he did "not find it easy to abandon lifetime habits of Democratic regularity," but in an election between a "real Republican nominated by the Republicans" and a "a crypto-Republican nominated by the Democrats," Anderson was "the only one of the three candidates with a Rooseveltian belief in affirmative government." Writing in the *Washington Star*, Rauh justified endorsing Anderson on the grounds that Carter had abandoned the Democratic Party and its policies. Echoing Schlesinger, Rauh noted that "though still a cautious man with a dollar—too tight-fisted for me—John Anderson has a deep belief in affirmative government." Furthermore, Rauh saw Anderson as the best bet to bring out the young people and independents whose votes would be necessary to save the seats of Church, McGovern, Nelson, and other liberals in the Senate.[61]

Schlesinger and Rauh also tried to assuage liberal concerns that voting for Anderson would help put Reagan in the White House by stressing that the negative consequences of a victory for the former California governor would not be enduring. Schlesinger pushed back against the influential argument among liberals that a vote for Carter was necessary to save the Supreme Court. Expressing a complacency that appears shocking in hindsight, he contended that "the basic issues about the reach of federal power have long since been resolved" and that a Senate Judiciary Committee led by Ted Kennedy and Birch Bayh would be "as capable of stopping bad appointments as it was when Mr. Nixon came up with Judges Haynsworth and Carswell." Similarly, Rauh believed that the federal judiciary had come to accept the federal power that had been challenged during the New Deal era and charged that "the view that a Reagan court would, for years into the future, block the historically overdue liberal upsurge" was "more fright than substance."[62]

The perspective that led Schlesinger to endorse Anderson also shaped his understanding of what the results of the 1980 election meant. Writing in the weeks after the election, Schlesinger swatted away the notion that the electorate had voted against liberalism, retorting, "Liberal policies haven't prevailed in Washington since 1966, when Lyndon Johnson decided to sacrifice the Great Society to the Vietnam War." Careful to guard against charges that he was mired in the past and beholden to a static conception of liberalism, he noted that "commanding domestic issues of our time— chronic inflation and the passing of the age of low-cost energy—are novel issues and demand novel remedies." Still, Schlesinger provided decidedly few specifics on what these remedies might look like, and his basic insistence on "affirmative government" as the answer suggested that any changes to his vision for liberalism amounted to little more than window dressing.[63]

While the last time the Democrats lost both the White House and Senate, in 1952, had led him to rethink liberal principles and advance the ideas of what became qualitative liberalism in hopes of Democratic electoral salvation, the aging Schlesinger undertook no serious political introspection in 1980. As a result, his understanding of the election changed little when he returned to its meaning more than two years later. Putting it bluntly, Schlesinger maintained that "the voters turned to Reagan in 1980 not because they wished to give laissez-faire an ideological license, but because they could not abide the thought of four more years of Jimmy Carter. And, whatever else Carter may have been, he was hardly a New Deal advocate of affirmative government." For Schlesinger, Carter's lack of any kind of New Deal bona fides rendered ridiculous the claim made by Tsongas and others that the election represented the death of the New Deal.[64]

Though his interpretation of the 1980 election was in many ways diametrically opposed to that of Schlesinger, Tsongas's reading also changed little in the years that followed his initial assessment. The day after the election, he had bluntly pronounced the New Deal dead.[65] The following year Tsongas published a book titled *The Road from Here*, which further developed his view that the New Deal had run dry intellectually and electorally. He began writing his treatise on "liberalism and realities in the 1980s" on the back of his highly publicized speech at the 1980 ADA national convention, which stressed the need for liberalism to adapt to new circumstances or perish in irrelevance.⁶⁶

Tsongas conceived of his book, like his ADA speech, as a warning for fellow liberals, and for the Massachusetts senator, the 1980 election confirmed the urgency of that warning. The election had brought the conservative wing of the Republican Party into power and ended "the fifty-year legacy of Franklin Delano Roosevelt." With no mention of Carter's conservatism or unpopularity, he concluded that "the demise of Democratic Party rule was due to one basic fact: reality does not bend to fit political theory. Much of the thrust of the 1980 Democratic platform reflected the realities of the 1930s and 1960s, not those of the decade ahead." While Schlesinger rejected the idea that liberalism had even been an option for voters to reject in 1980, Tsongas saw the election as one in which "the country decided to replace liberals with conservatives" and insisted that the task for liberals was to "understand that voters felt threatened by events and situations, and they voted accordingly." This meant that Tsongas, unlike Schlesinger, stressed the need for a fundamental rethinking of liberal assumptions and positions.⁶⁷

The 1980 election also made a distinct impression on Gary Hart, though for more immediate reasons. While Tsongas did not face the voters in 1980, Hart was up for reelection and regularly featured on lists of endangered Democratic senators with the likes of Church, McGovern, and Nelson. Facing a tough challenge in the growing state of Colorado, Hart didn't just try to redefine what it meant to be a liberal; he tried to distance himself from the label altogether. During the campaign, he stressed that while he had been McGovern's campaign manager, he had never agreed with all of the presidential candidate's views. Hart also sometimes attacked his conservative Republican opponent from the right, particularly on defense issues. Hart had run for his Senate seat in 1974 promising to push for cuts in the military budget. In 1980 he insisted that he would support increases in defense spending if it would produce improvements to the nation's security. Hart's rightward shift on defense issues attracted the attention of the conservative columnist Jeffrey Hart, no relation, who produced a blurb for the senator's campaign literature declaring that while "he first achieved national notice as George McGovern's campaign manager, the young senator is anything but a 1960s style New Left anti-American. He is informed, analytical, and he is worried about the state of our forces."⁶⁸ When the votes were tallied, the liberal stalwarts on the list of endangered Democratic senators lost their seats while Hart retained his. The nature of Hart's electoral survival was not lost on him as he and other young Democrats keen to challenge liberal dogmas moved to the center of the political stage in the coming years.[69]

THE RISE OF DEMOCRATIC NEOLIBERALISM

As Ronald Reagan settled into the White House, the Watergate babies and other like-minded young Democrats found a reeling Democratic Party receptive to their ideas and a political press interested in their prospects. Increasingly dubbed "Atari Democrats" or neoliberals, these young Democrats continued to develop their ideas as they sought to bring greater coherence to their vision for a pragmatic liberalism attuned to the challenges and realities of the 1980s. Aiming both to chart what they saw as a sustainable path for liberalism and advance their political careers, Paul Tsongas and Gary Hart wrote books laying out their vision for neoliberalism. Meanwhile, Charles Peters's *Washington Monthly* became the foremost outlet for neoliberal writers. While neoliberal politicians and writers differed in many of the particulars of their proposals, they shared an insistence that despite their skepticism toward the feasibility of traditional liberal means, they remained fully committed to liberal ends. According to Peters, neoliberals recognized "that there were a lot of things wrong with a lot of the Big Government solutions we tried but there was never anything wrong with the ends we were seeking—justice, fair play, and liberal ideals."[70] Still, in the immediate aftermath of Reagan's election it was not clear that neoliberalism would win out as the prevailing form of liberalism with roots in the New Politics. The ongoing renewal of the liberal–labor coalition offered a path for the New Politics at odds with the combination of social liberalism and economic conservatism championed by neoliberals.

The prospects for a legacy of the New Politics that maintained its economic progressivism benefited from changes in leadership at the highest ranks of organized labor in the late 1970s. The growing cooperation between organized labor and New Politics forces seen during the mid-1970s with the push for Humphrey–Hawkins picked up steam with the end of George Meany's almost quarter-century reign as president of the AFL-CIO in 1979 and Lane Kirkland's succession to the top post in US organized labor. Meany had staunchly supported the Vietnam War, refused to throw the AFL-CIO's weight behind George McGovern's 1972 presidential campaign despite the South Dakota senator's sterling voting record on labor issues, and viscerally opposed the New Politics forces in the Democratic Party. While Kirkland had been Meany's lieutenant and anointed successor, he was willing—unlike his predecessor—to join with New Politics forces to try to arrest the decline of organized labor.[71]

Kirkland's willingness to work with New Politics groups and figures was put on vivid display when the AFL-CIO organized a Solidarity Day rally in Washington, DC, in September 1981 to protest the policies of the Reagan administration, a demonstration that attracted around 260,000 people. Speakers at the rally included figures with ties to the New Politics who had been involved in the struggle for Humphrey–Hawkins such as Eleanor Smeal, president of NOW, and Coretta Scott King, president of the Martin Luther King Jr. Center for Social Change. The crowd of over a quarter-million people featured, according to the *Washington Post*, "burly machinists and mine workers in T-shirts, nylon windbreakers and baseball caps" standing "side-by-side with antinuclear activists, gay rights advocates and thousands of municipal workers." Political columnist David Broder opined that Kirkland had managed to "put the oft-scorned labor movement, and himself at its head, out front of what might become the most powerful grass-roots progressive coalition since the civil rights and anti-Vietnam war days."[72]

Instead of becoming a launching pad for a powerful progressive coalition that maintained the economic progressivism of the New Politics, Solidarity Day became largely forgotten despite being one of the largest mass protests organized in the nation's capital up to that point.[73] Deindustrialization, declining membership, and the rise of right-wing anti-labor attacks in the 1980s combined to put organized labor on the defensive and made it less able or willing to undertake new initiatives and expend resources on forging new coalitions. As organized labor retreated into a defensive posture, the Democratic establishment increasingly saw unions as relics or special interests and looked to the neoliberal "Atari Democrats" for the new ideas that would bring the party electoral salvation.

With Democratic insiders hungry for fresh ideas and the 1984 election looming on the horizon, Tsongas and Hart laid out in their books their comprehensive visions for a reformed liberalism that they believed would be necessary to meet the electoral and economic challenges of the late twentieth century. Tsongas's book, *The Road from Here*, which featured the telling subtitle *Liberalism and Realities in the 1980s*, grew out of his 1980 keynote speech before the ADA national convention. In his address he insisted that the existing form of liberalism, with its myopic commitment to government as the answer to society's challenges, offered little hope of addressing the problems of international competitiveness, rising energy costs, limited resources, and other pressing issues that would define the decade's political agenda.[74] Unsurprisingly, Tsongas received a cool response from his audience. Speaking to reporters afterwards, he offered a more pointed articulation of his views when he deemed government to have a "deadening impact" and derided the "Johnson–Humphrey Great Society approach" to politics and governance. Traditional liberals, Tsongas asserted, were "mired in yesterday's truisms. Listening to them is like going to an old movie."[75]

Tsongas's intentionally provocative speech to the country's foremost liberal organization received significant attention and produced a variety of strong responses. The *New York Times* ran an article that paraphrased the speech, and David Broder's discussion of it in his syndicated column appeared in forty-four newspapers. Interestingly, as Tsongas detailed in his own book, conservatives such as former defense secretary James Schlesinger and Republican senators Richard Lugar, James McClure, and Alan Simpson offered words of praise for the speech.[76] In contrast, Leon Shull responded to Tsongas's speech and his remarks to the press with the simple insistence that "the essence of liberalism is the use of government to intervene on behalf of people." Shull readily admitted that liberalism needed to change to meet the challenges of new issues and circumstances but also made clear his concern that neoliberals like Tsongas were losing sight of the basic commitment to the underprivileged that had long served as the guiding principle for liberals. "To say these are old battles," Shull contended, "is not an excuse to stop fighting them."[77] Schlesinger fired off a snarky letter to Tsongas asking him to provide an example of "some remedies for inflation, unemployment and the energy stringency that do not call on affirmative government and intelligent public purpose." After several more letters to Tsongas but no response, Schlesinger scolded the Massachusetts senator, "Your refusal to offer even the courtesy of acknowledgment leaves the inevitable conclusion that your neo-liberalism is so empty that you have nothing at all to say in explanation of it." He then relayed the details of his attempted correspondence to the readers of his *Wall Street Journal* column.[78]

In reaction to criticism that the vision of neoliberalism offered in his ADA speech was hollow, Tsongas set out to write a book that would offer a constructive and detailed take on his political outlook. While he had already written two hundred pages of his book before returns in the 1980 election came in, the eventual results served to reinforce rather than challenge his conviction that liberalism was in trouble and needed to change dramatically to address contemporary problems and remain politically viable. Organizing his book around "new realities" such as the energy crisis, international trade, the environment, and inflation, Tsongas sought to distinguish his vision from both Reagan's free market fundamentalism and the "big government" approach of "traditional" liberalism. Like many of his fellow Watergate babies, Tsongas projected himself and his political vision as non-ideological or even anti-ideological. Paradoxically, Tsongas insisted in the preface of the book that his effort to redefine the ideology of liberalism was not an ideological project but instead simply an effort to apply "realism—non-ideological, clear-eyed realism."[79]

Tsongas attempted to apply his pragmatic perspective to a wide range of issues in *The Road From Here*, but the heart of the book could be found in its assessment of the country's economic malaise and its prescriptions for rebuilding the US economy. To foster the growth and productivity needed for an economic rebound, Tsongas looked to Japan—with its recent track record of explosive economic growth and example of state-directed capitalism—as a model. Some aspects of Tsongas's modified "Japan, Inc." model involved greater government intervention in the economy, such as the development of an industrial policy that would bring more planning and coherence to the efforts of US companies to compete internationally. Other aspects of his repurposing of Japanese economic policies entailed less government involvement in the economy and called into question some of the basic architecture of the New Deal. For example, Tsongas argued that while the Glass–Steagall Act—which prevented US banks from risking Americans' savings by investing in commercial enterprises—had made sense in the context of the Great Depression, it hampered US competitiveness in international markets in the 1980s. To make his case, Tsongas cited the example of a Japanese entrepreneur who could join forces with a Japanese bank with overseas branches and an export trading company to sell his product in foreign markets. This sort of arrangement, he noted, would be impossible in the United States because Glass–Steagall prevented banks with valuable international outreach experience from using most of their assets to assist American entrepreneurs trying to do business abroad. Throughout his ideas on adapting Japanese economic policies to US circumstances and his broader economic vision, Tsongas wove an emphasis on the importance of high technology for the future of the American economy. For Tsongas, the growth of high-tech companies in the Route 128 corridor around Boston in the decades after World War II showed the way out of the economic malaise of the 1970s.[80]

From latching onto Japanese economic policies to championing entrepreneurship and the high-tech industry, Gary Hart's book *A New Democracy* touched on many of the same themes as Tsongas's volume. Though it avoided explicit discussion of liberalism—the New Deal and the Great Society go unmentioned in its pages—and was more clearly a justification for a presidential campaign, Hart's book also sought to revive Democratic electoral prospects by redefining liberalism. Like Tsongas, Hart placed the need for economic recovery at the center of that project. For instance, he looked to the role played by the Bank of Japan in pouring huge sums of money into leading Japanese companies and proposed that similar results could be achieved in the United States if laws governing the investments made by public pension funds were loosened so that some of the enormous assets held in those funds could be invested in potentially dynamic smaller firms. Throughout *A New Democracy*, he connected Japan-inspired economic and industrial policies to the needs of entrepreneurs and the importance of their dynamism in an otherwise largely stagnant American economy. Hart differed from Tsongas on entrepreneurship only in his even more enthusiastic embrace of what would later become known as "startups" and rewarding those who take risks in pursuing business opportunities. Instead of Route 128 companies, he celebrated the Silicon Valley "high fliers" of Apple Computer and Atari, which had given rise to the label "Atari Democrats" in the first place.[81]

Hart did, however, distinguish himself from Tsongas and many other neoliberals of the period with his detailed attention to issues of national security and military preparedness. Having applied for and received a US Naval Reserve commission in what was at least partly an effort to bolster his presidential prospects, Hart devoted half of his book to national security issues, which he analyzed at times on a granular level. A chapter that opens with the insistence that the US Navy needed far more—though smaller—ships to counter Soviet naval power encapsulates much of Hart's approach to military reform. In this chapter, he sought to offer some appeal to peace-oriented voters with his criticism of the B-1 bomber project and expensive aircraft carriers, and his rejection of the "bigger is better" mentality that had long prevailed in national security. Still, his very insistence that the national security debate should not be about the size of the military or its budget but rather its effectiveness precluded the kind of demand to slash defense spending and "reorder national priorities" that had been integral to the foreign policy outlook of the New Politics movement in the late 1960s and early 1970s.[82]

During the same years when Tsongas and Hart emerged among the most visible and influential neoliberal Democratic politicians, Charles Peters established the *Washington Monthly* as the go-to outlet for neoliberal writers. Like Tsongas, Peters had served in the Peace Corps. Peters's experience in the Evaluation Division of the Peace Corps, examining the operations of a government agency from top to bottom and determining why programs succeeded or failed, informed the basic outlook that he brought to the *Washington Monthly* as its editor in chief. Peters wanted his new magazine to cover politics, government, and the world similarly to the way the Evaluation Division analyzed the Peace Crops: by emphasizing institutional dynamics and results. Staffed primarily by veterans of the Peace Corps, the *Washington Monthly* started publishing in 1969. The Vietnam War was a constant presence in the magazine during its early years.[83]

By the mid-to-late 1970s, the importance of entrepreneurship became a kind of rallying cry for the *Washington Monthly*. After the magazine survived a Chapter 11 bankruptcy proceeding in 1972, entrepreneurship became, in Peters's own words, "practically a religion" with him. He saw it as the key to overcoming economic stagnation and was troubled by the scorn that liberals tended to heap on it. From Peters's perspective, most liberals "thought of the businessman as a Babbitt at best and a cruel exploiter at worst." Increasingly, he saw the *Washington Monthly* as a means for convincing liberals that without the jobs and wealth produced by businessmen, it would be impossible to finance the social programs they believed in. In response to accusations from liberals that Peters and his stable of writers at the magazine were little more than neoconservatives, the *Washington Monthly* editor coined the term "neoliberal" to distinguish their politics from both neoconservatism and what he called "traditional" liberalism.[84]

While Peters later wished he had come up with a more accessible label, "neoliberal" stuck and came to be used regularly in the press to describe him and politicians like Tsongas and Hart.[85] Resigning himself to the term, Peters wrote "A Neo-Liberal's Manifesto," which ran in the *Washington Post* in 1982 and succinctly laid out his political vision for an audience that reached far beyond the readership of the *Washington Monthly*. In the manifesto, he explained that "if neo-conservatives are liberals who took a critical look at liberalism and decided to become conservatives, we are liberals who took the same look and decided to retain our goals but to abandon some of our prejudices." For Peters, those prejudices included liberals' automatic support for unions and government social programs along with their blanket opposition to the military and big business. Emphasizing the importance of economic growth for liberal goals, he bluntly declared, "Our hero is the risk-taking entrepreneur who creates new jobs and better products."[86]

Still, Peters was keen to distinguish neoliberal championing of entrepreneurship from Republican free market fundamentalism. He argued that neoliberals want to encourage entrepreneurship "not with Reaganite policies that simply make the rich richer" but with legislation that helps attract investment and an educational system that fosters creativity and high-tech endeavors. Peters looked to education policy, in particular, as a key example of how neoliberals differed from "traditional" liberals. Contrasting the knee-jerk support for organized labor that he saw among "traditional" liberals with neoliberals' "criticism of white-collar unions for their resistance to performance standards," Peters stressed the need for greater accountability among public school teachers. In his estimation, "public schools have to be made better, much better, if we are to compete economically with other technologically advanced countries, if we are to have more Route 128s and Silicon Valleys."[87]

Hart and Tsongas shared Peters's insistence that while the means they proposed—particularly those in the economic realm—differed in many ways from those offered by "traditional" liberals, they remained committed to the ends that had long defined American liberalism. Both senators firmly believed that liberals and Democrats needed to prove that they were serious about regaining US economic competitiveness in order to maintain the viability of the liberal goal of social justice. Hart insisted at the outset of *A New Democracy* that if the country was to maintain its traditional commitment to social justice, Americans had to "find *new* ways to realize them."[88] In *The Road from Here*, Tsongas rejected the assertion that his economic views meant that he had become a conservative and underscored his "unbending views on social issues" such as capital punishment, gay rights, and civil rights. The Massachusetts senator insisted that his acceptance of the "critical role in our collective well-being" played by the business community had helped to gain their tolerance of his "social liberalism" and made it more politically viable.[89] Months after his speech at the 1980 ADA national convention urging liberals to embrace a greater role for the free market, Tsongas became the first senator in history to propose a law securing gay rights when he introduced a bill to prevent employment discrimination on the basis of sexual orientation.[90] Still, as much as neoliberals like Peters, Hart, and Tsongas insisted on their liberal bona fides, veteran ADA liberals remained unconvinced that a commitment to social liberalism alone made one a liberal or that neoliberal means were adequate to achieve liberal ends.

DEMOCRATIC NEOLIBERALISM AND ITS COMPLICIT CRITICS

The intensity of the criticism lobbed at neoliberal Democrats by the ADA and its veteran figures grew alongside the continued growth of power and influence wielded by neoliberals in the Democratic Party. In the years following the 1980 election, neoliberals expanded their numbers and influence among congressional Democrats. In 1984 Gary Hart came up just short of winning the Democratic presidential nomination. Unsurprisingly, veteran ADAers such as Arthur Schlesinger Jr. were not impressed with the changing winds in the Democratic Party. In 1986 Schlesinger described neoliberal Atari Democrats as "Me-Too" Reaganites.[91] The increasingly strident criticism of Schlesinger and other like-minded liberals toward neoliberal Democrats did little to stem the neoliberal tide in the party. Four years after Hart's near miss for the party nomination, Michael Dukakis—a Watergate baby and prototypical technocratic neoliberal who ran on the issue of "competency"—became the Democratic nominee for president. With no viable political alternative available, the ADA and its veteran figures ultimately got behind Dukakis's bid for the presidency, but they remained ever critical of the Democratic Party's neoliberal turn.[92] Still, for all their avowed hostility to Democratic neoliberalism, the path to the synthesis of economic conservatism with liberal social and cultural values advanced by neoliberals during the 1980s can be traced back to ideas long advanced by veteran ADA intellectuals.

The debate between ADA liberals and neoliberals that played out in the pages of books, magazines, and newspapers reached a much wider audience when it became a significant element in the 1984 Democratic primaries. The two candidates who won the most delegates in the primaries crystallized much of what had distinguished neoliberals from ADA liberals and other economic progressives over the preceding years. Hart came in a close second, running an antiestablishment campaign rooted in the neoliberal agenda he had laid out in *A New Democracy* and winning the support of younger New Class voters, who in the 1980s were increasingly dubbed young urban professionals or "yuppies." Walter Mondale—a longtime protégé of Hubert Humphrey with close ties to organized labor—clinched the nomination by cobbling together what remained of the New Deal–Great Society coalition. During a televised debate, Mondale echoed Schlesinger's earlier criticism of Tsongas's ideas as empty when he famously responded to Hart's talk of "new ideas" by quoting the then-ubiquitous Wendy's slogan "Where's the beef?"[93] Prior to winning the Democratic nomination, Mondale received the endorsement of the ADA on the basis of his longtime connections to the organization and his perceived electability.[94]

While Mondale's New Deal–oriented economic progressivism won the battle for the Democratic nomination over the neoliberal campaign of Hart, neoliberalism ultimately won the war for the legacy of liberalism and the reins of the Democratic Party. During the 1984 primaries, the venerable liberal magazine *The New Republic* ran a column sketching the contours of the debate between Hart's neoliberals and Mondale's "paleoliberals." The column offered a favorable assessment of the agenda offered by Hart and implicitly accepted the neoliberal framework with the insistence that this debate "doesn't easily break down into right and left because it's about means, not ends." The "Neoliberals, Paleoliberals" column pointed the ways toward a growing embrace of neoliberalism among *New Republic* editors and writers in the years to come.[95] Over the latter half of the 1980s, the ideas and perspective of neoliberalism increasingly became part of the furniture of the liberalism found in *The New Republic* and ceased to be regularly denoted as such. Meanwhile, in electoral politics, Mondale's landslide loss to Ronald Reagan in the general election—he won only thirteen Electoral College votes, even fewer than George McGovern picked up in his loss against

Richard Nixon in 1972—crushed the political influence of New Deal–style economic progressives in the Democratic Party and boosted the stock of neoliberals even further.[96] Hart emerged out of the electoral wreckage of the 1984 election as the clear front-runner for the Democratic nomination in 1988 and laid the groundwork for his campaign by founding a think tank named after his 1983 book: Hart's Center for a New Democracy.[97]

As the power and influence of neoliberals in the Democratic Party grew in the wake of the 1984 election, the ADA and its veteran figures upped the vitriol in their criticism of neoliberalism, but the basis of their criticism remained largely the same. ADA liberals such as John Kenneth Galbraith, Joseph Rauh, and Arthur Schlesinger Jr. attacked the economic turn to the right among Democrats on both moral and political grounds. From a moral perspective, they stressed that a move to the right on economic issues would have a detrimental impact on racial minorities and other vulnerable populations. When examining the conservative economic turn of Democrats from a political perspective, they frequently offered variations on Harry Truman's observation that "given the choice between two conservative parties, people will always choose the one that is honestly and deliberately so."[98] Following the 1984 election, the ADA and its veteran figures simply offered more strident versions of criticism in that vein. In 1986, for instance, Schlesinger took neoliberals to task for "worshiping at the shrine of the free market" and described them as "Reaganite fellow-travelers" who "would have the Democratic Party stand for Reaganism with a human face."[99]

The often bitter condemnation of neoliberal Democrats offered by Schlesinger and other veteran figures can obscure the role those intellectuals played in paving the way to the synthesis of economic conservatism with liberal social and cultural values that gained ascendency during the 1980s. The self-professed non-ideological approach of the neoliberals that helped to justify on pragmatic grounds their turn to more conservative economic positions owed much to some of the best-known and most influential concepts developed by Schlesinger and Galbraith. Although Daniel Bell is most frequently associated with the "end of ideology" thesis that Atari Democrat role model John F. Kennedy drew on with his technocratic approach to politics, he was far from the only thinker to contribute to the notion that the "traditional" ideologies of the left and the right had become exhausted and largely irrelevant to the circumstances of the postwar era. Bell's "end of ideology" thesis rested on the idea that developments over the past decades such as the Moscow trials and the suppression of Hungarian workers had discredited the foundations of socialist ideology on the left, while the establishment and success of welfare states had undermined the basis for laissez-faire economics on the right. According to Bell, in a world in which few serious Western intellectuals believed that it was possible to plan and socially engineer a "new utopia of social harmony" or that the welfare state was the "road to serfdom," a "rough consensus" on the mixed economy and political pluralism had taken hold.[100]

Bell's "rough consensus" had much in common with Schlesinger's "vital center" and Galbraith's concept of "countervailing power." In making the case for the "vital center" in his seminal 1949 book of the same name, Schlesinger devoted sustained attention to the "failure of the right" and the "failure of the left." For Schlesinger, as for Bell, the politics of serious-minded people lay within the mixed economy and political pluralism of the New Deal state.[101] Galbraith advanced similar ideas with the notion of "countervailing power" that he had introduced in his influential 1952 book *American Capitalism*, which held that with increasing industrial concentration, the idea in classical economics that the power of businesses was held in check by their competition with one another had given way to a system in which the power of large industrial corporations was limited by the opposing force—the countervailing power—of strong unions and retailers with significant purchasing power. He rejected laissez-faire economics with the insistence that the role of the government in such a system should be to support and encourage the growth of the countervailing forces required to maintain equilibrium in the economy and enable it to respond to the interests and needs of different groups and classes of people. At the same time, Galbraith rejected the socialist demand for public ownership of the means of production in favor of "leaving authority of production decisions in private hands" on the grounds that "countervailing power operates to prevent the misuse of such power." With the assumptions of laissez-faire economics and Marxism at odds with the reality of an economy defined by countervailing power, Galbraith believed that "the ancient and useful distinction between Left and Right" had "developed a color that makes it nearly useless."[102]

Through their involvement in the Congress for Cultural Freedom, Bell, Schlesinger, and Galbraith all helped to shape and popularize the "end of ideology" thesis, which gained significant intellectual currency in the late 1950s and early 1960s. All three participated in the organization's 1955 conference in Milan, which had the "Future of Freedom" in its official name and the "end of ideology" as its unofficial theme. The Milan conference played a pivotal role in the acceptance won by the "end of ideology" concept among intellectuals on both sides of the Atlantic. Bell's experience at this consequential conference provided the foundation for the book that would come to be most commonly associated with the "end of ideology" concept. Bell based his first two chapters of the book on papers he presented in Milan. In a paper he delivered at the conference, Galbraith drew on concepts that he had developed in *American Capitalism* to debunk the positions of doctrinaire laissez-faire conservatism and socialism on the basis of the successful track record of the mixed economy.[103] With their rejection of what they saw as the discredited and all-consuming ideologies of the right and left, Bell, Schlesinger, and Galbraith often came to see the job of politics and politicians in the late 1950s and early 1960s as the technocratic management of the economy within the boundaries of the New Deal state. While Schlesinger and Galbraith did develop some positions critical of technocratic approaches to foreign policy and the insulation of the national security bureaucracy from democratic pressures with the escalation of the US war in Vietnam, their enduring preference in mode and style of governance remained overwhelmingly technocratic. For Schlesinger, Galbraith, and many other ADAers, ideology entailed dogmatic imprisonment within a political extreme of one kind or another. In contrast, the "vital center" of liberalism advanced by the ADA was free from such ideological shackles and simply represented an attempt to respond to and address the realities of the world.

When Tsongas, Hart, and other neoliberal Democrats attracted the ire of Schlesinger and veteran ADA liberals in the 1980s, they were voicing many of the same ideas and assumptions those liberals had advanced for decades, even if the specifics of the policies they proposed differed. Schlesinger and Galbraith had made their cases against the ideologies of laissez-faire conservatism and socialism. By the 1980s, the political landscape had shifted to the right, and socialism was no longer even a peripheral part of the discussion. While Schlesinger had located his "vital center" between the laissez-faire economics of the right and the socialist left, neoliberal Democrats in the 1980s found their own kind of "vital center" between the right and the kind of liberalism advanced by Schlesinger and the ADA. Their "vital center" was considerably to the right of Schlesinger's, but they frequently advanced it on the same kinds of pragmatic grounds the historian had used. Tsongas, for example, ended *The Road from Here* by stating that he had "tried to show that there are certain realities facing America and that they will prevail over dogma, whether of the liberal or conservative variety."[104]

The transformation of the New Politics movement into a neoliberalism with more limited notions and goals of social and economic justice also highlighted some of the misguided assumptions that had underpinned the contributions of Galbraith, Schlesinger, and other leading ADA intellectuals to that movement. Those veteran intellectuals had seen the growing ranks of the New Class as a "constituency of conscience" that would approach politics less in terms of its own material self-interest than in terms of a moral concern with the Vietnam War, the military-industrial complex, chronic racial and gender inequality, and other sources of social injustice. Many of the New Class voters whom Galbraith, Schlesinger, and other like-minded ADA liberals had looked to as the key to the post–New Deal liberal coalition when they parted ways with organized labor maintained a commitment to the abstract moral values that had drawn them to the New Politics in the first place. Their political outlook and priorities, however, were ultimately shaped far more by their own economic concerns than their champions in the ADA had anticipated. In the 1950s and early 1960s, when Galbraith and Schlesinger sketched the contours of qualitative liberalism in response to growing American affluence, they grossly overestimated the reach of the affluent society. Similarly, in the late 1960s and early 1970s, they misjudged the degree to which the attainment of a certain degree of affluence among individuals of the New Class would render them indifferent to the economic issues that affected them and free them to act out of a seemingly disinterested moral concern for social progress.

In the late 1970s and early 1980s, deindustrialization, the energy crisis, inflation, and high unemployment brought precarity, or a sense of precarity, to New Class voters whom ADA liberals had seen as secure members of the affluent society and the linchpin of liberalism's future. In California—a state that featured frequently in analyses of the New Class—significant numbers of white-collar suburban voters joined the "tax revolt" that passed Proposition 13 by a two-to-one margin in 1978. The proposition, which rolled back property taxes to 1 percent of market value based on 1975 assessments, ensured that raising property taxes in the future would be exceedingly difficult, requiring supermajorities for any changes to tax rates. With an immediate reduction in property tax revenues of more than $7 billion, funding available for public services in California plummeted.[105]

During the same period, many of those California New Class voters supported advances in gay rights and helped to defeat efforts to roll back those advances. In 1975 California's budding neoliberal governor Jerry Brown signed into law legislation that repealed the state's sodomy statutes and protected teachers from being fired for private consensual sex acts. Three years later, in the same election that saw the passage of Proposition 13, California voters defeated by more than 1 million votes a ballot initiative that would have repealed those protections for teachers and required the firing of gay and lesbian educators.[106] Like those in California, New Class voters across the country during the late 1970s and 1980s were frequently supportive of liberal social and cultural initiatives that required little sacrifice from them as taxpayers. Galbraith, Schlesinger, and other veteran ADA intellectuals, however, had assumed that New Class voters would be as liberal on economic matters as they were on social and cultural issues. When they exerted considerable political energy to establish the New Class as the core constituency of the new liberal coalition on the basis of that misplaced assumption, those influential ADAers made inadvertent—yet crucial—contributions to the foundations of the economically conservative and socially liberal neoliberalism that gained ascendency in the Democratic Party in the 1980s.

Although neoliberalism became pervasive in liberal and Democratic politics during the 1980s, it never became universal. By drawing on the energy of the civil rights movement and running campaigns with thoroughly social democratic impulses, Jesse Jackson finished third in the 1984 Democratic primaries and second in the 1988 Democratic primaries.[107] Jackson's campaigns drew on a tradition of stressing the relationship between economic inequality and racial inequality that was very much in line with the politics advanced by the ADA over the two preceding decades. Walter Mondale's long history with the ADA, however, ensured him the organization's nomination in 1984, and an increasingly cautious electoral pragmatism in the ADA led it to back Michael Dukakis in 1988. In the same years when the ADA and its leading figures failed to support Jackson campaigns that drew on New Politics constituencies and embodied much of their political outlook, they heaped scorn on neoliberal Democrats despite their own contributions to the intellectual underpinnings of Democratic neoliberalism. The ADA's increasingly complicated relationship with these different trajectories of American liberalism in the 1980s developed against the backdrop of a broader conservative turn in American politics. The decade that saw three presidential elections won decisively by Republicans took its toll on the intellectual influence and political prospects of American liberalism. It took an even greater toll on the ADA. While American liberalism survived as a diminished—though still meaningful and viable—political ideology in the wake of the 1980s, the ADA began its steep descent into irrelevance. Nevertheless, the dual legacies of liberalism carried through the decade by the likes of Jackson and Ted Kennedy on the one hand and the neoliberal Atari Democrats on the other, both bore the intellectual imprint of the ADA and its influential thinkers.

EPILOGUE

NEW POLITICS, NEW DEMOCRATS, AND AMERICAN LIBERALISM IN THE TWENTY-FIRST CENTURY

The shift in liberal and Democratic politics from the union halls to the suburbs that began with the rise of the New Politics movement in the late 1960s had become unmistakable by the time of the 1992 Democratic National Convention. On the last day of the convention, the centrist Arkansas governor and recent Democratic Leadership Council (DLC) chair Bill Clinton accepted the Democratic nomination for president at Madison Square Garden in New York City. Two days earlier, convention delegates had adopted a platform that reflected the presumptive nominee's policy preferences. Titled "A New Covenant with the American People," the platform sought to distance the party from its liberal "tax and spend" reputation by offering a vision for the country in which the American people could expect to rely less on their government and shoulder more individual responsibility. With a keen desire to demonstrate that the Democratic Party was no longer the captive of a labor movement frequently attacked during the 1980s and 1990s as a "special interest," the platform also expressed support for the North American Free Trade Agreement (NAFTA) in the face of widespread opposition from labor unions.[1]

The celebration of individual responsibility over government programs and enthusiasm for free trade found in the 1992 Democratic Party platform would not have been out of place in a platform of the Republican Party. The Democratic platform, however, coupled these turns to the right on economic issues with support for liberal social issues such as abortion rights and gay rights which formed the basis for a quiet social liberalism that stood in contrast to an increasingly noisy GOP social conservatism. This contrast and its electoral ramifications came into sharper relief as the 1992 presidential election wore on. After George H. W. Bush campaigned in Denver suburbs that had long been a GOP stronghold, Democratic Colorado governor Roy Romer predicted that the absolutist opposition to abortion and attacks on homosexuals put on display at the Republican National Convention would do the incumbent president few favors with the state's suburban "pro-choice, two-job yuppies, who tend to be conservative on fiscal issues but libertarian on social questions."[2]

When the votes were tallied, Clinton prevailed over Bush in the Denver suburbs, turned Colorado blue in a presidential election for the first time in almost three decades, and won the White House.[3] By bringing the Democrats out of the presidential wilderness and securing two terms in the White House, Clinton and his fellow New Democrats of the DLC secured a degree of influence in Democratic politics that had eluded the neoliberal Atari Democrats. The power that Clinton and the New Democrats came to wield in the Democratic Party dramatically narrowed the horizons of American liberalism. With the New Democrats' near total hold on the Democratic Party in the 1990s, pro–free market and free trade policies came to the forefront and the vestiges of social democratic impulses that remained in the party largely fell by the wayside. With little room to maneuver on economic issues, liberals increasingly focused their attention on social and cultural issues. The circumscription of liberalism to mostly social and cultural matters and the accompanying shift to New Class suburbanites as the primary base for liberal politics did much to define what American liberalism was and who it was for in the late twentieth and early twenty-first centuries.

The ascendency of Clinton and the DLC also put the ADA in a difficult position and highlighted just how marginal the group had become by the early 1990s. The ADA had initially supported liberal Iowa senator Tom Harkin in the 1992 Democratic primaries before backing Clinton in the general election. When questioned about the party platform spearheaded by Clinton's forces at the 1992 Democratic National Convention that criticized "big government" and promoted market-friendly policies, Joseph Rauh expressed his deep disappointment that "the spectrum of [his] party has moved so far to the right." Still, Rauh supported the Arkansas governor's candidacy and held out hope that he was more liberal than he appeared and was simply campaigning on a more moderate position to capture the center. Others in the ADA, though, were even less hopeful in their approach to the 1992 election. ADA program director Ron Zucker expressed the resignation felt by many in the organization when he stated: "I don't feel like losing again. I'm tired of it. I'd rather vote for Clinton, who I consider to be a Republican."[4] Amid its rapidly deteriorating relevance, the ADA threw what weight it still had behind a Clinton candidacy that represented a repudiation of many of the principles the organization had long fought for. While the ADA was effectively out of the picture and the American political landscape drifted to the right over the course of the 1990s, the liberalism that did survive carried on the neoliberal legacy of the New Politics movement the group had helped to shape decades earlier. The New Politics movement had left behind both social democratic and neoliberal legacies, but for more than two decades it appeared as though only the latter would be its enduring legacy.

LIBERALISM IN THE ERA OF THE NEW DEMOCRATS

In his 1996 State of the Union address, President Bill Clinton famously declared that "the era of big government is over" before highlighting the sweeping welfare reforms he was negotiating with a Republican-controlled Congress. Clinton's long-standing pledge to "end welfare as we know it" and his attack on "big government" represented the culmination of efforts to move the Democratic Party to the political center that the DLC initiated with its founding in 1985.[5] While the neoliberal Atari Democrats had always insisted that they were reforming and modernizing liberalism, not abandoning it, Clinton and the New Democrats of the DLC made no such claims. The New Democrats considered liberalism to be an electoral liability for their party and sought to dispel the popular association of the Democratic Party with welfarism that they saw as detrimental to its prospects with the moderate majority in the American electorate. This means that even by the broadest definitions of liberalism, the New Democrats were hardly liberals.

Still, when they were in office, New Democrats often had to grapple with pressure from liberal activists and constituencies. When New Democrats made liberal gestures in response to such pressure, it was typically on issues seen as social and cultural rather than economic. The DLC had long sought to moderate the liberal positions of the Democratic Party in the realm of social policy as much as economic policy, but New Democrats frequently found social liberalism easier to accommodate than economic progressivism. Clinton, for example, largely remained a supporter of abortion and gay rights amid his efforts to "end welfare as we know it" during his first term in the White House.[6] As a result, the young president and other prominent New Democrats in the 1990s often ended up governing or legislating in ways that shared much in common with the synthesis of social liberalism and economic conservatism advanced by neoliberal Atari Democrats in the 1980s.

Founded in the wake of Walter Mondale's staggering loss in the 1984 presidential election, the DLC sought to end what its members saw as the hold of "special interests" such as organized labor and civil rights groups on the party in order to capture the center in American politics. With political strategist Al From as its executive director and Missouri congressman Dick Gephardt as its chair, the DLC established itself as an unofficial party group that sought to influence the direction of the national Democratic Party from outside the formal party machinery. Unlike the ADA—which continually exhibited ambivalence about whether it should be a small organization of influential elites or a mass organization with significant grassroots participation—the DLC clearly opted for the former. The elected officials and political strategists who filled the ranks of the DLC in its early years were almost universally white and hailed predominantly from the South. Early DLC leaders were convinced that a move to the center on economic policy alone would not be enough to win back the mass of moderate voters who had abandoned the Democratic Party. They insisted that the party also needed to mute or downplay its support for divisive social and cultural issues born out of the 1960s "rights revolution," such as affirmative action and gay rights, which they saw as alienating wide swaths of the American electorate. For the DLC, moving the Democratic Party toward the center on these issues in both substance and public perception was necessary if the party hoped to become competitive again in presidential elections and forestall further losses in Congress.[7]

A founding member of the DLC who chaired the organization from 1990 to 1991, Clinton embraced much of the organization's politics and leveraged its rebranding of the Democratic Party to present himself as a "different kind of Democrat" in his successful 1992 presidential campaign. A white southerner who had a long history with the organization, Clinton was in many ways an archetypal member of the DLC. Clinton also stood out from many of his fellow DLCers, however, in terms of his embrace of some social and cultural values popularly associated with the 1960s. The Arkansas governor had opposed the Vietnam War, worked for George McGovern's 1972 presidential campaign, and admitted to smoking, if not inhaling, marijuana.[8] Clinton's differences with DLC dogma became readily apparent early on in his presidency. While his support for cracking down on crime, reforming welfare, revamping government bureaucracy, and passing NAFTA were very much in line with the DLC program, the new president's positions on a variety of issues widely seen as social in nature put him decidedly at odds with the group. On his first day in the White House, Clinton signed executive orders that lifted a variety of federal restrictions on abortion. Later in his first week in office, Clinton announced that his administration would begin the process of ending the outright ban on gay men, bisexuals, and lesbians in the military, which resulted in the "Don't Ask, Don't Tell" policy. Along with the overt allocation of cabinet positions for members of specific minority groups, Clinton's early actions in the White House signaled that social liberalism would be a key component of his administration's governing philosophy.[9]

The Clinton administration's embrace of aspects of social liberalism alongside its consistent push for market-friendly economic policies established the basic framework that American liberalism operated under during the 1990s. The hegemonic control over the Democratic Party established by Clinton and his fellow New Democrats over the course of the decade rendered meaningful social democratic or economically progressive initiatives virtually unimaginable. By signing NAFTA into law, deregulating a number of industries, replacing Aid to Families with Dependent Children with the drastically scaled backed welfare measures of the Temporary Assistance for Needy Families program, cutting the capital gains tax rate, and repealing significant provisions of the Glass–Steagall Act, among other neoliberal initiatives, Clinton moved US economic policy significantly to the right and dismantled key elements of the New Deal state. The implementation of neoliberal measures in trade policy and at home by a Democratic president profoundly limited the possibilities open to American liberals and their aspirations. In this sense, Clinton did far more to limit the possibilities for American liberalism than Ronald Reagan ever managed. While Clinton trimmed his sails even on social liberalism after a disastrous midterm election in 1994 that saw Republicans take control of Congress and right-wing Georgia congressman Newt Gingrich become speaker of the

House, the course of events in the 1990s demonstrated that if there was any room for liberalism in American politics, it would be found in social or cultural realms rather than the economic arena.[10]

Still, despite Clinton's role in these developments, the ADA found itself with little choice but to support the president's reelection in 1996. ADA national director Amy Isaacs claimed to see Clinton's welfare reform legislation as a strategic retreat and urged liberals to forgo purity in favor of pragmatism. "Purity," she claimed, had gotten her "Richard Nixon and Ronald Reagan."[11] However craven the ADA's position may have been in 1996, it made little difference one way or another. Unlike in previous decades, the ADA had little to no bearing on presidential elections by the late 1990s.

THE FADING FORTUNES OF THE ADA

In recent decades, the news media have made occasional references to ADA ratings to indicate where a member of Congress falls on the political spectrum, but the organization has featured most frequently in obituaries for its leading figures from earlier years. The passing of many from a previous generation of ADA leadership has also meant that bequests have become a significant source of funding for the group.[12] While it continues to hold annual awards banquets that nostalgically celebrate its storied past, the years of consequential ADA national conventions that drew large numbers of notable and grassroots participants from across the country have long since passed. This is a dramatic decline for what was the most prominent liberal organization in the United States for a quarter century after World War II. The effective demise of the ADA should not, however, be seen as implying the end of liberalism. If anything, liberalism—in its various forms—has gained momentum in the years since the ADA faded from the scene. Whether tagged with the "liberal" or "progressive" label, left-of-center activists and voters have grown in energy and numbers in the wake of the successes and failures of Barack Obama's presidency and Bernie Sanders's insurgent presidential campaigns. While the politics of many of those voters and activists share much in common with that of the ADA, few of them are likely to have heard of an organization that has had no meaningful presence in liberalism's twenty-first-century revival.

The current predicament of the ADA is the result of a long and steady decline that began not long after it scored some of its greatest successes.

Following its endorsement of Eugene McCarthy in 1968, the ADA attracted as much press coverage as it had at any point in its history and enjoyed a sizable increase in membership. This new influx of members skewed young, and their membership dues helped to offset the lost financial contributions from labor unions that parted ways with the ADA after the McCarthy endorsement.[13] But these developments did not last. Despite seeing a temporary uptick in youth involvement under the leadership of Joe Duffey and Allard Lowenstein in the late 1960s and early 1970s, the ADA found itself unable to attract subsequent generations of liberal activists in the 1980s and 1990s. Similarly, the ADA's funding model of depending on member dues and small contributions proved to be unsustainable. This turned out to be the case even with the ADA's considerable success in raising funds via targeted direct mail campaigns using many of the same new technologies famously exploited by conservative groups in the late twentieth century.[14] Because of the relative unpredictability of membership numbers and small contributions, the ADA began to aggressively court big donors in the mid-1970s in hopes of putting the organization on a more secure financial foundation. With the Vietnam War over and the ADA having mended fences with a number of labor unions, the group increasingly looked once again to organized labor as a source of dependable financial contributions and political support.[15] The ADA, however, had hitched its financial and political fortunes to labor unions during a period of significant decline for organized labor in the United States. Between 1953 and 2000, union membership declined from almost one third of all workers to around 13.5 percent of the entire workforce and a mere 9.5 percent of workers in the private sector.[16] Lower union density meant that labor unions have had less money to throw at the ADA and less pull with the Democratic Party. Moreover, the aging labor union leaders who gained an increased presence in the ADA in the 1980s and 1990s did little to help the organization attract the next generation of liberal activists.

With a fraction of its former membership numbers, few active chapters, limited press attention, and the absence of figures who bring the kind of stature and influence possessed by former leaders like John Kenneth Galbraith and Arthur Schlesinger Jr., the ADA limps on as a shadow of its former self. The decline of the organization has coincided with the growing balkanization of liberal activism. Since the 1980s, liberal activism has increasingly shifted from multi-issue organizations like the ADA to a diverse array of groups committed to more specific issues, such as the American Civil Liberties Union, the Human Rights Campaign, the National Abortion Rights Action League, People for the Ethical Treatment of Animals, and the Sierra Club. Multi-issue liberal organizations that have formed and gained significant traction in recent years—such as Our Revolution, which grew out of Sanders's 2016 presidential campaign—have tended to be more directly tied to specific politicians and more narrowly focused on electoral politics than the ADA. This means that no liberal organization has emerged to provide the intellectual influence once wielded by the ADA and its leading figures on the direction and development of American liberalism. The absence of an organization with an intellectual focus and influence comparable to that of the ADA during the long postwar era from the mid-1940s to the mid-1970s has left liberalism largely bereft of bold new ideas or direction. As a result, the legacy of the liberal transformation ushered in by the New Politics movement has retained an outsized influence on liberal politics long after anything known as the "New Politics" ceased to be a regular feature of the nation's political vocabulary.

THE NEW CLASS AND THE NEW POLITICS IN THE TWENTY-FIRST CENTURY

A Gallup poll in 2018 found that majorities of both young Americans and self-identified Democrats held a more favorable view of socialism than capitalism.[17] Of course, it is important not to read too much into the variety of polls that have highlighted the growing popularity of socialism with significant segments of the American electorate in recent years. How respondents to these polls understood or defined the terms "socialism" and "capitalism" is likely all over the map. Nevertheless, the American political environment has clearly undergone a sea change since the years of the Cold War, when ADA leaders advanced a politics that had much in common with that of those who embrace the "socialist" label in the twenty-first century but—with the notable exception of Michael Harrington—assiduously avoided any association with the label themselves. With the Cold War receding into the distance, contemporary notions of "socialism" tend to evoke something akin to Scandinavian social democracy rather than Soviet gulags. The collapse of the Soviet Union and its disappearance as a specter in American politics made the rhetorical rehabilitation of the "socialist" label possible in the United States, but does not—by itself—account for the rising popularity of progressive economic policies associated with the label. The growth in support for economic progressivism seen in recent years owes much to profound changes in the circumstances and views of the New Class voters whom the ADA and its leading figures long prioritized as the future social base for American liberalism.

Against the backdrop of the civil rights revolution and Vietnam antiwar movement of the 1960s, Arthur Schlesinger Jr. bluntly opined that the affluent and well-educated members of the New Class tended to "care more about rationality, reform and progress" than the "emotional and primitive champions of conservatism" common in the white working class.[18] Whether or not they expressed their views as indelicately as Schlesinger, ADA liberals during the 1960s and 1970s looked to the New Class to bolster or replace a New Deal coalition that could no longer be counted on to deliver victories for liberals at the polls. Many of those New Class voters embraced the neoliberalism of the Atari Democrats in response to the stagflation of the 1970s and early 1980s. Considerable numbers of New Class voters similarly threw their weight behind Bill Clinton and other New Democrats in the wake of the early 1990s recession. Throughout the late twentieth century, New Class voters tended to embrace fiscal conservatism in response to the economic precarity they experienced or perceived. This phenomenon appeared to dash the expectation articulated by Schlesinger and other veteran ADA intellectuals such as John Kenneth Galbraith that New Class voters would be as liberal on economic matters as they were on social and cultural issues.

The twenty-first century, however, has given some signs of hope for the expectations that ADA intellectuals placed on the New Class. In contrast to conditions in the late twentieth century, economic precarity and the accelerating erosion of the middle class in the years since the Great Recession led to a resurgence of support for progressive economic policies. The downward mobility of New Class voters and their children—who expect a lower standard of living than their parents enjoyed—propelled the unexpected successes of Bernie Sanders's presidential campaigns. The children of the New Class have been central to this phenomenon. Sanders's scathing critique of the economic status quo along with his call to make college education at state institutions tuition-free and forgive all federal student loans understandably appealed to millennials saddled with student debt and struggling to make ends meet in a capitalist system that has failed to offer them the kinds of opportunities it once provided to baby boomers.[19]

If Sanders's successes and the meaningful return of economic progressivism to liberal politics in recent years has given some vindication for the expectations ADA intellectuals placed on the New Class, the same cannot be said of their notion of the New Class as a "constituency of conscience." ADA intellectuals believed that the attainment of a certain degree of affluence among individuals in the New Class would allow them to approach politics less in terms of their own economic self-interest than in terms of a moral concern with the Vietnam War and the injustices suffered by the "constituency of the oppressed." The turn of New Class voters to the right on economic issues during the late twentieth century proved that ADA intellectuals had grossly misjudged the degree to which the seeming affluence of New Class voters would free them to disinterestedly support policies understood as primarily benefiting others. Despite the revival of economic progressivism, the twenty-first century has provided little evidence of the New Class as a "constituency of conscience." The rising popularity of progressive economic policies associated with "socialism" and the Sanders campaigns has primarily resulted from the material concerns of New Class voters whom ADA intellectuals had seen as somehow being above such concerns.

Take, for example, the case of Carla Bellamy, a New York–based anthropology professor highlighted by journalist Alissa Quart in her 2018 book *Squeezed*. Even with her PhD from Columbia University, a tenure-track faculty position, and a husband with similar professional employment, Bellamy and her family had to take on significant debt in order to pay for day care for their two children and keep a roof over their heads. The difficult financial circumstances Bellamy faced politicized her. She became a committed Sanders supporter during the 2016 Democratic primaries. Bellamy went to his rallies in the Bronx and volunteered for the campaign by phone banking and canvassing for the candidate door-to-door.[20] While Bellamy may very well have been concerned about the injustices suffered by others in circumstances more difficult than her own, her support for Sanders was sparked and driven primarily by her own economic anxieties and concerns. As millions of individuals in the New Class grapple with economic challenges similar to those faced by Bellamy—even if they do not have to deal with New York City's extraordinarily high cost of living—a resurgent economic progressivism based on material conditions rather than moral rectitude has taken shape in the United States.

Throughout the early decades of the twenty-first century, the New Class, the New Politics, and the ADA have had little resonance and seldom featured in political discourse. They are nevertheless central to understanding the circumstances of twenty-first-century American liberalism and the tensions that run through it. The deteriorating economic condition of the New Class enabled the return of economic progressivism to the liberal agenda and brought the social democratic legacy of the New Politics that the ADA and its leading figures helped to shape back into the mainstream of American politics. The enduring pull of a liberalism that prioritizes social issues and the return of a meaningful economic progressivism formed the basic contours of the divisions in liberal politics highlighted by political commentators during the contest between Hillary Clinton and Bernie Sanders in the 2016 Democratic primaries. Social liberalism and economic progressivism are by no means inherently antithetical, but they have often been difficult to reconcile in practice. This reconciliation has not been helped by unresolved contradictions inherited from a New Politics movement rooted in both a qualitative liberalism shaped by the presumptions of a postwar "affluent society" and a social democratic outlook that grew out of the demands of the civil rights movement.

At first glance, the present century appears to offer little hope for reconciling these tensions. In 2016 Clinton's critics attacked her "neoliberal identity politics," while Sanders faced accusations of "class reductionism."[21] In the years that followed, "In This House" yard signs signaling in capital letters a commitment to the belief that "Black Lives Matter / Women's Rights Are Human Rights / No Human Is Illegal / Science Is Real / Love Is Love / Kindness Is Everything" became ubiquitous on the front lawns of liberal homeowners around the country. At the same time, many of those homeowners have opposed tax increases and changes in zoning laws that would materially benefit the marginalized groups highlighted by those signs.[22] Drawing on these kinds of examples, critics have frequently framed social liberalism and economic progressivism as though they were mutually exclusive. These tensions are not, however, irreconcilable. From Sanders himself to a newly energized labor movement and the Black Lives Matter movement, a growing number of voices in American liberalism have insisted that commitments to civil rights, gay rights, women's rights, and other important social causes ultimately remain limited without the economic justice that enables individuals to exercise those rights. Still, whether the contemporary resurgence of economic progressivism proves more durable than the one initially sparked by the New Politics movement and can be reconciled with social liberalism in the real world of politics remains to be seen.

NOTES

INTRODUCTION: FROM UNION HALLS TO THE SUBURBS VIA THE NEW POLITICS MOVEMENT

1 Todd S. Purdum, "Do the Democrats Have a Next Act?," *Politico*, January 15, 2016.
2 For an example, see Chris Megerian and Evan Halper, "Dem Foes Talk Race, Walk Parallel Paths: Sanders Focuses on Class as Clinton Confronts Privilege," *Chicago Tribune*, February 26, 2016. "Identity politics" has come to be used primarily as a pejorative by those who see what they deem to be an excessive emphasis on issues of race, gender, and sexuality as undermining universal political projects and encouraging the balkanization of political initiatives. Chapter 5 will engage more deeply with these criticisms and the broader debate surrounding what can more fairly be characterized as the politics of race, gender, and sexuality. For the sake of brevity and clarity prior to engagement with this debate, however, this introduction uses "identity politics"—in quotation marks—as shorthand for the politics of race, gender, and sexuality.
3 For more on Roosevelt's "Forgotten Man" speech, see Jefferson Cowie, *The Great Exception: The New Deal and the Limits of American Politics* (Princeton: Princeton University Press, 2016), 91–93.
4 For examples, see Allen J. Matusow, *The Unraveling of America: A History of Liberalism in the 1960s* (New York: Harper & Row, 1984); Gareth Davies, *From Opportunity to Entitlement: The Transformation and Decline of Great Society Liberalism* (Lawrence: University Press of Kansas, 1996); Kevin Mattson, *When America Was Great: The Fighting Faith of Postwar Liberalism* (New York: Routledge, 2004); Dominic Sandbrook, *Eugene McCarthy: The Rise and Fall of Postwar American Liberalism* (New York: Alfred A. Knopf, 2004), esp. 221–23; Michael W. Flamm, *Law and Order: Street Crime, Civil Unrest, and the Crisis of Liberalism in the 1960s* (New York: Columbia University Press, 2005); Jeffrey Bloodworth, *Losing the Center: The Decline of American Liberalism, 1968–1992* (Lexington: University Press of Kentucky, 2013). Matusow's *Unraveling of America* influenced a generation of historians with its emphasis on liberal decline during the late 1960s and its metaphor of liberal "unraveling" as central to that decline. Davies, Mattson, Sandbrook, Flamm, Bloodworth, and other scholars who follow the general contours of the declension narrative differ as to the relative importance of various contributory factors but nevertheless direct their narrative toward a point of eventual demise in the 1980s; this serves to marginalize the important and lasting changes in liberal politics seen

over the course of the late 1960s and the 1970s. This book joins more recent scholarship such as Lily Geismer's 2015 *Don't Blame Us* and Leandra Ruth Zarnow's 2019 *Battling Bella* in challenging the declension narrative established by Matusow. Still, despite the contributions of these books and other scholarship produced since the mid-2010s, *The Unraveling of America* continues to be regularly cited by a wide variety of scholars as the authoritative account of postwar American liberalism. While not all of those scholars explicitly deploy Matusow's declension narrative, some—such as Jon Cowans in *Film and Colonialism in the Sixties*—rely on *The Unraveling of America* for their depiction of the trajectory of American liberalism during the second half of the twentieth century. Lily Geismer, *Don't Blame Us: Suburban Liberals and the Transformation of the Democratic Party* (Princeton: Princeton University Press, 2015); Leandra Ruth Zarnow: *Battling Bella: The Protest Politics of Bella Abzug* (Cambridge: Harvard University Press, 2019); Jon Cowans, *Film and Colonialism in the Sixties: The Anti-Colonialist Turn in the US, Britain, and France* (New York: Routledge, 2019).

5 The *New York Times* pronounced the address "a robust articulation of modern liberalism in America," while the *Los Angeles Times* saw it as offering "a sweeping liberal vision." According to the *Washington Post*, Obama's address represented "something approaching a liberal manifesto." "President Obama's Inaugural Address," *New York Times*, January 22, 2013; Peter Baker, "Obama Offers a Liberal Vision in Inaugural Address: 'We Must Act,'" *New York Times*, January 22, 2013; Paul West and Christi Parsons, "For His Second Term, a Sweeping Liberal Vision," *Los Angeles Times*, January 22, 2013; "Mr. Obama Reboots," *Washington Post*, January 22, 2013.

6 For more on the form of "identity politics" that took hold in the Democratic Party and among elites at the helm of a wide variety of powerful institutions, see Olúfẹ́mi Táíwò's *Elite Capture*. Táíwò traces "identity politics" from the origins of the term in the Combahee River Collective—an organization of Black queer feminist socialists—to its eventual "capture" by political parties, corporations, universities, and other institutions that use its vocabulary in ways that can bolster their reputation but are "irrelevant or even counter to the interests of the marginalized people whose identities are being deployed." Crucially, he sees this phenomenon as a result of how "identity politics" has been employed rather than something that is intrinsic to its nature. For Táíwò, the problem is not "identity politics" itself but the "elite capture" of "identity politics." Olúfẹ́mi O. Táíwò, *Elite Capture: How the Powerful Took Over Identity Politics (and Everything Else)* (Chicago: Haymarket, 2022), esp. 1–13.

7 The term "neoliberalism" has been used to describe so many different phenomena in late-stage capitalism that it has almost become devoid of any meaning. Chapter 6 will dive deeper into the varied definitions of neoliberalism and the more specific usage of the term to describe Atari Democrats in the 1980s.

8 "Founders of Americans for Democratic Action," folder 3, box 9, M97-135, Americans for Democratic Action Records, Additions, 1943–1995, Wisconsin Historical Society, Madison (hereafter cited as M97-135, ADA).

9 Arthur D. Morse, "ADA's New New Deal," *The Survey*, July 1949, 354.

10 James Burnham, "Does the ADA Run the New Frontier?," *National Review*, May 7, 1963, 355–62.

11 Arthur M. Schlesinger Jr., *The Vital Center: The Politics of Freedom* (Cambridge: Riverside Press, 1949), 11–34, 35–50, 166.
12 For a succinct examination of liberalism in its many forms that attempts to define the ideology, see Michael Freeden and Marc Stears, "Liberalism," in *Oxford Handbook of Political Ideologies*, ed. Michael Freeden, Lyman Tower Sargent, and Marc Stears (New York: Oxford University Press, 2013), 329–47.
13 Ben Jackson, "Social Democracy and Democratic Socialism," in Freeden, Sargent, and Stears, *Oxford Handbook of Political Ideologies*, 348–62.
14 Nelson Lichtenstein, *State of the Union: A Century of American Labor* (Princeton: Princeton University Press, 2002), 30–35.
15 For example, see Jason Scott Smith, "Saving Capitalism, 1933–1934," in *A Concise History of the New Deal* (New York: Cambridge University Press, 2014), 30–61.
16 Steven M. Gillon, *Politics and Vision: The ADA and American Liberalism, 1947–1985* (New York: Oxford University Press, 1987), esp. 223–43. Gillon's analysis of the ADA has continued to shape representations of the organization in a wide variety of scholarship. For a more recent example, see Michael Kazin, *What It Took to Win: A History of the Democratic Party* (New York: Farrar, Straus and Giroux, 2022), 238.
17 The concept of a "New Class" has complicated intellectual roots, and those who make up the class have been conceived of in a variety of ways by different theorists and writers. Chapters 4 and 5 will offer a fuller analysis of the history of the idea as well as the ways in which it has been employed and viewed across the political spectrum.
18 For more on the various labels that have been used to describe the New Class, see Geismer, *Don't Blame Us*, 6–7; and Suleiman Osman, *The Invention of Brownstone Brooklyn: Gentrification and the Search for Authenticity in Postwar New York* (New York: Oxford University Press, 2011), 12.
19 For example, see Kenneth S. Baer, *Reinventing Democrats: The Politics of Liberalism from Reagan to Clinton* (Lawrence: University Press of Kansas, 2000), esp. 19–20; Richard D. Kahlenberg, *Tough Liberal: Albert Shanker and the Battles over Schools, Unions, Race, and Democracy* (New York: Columbia University Press, 2007), esp. 145–65; Justin Vaïsse, *Neoconservatism: The Biography of a Movement* (Cambridge: Belknap Press of Harvard University Press, 2010), esp. 81–109; Ronald Radosh, *Divided They Fell: The Demise of the Democratic Party, 1964–1996* (New York: Free Press, 1996), esp. 133–82; Sidney M. Milkis, "Lyndon Johnson, the Great Society, and the 'Twilight' of the Modern Presidency," in *The Great Society and the High Tide of Liberalism*, ed. Sidney M. Milkis and Jerome M. Mileur (Amherst: University of Massachusetts Press, 2005), 33; Doug Rossinow, *Visions of Progress: The Left-Liberal Tradition in America* (Philadelphia: University of Pennsylvania Press, 2008), 252. Leandra Zarnow's 2019 book *Battling Bella* offers a somewhat different interpretation that examines the New Politics movement through the career of Bella Abzug. Zarnow emphasizes Abzug's influence on the New Politics and explicitly situates the congresswoman's politics within a radical tradition that spanned the "Old Left" and the New Left. Zarnow, *Battling Bella*, esp. 1–11, 39–63.
20 For the most influential example, see Matusow, *The Unraveling of America*, 270, 343–44. Matusow's book left a lasting mark on the scholarship of American postwar

liberalism with its portrayal of liberalism as fundamentally ill-equipped to deliver on the promises of orderly social progress made by liberal politicians. Matusow argues that liberals raised expectations that they could not possibly meet because they "were constrained to act within a political culture that imposed severe limits on the extent of permissible change." Accordingly, he looks to the youthful rage of the New Left as the primary cause of the leftward movement among mainstream liberals in the late 1960s who desperately sought to maintain their "capacity to shape events."

21 For example, see Gillon, *Politics and Vision*, esp. 177–224; and Bloodworth, *Losing the Center*, 136. Gillon does not discount the role of Galbraith, Rauh, Schlesinger, and other ADA veterans in the changes seen in the organization during the late 1960s. Nevertheless, he still emphasizes their hesitancy toward those changes and looks instead to a new generation of leadership and the influx of younger grassroots members as the primary factors responsible for the ADA's turn to the New Politics. With a greater propensity to see the labels "postwar liberal" and "Cold War liberal" as interchangeable, Bloodworth assumes that few changes in the political outlook of the ADA's established leadership took place during the years since onset of the Cold War in delivering a blunt assessment of the transformation of the organization. According to Bloodworth, "New Politics activists gained effective control of the ADA" during the mid-1960s and used "the organization's considerable heft as a launching pad" to take over the Democratic Party.

22 Alan Rappeport, "Sanders, Long-Serving Independent, Enters Presidential Race as a Democrat," *New York Times*, May 1, 2015.

CHAPTER 1: THE ORIGINS OF A LIBERAL DIVIDE

1 Arthur Schlesinger Jr., "The Challenge of Abundance," *Reporter*, May 3, 1956, 9.
2 See John Kenneth Galbraith, *The Affluent Society* (Cambridge: Riverside Press, 1958), esp. 194, 251–69. All subsequent citations refer to this edition.
3 Arthur M. Schlesinger Jr., *The Crisis of Confidence: Ideas, Power, and Violence in America* (Boston: Houghton Mifflin, 1969), 248.
4 Alonzo L. Hamby, *Beyond the New Deal: Harry S. Truman and American Liberalism* (New York: Columbia University Press, 1973), 16–17, 29.
5 William R. Conklin, "Wallace Charts Policies for 1948 in Liberal Merger," *New York Times*, December 30, 1946.
6 "130 Liberals Form a Group on Right," *New York Times*, January 5, 1947.
7 John Nichols, *The Fight for the Soul of the Democratic Party: The Enduring Legacy of Henry Wallace's Antifascist, Antiracist Politics* (New York: Verso, 2020), 82–106.
8 Joseph P. Lash, *Eleanor: The Years Alone* (New York: W. W. Norton, 1972), 79.
9 Kevin Mattson, *When America Was Great: The Fighting Faith of Postwar Liberalism* (New York: Routledge, 2004), 47. Mattson's study—like much of the scholarship on American postwar liberalism—frames the ADA's attack on Henry Wallace's 1948 presidential campaign as the formative event of Cold War liberalism.
10 For more on the influence wielded by communists in the PCA and the Progressive Party, see Graham White and John Maze, *Henry A. Wallace: His Search for a*

New World Order (Chapel Hill: University of North Carolina Press, 1995), 257–59, 261–62.
11 John C. Culver and John Hyde, *American Dreamer: The Life and Times of Henry A. Wallace* (New York: W. W. Norton, 2000), 501.
12 Clifton Brock, *Americans for Democratic Action: Its Role in National Politics* (Washington, DC: Public Affairs, 1962), 24; "Paid Up ADA Members," July 8, 1947, folder 60, Americans for Democratic Action Records, 1932–1965 (Microfilm Corporation of American Microfilm Publication, roll 43) (hereafter cited as ADA-MF), box 2, series 2, ms. 3, Wisconsin Historical Society, Madison (hereafter cited as ms. 3, ADA).
13 Brock, *Americans for Democratic Action*, 17–24.
14 Highly critical of the conservative nature of Truman's presidency in its early years, the ADA sought to draft either Dwight D. Eisenhower—whose politics were largely unknown in the late 1940s—or Supreme Court Justice William O. Douglas to challenge Truman for the Democratic presidential nomination in 1948. Understandably, the ADA's dedicated efforts to throw Truman off the Democratic ticket strained the relationship between the president and the organization. Eventually, however, the vigorous campaigning of the ADA against Wallace's Progressive Party and Truman's turn toward a more liberal posture in the later stages of his 1948 campaign and during his full term as president made the repair of their relationship possible. Brock, *Americans for Democratic Action*, 11, 24–27, 88, 91, 100–104.
15 Jeff Broadwater, *Adlai Stevenson and American Politics: The Odyssey of a Cold War Liberal* (New York: Twayne, 1994), 119–20.
16 For the most influential expression of the postwar era as a period of liberal consensus, see Godfrey Hodgson, *America In Our Time: From World War II to Nixon—What Happened and Why* (New York: Vintage, 1976). For a more recent consideration of the postwar era as a period of liberal consensus and the historiography of that framework, see Robert Mason and Iwan Morgan, eds., *The Liberal Consensus Reconsidered: American Politics and Society in the Postwar Era* (Gainesville: University Press of Florida, 2017).
17 Galbraith, *The Affluent Society*, 122.
18 Robert M. Collins, *More: The Politics of Growth in Postwar America* (New York: Oxford University Press, 2000), x.
19 Collins, *More*, x, 4–6, 10.
20 Collins, *More*, 16; Stephen Kemp Bailey, *Congress Makes a Law: The Story Behind the Employment Act of 1946* (New York: Columbia University Press, 1950), 228–32.
21 Donald K. Pickens, *Leon H. Keyserling: A Progressive Economist* (Lanham, MD: Lexington Books, 2009), 94–95; "The Proceedings in Washington," *New York Times*, October 20, 1949.
22 Collins, *More*, 20–21; Hamby, *Beyond the New Deal*, 297, 302, 415, 453–54.
23 Galbraith, *The Affluent Society*, 96–97, 119–20, 188–89; Collins, *More*, 240.
24 "Economic Policy: Full Production and Employment," *ADA World*, April 1950, 1-A.
25 "Full Employment in an Expanding Economy," *ADA World*, May 1954, 2M.
26 "Full Employment in an Expanding Economy," 1M–2M.
27 "Full Employment in an Expanding Economy," 2M; "Building Military Strength," *ADA World*, April 1955, 2M.

28 Leon H. Keyserling, "For a National Prosperity Budget," *New York Times*, March 25, 1956.
29 Arthur M. Schlesinger Jr., "Which Road for the Democrats," *Reporter*, January 20, 1953, 32.
30 Schlesinger, "Which Road for the Democrats," 32, 34.
31 Leon H. Keyserling, "Looking Ahead on Economics and Politics," memorandum, June 12, 1953, 1–3, 7–8, 13, box P-17, Arthur M. Schlesinger Jr. Personal Papers, John F. Kennedy Presidential Library, Boston (hereafter cited as AMS-JFK).
32 Arthur Schlesinger Jr. to Leon Keyserling, July 5, 1953, box P-17, AMS-JFK; Leon Keyserling to Arthur Schlesinger Jr., July 10, 1953, 2, box P-17, AMS-JFK.
33 Arthur Schlesinger Jr. to Leon Keyserling, August 18, 1953, box P-17, AMS-JFK.
34 Schlesinger, "The Challenge of Abundance," 8–9.
35 Schlesinger, "The Challenge of Abundance," 9.
36 Schlesinger, "The Challenge of Abundance," 9–10.
37 Seymour Harris to Arthur Schlesinger Jr., November 14, 1955, box P-16, AMS-JFK.
38 Leon Keyserling to Arthur Schlesinger Jr., December 12, 1955, 1–2, box P-17, AMS-JFK; Leon H. Keyserling, "'Liberal' Government Is Not Enough," *Reporter*, May 31, 1956, 17–18.
39 For example, see Lily Geismer, *Don't Blame Us: Suburban Liberals and the Transformation of the Democratic Party* (Princeton: Princeton University Press, 2015), esp. 1–16.
40 John Kenneth Galbraith, *The Affluent Society*, 2nd ed. (Boston: Houghton Mifflin, 1969), xxviii.
41 For example, see Kevin Mattson, *When America Was Great: The Fighting Faith of Postwar Liberalism* (New York: Routledge, 2006), 140–71. One of the most extensive studies of qualitative liberalism, Mattson's chapter "Hopes: Liberalism and the Quality of Public Life" characterizes the qualitative liberalism of Galbraith and Schlesinger as reflecting a desire to renegotiate American engagement with the Cold War on less militaristic terms.
42 Adlai Stevenson, "America's Image of Greatness," *Life*, May 30, 1960, 97.
43 Arthur M. Schlesinger Jr., "Military Force: How Much and Where?," *Reporter*, August 4, 1953, 13, 15.
44 Arthur M. Schlesinger Jr., "The New Mood in Politics," *Esquire*, January 1960, 58.
45 Collins, *More*, 24.
46 Galbraith, *The Affluent Society*, 164, 166.
47 Galbraith, *The Affluent Society*, 167–68.
48 Arthur M. Schlesinger Jr., "America's Domestic Future: Its Perils and Prospects," *Spelman Messenger*, February 1961, 17.
49 On the myth of the "missile gap," see Christopher A. Preble, *John F. Kennedy and the Missile Gap* (DeKalb: Northern Illinois University Press, 2004).
50 Arthur M. Schlesinger Jr., "The Coming Shape of American Politics," *Progressive*, September, 1959, 26.
51 Scott C. Kamen, "The Demise of the Congress for Cultural Freedom: Transatlantic Intellectual Consensus and 'Vital Center' Liberalism, 1950–1967" (MA thesis, University of Maryland, 2011), 1–4, 10–13.
52 Mattson, *When America Was Great*, 147.

53 John Kenneth Galbraith, "How Much Should a Country Consume?," in *Perspectives on Conservation*, ed. Henry Jarrett (Baltimore: Johns Hopkins University Press, 1958), 96; Cristina Carbone, "Staging the Kitchen Debate: How Splitnik Got Normalized in the United States," in *Cold War Kitchen: Americanization, Technology, and European Users*, ed. Ruth Oldenziel and Karin Zachmann (Cambridge: MIT Press, 2009), 70–71.
54 Max Ascoli, "The Scarcity of Ideas," May 3, 1956; Keyserling, "'Liberal' Government Is Not Enough," 18; Schlesinger, "The Coming Shape of American Politics," 26, 29.
55 Schlesinger, "The Coming Shape of American Politics," 25.
56 Arthur Schlesinger Jr., "Where Does the Liberal Go from Here?," *New York Times Magazine*, August 4, 1957, 38.
57 Mattson, *When America Was Great*, 145.
58 Giles Scott-Smith, *The Politics of Apolitical Culture: The Congress for Cultural Freedom, the CIA and Post-war American Hegemony* (New York: Routledge, 2002), 14, 42–44, 114.
59 Schlesinger, "Where Does the Liberal Go from Here?," 38.
60 Arthur Schlesinger Jr., "Our New-Found Leisure Won't Bore Us If Some of It Is Employed in Reading," *Saturday Evening Post*, April 18, 1959, 10.
61 Galbraith, *The Affluent Society*, 152–60.
62 Schlesinger, "Where Does the Liberal Go from Here?," 7.
63 Arthur Schlesinger Jr., "The Challenge to Liberalism," in *An Outline of Man's Knowledge of the Modern World*, ed. Lyman Bryson (Garden City, NY: Nelson Doubleday, 1960), 472–73.
64 Leon Keyserling, "Eggheads and Politics," *New Republic*, October 27, 1958, 17.
65 Schlesinger, "The Coming Shape of American Politics," 24.
66 Schlesinger, "The Coming Shape of American Politics," 22–24.
67 Schlesinger, "The Coming Shape of American Politics," 24.
68 Christopher Lasch, *The New Radicalism in America, 1889–1963: The Intellectual as a Social Type* (New York: Alfred A. Knopf, 1965), 310.
69 Richard H. Pells, *The Liberal Mind in a Conservative Age: American Intellectuals in the 1940s and 1950s* (New York: Harper & Row, 1985), 173.
70 John Kenneth Galbraith, *The Liberal Hour* (Cambridge, MA: Riverside Press, 1960), 27, 62.
71 Collins, *More*, 132.
72 Galbraith, *The Affluent Society*, 253.
73 Galbraith, *The Affluent Society*, 2, 3, 133–34, 255, 267.
74 Schlesinger, "The Coming Shape of American Politics," 24, 26.
75 Paul H. Douglas, "How Affluent Is Our Society?," *New Leader*, February 2, 1959, 17; "Founders of Americans for Democratic Action," 2, folder 3, box 9, M97-135, ADA. Douglas served on the faculty of the Department of Economics at the University of Chicago before the department's near universal turn to conservative economic perspectives. In the 1920s and 1930s Douglas earned significant recognition for his groundbreaking work on growth economics. For more, see Richard Parker, *John Kenneth Galbraith: His Life, His Politics, His Economics* (New York: Farrar, Straus and Giroux, 2005), 324.

76 Carl Auerbach, "Economic Realities," *Progressive*, August 1958, 25; "ADA's Co-Founder Resigns," *New York Times*, February 28, 1968.
77 Leon Keyserling to John Kenneth Galbraith, July 3, 1963, box 40, John Kenneth Galbraith Personal Papers, John F. Kennedy Presidential Library, Boston (hereafter cited as JKG); Leon Keyserling to John Kenneth Galbraith, November 14, 1958, box 40, JKG.
78 Edward D. Hollander, speech delivered in Akron to the ADA Ohio state convention, December 5, 1964, 1, folder 3, box 33, M97-135, ADA.
79 Galbraith, *The Affluent Society*, 215-16, 265-66, 291, 293
80 John Kenneth Galbraith, "The State of Liberalism," address at the annual Roosevelt Day Dinner, January 31, 1959, Washington, DC, 8-9, box 862, JKG. Excerpts from this address were published in J. K. Galbraith, "Some Unfinished Business of Liberals," *New Republic*, February 9, 1959, 7.
81 Galbraith, *The Affluent Society*, 312-16.
82 Douglas, "How Affluent Is Our Society?," 17.
83 ADA board meeting, discussion summary, October 1959, 1, folder 199 (ADA-MF, roll 46), box 67, series 2, ms. 3, ADA).
84 Keyserling, "Eggheads and Politics," 14-17.
85 Leon Keyserling, "Leon Keyserling on Economic Expansion," *New Republic*, November 17, 1958, 17.
86 Leon H. Keyserling, "Less for Private Spending," *New Republic*, May 23, 1960, 15-16. The issues that defined Keyserling's criticism of *The Affluent Society* in the late 1950s and early 1960s would continue to inform his insistence on the fundamental inadequacies of existing antipoverty programs for years to come. For examples of how his critical perspective on *The Affluent Society* and Galbraith's general emphasis on improved social balance as a means of addressing poverty shaped his later criticism of the Johnson administration's War on Poverty, see A. Philip Randolph Institute, *A "Freedom Budget" for All Americans: Budgeting Our Resources, 1966-1975, to Achieve Freedom from Want* (New York: A. Philip Randolph Institute, 1966), esp. 38-42; Leon H. Keyserling, "What Has Happened to ADA?," memorandum, January 17, 1968, 12C-21, folder 16, box 36, M97-135, ADA.
87 Collins, *More*, 16.
88 Précis of pamphlet on the budget and inflation, January 18, 1960, 1, folder 200 (ADA-MF, roll 46), box 68, series 2, ms. 3, ADA.
89 Leon Keyserling to editor of *ADA World*, March 28, 1959, 2, folder 117 (ADA-MF, roll 83), box 13, series 4, ms. 3, ADA.
90 "Goals for America," *ADA World*, May, 1959, 3A; "Domestic Policy, Fully Employment," *ADA World*, February-March 1959, 1A.
91 "Domestic Policy, an Expanding Dynamic Economy," *ADA World*, February, 1960, 1A, 2A.
92 "Call to the ADA XV Anniversary Convention, Mayflower Hotel, Washington D.C., April 27-29," convention pamphlet, folder 134 (ADA-MF, roll 84), box 14, series 4, ms. 3, ADA.
93 Robert Lekachman, "Liberals and the U.S. Economy," *New Leader*, January 26, 1959, 6.
94 Lekachman, "Liberals and the U.S. Economy," 6.

95 See Allen J. Matusow, *The Unraveling of America: A History of Liberalism in the 1960s* (New York: Harper & Row, 1986), esp. 11; Doug Rossinow, *Visions of Progress: The Left-Liberal Tradition in America* (Philadelphia: University of Pennsylvania Press, 2008), esp. 9.
96 Arthur Schlesinger Jr. to John Kenneth Galbraith, March 29, 1960, box 59, JKG.
97 John Kenneth Galbraith to Leon Keyserling, May 24, 1960, 1, box 40, JKG.
98 Leon Keyserling to John Kenneth Galbraith, May 31, 1960, 1–2, box 40, JKG.
99 John Kenneth Galbraith to Leon Keyserling, June 7, 1960, box 40, JKG.
100 Leon Keyserling to John Kenneth Galbraith, June 9, 1960, box 40, JKG.
101 Leon Keyserling to John Kenneth Galbraith, June 13, 1960, box 40, JKG.
102 Leon Keyserling to John Kenneth Galbraith, March 11, 1961, box 40, JKG. Until the latter half of the 1960s, Galbraith, Keyserling, Schlesinger, and fellow ADA member Seymour Harris frequented dined with and visited one another in Cambridge, in Washington, DC, and at Galbraith's summer retreat in Vermont.
103 Keyserling, "What Has Happened to ADA?," 2.

CHAPTER 2: RETHINKING THE COLD WAR

1 "Foreign Policy: Viet Nam," *ADA World*, April–May 1962, 2A; David Halberstam, "The Importance of Being Galbraith," *Harper's Magazine*, November 1967, 54.
2 Noam Chomsky, "The Responsibility of Intellectuals," *New York Review of Books*, February 23, 1967, 16–18, 24–25.
3 For examples, see Allen J. Matusow, *The Unraveling of America: A History of Liberalism in the 1960s* (New York: Harper & Row, 1984), 378–79; and Steven M. Gillon, *Politics and Vision: The ADA and American Liberalism, 1947–1985* (New York: Oxford University Press, 1987), esp. 180–82, 193–95. In his influential study of American liberalism in the 1960s, Matusow depicts veteran ADA leaders and other liberal critics of the Johnson administration's Vietnam War policies as differing little from the administration they pilloried when it came down to the fundamental issues at stake. Gillon characterizes the established leaders of the organization as less committed than their younger colleagues to opposing the Vietnam War and more likely to see the conflict as part of the Cold War struggle with the Soviet Union. Gillon's characterization of veteran ADA leaders as less committed in their opposition to the Vietnam War than younger leaders in the organization owes much to the distinction he draws between the "traditional," "moderate," and "reform" factions in order to describe and explain the tensions in the ADA during the latter half of the 1960s. The inflexible and limiting nature of that framework leads him to overstate the differences that distinguished Galbraith, Schlesinger, and other older leaders whom he groups under the "moderate" banner from younger leaders in the ADA whom he places under the "reform" banner. For examples of other scholars who call into question the antiwar credentials of the ADA and its leaders—including both those who participated in the antiwar movement and those who had no personal connection to it—see Fred Halstead, *Out Now! A Participant's Account of the American Movement against the Vietnam War* (New York: Monad Press, 1978), 291; Todd Gitlin, *The Sixties: Years of Hope, Days of Rage* (New York: Bantam Books, 1993), esp. 294; Lloyd C. Gardner, *Pay Any Price: Lyndon Johnson*

and the Wars for Vietnam (Chicago: Ivan R. Dee, 1995), 193; and Louis B. Zimmer, "Morgenthau and Schlesinger and the National Interest," in *The Vietnam War Debate: Hans J. Morgenthau and the Attempt to Halt the Drift into Disaster* (Lanham, MD: Lexington Books, 2011), 117–66.

4 Schlesinger first sketched out the concept of a "vital center" in American politics in an article published in the run-up to the 1948 presidential election which brought the term into regular usage. Published the following year, Schlesinger's book-length treatment of the topic is his most comprehensive articulation of the concept and became a playbook for many American liberals during the postwar era. Arthur M. Schlesinger Jr., "Not Left, Not Right, but a Vital Center," *New York Times Magazine*, April 4, 1948, 7, 44–47; Arthur Mr. Schlesinger Jr., *The Vital Center: The Politics of Freedom* (Cambridge: Riverside Press, 1949).

5 That petition-gathering campaign, Negotiation Now!, has been depicted by a number of historians as irresolute in its opposition to the Vietnam War or even as an attempt to co-opt the antiwar movement by individuals and groups who did not actually oppose the Johnson administration's prosecution of the war. Negotiation Now! has often been highlighted in scholarship that challenges the commitment of liberals—both within and outside the ADA—to opposing the Vietnam War. For examples of studies that question the integrity, aims, or effectiveness of the Negotiation Now! campaign, see Maurice Isserman, *The Other American: The Life of Michael Harrington* (New York: Public Affairs, 2000), 271–72; Gillon, *Politics and Vision*, 194; Andrew E. Hunt, *The Turning: A History of Vietnam Veterans against the War* (New York New York University Press, 1999), 20–21; Halstead, *Out Now!*, 291.

6 Characterizations of the ADA's position on the Vietnam War by historians have often highlighted Schlesinger's defense of administration policy at a national teach-in in Washington, DC, in early 1965. For his part, Schlesinger, in the months that followed his display of support for the administration line on the war in early 1965, became a vocal opponent of both the escalation of the US war effort and the reasoning that had led to American military intervention in Southeast Asia in the first place. Charles DeBenedetti, with the assistance of Charles Chatfield, *An American Ordeal: The Antiwar Movement of the Vietnam Era* (Syracuse: Syracuse University Press, 1990), 115; Tom Wells, *The War Within: America's Battle over Vietnam* (New York: Henry Holt, 1994), 32.

7 For example, see Ronald Radosh, *Divided They Fell: The Demise of the Democratic Party, 1964–1996* (New York: Free Press, 1996), 75; Matusow, *The Unraveling of America*, 344. With frequent attention given to the divide between liberals and radicals in the antiwar movement, the historiography of the movement generally mitigates New Left pressure as a principal factor in the development of liberal positions on the war. Interpretations of liberals as moving toward the left and a more critical position on the Vietnam War in response to New Left pressure can, however, be found throughout the historiography of postwar liberalism. One of the most developed expressions of this interpretation is in Matusow's influential volume *The Unraveling of America*, where he contends that the insistent challenge of the New Left put mainstream liberals on the defensive and required them to move left or lose their capacity to shape events.

8 Larry Berman, *Planning a Tragedy: The Americanization of the War in Vietnam* (New York: W. W. Norton, 1982), 10; George McT. Kahin, *Intervention: How America Became Involved in Vietnam* (Alfred A. Knopf: New York, 1986), 139; DeBenedetti, *An American Ordeal*, 82–85.
9 Halberstam, "The Importance of Being Galbraith," 54.
10 John Kenneth Galbraith to President John F. Kennedy, March 2, 1962, 1–2, folder 35, box 1, M97-135, Americans for Democratic Action Records, Additions, 1943–1995, Wisconsin Historical Society, Madison (hereafter cited as M97-135, ADA).
11 "Foreign Policy: Viet Nam," 2A.
12 "Southeast Asia," Foreign Policy Resolutions, *ADA World*, May 1963, 3.
13 Melvin Small, *At the Water's Edge: American Politics and the Vietnam War* (Chicago: Ivan R. Dee, 2005), 28–30; "Message and Draft Text in Congress," *New York Times*, August 6, 1964.
14 Melvin Small, *Johnson, Nixon, and the Doves* (New Brunswick: Rutgers University Press, 1988), 28; "Board Endorses Johnson-Humphrey," *ADA World*, September 1964, 1.
15 DeBenedetti, *An American Ordeal*, 98, 104.
16 "Halt Viet Nam Bombs; Negotiate Instead," *ADA World*, March 1965, 1, 6.
17 John Kenneth Galbraith, "Suspension of Air Attacks Urged," *New York Times*, April 27, 1965.
18 "Text of the President's Address on U.S. Policies in Vietnam," *New York Times*, April 8, 1965.
19 "Initiatives In Viet-Nam," *ADA World*, April 1965, 2.
20 Roy Bennett, "President's Speech Sheds Light on Viet-Nam Crisis," *ADA World*, April 1965, 2. *The Correspondent* played an early and important—though often neglected—role in distancing liberalism from the reflexive anticommunism that had suffused mainstream American politics since the start of the Cold War. The short-lived journal also pointed the way toward collaboration between liberals and the New Left with contributions from prominent left-of-center intellectuals such as Daniel Bell, Lewis Coser, and David Riesman as well as younger leftists such as Todd Gitlin, Tom Hayden, Staughton Lynd, and Howard Zinn. For more on *The Correspondent*, its relationship to the New Left, and its impact on both liberal and radical politics, see Daniel Geary, "The New Left and Liberalism Reconsidered: The Committee of Correspondence and the Port Huron Statement," in *The Port Huron Statement: Sources and Legacies of the New Left's Founding Manifesto*, ed. Richard Flacks and Nelson Lichtenstein (Philadelphia: University of Pennsylvania Press, 2015), 83–94.
21 Bennett, "President's Speech Sheds Light on Viet-Nam Crisis," 2.
22 For example, see Arthur Schlesinger Jr., keynote address at the annual ADA national convention, Washington, DC, April 2, 1965, 9, folder 7, box 328, Arthur M. Schlesinger Jr. Papers, 1922–2007, Manuscripts and Archives Division, Stephen A. Schwarzman Building, New York Public Library (hereafter cited as AMS); John Kenneth Galbraith, keynote address at the ADA national convention, April 22, 1966, 5, box 868, John Kenneth Galbraith Personal Papers, John F. Kennedy Presidential Library, Boston (hereafter cited as JKG).

23 Schlesinger, keynote address, 9.
24 Galbraith, keynote address, 5.
25 John Kenneth Galbraith, address at Roosevelt Day dinner, Philadelphia, January 30, 1965, 4–5, box 866, JKG.
26 Galbraith to Kennedy, March 2, 1962.
27 "Foreign Policy: Viet Nam," 2A.
28 Arthur M. Schlesinger Jr., *The Bitter Heritage: Vietnam and American Democracy, 1941–1966* (Boston: Houghton Mifflin, 1967), 68.
29 During the early postwar period, Schlesinger—like most political observers—accepted the monolithic nature of the communist world as a virtually unquestionable fact. A large body of scholarship that began to take shape during the 1960s has since demonstrated that disharmony had always existed in the communist world. An early analysis of the historic disunity in what many had assumed to be a monolithic communist bloc can be found in Norman J. G. Pounds, "Fissures in the Eastern European Bloc," *Annals of the American Academy of Political and Social Science* 372 (July 1967): 40–58. Schlesinger, *The Bitter Heritage*, 68.
30 Schlesinger, *The Bitter Heritage*, 68–69.
31 Arthur Schlesinger Jr. in "Liberal Anti-Communism Revisited: A Symposium," *Commentary*, September 1967, 69–70.
32 John Kenneth Galbraith, "The Galbraith Plan to End the War," *New York Times Magazine*, November 12, 1967, 124.
33 Galbraith, "The Galbraith Plan to End the War," 124.
34 "Vietnam and Political Policy," resolution adopted by the national board of Americans for Democratic Action, September 23, 1967, 1, folder 14, box 10, M97–135, ADA.
35 Schlesinger, *The Bitter Heritage*, 75.
36 Speech by Richard N. Goodwin at the national board meeting of Americans for Democratic Action, Washington, DC, September 17, 1966, 15, folder 3, box 33, M97–135, ADA.
37 Wells, *The War Within*, 24.
38 DeBenedetti, *An American Ordeal*, 111–12, 125.
39 See Schlesinger, "Not Left, Not Right, but a Vital Center," 7, 44–47.
40 Galbraith, address at Roosevelt Day Dinner, January 30, 1965, 4–5.
41 Schlesinger, *The Vital Center*, 169.
42 Lionel Trilling, *The Liberal Imagination: Essays on Literature and Society* (New York: Viking Press, 1950), ix.
43 Schlesinger, *The Vital Center*, 35, 38, 165–66; Stephen P. Depoe, *Arthur Schlesinger, Jr., and the Ideological History of American Liberalism* (Tuscaloosa: University of Alabama Press, 1994), 6; Reinhold Niebuhr, *The Children of Light and the Children of Darkness: A Vindication of Democracy and a Critique of Its Traditional Defense* (New York: Charles Scribner's Sons, 1944), ix–xiii, 1–41.
44 Schlesinger, *The Vital Center*, 166.
45 Arthur M. Schlesinger Jr., "McCarthyism Is Threatening Us Again," *Saturday Evening Post*, August 13, 1966, 12.
46 Founded in 1957 by a group of liberal "nuclear pacifists," SANE sought to bring attention to the danger of the nuclear arms race between the United States and the

Soviet Union. Like the ADA, SANE was an early critic of US military intervention in the Vietnam War. With the escalation of the US war effort in Vietnam, SANE increasingly focused its attention and efforts on mounting opposition to the war. For more on SANE, see Milton S. Katz, *Ban the Bomb: A History of SANE, the Committee for a SANE Nuclear Policy* (New York: Praeger, 1987).

47 "March on Washington for Peace in Vietnam: A Call to Mobilize the Conscience of America," 1–2, folder 39, box 21, M97–135, ADA.

48 Sanford Gottlieb, "March on Washington for Peace in Vietnam, Report No. III," 1–2, folder 39, box 21, M97–135, ADA.

49 Sanford Gottlieb, "March on Washington for Peace in Vietnam, Report No. IV," November 22, 1965, 1, folder 39, box 21, M97–135, ADA; John D. Morris, "Peace Marchers Bar Pacifist Signs," *New York Times*, November 21, 1965.

50 Sanford Gottlieb, "March on Washington for Peace in Vietnam, Report No. II," October 20, 1965, 1, folder 39, box 21, M97–135, ADA.

51 National board meeting minutes, September 28, 1965, 4, folder 36, box 9, M97–135, ADA.

52 Leon Shull to Chapters and Board, Re: March and rally in Washington, folder 19, box 22, M97–135, ADA.

53 "The Right to Dissent," *ADA World*, October 1965, 2; Ed Wynn, "Freedom to Demonstrate Supported," *ADA World*, October 1965, 3; "National Vietnam March Planned," *ADA World*, October 1965, 4; "The March Call," *ADA World*, October 1965, 4.

54 Henry Meigs to Leon Shull, October 14, 1965, folder 29, box 2, M97–135, ADA.

55 Samuel Beer and Paul Seabury to Don Edwards, October 20, 1965, 1, folder 14, box 36, M97–135, ADA.

56 For the text of the telegram sent to Ho, see "Burning of Cards at Protest Foiled," *New York Times*, October 29, 1965.

57 Samuel Beer and Paul Seabury to Don Edwards, October 20, 1965, 1–3.

58 Arthur Schlesinger Jr. to Don Edwards, October 21, 1965, folder 29, box 36, M97–135, ADA.

59 John Herbers, "Typical Marcher: Middle-Class Adult," *New York Times*, November 28, 1965; "Throng of 20,000 Marches in Protest of Vietnam War," *Washington Post*, November 28, 1965.

60 "The Antiwar Left and Its 'March on Washington,'" *National Observer*, November 22, 1965.

61 Thomas Powers, *Vietnam: The War at Home: Vietnam and the American People, 1964–1968* (Boston: G. K. Hall, 1984), 90.

62 Louis J. Braun to Fellow Sponsors, November 17, 1965, 1–2, folder 39, box 21, M97–135, ADA.

63 "March for Peace," *Christian Century*, December 8, 1965, 1501; Halstead, *Out Now!*, 112; Adam Garfinkle, *Telltale Hearts: The Origins and Impact of the Vietnam Antiwar Movement* (New York: St. Martin's Griffin, 1997), 79; Powers, *Vietnam*, 92; Small, *Johnson, Nixon, and the Doves*, 69; "The Biggest Peace Demonstration in the History of Washington," *I. F. Stone's Weekly*, December 6, 1965, 2; Wells, *The War Within*, 62. Though estimates of participation at the November 27 March on Washington vary from 20,000 to 50,000—with estimates around 25,000 most

prevalent—most sources describe the event as the single largest antiwar demonstration ever held in the nation's capital at the time it took place. Some sources go further and characterize the march as the single largest antiwar demonstration the country had ever seen, with a greater number of participants in one location than at any of the individual demonstrations that constituted the earlier International Days of Protest.

64 DeBenedetti, *An American Ordeal*, 131; John D. Morris, "March in Capital Selects Slogans," *New York Times*, November 24, 1965.
65 Sanford Gottlieb, "March on Washington for Peace in Vietnam, Final Report," December 9, 1965, 1, folder 39, box 21, M97–135, ADA.
66 Herbers, "Typical Marcher."
67 "March for Peace," 1501.
68 Melvin Small, *Antiwarriors: The Vietnam War and the Battle for America's Hearts and Minds* (Lanham, MD: SR Books, 2002), 42; Nancy Zaroulis and Gerald Sullivan, *Who Spoke Up? American Protest against the War in Vietnam, 1963–1975* (New York: An Owl Book, 1984), 64–65.
69 "A Band of New York Intellectuals Meets with Prof. Schlesinger for a Talk-In on Vietnam," *New York Times Magazine*, February 6, 1966, 79.
70 Schlesinger, "McCarthyism Is Threatening Us Again," 12.
71 Schlesinger, *The Vital Center*, 41.
72 Don Edwards to Paul Seabury and Samuel H. Beer, November 2, 1965, 1–2, box P-1, AMS-JFK; Gottlieb, "March on Washington for Peace in Vietnam, Report No. III," 1.
73 "King Asks Million Signers for Plea to End Bombing," *Washington Post*, April 25, 1967.
74 Negotiation Now! petition statement, *Negotiation Now! Bulletin*, June 21, 1967, 4.
75 For example, see Isserman, *The Other American*, 271–72; Gillon, *Politics and Vision*, 194. Socialist writer and activist Michael Harrington later charged leaders in the Socialist Party of America with using Negotiation Now! as a "front for effective sabotaging of efforts to end American intervention in Southeast Asia." Drawing on one of Vladimir Lenin's most oft-quoted lines, Harrington remarked that SPA leaders "supported Negotiations Now! the way a rope supports a hanging man." Michael Harrington in "Ronald Radosh and Michael Harrington: An Exchange," *Partisan Review* 56 (1989): 83.
76 Wells, *The War Within*, 94.
77 Simon Hall, *Peace and Freedom: The Civil Rights and Antiwar Movements in the 1960s* (Philadelphia: University of Pennsylvania Press, 2005), 105–6.
78 "King Plans Anti-War Campaign," *Washington Post*, April 24, 1967; DeBenedetti, *An American Ordeal*, 182.
79 Halstead, *Out Now!*, 291–92.
80 Halstead, *Out Now!*, 291.
81 "Negotiation Now! Campaign Underway; Millions of Signatures Is Goal," *ADA World*, July 1967, 11.
82 Leon Shull to National Board, Chapters, Officers, "Memorandum No. 6," May 22, 1967, box 497, JKG; "Negotiation Now! Campaign Underway; Millions of Signatures Is Goal," 11.

83 Andrew J. Glass, "Galbraith Offers Viet Plan," *Washington Post*, June 29, 1967; "Delegations at Washington Make Headway in Congress for Vietnam Bombing Halt," *Negotiation Now! Bulletin*, July 4, 1967, 1, 3; John Kenneth Galbraith, "Vietnam: The Moderate Solution," address at "Negotiations Now: A National Citizens Campaign to End the War in Vietnam," Washington, DC, June 28, 1967, 28, box 5, acc. 98A-048, Negotiation Now! Records (DG 196), Swarthmore College Peace Collection, Swarthmore, PA (hereafter cited as NEN).

84 "Paragraph to be included in the ADA response which will be signed by Leon Shull," box 497, JKG. Galbraith's well-received address reached an audience far beyond the Negotiation Now! gathering in Washington, DC, with the publication of two widely read articles based on the speech. For the initial adaptation of the address for publication, see John Kenneth Galbraith, "Vietnam: The Moderate Solution," *Christianity and Crisis*, August 7, 1967, 185–90. For the version that reached a more popular audience, see John Kenneth Galbraith, "Resolving Our Vietnam Predicament," *Playboy*, December 1967, 139, 142, 278–81.

85 Curtis Gans to Leon Shull, "Re: Mobilization," March 16, 1967, 1–2, folder 37, box 36, M97-135, ADA.

86 Douglas Robinson, "100,000 Rally at U.N. against Vietnam War," *New York Times*, April 16, 1967; "On Dissent," *ADA World*, May 1967, 2.

87 Curtis Gans to Leon Shull, "Re: Summer Programs," May 22, 1967, 1, folder 37, box 36, M97-135, ADA.

88 Curtis Gans to Leon Shull, "Re: Summer Programs," May 22, 1967, 1.

89 Leon Shull to John Kenneth Galbraith, June 20, 1967, box 498, JKG.

90 Paul Hodge, "Rauh Runs into Critics in Viet Policy Campaign," *Washington Post*, June 27, 1967.

91 Almost every issue of the *Negotiation Now! Bulletin* provides at least one example of the campaign's efforts to discredit positions advanced by individuals and organizations on the both the right and the left of the Vietnam War debate.

92 "Negotiation Now! Campaign Underway; Millions of Signatures Is Goal," 11; "Negotiation Now," *ADA World*, September 1967, 2; Sanford Gottlieb, "SANE's Relations with Negotiation Now," memorandum, September 25, 1967, 2, box 2, NEN; "Draft Statement," folder 4, box 99, AMS; "Negotiation Now! Pronounced Success," *ADA World*, November 1967, 1.

93 "Negotiation Now! A National Citizens' Campaign for New Initiatives to End the War in Vietnam," *ADA World*, May 1967, 16.

94 Fritzi Cohen to Don Keyes, August 23, 1967, folder 4, box 99, AMS.

95 Isserman, *The Other American*, 271–72. Isserman argues that despite featuring Galbraith, King, Schlesinger, and other prominent figures among its list of sponsors, Negotiation Now! was "organizationally little more than a front group for the Shachtmanite faction of the Socialist Party." With many individuals in its organization who were neither members of the SPA nor supporters of Max Shachtman, Negotiation Now! cannot be written off simply as a Shachtmanite front group. The position of Negotiation Now! on the Vietnam War and its fervent attacks on the wider antiwar movement did, however, make the organization appealing to Shachtman and his supporters in the SPA.

96 Despite the possibly insurmountable hurdles to reaching a negotiated settlement to the Vietnam War, the ADA's comparative flexibility toward the NLF did offer a more plausible starting point for negotiations than the rigidly anticommunist posture of the Johnson administration. Unlike the administration, the ADA stressed the need to include the NLF in negotiations and accepted the inevitability that they would have to be included in some form of coalition government in the South in order to get their representatives and Hanoi to the negotiating table.

97 With the benefit of hindsight, Schlesinger later confessed that unilateral withdrawal was "the position I should have taken from the start." Arthur Schlesinger Jr. quoted in Wells, *The War Within*, 137. Galbraith, "The Galbraith Plan to End the War," 128–30; Arthur Schlesinger Jr., "Thinking Aloud: Vietnam and the 1968 Election," *New Leader*, November 6, 1967, 12.

98 Galbraith, Schlesinger, and number of their veteran ADA colleagues left no question as to their agreement with the position on the Vietnam War adopted by the delegates at the organization's national convention when *The New Republic* published an editorial months later that mistakenly associated them with the continued opposition to unilateral withdrawal by the successor organization to Negotiation Now!, the National Committee for a Political Settlement in Vietnam. The editorial railed against them for supporting a cease-fire proposal at odds with the political and military reality of Vietnam which ultimately undermined genuine prospects for ending the war. In response, Galbraith, Rauh, Schlesinger, Shull, and others unhappy about being included among the targets of the editorial fired off letters to *The New Republic* making clear that they had had nothing to do with the committee for some time, had no knowledge of its recent cease-fire proposal, and believed the only realistic path to peace to be the unilateral withdrawal of US forces from Vietnam. "A.D.A. Parley Urges a Vietnam Pullout," *New York Times*, June 8, 1969; "ADA Asks Full Withdrawal of U.S. Troops in Vietnam," *Washington Evening Star*, June 8, 1969; "ADA—Its 25th Year," memorandum, 1, folder 1, box 18, M97-135, ADA; "The Cease-Fire Fallacy," *New Republic*, October 4, 1969, 5–6; "Correspondence: Cease-Fire Fallacy," *New Republic*, October 18, 1969, 31–32.

CHAPTER 3: BEYOND THE WAR ON POVERTY

1 John P. Roche to attendees of the 1964 ADA National Convention, memorandum, folder 24, box 16, M97-135, ADA.

2 For example, see Robin Marie Averbeck, *Liberalism Is Not Enough: Race and Poverty in Postwar Political Thought* (Chapel Hill: University of North Carolina Press, 2018), esp. 1–9. Averbeck acknowledges some "social democratic variations" of postwar liberalism and "the undeniable diversity of liberal political thought" but nevertheless paints postwar liberalism with a broad brush. Situating her book in a tradition of scholarship that views racism as central to rather than an aberration within American liberalism, she sees its postwar form as primarily a rationalization for racial capitalism. Averbeck maintains that postwar liberals' unbending commitment to individualism and decontextualized civil liberties left them unable to challenge racial capitalism and laid the foundation for the rise of the New Right. For more on the concept of racial capitalism, which has received significant attention

in the decades since Cedric Robinson popularized the term with his 1983 book *Black Marxism*, see Cedric J. Robinson, *Black Marxism: The Making of the Black Radical Tradition* (Chapel Hill: University of North Carolina Press, 1983); and Destin Jenkins and Justin Leroy, eds., *Histories of Racial Capitalism* (New York: Columbia University Press, 2021).

3 For examples, see Steven M. Gillon, *Politics and Vision: The ADA and American Liberalism, 1947-1985* (New York: Oxford University Press, 1987), 161-63, 175; Carol A. Horton, *Race and the Making of American Liberalism* (New York: Oxford University Press, 2005), 121-38.

4 "Annual Message to the Congress on the State of the Union. January 8, 1964," in *Lyndon B. Johnson, 1963-64: Containing the Public Messages, Speeches, and Statements of the President*, vol. 1 (Washington, DC: United States Government Printing Office, 1965), 114 (hereafter *LBJ, 1963-64*).

5 For more on UDA's support of the Full Employment Bill of 1945, see Robert Clayton Pierce, "Liberals and the Cold War: Union for Democratic Action and Americans for Democratic Action, 1940-1949" (PhD diss., University of Wisconsin–Madison, 1979), 106-7, 119-20. For examples of how the ADA looked to economic growth and properly regulated private industry to address the country's remaining poverty, see the ADA's 1948 economic policy in "Economic Policy," *ADA World*, March 2, 1948, 5; and its 1963 economic policy in "Compendium of ADA's Position," memorandum, 2, folder 136 (ADA-MF, roll 84), box 14, series 4, ms. 3, ADA.

6 For more on how Keyserling viewed the relationship between earlier initiatives and the Freedom Budget, see Leon Keyserling to Bayard Rustin, October 19, 1967, 2, folder 4, box 20, Bayard T. Rustin Papers, Manuscript Division, Library of Congress, Washington, DC (hereafter cited as BTR).

7 For example, see Gillon, *Politics and Vision*, 161-63; Horton, *Race and the Making of American Liberalism*, 121-38.

8 Arthur M. Schlesinger Jr., *Journals: 1952-2000* (New York: Penguin Press, 2007), 390. According to Schlesinger, while Humphrey's inspiring speech on behalf of civil rights proved to be crucial in attracting support among delegates for the civil rights plank, the Minneapolis mayor did not want to give the politically divisive speech. In his journals, Schlesinger described Humphrey as needing to be "shamed into it, and physically transported to the convention hall, by Joe Rauh, who had written the speech."

9 W. H. Lawrence, "Victory Sweeping," *New York Times*, July 15, 1948.

10 C. P. Trussell, "South Beaten on Race Issue as Rights Plank Is Widened," *New York Times*, July 15, 1948; "Truman's Plan Collapses," *Newsweek*, July 26, 1948, 20.

11 Michael E. Parrish, *Citizen Rauh: An American Liberal's Life in Law and Politics* (Ann Arbor: University of Michigan Press, 2010), 164-66; John Lewis, *Walking with the Wind: A Memoir of the Movement*, with Michael D'Orso (New York: Simon & Schuster, 1998), 277.

12 "Proceedings of the 17th Annual Convention of Americans for Democratic Action," May 15-17, 1964, 7, folder 24, box 16, M97-135, ADA.

13 "Massachusetts," *ADA World*, September 1964, 6.

14 "Cleveland," *ADA World*, September 1964, 7.

15 E. W. Kenworthy, "Mississippi Factions Clash before Convention Panel," *New York Times*, August 23, 1968.
16 William H. Chafe, *Never Stop Running: Allard Lowenstein and the Struggle to Save American Liberalism* (New York: BasicBooks, 1993), 197; Parrish, *Citizen Rauh*, 168–71; Joseph Rauh, interview by William Chafe, Washington, DC, June 9, 1988, transcript, 8–10, folder 7942, box 217, Allard K. Lowenstein Papers, 1924–1995, Southern Historical Collection, Wilson Library, University of North Carolina, Chapel Hill (hereafter cited as AKL); Joseph Rauh, interview by Todd Gitlin, Washington, DC, March 1985, transcript, 27–29, folder 7941, box 217, AKL; Richard Miller to Allard Lowenstein, May 31, 1967, folder 1230, box 34, AKL.
17 Chafe, *Never Stop Running*, 198; Joseph Rauh, interview by Todd Gitlin, 32–38; Joseph Rauh, interview by William Chafe, 11–18.
18 Lewis, *Walking with the Wind*, 280–81; Chafe, *Never Stop Running*, 198; Joseph Rauh, interview by Todd Gitlin, 41, 42; Joseph Rauh, interview by William Chafe, 18, 21.
19 Joseph Rauh, interview by Todd Gitlin, 28.
20 Arthur M. Schlesinger, "America's Domestic Future: Its Perils and Prospects," *Spelman Messenger*, February 1961, 16.
21 For example, see Arthur Schlesinger Jr. to John F. Kennedy, memorandum, June 8, 1963, WH-66, AMS-JFK.
22 Merle Miller, *Lyndon: An Oral Biography* (New York, G. P. Putnam's Sons, 1980), 337.
23 John Kenneth Galbraith, "Let Us Begin: An Invitation to Action on Poverty," *Harper's Magazine*, March 1964, 16.
24 For example, see Gillon, *Politics and Vision*, 161, 175; Horton, *Race and the Making of American Liberalism*, 121–38. Gillon argues that most liberals, including those in the ADA, overestimated the effect the 1964 Civil Rights Act would have on the daily lives of the majority of African Americans. Accordingly, he sees ADA liberals as responsible for overselling civil rights legislation that did little to help African Americans obtain the basic opportunities enjoyed by most whites. Horton finds the source of optimism among postwar liberals as to what the enactment of basic antidiscrimination laws could achieve in their rejection of the class-based politics of the New Deal, which led them to ignore the structural social and economic aspects of racial inequality. Horton builds her argument on the work of historians, such as Ira Katznelson and Nelson Lichtenstein, who stress the significance of what they see as the departure of postwar liberalism from the class-based approach and social democratic orientation found in some aspects of the New Deal. See Ira Katznelson, "Was the Great Society a Lost Opportunity?," in *The Rise and Fall of the New Deal Order, 1930–1980*, ed. Steve Fraser and Gary Gerstle (Princeton: Princeton University Press, 1989), 185–211; Nelson Lichtenstein, "From Corporatism to Collective Bargaining: Organized Labor and the Eclipse of Social Democracy in the Postwar Era," in Fraser and Gerstle, *The Rise and Fall of the New Deal Order*, 122–52.
25 John Kenneth Galbraith, *The Affluent Society* (Cambridge: Riverside Press, 1958), 325–27, 328.
26 Thomas J. Sugrue, *Sweet Land of Liberty: The Forgotten Struggle for Civil Rights in the North* (New York: Random House, 2008), 275–76; Maurice Isserman, *The Other*

American: The Life of Michael Harrington (New York: Public Affairs, 2000), 196–97, 209–10; Marion Magid, "The Man Who Discovered Poverty," *New York Herald Tribune Magazine*, December 27, 1964, 8.

27 Michael Harrington, *The Other America: Poverty in the United States* (New York: Macmillan, 1962), 11–12, 164.
28 Isserman, *The Other American*, 157–58, 183.
29 Harrington, *The Other America*, 61–81.
30 Harrington, *The Other America*.
31 Robert E. Baker, "200,000 Jam Mall in Mammoth Rally in Solemn, Orderly Plea for Equality," *Washington Post*, August 29, 1963.
32 Like Randolph, Bayard Rustin—who served as march director—saw economic issues as the "basic reason for the March." With the introduction of President Kennedy's civil rights bill in June, however, the emphasis of the August march broadened beyond a focus on economic issues to include greater attention to legal civil rights in an effort by organizers to generate pressure in support of the president's proposed legislation. For examples of studies that illuminate the economic aims of the March on Washington, see Paula F. Pfeffer, *A. Philip Randolph, Pioneer of the Civil Rights Movement* (Baton Rouge: Louisiana State University Press, 1990), 45–51, 240, 244–46; William P. Jones, *The March on Washington: Jobs, Freedom, and the Forgotten History of Civil Rights* (New York: W. W. Norton, 2013), esp. xv–xiii; Dona Hamilton and Charles V. Hamilton, *The Dual Agenda: Race and Social Welfare Policies of Civil Rights Organizations* (New York: Columbia University Press, 1997), 123–28; Jacquelyn Dowd Hall, "The Long Civil Rights Movement and the Political Uses of the Past," *Journal of American History* 91, no. 4 (2005): 1252–53.
33 Full transcripts of the speeches made by Randolph and Lewis can be found in *The March on Washington for Jobs and Freedom, August 28, 1963: Speeches by the Leaders* (New York: National Association for the Advancement of Colored People, 1963).
34 E. W. Kenworthy, "200,000 March for Civil Rights in Orderly Washington Rally; President Sees Gain for Negro," *New York Times*, August 29, 1963.
35 "Civil Rights Bill Passed 'Better Than Expected,'" *ADA World*, June–July 1964, 1, 3; "The 1964 Civil Rights Bill," *ADA World*, June–July 1964, 2.
36 For examples, see Gillon, *Politics and Vision*, 161, 175; Horton, *Race and the Making of American Liberalism*, 121–38.
37 "Civil Rights Resolution," May 16, 1964, 1, folder 27, box 16, M97-135, Americans for Democratic Action Records, Additions, 1943–1995, Wisconsin Historical Society, Madison (hereafter cited as M97-135, ADA).
38 "Civil Rights Resolution," May 16, 1964, 2–3.
39 "Annual Message to the Congress on the State of the Union. January 8, 1964," in *LBJ, 1963–64*, 1:114.
40 James T. Patterson, *America's Struggle against Poverty in the Twentieth Century* (Cambridge: Harvard University Press, 2000), 112–37.
41 "War on Poverty Welcomed," *ADA World*, March 1964, 2.
42 "Massive Efforts Required to Win War on Poverty," *ADA World*, February 1964, 1.
43 "Poverty in America," in "A Program for Americans: 1964," 21, 22–23, folder 9, box 35, M97-135, ADA.

44 "Civil Rights Resolution," May 16, 1964, 1.
45 Stephen Kemp Bailey, *Congress Makes a Law: The Story behind the Employment Act of 1946* (New York: Columbia University Press, 1950), 75, 166, 225, 228–32. The original Senate bill championed by the UDA declared a right to employment guaranteed by the federal government through economic policies that aimed to maximize private employment and public works to make up for any employment shortfall. When President Truman threw his support behind a far weaker House version and eventually signed into law the renamed Employment Act of 1946, gone were the explicit commitments and guarantees of the Senate bill. In their place, the act made a general declaration of the "continuing policy and responsibility" of the federal government to foster the conditions "to promote maximum employment" and created the Council of Economic Advisers to assist the president in carrying out a program toward that end.
46 Pierce, "Liberals and the Cold War," 119.
47 "Poverty in America," 22.
48 For Schlesinger in 1956 addressing the issues that would come to define qualitative liberalism, see Arthur Schlesinger Jr., "The Challenge of Abundance," *Reporter*, May 3, 1956, 9–10; and for Schlesinger offering praise for the approach of the Johnson administration's War on Poverty in 1965, see Arthur Schlesinger Jr., keynote address at the Americans for Democratic Convention National Convention, April 2, 1965, 9–10, box P-1, AMS-JFK.
49 Galbraith, "Let Us Begin," 16, 18, 23–24, 26.
50 John Kenneth Galbraith, "The Starvation of the Cities," *Progressive*, December 1966, 16.
51 Louis B. Schwartz, "Toward a Just and Compassionate Incomes Policy: An American Standard Family Income," 1, folder 25, box 3, M97-135, ADA; "Income Maintenance," *ADA World*, August 1966, 14; Sandra Wexler and Rafael J. Engel, "Historical Trends in State-Level ADC/AFDC Benefits: Living on Less and Less," *Journal of Sociology & Social Welfare* 26, no. 2 (1999): 44.
52 Brian Steensland, *The Failed Welfare Revolution: America's Struggle over Guaranteed Income Policy* (Princeton: Princeton University Press, 2011), 4, 18–19, 43–44; "Economists Urge Assured Income," *New York Times*, May 28, 1968.
53 For example, see Davies, *From Opportunity to Entitlement*, esp. 2–12, 88–89; Kenneth S. Baer, *Reinventing Democrats: The Politics of Liberalism from Reagan to Clinton* (Lawrence: University Press of Kansas, 2000), 24–25; Bloodworth, *Losing the Center*, 117–18. Davies argues that New Politics liberals fundamentally abandoned the American political tradition of individualism as embodied in the "opportunity liberalism" of the New Deal and the Great Society in favor of "manifestly unpopular definitions of income by right" characteristic of the ascendant "entitlement liberalism" of the late 1960s and early 1970s. Baer and Bloodworth cite and reproduce Davies's argument in their work.
54 Harrington, *The Other America*, 20.
55 *The March for Jobs and Freedom*, unpaginated.
56 Leon Keyserling, "Economy Not Meeting Needs," *ADA World*, December 1965, 2M.
57 Louis B Schwartz, "Toward a Just and Compassionate Incomes Policy," 1.
58 Schwartz, "Toward a Just and Compassionate Incomes Policy," 1.

59 Schwartz, "Toward a Just and Compassionate Incomes Policy," 2–3.
60 Later guaranteed annual income proposals such as the Nixon administration's Family Assistance Plan (FAP) coupled work requirements with a guaranteed annual income of $1,600—lower than the benefit levels provided by Aid to Families with Dependent Children in many northern states—in order to encourage those who received benefits to seek employment at the lower end of labor market. In contrast, the ADA resolution, which called for a guaranteed annual income of $4,000 per year, contained no specific work requirements for beneficiaries of the proposed program. Whereas the FAP primarily sought to encourage participation in a labor market assumed to have the capacity to absorb the unemployed, Schwartz saw the establishment of a guaranteed annual income not as a means of inducing able-bodied individuals to work but as a necessary response to a process of automation that was shrinking the size of the labor force required by private industry. From his perspective, the vast majority of unemployed able-bodied individuals were jobless not because they had been insufficiently prodded into seeking employment but because the American economy had failed to provide an adequate number of jobs, and thus they deserved nothing less than a "just and compassionate" income. Steensland, *The Failed Welfare Revolution*, 128–29; "National Economic Policy: Broadened and Expanded Public Services and the Guaranteed Annual Income," April 22–25, 1966, 1, folder 17, box 26, M97-135, ADA; Schwartz, "Toward a Just and Compassionate Incomes Policy," 1.
61 "National Economic Policy: Broadened and Expanded Public Services and the Guaranteed Annual Income," 2–3, 6.
62 "National Economic Policy: Broadened and Expanded Public Services and the Guaranteed Annual Income," 3.
63 "Slum Plea Made at Rights Parley," *New York Times*, November 18, 1965.
64 A. Philip Randolph Institute, *A "Freedom Budget" for All Americans: Budgeting Our Resources, 1966–1975 to Achieve Freedom from Want* (New York: A. Philip Randolph Institute, 1966), 2–4, 11–13. For more on the origins and legacy of Roosevelt's "Four Freedoms," see Jeffrey A. Engel, ed., *The Four Freedoms: Franklin D. Roosevelt and the Evolution of an American Idea* (New York: Oxford University Press, 2016).
65 "Twenty-One ADAers Sign Freedom Budget for All," *ADA World*, December 1966, 9; "Freedom Budget," *ADA World*, January 1966, 2.
66 Stokely Carmichael to Bayard Rustin, August 16, 1966, folder 16, box 19, BTR; "10-Year Plan Aims at Poverty's End," *New York Times*, October 27, 1966.
67 Leon Keyserling to Bayard Rustin, October 19, 1967, 2, folder 4, box 20, BTR.
68 *Freedom Budget*, intro., 5, 9, 22.
69 *Freedom Budget*, 19–20.
70 Leon Keyserling to Bayard Rustin, September 28, 1966, 1, folder 3, box 20, BTR.
71 Like ADA policy from the period, the Freedom Budget would strike some commentators as economically and politically radical, but the proposal nevertheless expressed a clear commitment to traditional middle-class cultural values. Reflecting the belief of its authors and supporters in the desirability of a male-breadwinner-centered family structure, the Freedom Budget emphasized full employment policy as vital to ensuring the ability of male family heads to

secure the income needed to support a decent standard of living for their families. In contrast to their overriding emphasis on full employment, contributors to and backers of the Freedom Budget saw guaranteed income as a necessary but supplemental measure that they envisioned only for the disabled, the elderly, and others unable to work or those who they believed should not be working outside the home, such as mothers with young children. *Freedom Budget*, 32, 63–64.

72 "10-Year Plan Aims at Poverty's End"; "Twenty-One ADAers Sign Freedom Budget for All," 9.

73 Bayard Rustin, "A Freedom Budget for All," *ADA World*, December 1966, 1M–4M; Leon Shull to Bayard Rustin, January 17, 1967, folder 23, box 21, M97-135, ADA.

74 David C. Carter, *The Music Has Gone Out of the Movement: Civil Rights and the Johnson Administration, 1965–1968* (Chapel Hill: University of North Carolina Press, 2009), 99–100; Paul Le Blanc and Michael D. Yates, *A Freedom Budget for All Americans: Recapturing the Promise of the Civil Rights Movement in the Struggle for Economic Justice Today* (New York: Monthly Review Press, 2013), 96–98; memorandum on "Recent Developments in Support of 'The Freedom Budget for All Americans,'" folder 23, box 21, M97-135, ADA.

75 Memorandum to endorsers of the Freedom Budget from Bayard Rustin, Re: Distribution of the popular edition of the Freedom Budget, folder 23, box 21, M97-135, ADA; "Rustin, Keyserling Push $185 Billion Poverty Budget," *Philadelphia Bulletin*, January 14, 1967.

76 Leon Shull to Bayard Rustin, January 17, 1967; Leon Shull to Bayard Rustin, November 18, 1966, folder 19, box 3, M97-135, ADA.

77 David L. Anderson, *The Columbia Guide to the Vietnam War* (New York: Columbia University Press, 2002), 286.

78 *Freedom Budget*, intro.

79 Herbert Gans to Bayard Rustin, December 12, 1966, folder 17, box 19, BTR.

80 Bayard Rustin to Herbert Gans, December 21, 1966, folder 17, box 19, BTR.

81 Leon Keyserling to Rev. Shirley E. Greene, February 24, 1967, 1–2, folder 4, box 20, BTR.

82 Robert Browne to A. Philip Randolph, October 26, 1966, folder 3, box 20, BTR.

83 Joseph Rauh quoted in Helene Slessarev, *The Betrayal of the Urban Poor* (Philadelphia: Temple University Press, 1997), 50.

84 Leon Keyserling to Bayard Rustin, October 19, 1967, 2.

85 Landon R. Y. Storrs, *The Second Red Scare and the Unmaking of the New Deal Left* (Princeton: Princeton University Press, 2013), 107–76.

86 Storrs, *The Second Red Scare and the Unmaking of the New Deal Left*, 107–76.

87 Davies, *From Opportunity to Entitlement*, 204.

88 *Report of the National Advisory Commission on Civil Disorders* (Washington, DC: United States Government Printing Office, 1968), 1.

89 *Report of the National Advisory Commission on Civil Disorders*, 1, 11–13.

90 ADA statement on the Report of the National Advisory Commission on Civil Disorders, box 497, JKG.

91 John Kenneth Galbraith to Carl Auerbach, March 14, 1968, box 496, JKG.

CHAPTER 4: THE COMING OF THE NEW POLITICS MOVEMENT

1 For example, see Steven M. Gillon, *Politics and Vision: The ADA and American Liberalism, 1947–1985* (New York: Oxford University Press, 1987), 204–24; and Michael Kazin, *What It Took to Win: A History of the Democratic Party* (New York: Farrar, Straus and Giroux, 2022), 62.
2 Arthur M. Schlesinger Jr., *The Bitter Heritage: Vietnam and American Democracy, 1941–1966* (Boston: Houghton Mifflin, 1967), 50.
3 "Vietnam Policy Resolution," *ADA World*, August 1966, 4.
4 Penny Lewis, *Hardhats, Hippies, and Hawks: The Vietnam Antiwar Movement as Myth and Memory* (Ithaca: Cornell University Press, 2013), 100–101; Nelson Lichtenstein, *State of the Union: A Century of American Labor* (Princeton: Princeton University Press, 2002), 116.
5 "A Halt to Bombing of North Vietnam Proposed by A.D.A.," *New York Times*, April 2, 1967.
6 "Political Resolution," *ADA World*, May 1967, 3.
7 ADA national board meeting, minutes, May 19, 20, and 21, 1967, 3, folder 10, box 10, M97-135, ADA; "ADA Independence Voted; Liberal for Peace Backed," *ADA World*, July 1967, 10.
8 "The Following Have Subscribed to the Essence of Gus Tyler's Letter of June 9, 1967, to the Members of the National Board of ADA on the 'Foreign Policy' Resolution," memorandum, box 498, JKG; Gus Tyler to Members of the ADA National Board, memorandum, June 9, 1967, 1–2, box 369, AMS.
9 Arthur Schlesinger Jr. to Members of the ADA National Board, memorandum, June 16, 1967, 1–2, folder 15, box 2, M97-135, ADA.
10 Arthur Schlesinger Jr. to Members of the ADA National Board, 2.
11 Leon Keyserling to Members of the ADA National Board, memorandum, July 3, 1967, 1–3, folder 16, box 36, M97-135, ADA.
12 John Kenneth Galbraith, "The Galbraith Plan to End the War," *New York Times Magazine*, November 12, 1967, 128–30.
13 Arthur Schlesinger Jr., "Thinking Aloud: Vietnam and the 1968 Election," *New Leader*, November 6, 1967, 11–12.
14 Schlesinger, "Thinking Aloud: Vietnam and the 1968 Election," 12.
15 Leon Shull, interview by William Chafe, Washington, DC, February 11, 1992, transcript, 3–5, folder 7420, box 207, AKL.
16 On January 27, 1968, SANE became the first nonpartisan organization to endorse McCarthy. The ADA's endorsement on February 10 represented the first from a national organization whose commitments were not limited to a particular set of issues. Milton S. Katz, "Peace Liberals and Vietnam: SANE and the Politics of 'Responsible Protest,'" *Peace & Change* 9, no. 20 (1983): 21, 27.
17 Gillon, *Politics and Vision*, 204–24; Paul R. Wieck, "ADA Goes for McCarthy," *New Republic*, February 24, 1968, 14.
18 John Kenneth Galbraith, *The Affluent Society* (Cambridge: Riverside Press, 1958), 340–46.
19 David T. Bazelon, *Power in America: The Politics of the New Class* (New York: New American Library, 1967), 307–32.

20 For more on the various terms that have been used to describe members of the New Class, see Lily Geismer, *Don't Blame Us: Suburban Liberals and the Transformation of the Democratic Party* (Princeton: Princeton University Press, 2015), 6–7; Suleiman Osman, *The Invention of Brownstone Brooklyn: Gentrification and the Search for Authenticity in Postwar New York* (New York: Oxford University Press, 2011), 12.

21 During the early twentieth century, Thorstein Veblen became perhaps the leading proponent of the idea that the country's growing technical intelligentsia were a class that would play an increasingly important social role on the basis of its indispensability to the operation of an advanced industrial society. Veblen's ideas and work influenced the thinking of many ADA intellectuals and Galbraith in particular. In his influential 1941 book *The Managerial Revolution*, James Burnham helped to lay further groundwork for the idea of a "New Class" with his thesis that the nations typically considered to be the most advanced examples of capitalism had transitioned, or were in the process of transitioning, from capitalist societies in which the bourgeoisie held power to "managerial" societies in which managers who lacked meaningful formal ownership of property held power. Although his conception of the "managerial class" in a "managerial society" differed in various ways from the conception of the "New Class" that developed in the following decades, Burnham's recognition of the growing divergence between formal property ownership and social power shaped the thinking of Galbraith and other influential theorists of the New Class. Likewise, the bureaucrats and Communist Party officials identified by Milovan Đilas as a "New Class" in his 1957 book *The New Class: An Analysis of the Communist System* possessed both similarities to and differences from the individuals later grouped under the "New Class" label in capitalist states. Đilas brought significant attention to what he saw as the inevitable development of a New Class in communist states, which controlled the means of production not through direct ownership but by way of a political and organizational position that demanded high levels of education. The diverse intellectual origins and contexts of the term "New Class" have meant that different theorists and writers have often had quite different meanings in mind when using the term. Thorstein Veblen, *The Engineers and the Price System* (New York: B. W. Huebsch, 1921); Christopher Lasch, *The True and Only Heaven: Progress and Its Critics* (New York: W. W. Norton, 1991), 509; James Burnham, *The Managerial Revolution: What Is Happening in the World* (New York: John Day, 1941); John Kenneth Galbraith, *The New Industrial State*, 2nd ed. (New York: Signet, 1971), 124; Milovan Đilas, *The New Class: An Analysis of the Communist System* (New York: Praeger, 1957); Lawrence Peter King and Iván Szelényi, *Theories of the New Class: Intellectuals and Power* (Minneapolis: University of Minnesota Press, 2004), xx, 57–61, 149–51.

22 For the earliest example, see Arthur M. Schlesinger Jr., "Which Road for the Democrats," *Reporter*, January 20, 1953, 31–34.

23 Schlesinger addressed the meaning of the collapse of the New Deal coalition for liberals across a variety of forums in the late 1960s. See Arthur Schlesinger Jr., "Is Liberalism Dead?," address at Roosevelt Day Dinner, New York City, January 1, 1967, folder 4, box 4, AMS; Arthur Schlesinger Jr., "The New Liberal Coalition," *Progressive*, April 1967, 15–19; Arthur M. Schlesinger Jr., *The Crisis of Confidence: Ideas, Power, and Violence in America* (Boston: Houghton Mifflin, 1969), 244–53.

24 Schlesinger, *The Crisis of Confidence*, 248–49.
25 In the 1970s, Andrew Levison and Cayo and Brendan Sexton produced studies that drew on polling data and other evidence to dispel the myth that a fundamentally reactionary white working class overwhelmingly supported the Vietnam War. Barbara Ehrenreich and Jefferson Cowie demonstrate that contrary to the image of the Vietnam War era working class as complacent defenders of the status quo, workers in the late 1960s and early 1970s engaged in the greatest wave of labor militancy since World War II. Penny Lewis examines the ways in which intellectuals, activists, politicians, and the media contributed to an enduring image of the flag-waving, pro-war blue-collar worker that would ultimately be put to use by Richard Nixon and other Republicans to appeal to the "silent majority" of Americans who supposedly did not vocally express their views but were depicted in such rhetoric as supporting US involvement in the Vietnam War. For a survey of polling dating and subsequent studies on support for and opposition to the Vietnam War among different demographic groups, see Lewis, *Hardhats, Hippies, and Hawks*, 50–54. Patricia Cayo Sexton and Brendan Sexton, *Blue Collars and Hard-Hats: The Working Class and the Future of American Politics* (New York: Vintage, 1971); Andrew Levison, *The Working-Class Majority* (New York: Coward, McCann, and Geoghegan, 1974); Barbara Ehrenreich, *Fear of Falling: The Inner Life of the Middle Class* (New York: Pantheon Books, 1989), 10; Jefferson Cowie, "'Vigorously Left, Right, and Center': The Crosscurrents of Working-Class America in the 1970s," in *America in the Seventies*, ed. Beth Bailey and David Farber (Lawrence: University Press of Kansas, 2004), 84; Lewis, *Hardhats, Hippies, and Hawks*, 141–85.
26 Schlesinger, "The New Liberal Coalition," 17.
27 John Kenneth Galbraith, "The Galbraith Acceptance," *ADA World*, May 1967, 6M–7M.
28 Arthur Schlesinger Jr. to Members of the ADA National Board, 2. Schlesinger did not use the term "New Class" in this memorandum but referred instead to "independent liberals" and "the young." In his writing during the period, however, Schlesinger often used labels such as "well-informed," "issue-oriented," and "independent" to describe and refer to the New Class and makes a similar implicit reference to the New Class in this memorandum. For a typical example of the various ways in which Schlesinger referred to the New Class, see Schlesinger, *The Crisis of Confidence*, 249–50.
29 John Kenneth Galbraith to Walter Reuther, November 10, 1967, folder 36, box 1, M97-135, ADA.
30 Daniel T. Rodgers, *Age of Fracture* (Cambridge: Belknap Press of Harvard University Press, 2011), 83.
31 Curtis Gans, interview for *Citizen*, a documentary film on Allard Lowenstein, transcript, 8–10, folder 7442, box 207, AKL; Allard K. Lowenstein, "Three Views, Politics 1968," *ADA World*, December 1967, 6M; Joseph Rauh, "The Debate Continued," *ADA World*, September 1967, 1M–2M; "ADA Leads Drive for Peace Caucuses," *ADA World*, November 1967, 1.
32 "ADA Defers," *New Republic*, October 7, 1967, 6; Allard Lowenstein, interview for McCarthy Historical Project Oral History Interview Series, transcript, 2–3, folder 7465, box 207, AKL; Curtis Gans, interview for *Citizen*, 14; John Kenneth Galbraith,

"Vietnam: Public Opinion and the Political Prospect," keynote convention of the California Democratic Council, Long Beach, CA, September 30, 1967, 24, box 872, JKG; John Kenneth Galbraith to Americans for Democratic Action National Board, memorandum, November 30, 1967, box 497, JKG.

33 "McCarthy Statement on Entering the 1968 Primaries," *New York Times*, December 1, 1967; Leon Shull to Arthur Schlesinger Jr., December 11, 1967, folder 15, box 2, M97-135, ADA; Joseph Rauh, interview by William Chafe, Washington, DC, June 9, 1988, transcript, 37, folder 7942, box 217, AKL.
34 John Kenneth Galbraith to Eugene McCarthy, December 8, 1967, box 139, JKG.
35 Leon Shull to John Kenneth Galbraith, January 17, 1968, box 498, JKG.
36 Dominic Sandbrook, *Eugene McCarthy: The Rise and Fall of Postwar American Liberalism* (New York: Alfred A. Knopf, 2004), xi, 94–96, 108, 114, 157–58; Leon Shull to John Kenneth Galbraith, January 19, 1968, folder 36, box 1, M97-135, ADA; Joseph Rauh to Eleanor Clark French, April 16, 1968, folder 2, box 49, AMS.
37 Joseph Rauh, interview by William Chafe, 38.
38 Arthur Schlesinger Jr., "The Old Politics and the New," April 9, 1968, 2, folder 6, box 413, AMS.
39 Joseph Rauh quoted in Gillon, *Politics and Vision*, 208; Joseph Rauh to Eleanor Clark French, April 16, 1968.
40 Melvin Small, *Johnson, Nixon, and the Doves* (New Brunswick: Rutgers University Press, 1988), 133–34.
41 Arthur Schlesinger to James Wechsler, "ADA Board Meeting," memorandum, folder 4, box 4, AMS.
42 ADA national board meeting, minutes, February 10 and 11, 1967, folder 14, box 10, M97-135, ADA; "Board Endorses McCarthy," *ADA World*, February 1968, 1, 4; "Resolution on McCarthy Candidacy," *ADA World*, February 1968, 4.
43 Marjorie Hunter, "McCarthy Backed by Board of A.D.A.," *New York Times*, February 11, 1968.
44 "ADA's Co-Founder Resigns," *New York Times*, February 28, 1968; "Board Member Resigns," *New York Times*, February 14, 1968; "ADA Goes for McCarthy," 15.
45 David R. Jones, "3 Union Leaders Quit A.D.A. Board," *New York Times*, February 13, 1968.
46 Leon Shull, "ADA for the Past Year," memorandum, April 30, 1970, 11, folder 38, box 17, M97-135, ADA.
47 Leon Shull, "National Director's Report to National Board," December 7, 1968, box 498, JKG.
48 Schlesinger, *The Crisis of Confidence*, 268.
49 Jack Bell, "Moral Support, Little Else, That's What Sen. McCarthy Gets," *Rhinelander (WI) Daily News*, January 9, 1968.
50 "LBJ Critics Desert McCarthy," *Wisconsin State Journal*, January 9, 1968.
51 "McCarthy and the ADA," *Marshfield (WI) News-Herald*, February 8, 1968.
52 "McCarthy Moves Up," *New York Times*, February 14, 1968.
53 "ADA Endorses McCarthy, LBJ Aide Quits Organization," *Washington Post*, February 11, 1968.
54 "ADA Chapters on McCarthy Candidacy," memorandum, January 31, 1968, folder 14, box 10, M97-135, ADA; Leon Shull to National Board, Chapters, and

Officers, "1968 Primaries Campaign Report," memorandum, March 1, 1968, folder 41, box 21, M97-135, ADA; Leon Shull to John Kenneth Galbraith, March 4, 1968, folder 35, box 1, M97-135, ADA; "Endorsement Triggers Intense Campaigning," *ADA World*, March–April 1968, 1.

55 "Unforeseen Eugene," *Time*, March 22, 1968, 12.
56 Warren Weaver Jr., "To M'Carthy, Now, It's 'On, Wisconsin,'" *New York Times*, February 19, 1968.
57 Lewis Chester, Godfrey Hodgson, and Bruce Page, *An American Melodrama: The Presidential Campaign of 1968* (New York: Viking Press, 1969), 4, 133–37.
58 Arthur Schlesinger Jr. quoted in James A. Burkhart and Frank J. Kendrick, introduction to *The New Politics: Mood or Movement?*, ed. James A. Burkhart and Frank J. Kendrick (Englewood Cliffs, NJ: Prentice-Hall, 1971), 1.
59 Charles DeBenedetti, *An American Ordeal: The Antiwar Movement of the Vietnam Era*, with the assistance of Charles Chatfield (Syracuse: Syracuse University Press, 1990), 191.
60 Jack Newfield, "New Group Seeks to Wed New Politics to New Left," *Village Voice*, July 17, 1966.
61 Joseph Rauh, "A Proposal to Maximize Political Support for an End to the War in Vietnam," July 28, 1967, 1-2, folder 19, box 22, M97-135, ADA.
62 For examples from 1968 of the term "New Politics" used in reference to the political movement that coalesced around the campaigns of McCarthy and Kennedy, see David Halberstam, "Politics 1968: McCarthy and the Divided Left," *Harper's Magazine*, March 1968, 32, 34, 36, 38-44; Marquis Childs, "The New Politics of Sen. McCarthy," *Washington Post*, March 27, 1968; Richard Harwood, "Can 'New Politics' Retain Its Luster?," *Washington Post*, May 23, 1968; Arthur Schlesinger Jr., "The 1968 Election: An Historical Perspective," *Vital Speeches of the Day*, December 15, 1968, 148-54. McCarthy articulated his understanding of what the New Politics represented throughout his campaign. For example, see Eugene McCarthy, "Politics as the 'Art of the Impossible,'" address at Purdue University, April 29, 1968, folder 7, box 4, ms. 246, McCarthy for President Papers, Wisconsin, 1967-68, Wisconsin Historical Society, Madison.
63 Schlesinger, *The Crisis of Confidence*, 252.
64 For example, see Allen J. Matusow, *The Unraveling of America: A History of Liberalism in the 1960s* (New York: Harper & Row, 1984), 392; George Rising, *Clean for Gene: Eugene McCarthy's 1968 Presidential Campaign* (Westport, CT: Praeger, 1997), esp. xiii–xiv, 61, 67–68. Rising does well to note that the bulk of New Left radicals refused to "sell out" to the "system" by going "Clean for Gene." Nevertheless, the very title of Rising's book and the broader thrust of his arguments convey the notion that a significant number of McCarthy's youthful volunteers adopted a clean-cut image and more moderate political views presumably at odds with their earlier appearance and politics in order to volunteer for the Minnesota senator's campaign.
65 Sandbrook, *Eugene McCarthy*, 180-81.
66 James Q. Wilson, *The Amateur Democrat: Club Politics in Three Cities* (Chicago: University of Chicago Press, 1966), 2-4, 52-58, 287-88.
67 Wilson, *The Amateur Democrat*, 1, 44, 77-85.

68 David Halberstam, "The Importance of Being Galbraith," *Harper's Magazine*, November 1967, 54.
69 James N. Giglio, *The Presidency of John F. Kennedy* (Lawrence: University Press of Kansas, 1991), 22.
70 Halberstam, "The Importance of Being Galbraith," 54; Noam Chomsky, "The Responsibility of Intellectuals," *New York Review of Books*, February 23, 1967, 16–19.
71 Joseph Rauh, interview by William Chafe, 37–38.
72 "The Military-Industrial Complex," in "1969 National ADA Policy," pamphlet, 88, folder 1, box 35, M97-135, ADA.
73 Arthur Schlesinger Jr., "Vietnam and the End of the Age of Superpowers," *Harper's Magazine*, March 1969, 44.
74 John Kenneth Galbraith, *How to Control the Military* (New York: Signet Books, 1969), 16–17, 26–27.
75 David Halberstam, *The Best and the Brightest* (New York: Random House, 1972), 152.
76 Arthur M. Schlesinger Jr., "McCarthyism Is Threatening Us Again," *Saturday Evening Post*, August 13, 1966, 11–12; "A Band of New York Intellectuals Meets with Prof. Schlesinger for a Talk-In on Vietnam," *New York Times Magazine*, February 6, 1966, 79.
77 Arthur Schlesinger Jr. to Hubert H. Humphrey, July 24, 1968, 3, folder 3, box 67, AMS.
78 John Kenneth Galbraith, "New Foreign Policy, Old Politics," Address at the Yale Political Union, April 15, 1968, 14, 16, box 873, JKG.
79 Schlesinger, "Vietnam and the End of the Age of Superpowers," 44.
80 "Galbraith Assails War Machine for U.S. Action in Cambodia," *ADA World*, May–June 1970, 3, 16.
81 John Kenneth Galbraith quoted in "Paths to Peace in Vietnam," *Progressive*, June 1969, 46.
82 Schlesinger, *Crisis of Confidence*, 249–50, 262–63.
83 Lanny J. Davis, *The Emerging Democratic Majority: Lessons and Legacies from the New Politics* (New York: Stein and Day, 1974), 15–28.
84 Halberstam, "Politics 1968: McCarthy and the Divided Left," 36.
85 ADA national board meeting, minutes, March 31 and April 1, 1973, 3, folder 35, box 10, M97-135, ADA; Davis, *The Emerging Democratic Majority*, 253.
86 Eugene McCarthy, "Why I'm Battling LBJ," *Look*, February 6, 1968, 24.
87 George McGovern, *An American Journey: The Presidential Campaign Speeches of George McGovern* (New York: Random House, 1974), 121.
88 James A. Wechsler, "Liberals and the New Left," *Progressive*, May 1969, 19.
89 For example, see Gillon, *Politics and Vision*, esp. 180–82, 193–95, 224; Gareth Davies, *From Opportunity to Entitlement: The Transformation and Decline of Great Society Liberalism* (Lawrence: University Press of Kansas, 1996), 167; Justin Vaïsse, *Neoconservatism: The Biography of a Movement* (Cambridge: Belknap Press of Harvard University Press, 2010), 47–48. Rooted in the limiting distinction he draws between "traditional," "moderate," and "reform" groups in the ADA, Gillon emphasizes and overstates the differences between younger "reformers" like Duffey and older "moderates" like Galbraith. Davies and Vaïsse cite and reproduce Gillon's framework in their volumes.

90 Joseph Rauh, interview by Todd Gitlin, Washington, DC, March 1985, transcript, 20–21, folder 7941, box 217, AKL; Richard Miller to Allard Lowenstein, May 31, 1967, folder 1230, box 34, AKL; Joseph Rauh, interview for *Citizen*, a documentary film on Allard Lowenstein, transcript, 17, folder 7455, box 207, AKL; James A. Wechsler, introduction to *Lowenstein: Acts of Courage and Belief*, ed. Gregory Stone and Douglas Lowenstein (New York: Harcourt Brace Jovanovich, 1983), xxxvi.

91 Eric Rennie, *A Campaign Album: A Case Study of the New Politics* (Philadelphia: United Church Press, 1973), 12–13; Milton Bracker, "27 Pickets Seized with 17 Children In Street Blockade," *New York Times*, July 20, 1963.

92 Joseph Duffey, interview by author, Washington, DC, August 15, 2014; Ellen Hoffman, "Joseph Duffey Will Succeed Galbraith as ADA Chairman," *Washington Post*, June 9, 1969.

93 Wechsler, introduction to *Lowenstein*, xxxvi–xxxvii.

94 James Wechsler to Joe Duffey, March 31, 1971; Wechsler, introduction to *Lowenstein*, xxxvi–xxxvii.

95 Robert C. Maynard, "Left-of-ADA Democrats Nursing a Coalition," *Washington Post*, April 27, 1969.

96 Acceptance speech of Joseph Duffey, newly elected chairman of Americans for Democratic Action, Washington, DC, June 7, 1969, 1, folder 23, box 28, M97-135, ADA.

97 "ADA Pushes Youth Vote," *ADA World*, September 1971, 1.

98 For example, see Gillon, *Politics and Vision*, 181; John Ehrman, *The Rise of Neoconservatism: Intellectuals and Foreign Affairs, 1945–1994* (New Haven: Yale University Press, 1995), 48–49.

99 Impressed by his articles for *Christianity and Crisis*, Niebuhr later provided a recommendation for Duffey that proved instrumental to his appointment to the faculty of Hartford Seminary. Joseph Duffey, interview by author, March 4, 2014; Rennie, *A Campaign Album*, 11.

100 Acceptance speech of Joseph Duffey, newly elected chairman of Americans for Democratic Action.

101 Joseph Rauh, interview for *Citizen*, a documentary film on Allard Lowenstein, 1; Chafe, *Never Stop Running*, 368–83; Lanny Davis, interview by William Chafe, Washington, DC, February 25, 1992, transcript, 12, folder 7356, box 205, AKL; Leon Shull, interview by William Chafe, 39–40.

102 Foreign Policy Commission—Majority Report to Convention, "Vietnam," memorandum, June 6, 1969, box 2, acc. 98A-048, NEN; Foreign Policy Commission—Minority Report to Convention, "Vietnam," memorandum, June 6, 1969, box 2, acc. 98A-048, NEN; "Foreign Policy Commission Members," June 6, 1969, box 2, acc. 98A-048, NEN.

103 The same day as the ADA National Convention vote on the unilateral withdrawal resolution, the SANE national board passed a resolution representing a somewhat weaker position that urged the US government to "withdraw immediately and unilaterally 250,000 troops form South Vietnam" and reiterated its support for the withdrawal of the remaining US troops as part of a political settlement. "A.D.A. Parley Urges a Vietnam Pullout," *New York Times*, June 8, 1969; "ADA Asks

Full Withdrawal of U.S. Troops in Vietnam," *Washington Evening Star*, June 8, 1969; "ADA—Its 25th Year," memorandum, 1, folder 1, box 18, M97-135, ADA; Milton S. Katz, *Ban the Bomb: A History of SANE, the Committee for a SANE Nuclear Policy* (New York: Praeger, 1987), 112.

104 Galbraith, Rauh, Schlesinger, and Shull left no question as to their agreement with the position on the Vietnam War adopted by the delegates at the ADA's national convention when *The New Republic* published an editorial months later that mistakenly associated them with the successor organization to Negotiation Now!, which continued to oppose unilateral withdrawal. The editorial railed against the sponsors of the National Committee for a Political Settlement in Vietnam, formerly Negotiation Now!, for supporting a cease-fire proposal that was at odds with the political and military reality of Vietnam and that would ultimately undermine genuine prospects for ending the war. In response to the editorial's tarnishing them with the other organization's position on the Vietnam War, Galbraith, Rauh, Schlesinger, and Shull fired off letters to *The New Republic* making clear that they had had nothing to do with the committee for some time, had no knowledge of its recent cease-fire proposal, and believed the only realistic path to peace to be the unilateral withdrawal of American forces from Vietnam. "The Cease-Fire Fallacy," *New Republic*, October 4, 1969, 5–6; "Correspondence: Cease-Fire Fallacy," *New Republic*, October 18, 1969, 31–32.

105 Shull, "ADA for the Past Year"; "National Convention Elects Lowenstein," *ADA World*, May–June 1971, 1.

CHAPTER 5: THE EVOLUTION OF THE NEW POLITICS

1 Norman Podhoretz, *Breaking Ranks: A Political Memoir* (New York: Harper & Row, 1979), 339.
2 "The NDC . . . a History," folder 30, box 4, Donald O. Peterson Papers, 1947–1980, Eau Claire ms. BB, Eau Claire Area Research Center, Eau Claire, WI (hereafter cited as DOP).
3 "Steering Committee of the New Democratic Coalition," folder 5, box 2, M97-135, ADA; "Duffey Named Chairman at 22nd Convention, Call for Shift to Greater Local Political Action," *ADA World*, July 1969, 3; Robert C. Maynard, "Left-of-ADA Democrats Nursing a Coalition," *Washington Post*, April 27, 1969; Paul R. Wieck, "The New Politics Still Lives," *New Republic*, December 14, 1968, 21.
4 ADA-NDC Conference Committee meeting, minutes, March 1, 1973, folder 1316, box 36, AKL.
5 Kevin Boyle, *The UAW and the Heyday of American Liberalism, 1945–1968* (Ithaca: Cornell University Press, 1995), 156, 207–10, 243, 245–47.
6 Don Peterson and Paul Schrade to NDC Steering Committee Members and State Affiliates, memorandum, July 22. 1969, 1, folder 33, box 4, DOP; "A Provisional Statement of Purposes," November 24, 1968, folder 30, box 4, DOP; Maynard, "Left-of-ADA Democrats Nursing a Coalition."
7 Douglas E. Kneeland, "New Democratic Coalition Says It Will Seek a Wide Following," *New York Times*, November 25, 1968; Peterson and Schrade to Steering Committee Members and State Affiliates, July 22. 1969, 2.

8 Stephen C. Schlesinger, *The New Reformers: Forces for Change in American Politics* (Boston: Houghton Mifflin, 1975), 4–5, 112–13, 135.
9 R. W. Apple Jr., "Coalition of 1968 Ponders Its Role," *New York Times*, February 15, 1970.
10 "Badger Dems Urge Troop Pull-Out," *St. Paul Sunday Pioneer Press*, June 15, 1969; James D. Selk, "Democrats Feather Doves' Nest," *Wisconsin State Journal*, June 15, 1969.
11 Michael Harrington, "New Democrats Going Where the People Are," *Washington Star*, undated newspaper clipping, folder 30, box 4, DOP; "Duffey Scores Upset in Connecticut Race," *ADA World*, September 1970, 23; Joseph Duffey, "Forging a Winning Coalition," keynote speech at the New Democratic Coalition Western States Political Action Conference, 8, folder 23, box 28, M97-135, ADA.
12 Peterson and Schrade to Steering Committee Members and State Affiliates, July 22, 1969, 1.
13 Penny Lewis, *Hardhats, Hippies, and Hawks: The Vietnam Antiwar Movement as Myth and Memory* (Ithaca: Cornell University Press, 2013), 50–54.
14 Bella Abzug quoted in Schlesinger, *The New Reformers*, 135.
15 Statement by Arthur Schlesinger Jr., national vice chairman of the Americans for Democratic Action, February 26, 1969, folder 1, box 7, M97-135, ADA.
16 Statement of John Kenneth Galbraith at the opening session of the Congressional Conference on the Military Budget and National Priorities, March 28, 1969, 1, box 140, JKG.
17 "McCarthy Statement on Entering the 1968 Primaries," *New York Times*, December 1, 1967.
18 Doug Rossinow, *The Politics of Authenticity: Liberalism, Christianity, and the New Left in America* (New York: Columbia University Press, 1998), 219.
19 Statement of John Kenneth Galbraith at the opening session of the Congressional Conference on the Military Budget and National Priorities, 1.
20 "'National Security' Revisited," *ADA World*, August–September 1969, 2.
21 "'National Security' Revisited," 2.
22 "The Military-Industrial Complex," in "1969 National ADA Policy," pamphlet, 87–88, folder 1, box 35, M97-135, ADA.
23 Resolution on the Military-Industrial Complex, adopted at the 1969 ADA convention, 1969 ADA National Policy, folder 1, box 35, M97-135, ADA.
24 John Kenneth Galbraith quoted in "The People versus the Pentagon" *Progressive*, June 1969, 16.
25 "U.S. Priorities Views Sought," *Washington Sunday Star*, November 16, 1969; Coalition on National Priorities and Military Policy, memorandum, box 11, ms. 577, Social Action Vertical File, ca. 1960–2002, Wisconsin Historical Society, Madison; Meeting of the Coalition on National Priorities and Military Policy, minutes, January 22, 1970, box 44, series G, SANE, Inc., Records, 1957–1987 (DG 58), Swarthmore College Peace Collection, Swarthmore, PA.
26 Newsletter from the coordinators of the Vietnam Moratorium Committee, April 20, 1970, 1, box 176, JKG.
27 Memorandum from the Vietnam Moratorium Committee, 1969, 1, folder 20, box 22, M97-135, ADA.

28 Lewis, *Hardhats, Hippies, and Hawks,* 132; Charles DeBenedetti, with the assistance of Charles Chatfield, *An American Ordeal: The Antiwar Movement of the Vietnam Era* (Syracuse: Syracuse University Press, 1990), 260, 261, 267; "Protests Planned in 40 Cities," *Washington Post,* December 7, 1969; "2 Groups Plan December Moratorium," *New York Times,* December 7, 1969.
29 "2 Groups Plan December Moratorium"; "Town-Meeting Fight on War Costs Asked," *Washington Post,* November 16, 1969; Anne Hebald and Robert F. Levey, "Moratorium Renewed on Smaller Scale," *Washington Post,* December 13, 1969.
30 DeBenedetti, *An American Ordeal,* 268–69.
31 Memorandum from Sam Brown, David Hawk, David Mixner, and Marge Sklencar, co-coordinators of the VMC, April 20, 1970, box 176, JKG; James Doyle, "Political Coalition Is Formed by Peace, Welfare Forces," *Washington Star,* January 5, 1970.
32 Arthur Schlesinger Jr. to John Kenneth Galbraith, March 4, 1969, 1, folder 2, box 49, AMS; Leon Shull, "Staff Report, ADA in 1970," memorandum, January 14, 1971, 5–6, folder 17, box 9, M97-135, ADA; Edward Lippert, Foreign Policy Specialist, memorandum, May 9, 1969, box 494, JKG; Leon Shull, "Beyond Politics: ABM Significance," *ADA World,* May 1969, 2W.
33 The struggle in the Senate ultimately centered on an amendment to the military authorization bill that would have halted the Safeguard system then in the process of being deployed and prohibited the deployment of other "advanced" ABM systems. Since Senate rules meant that the 50–50 tie vote would defeat the proposed amendment, Vice President Spiro Agnew's decision to cast a tiebreaking vote amounted to an unnecessary symbolic gesture. Lily Geismer, *Don't Blame Us: Suburban Liberals and the Transformation of the Democratic Party* (Princeton: Princeton University Press, 2015), 134–38; Thomas A. Halsted, "Lobbying against the ABM, 1967–1970," *Bulletin of the Atomic Scientists* 27, no. 4 (April 1971): 26, 28; "Close ABM Vote Foretells Tough Battles Ahead for Military, Renewed Attacks on ABM, Other Items," *ADA World,* August–September 1969, 1; Warren Weaver Jr., "Nixon Missile Plan Wins in Senate by a 51–50 Vote; House Approval Likely," *New York Times,* August 7, 1969.
34 Arthur Schlesinger Jr., "The Challenge of Abundance," *Reporter,* May 3, 1956, 9.
35 See Arthur M. Schlesinger Jr., *The Disuniting of America: Reflections on a Multicultural Society* (New York: W. W. Norton, 1991).
36 For example, see Todd Gitlin, "The Rise of Identity Politics," *Dissent,* Spring 1993, 175–76; Todd Gitlin, *The Twilight of Common Dreams: Why America Is Wracked by Culture Wars* (New York: Henry Holt, 1995).
37 Rossinow, *The Politics of Authenticity,* 243.
38 Jonathan Bell, *California Crucible: The Forging of Modern Liberalism* (Philadelphia: University of Pennsylvania Press, 2012), esp. 5–6, 164–65, 196, 279–80.
39 "Mexican Americans," in "1970 National ADA Policy," pamphlet, 6–7, folder 1, box 35, M97-135, ADA.
40 "United States Latinos," in "1973 National ADA Policy," pamphlet, 149–50, folder 1, box 35, M97-135, ADA.
41 "Southwest Council of La Raza Statement of Aims and Objectives," memorandum, folder 21, box 4, Christine Marie Sierra Papers, University of New Mexico Center for Southwest Research & Special Collections, Albuquerque (hereafter cited as

CMS); "Southwest Council of La Raza," 1969 Annual Report, pamphlet, folder 22, box 4, CMS; "Southwest Council of La Raza," in "1970 National ADA Policy," pamphlet, 6–7, folder 1, box 35, M97-135, ADA.

42 "Civil Liberties and Sexual Practices," in "1968 National ADA Policy," pamphlet, 7, folder 1, box 35, M97-135, ADA; "Civil Liberties and Sexual Practices," in "1971 National ADA Policy," pamphlet, 21, folder 1, box 35, M97-135, ADA; "Gay Rights, Civil Liberties and Sexual Practices," in "1973 National ADA Policy," 132, folder 1, box 35, M97-135, ADA; Kelsy Kretschmer, *Fighting for Now: Diversity and Discord in the National Organization for Women* (Minneapolis: University of Minnesota Press, 2019), 48–49.

43 "Women's Rights," in "1970 National ADA Policy," pamphlet, 8–9, folder 1, box 35, M97-135, ADA; "Women's Rights," in "1971 National ADA Policy," pamphlet, 14, folder 1, box 35, M97-135, ADA.

44 Kretschmer, *Fighting for Now*, 43–45, 48–49.

45 "Women's Rights," in "1972 National ADA Policy," pamphlet, 17, folder 1, box 35, M97-135, ADA; "Women's Rights," in "1973 National ADA Policy," pamphlet, 131, folder 1, box 35, M97-135, ADA.

46 John Kenneth Galbraith, Edwin Kuh, and Lester Thurow, "The Minority Advancement Plan: A Practical Proposal for Breaking the Monopoly of Good Jobs by White Males," folder 37, box 1, M97-135, ADA; Leon Shull to John Kenneth Galbraith, November 11, 1971, folder 37, box 1, M97-135, ADA; Leon Shull to John Kenneth Galbraith, September 29, 1971, folder 37, box 1, M97-135, ADA.

47 ADA national board meeting, minutes, October 16 and 17, 1971, 6, folder 29, box 10, M97-135, ADA.

48 Israel Shenker, "So What's the Bad Word?," *New York Times*, February 24, 1977; "A Quarter Century of Gay Life in New York: A Photo Essay," *New York Magazine*, June 20, 1994, 48; Arthur Schlesinger Jr., "Flip Remarks," *New York Magazine*, July 25, 1994, 6.

49 Schlesinger, *The Disuniting of America*, esp. 9, 15–16, 68, 108; Arthur Schlesinger Jr., "A Dissenting Opinion," in New York State Social Studies Review and Development Committee, *One Nation, Many Peoples: A Declaration of Cultural Interdependence* (Albany: New York State Education Department, 1991), 45–47; John F. Harris, "Arthur Schlesinger's Education in Controversy," *Washington Post*, June 1, 1992.

50 *For the People: The Platform of the Democratic Party, 1972* (Washington, DC: Democratic Party, 1972); "ADA—Its 26th Year," 1, folder 3, box 18, M97-135, ADA.

51 "ADA Endorses McGovern," *ADA World*, June 1972, 3; "A.D.A. Backs McGovern, Bars Humphrey Rebuff," *New York Times*, April 24, 1972; "Endorsement Resolution," *ADA World*, June 1972, 3.

52 Byron E. Shafer, *Quiet Revolution: The Struggle for the Democratic Party and the Shaping of Post-Reform Politics* (New York: Russell Sage Foundation, 1983), 35–40; Judith Stein, *Pivotal Decade: How the United States Traded Factories for Finance in the Seventies* (New Haven: Yale University Press, 2010), 51–55. Despite its age, Shafer's book remains the definitive study of the reform of the Democratic Party between 1968 and 1972 and lasting legacies of the party reform process.

53 Shafer, *Quiet Revolution*, 413–14, 420, 473.

54 "ADA Works for Party Reform," *ADA World*, September 1971, 1, 16.
55 Ultimately, the widespread use of primaries and open party caucuses necessitated by the reforms of the McGovern–Fraser commission largely survived efforts to roll back party reform in the wake of the Democratic Party's 1972 national convention, while the demographic requirements implemented by the commission were weakened or eliminated entirely. Those efforts led to the removal of mandatory demographic requirements for African Americans, women, and youth derided by critics as quotas and the establishment of new reforms that retained many of the measures that had necessitated more participatory methods of delegate selection, but restored some of the power party officials had lost with the implementation of the McGovern–Fraser reforms. For more on the lasting legacies of the commission and subsequent efforts to scale back its reforms, see William Crotty, *Party Reform* (New York: Longman, 1983), 63–100.
56 Shafer, *Quiet Revolution*, 131, 530–31; Jefferson Cowie, *Stayin' Alive: The 1970s and the Last Days of the Working Class* (New York: New Press, 2010), 88–89.
57 Arthur Schlesinger Jr., "Can We Improve Our Method of Nominating Presidential Candidates?," notes for conference talk at CUNY, May 10, 1969, 5, folder 6, box 413, AMS; Samuel Beer quoted in Shafer, *Quiet Revolution*, 129.
58 For example, see Arthur M. Schlesinger Jr., *The Crisis of Confidence: Ideas, Power, and Violence in America* (Boston: Houghton Mifflin, 1969), 248–49.
59 Michael Harrington, *Toward a Democratic Left: A Radical Program for a New Majority* (New York: Macmillan, 1968), 266, 282–91. *Toward a Democratic Left* expanded on many of the ideas originally advanced in Harrington's widely read 1967 article for the *Village Voice*. See Michael Harrington, "The New Middle Class: Whose Camp Is It In?," *Village Voice*, June 1, 1967. For insight into the influence of Galbraith's work on how Harrington approached the New Class, see his review of *The New Industrial State*, Michael Harrington, "Liberalism According to Galbraith," *Commentary*, October 1967, 77–83.
60 Schlesinger, "Can We Improve Our Method of Nominating Presidential Candidates?," 6–9.
61 John Kenneth Galbraith, "American Politics: The New Context," Princeton, December 2, 1968, 1, 6–10, folder 36, box 1, M97-135, ADA.
62 Haynes Johnson, "A Portrait of Democrats' New Delegate," *Washington Post*, July 8, 1972.
63 Bruce Miroff, *The Liberals' Moment: The McGovern Insurgency and the Identity Crisis of the Democratic Party* (Lawrence: University Press of Kansas, 2009), 69.
64 Geismer, *Don't Blame Us*, 149, 150; Schlesinger, *The New Reformers*, 119; Arthur Schlesinger Jr., "The Case for George McGovern," *New Republic*, February 26, 1972, 17.
65 For the "Come Home, Democrats" advertisement, see "Come Home, Democrats," *New York Times*, December 7, 1972, or "Come Home, Democrats," *Washington Post*, December 7, 1972.
66 For examples of writers who describe their own turn to neoconservatism principally as a response to the New Left, see Podhoretz, *Breaking Ranks*, esp. 306–11; Ben J. Wattenberg, *Fighting Words: A Tale of How Liberals Created Neo-Conservatism* (New York: Thomas Dunne, 2008), esp. 77, 110, 137, 146, 219. For

examples of historians who emphasize the New Left as an impetus for neoconservatism, see Peter Steinfels, *The Neoconservatives: The Origins of a Movement* (New York: Simon & Schuster, 2013), esp. 46–51; John Ehrman, *The Rise of Neoconservatism: Intellectuals and Foreign Affairs, 1945–1994* (New Haven: Yale University Press, 1995), 35–45; Justin Vaïsse, *Neoconservatism: The Biography of a Movement* (Cambridge: Belknap Press of Harvard University Press, 2010), esp. 4, 43–46, 86–90. In contrast to the findings of Steinfels and Ehrman, Vaïsse's portrayal of neoconservatism as largely a response to the New Left—particularly in his treatment of the CDM—owes much to a fundamental failure to adequately distinguish the New Politics from the New Left.

67 Wattenberg, *Fighting Words*, 138; "Come Home, Democrats"; Vaïsse, *Neoconservatism*, 90, 93.
68 "Come Home, Democrats"; Justin Vaïsse, "Complete List of CDM Members and Directors (1972–1992)," *Neoconservatism: The Biography of a Movement*, companion website to the book, http://neoconservatism.vaisse.net/doku.php?id=complete_list_of_cdm_members_and_directors_1972-1992 (accessed November 14, 2015).
69 Miroff, *The Liberals' Moment*, 264; Vaïsse, *Neoconservatism*, 87; Rowland Evans and Robert Novak, "Anti–New Politics Liberals," *Washington Post*, November 12, 1972; Wattenberg, *Fighting Words*, 137.
70 Podhoretz, *Breaking Ranks*; Wattenberg, *Fighting Words*.
71 The tendency to stress the continuity and similarity of the New Politics and the New Left or even to treat the two terms as nearly synonymous is pervasive in scholarship that examines neoconservatism. For example, see Kenneth S. Baer, *Reinventing Democrats: The Politics of Liberalism from Reagan to Clinton* (Lawrence: University Press of Kansas, 2000), esp. 19–20, 33; Richard D. Kahlenberg, *Tough Liberal: Albert Shanker and the Battles over Schools, Unions, Race, and Democracy* (New York: Columbia University Press, 2007), esp. 145–65; Vaïsse, *Neoconservatism*, esp. 81–109.
72 Vaïsse, *Neoconservatism*, 50; Peter Steinfels, *The Neoconservatives: The Origins of a Movement* (New York: Simon & Schuster, 2013), 61–67, 71–72.
73 John Kenneth Galbraith, "The Case for George McGovern," *Saturday Review*, July 1, 1972, 26.
74 "Come Home, Democrats."
75 Penn Kemble and Josh Muravchik, "The New Politics & the Democrats," *Commentary*, December 1972, 84.
76 Michael Novak, "Needing Niebuhr Again," *Commentary*, September 1972, 60.
77 Irving Kristol, "About Equality," Commentary, November 1972, 43; Podhoretz, *Breaking Ranks*, 288.
78 "Come Home, Democrats."
79 Vaïsse, *Neoconservatism*, 97.
80 "Come Home, Democrats"; Podhoretz, *Breaking Ranks*, 338–39.
81 "Come Home, Democrats."
82 Kahlenberg, *Tough Liberal*, 1–3, 156, 292, 400–401.
83 Midge Decter in "What Is a Liberal—Who Is a Conservative? A Symposium," *Commentary*, September 1976, 50–51.

84 Michael Harrington, "The Welfare State and Its Neoconservative Critics," *Dissent*, September 1973, 435–54.
85 David Halberstam, "Travels with Bobby Kennedy," *Harper's Magazine*, July 1968, 58.
86 Marjorie Hunter, "Democratic Rules Panel Backs Sweeping Changes," *New York Times*, June 25, 1972.
87 "Democratic Homecoming," *Wall Street Journal*, December 8, 1972.
88 Elliot Abrams in "What Is a Liberal—Who is a Conservative?," 34.
89 Gus Tyler in "What Is a Liberal—Who is a Conservative?," 101.
90 "Come Home, Democrats."
91 Vaïsse, *Neoconservatism*, 10–13.

CHAPTER 6: FROM NEW POLITICS TO NEOLIBERALISM

1 Paul E. Tsongas, keynote address at the Americans for Democratic Action national convention, June 14, 1980, 3, folder 6, box 19, M97-135, ADA.
2 Remarks of Senator Edward M. Kennedy, Americans for Democratic Action national convention, June 14, 1980, folder 6, box 18.
3 Randall Rothenberg, *The Neoliberals: Creating the New American Politics* (New York: Simon & Schuster, 1984), 42; David S. Broder, "Politically Passé?," *Washington Post*, June 25, 1980.
4 Andrew Gamble "Economic Libertarianism," in *The Oxford Handbook of Political Ideologies*, ed. Michael Freeden, Lyman Tower Sargent, and Marc Stears (New York: Oxford University Press, 2013), 206–7
5 Arthur M. Schlesinger Jr., "Requiem for Neoliberalism," *New Republic*, June 6, 1983, 28.
6 Lily Geismer, *Left Behind: The Democrats' Failed Attempt to Solve Inequality* (New York: Public Affairs, 2022), esp. 1–13.
7 Arthur Schlesinger Jr., "For Democrats, Me-Too Reaganism Will Spell Disaster," *New York Times*, July 6, 1986.
8 William Schneider, "JFK's Children: The Class of '74," *Atlantic Monthly*, March 1989, 35–38, 46; Diane Granat, "The Class of 1974: Whatever Happened to the Watergate Babies?," *Congressional Quarterly Weekly Report*, March 3, 1984, 498.
9 Schneider, "JFK's Children," 35–38.
10 Granat, "The Class of 1974," 498–99.
11 Schneider, "JFK's Children," 42.
12 For the clearest expression of Bell's widely influential "end of ideology" thesis, see Daniel Bell "An Epilogue: The End of Ideology in the West," in *The End of Ideology: On the Exhaustion of Political Ideas in the Fifties* (Glencoe, IL: Free Press, 1960), 369–75.
13 Schneider, "JFK's Children," 37; Ronald D. Elving, "Watergate Babies Take Power," *Congressional Quarterly Weekly Report*, September 2, 1995, 2658; Granat, "The Class of 1974," 499–502.
14 Mary Russell, "'Freshman Class' Is Running Scared," *Washington Post*, January 12, 1976.
15 Granat, "The Class of 1974," 498–99; David E. Rosenbaum, "The Senate's Revolution Is Without an R," *New York Times*, February 2, 1975.

16 John A. Lawrence, *The Class of '74: Congress after Watergate and the Roots of Partisanship* (Baltimore: Johns Hopkins University Press, 2018), 127–28.
17 "The AFL-CIO: How Much Clout in Congress?," *Congressional Quarterly Weekly Report*, July 19, 1975, 1531–32.
18 "A Job for Everyone," *New Republic*, March 27, 1976, 3–4.
19 Taylor E. Dark III, "From Resistance to Adaptation: Organized Labor Reacts to a Changing Nominating Process," in *The Making of the Presidential Candidates, 2004*, ed. William G. Mayer (Lanham, MD: Rowman & Littlefield, 2004), 194.
20 ADA Finance Committee meeting, minutes, January 28, 1975, folder 38, box 6, M97–135, ADA; Americans for Democratic Action balance sheet, June 1, 1989, folder 33, box 8, M97–135, ADA; Labor Officers on ADA national board, March 28, 1979, folder 34, box 18, M97–135, ADA; Amy Isaacs, telephone interview by author, October 15, 2020.
21 Timothy Stanley, *Kennedy vs. Carter: The 1980 Battle for the Democratic Party's Soul* (Lawrence: University Press of Kansas, 2010), 26–27.
22 David L. Chappell, *Waking from the Dream: The Struggle for Civil Rights in the Shadow of Martin Luther King, Jr.* (Durham: Duke University Press, 2016), 65; Jefferson Cowie, *Stayin' Alive: The 1970s and the Last Days of the Working Class* (New York: New Press, 2010), 274.
23 "Guide to Media Access for Local Full Employment Coalition," folder 10, box 23, M97–135, ADA; John Carr to Full Employment Task Force, March 28, 1978, folder 10, box 23, M97–135, ADA.
24 Murray Finley and Coretta Scott King to Hon. Hubert Humphrey, August 1, 1975, folder 7, box 23, M97–135, ADA; written testimony of Murray Finley on the Full Employment and Balanced Growth Act before the House Subcommittee on Employment Opportunities, January 18, 1978, folder 9, box 23, M97–135, ADA; Byron E. Shafer, *Quiet Revolution: The Struggle for the Democratic Party and the Shaping of Post-Reform Politics* (New York: Russell Sage Foundation, 1983), 412; Arthur Schlesinger Jr., *Robert Kennedy and His Times*, vol. 2 (Boston: Houghton Mifflin, 1978), 954.
25 Murray Finley and Coretta Scott King to Hon. Hubert Humphrey, August 1, 1975; "A Job for Everyone," *New Republic*, March 27, 1976, 3–4; Leon H. Keyserling, "The Possible Dream," *New Republic*, May 1, 1976, 32.
26 Robert M. Collins, *More: The Politics of Growth in Postwar America* (New York: Oxford University Press, 2000), 167–68.
27 Cowie, *Stayin' Alive*, 272.
28 "Jobs Bill Divides House Democrats," *Washington Post*, August 6, 1976.
29 Office of Paul E. Tsongas, "Humphrey-Hawkins Full Employment Act (H.R. 50)," folder 2, box 196B, Washington Files, Paul E. Tsongas Collection, UMass Lowell Libraries Center for Lowell History, Lowell, MA.
30 Gary Mucciaroni, *The Political Failure of Employment Policy, 1945–1982* (Pittsburgh: University of Pittsburgh Press, 1990), 96–99.
31 Committee on Banking, Housing, and Urban Affairs, *Hearings on S. 50*, 94th Cong., 1st sess., May 20, 21, and 25, 1976 (Washington, DC: US Government Printing Office, 1976), 84–88; Richard Parker, *John Kenneth Galbraith: His Life, His Politics, His Economics* (New York: Farrar, Straus and Giroux, 2005), 140.

32 "Full Employment Bill," in *CQ Almanac, 1976*, 32nd ed. (Washington, DC: Congressional Quarterly, 1977), 371–73.
33 Leon Shull to the Hon. Hubert Humphrey, March 8, 1977, folder 9, box 23, M97-135, ADA.
34 Cowie, *Stayin' Alive*, 279–83.
35 "Full Employment Week: A Call to Action," folder 10, box 23, M97-135; Viva Baylinson and Page Gardner to All Chapter Chairpersons and Executives, August 18, 1977, folder 10, box 23, M97-135, ADA; Leon Shull to Officers, National Board, Chapters, December 12, 1977, folder 10, box 23, M97-135, ADA; Murray Finley and Coretta Scott King to National Organization Supporting Humphrey-Hawkins, folder 10, box 23, M97-135, ADA.
36 Edward Walsh, "Humphrey-Hawkins Measure Is Signed by the President," *Washington Post*, October 28, 1978; Hobart Rowen, "A Useful Exercise," *Washington Post*, January 28, 1979.
37 "A.D.A. Votes to Oppose Carter and Press Kennedy," *New York Times*, June 25, 1979; Bill Peterson, "ADA Joins Draft-Kennedy Movement," *Washington Post*, June 25, 1979.
38 For more on the significance of Ted Kennedy's 1980 campaign in demonstrating the popular appeal of liberalism during the late 1970s and early 1980s in spite of the widely presumed conservative turn in US politics, see Stanley, *Kennedy vs. Carter*.
39 Collins, *More*, 159; Cowie, *Stayin' Alive*, 301; Judith Stein, *Pivotal Decade: How the United States Traded Factories for Finance in the 1970s* (New Haven: Yale University Press, 2010), 225–31.
40 Haynes Johnson, "ADA Warns against Promises Unkept," *Washington Post*, May 8, 1977.
41 Arthur Schlesinger Jr. to Robert G. Lewis, February 28, 1979, box 59, JKG.
42 David S. Broder and Bill Peterson, "Key Democrats to Shun Midterm Parley," *Washington Post*, December 4, 1978; David S. Broder and Bill Peterson, "Kennedy Warns of a Party Split by Arms Outlays," *Washington Post*, December 10, 1978.
43 Barney Frank, "How Ted Got Drafted," *New Republic*, October 6, 1979.
44 Bill Peterson, "ADA Struggles with How to Avoid Fracturing Democrats," *Washington Post*, June 24, 1979.
45 Arthur Schlesinger Jr., "Who Needs Grover Cleveland?," *New Republic*, July 7, 1979, 15.
46 "A.D.A. Votes to Oppose Carter and Press Kennedy"; Ken Bode, "Dumpsters Convention," *New Republic*, July 7, 1979.
47 Warren Weaver Jr., "The Time for a Decision Is Getting Near for Kennedy," *New York Times*, August 26, 1979; George Gallup, "Democrats Favor Kennedy in Field of 9 Contenders," *Washington Post*, June 24, 1979; T. R. Reid, "Staking Out Left, Kennedy Assails Carter's Policies," *Washington Post*, January 29, 1980; Rowland Evans and Robert Novak, "Camelot McGoverned," *Washington Post*, November 7, 1979.
48 Reid, "Staking Out Left, Kennedy Assails Carter's Policies;" B. Drummond Ayres Jr., "Kennedy's Campaign Shift," *New York Times*, January 30, 1980; "Transcript of Kennedy's Speech at Georgetown University on Campaign Issues," *New York Times*, January 29, 1980.
49 Stanley, *Kennedy vs. Carter*, 6–7.

50 James Tobin, "11 Top State UAW Leaders Go 9 for Kennedy, 2 for Carter," *Detroit News*, February 5, 1980; Philip Shabecoff, "Carter Forces Find Labor's Mood Warm," *New York Times*, February 21, 1980.
51 Milton Coleman, "Gay Advocates Part with Barry, Endorse Kennedy," *Washington Post*, January 10, 1980; T. R. Reid and David S. Broder, "Kennedy Takes Tougher A-Plant Stand," *Washington Post*, February 21, 1980; "Ratings by Conservationists Put Kennedy at the Top," *New York Times*, April 19, 1980; Judith Valente, "Specter of the Draft Revives Old Slogans at Universities Here," *Washington Post*, February 2, 1980.
52 Stanley, *Kennedy vs. Carter*, 2–3, 152–57; Hedrick Smith, "Carter and Kennedy to Meet Today to Cope with Democratic Breach," *New York Times*, June 5, 1980.
53 Arthur M. Schlesinger Jr. and Joseph L. Rauh to ADA Board Colleague, September 13, 1980, folder 1, box 5, AMS.
54 National board meeting minutes, September 21, 1980, folder 43, box 10, M97–135, ADA; "Re-Electing President Jimmy Carter and Vice-President Walter F. Mondale," folder 43, box 10, M97–135, ADA.
55 Amy Isaacs, telephone interview by author, October 15, 2020.
56 Bill Peterson, "Democrats Hope, but Mostly Hurt after Worst Beating in 27 Years," *Washington Post*, November 6, 1980.
57 Arthur Schlesinger Jr., "The End of an Era?," *Wall Street Journal*, November 20, 1980.
58 For a succinct examination of what the Reagan Revolution did and did not achieve as well as how it has been interpreted and understood, see Gil Troy, *The Reagan Revolution: A Very Short Introduction* (New York: Oxford University Press, 2009).
59 Stanley, *Kennedy vs. Carter*, 175–79.
60 David S. Broder, "The Halo Syndrome," *Washington Post*, March 9, 1980.
61 Arthur Schlesinger Jr., "Casting a Vote for Anderson," *Wall Street Journal*, October 10, 1980; Joseph L. Rauh Jr., "A Chance to Follow the Idealistic Path," *Washington Star*, October 26, 1980.
62 Schlesinger, "Casting a Vote for Anderson"; Rauh, "A Chance to Follow the Idealistic Path." President Nixon nominated a conservative judge from South Carolina, Clement Haynsworth, to the Supreme Court in 1969. After Haynsworth was rejected by the Senate under a cloud of corruption allegations, Nixon nominated another conservative southern judge, G. Harrold Carswell, to the Supreme Court the following year. Carswell's nomination was rejected by the Senate amid attacks on the judge's long history of support for segregation. Both of Nixon's unsuccessful Supreme Court nominations were rejected by the full Senate, rather than the Senate Judiciary Committee. Rick Perlstein, *Nixonland: The Rise of a President and the Fracturing of America* (New York Scribner, 2008), 421–22, 427, 443, 459, 462, 474.
63 Schlesinger, "The End of an Era?"
64 Schlesinger, "Requiem for Neoliberalism," 28.
65 Peterson, "Democrats Hope, but Mostly Hurt after Worst Beating in 27 Years."
66 Paul Tsongas, *The Road from Here: Liberalism and Realities in the 1980s* (New York: Alfred A. Knopf, 1981), 30–36.
67 Tsongas, *The Road from Here*, xiii, 249.

68 Kenneth T. Walsh, "Hart Trouble. Colorado," *New Republic*, October 25, 1980.
69 Michael Getler, "Direct Hit Scored on Defense Policy," *Washington Post*, November 6, 1980.
70 Schneider, "JFK's Children," 40; Miroff, *The Liberals' Moment*, 268; Charles Peters quoted in Rothenberg, *The Neoliberals*, 20.
71 Nelson Lichtenstein, *State of the Union: A Century of American Labor* (Princeton: Princeton University Press, 2002), 247–49.
72 David S. Broder, "AFL-CIO Leader Riding a Big Bet," *Washington Post*, September 20, 1981; Seth S. King, "260,000 in Capital Rally for Protest of Reagan Policies," *New York Times*, September 20, 1981; Eric Pianin and Warren Brown, "Crowd Proclaims Labor's Solidarity," *Washington Post*, September 20, 1981.
73 Pianin and Brown, "Crowd Proclaims Labor's Solidarity."
74 Tsongas, keynote address, June 14, 1980.
75 Rothenberg, *The Neoliberals*, 42; Steven V. Roberts, "A.D.A. Debates Role of Liberalism in a Year of Losses and Budget Cuts," *New York Times*, June 15, 1980; Robert Healy, "New Liberalism, Old Politics," *Boston Globe*, September 12, 1980.
76 Tsongas, *The Road from Here*, 33–34.
77 Roberts, "A.D.A. Debates Role of Liberalism in a Year of Losses and Budget Cuts."
78 Arthur Schlesinger Jr. to Senator Paul Tsongas, July 8, 1980, box 225, JKG; Arthur Schlesinger Jr. to Honorable Paul Tsongas, September 12, 1980, box 225, JKG; Schlesinger, "The End of an Era?"
79 Tsongas, *The Road from Here*, x, 35; David Shribman, "Massachusetts' 'Other Senator' Urging a Realistic Liberalism," *New York Times*, October 6, 1981.
80 Tsongas, *The Road from Here*, esp. 127–31, 202–5.
81 Gary Hart, *A New Democracy: A Democratic Vision for the 1980's and Beyond* (New York: Quill, 1983), esp. 54–60,
82 "Hart Tells of Getting Navy Commission in '80," *New York Times*, March 10, 1984; Hart, *A New Democracy*, esp. 125–40.
83 Charles Peters, *Tilting at Windmills: An Autobiography* (Reading, MA: Addison-Wesley, 1988), 141–43, 154, 162.
84 Peters, *Tilting at Windmill*, 181–85, 205–7.
85 Peters, *Tilting at Windmills*, 207.
86 Charles Peters, "A Neo-Liberal's Manifesto," *Washington Post*, September 5, 1982.
87 Peters, "A Neo-Liberal's Manifesto."
88 Hart, *A New Democracy*, 8, 14.
89 Tsongas, *The Road from Here*, 10–11, 134.
90 Lloyd Grove, "Paul Tsongas's Precarious Stand," *Washington Post*, March 6, 1992.
91 Schlesinger, "For Democrats, Me-Too Reaganism Will Spell Disaster."
92 "DNC Follows ADA Lead—Endorses Dukakis!!," *ADA Today*, Summer 1988, 1.
93 Steven M. Gillon, *The Democrats' Dilemma: Walter F. Mondale and the Liberal Legacy* (New York: Columbia University Press, 1992), 340–43.
94 "Fritz Mondale Is ADA's Choice," *ADA World*, March 1984, 1.
95 "Neoliberals, Paleoliberals," *New Republic*, April 9, 1984, 6, 41.
96 Gillon, *The Democrats' Dilemma*, 389.
97 Robert Kuttner, "What's the Big Idea?," *New Republic*, November 18, 1985, 23.

98 For examples, see John Kenneth Galbraith, "The Conservative Majority Myth," *Dissent*, April 1976, 123–26; and Arthur Schlesinger Jr. to Walter Mondale, September 21, 1984, box 225, JKG.
99 Schlesinger, "For Democrats, Me-Too Reaganism Will Spell Disaster."
100 Bell, "An Epilogue," 373.
101 Arthur Mr. Schlesinger Jr., *The Vital Center: The Politics of Freedom* (Cambridge, MA: Riverside Press, 1949), esp. 11–50. For more on the continuity between the thought of Schlesinger and Bell, see Allen Paul Fisher, "Ideological Continuities in 'The End of Ideology': An Analysis of the Thought of Arthur Schlesinger, Jr., and Daniel Bell, 1940–1970" (PhD diss., Purdue University, 1977).
102 John Kenneth Galbraith, *American Capitalism: The Concept of Countervailing Power* (Boston: Houghton Mifflin, 1952), esp. ix, 115–57, 171–81.
103 Giles Scott-Smith, *The Politics of Apolitical Culture: The Congress for Cultural Freedom, the CIA and Post-war American Hegemony* (New York: Routledge, 2002), 145–53.
104 Tsongas, *The Road from Here*, 237.
105 Bruce J. Schulman, *The Seventies: The Great Shift in American Culture, Society, and Politics* (New York: Free Press, 2001), 211–12.
106 Gerald Hansen, "Brown Signs Sex Reforms," *Contact*, June 18, 1975; "California," *Contact*, May 7, 1975; Amy L. Stone, *Gay Rights at the Ballot Box* (Minneapolis: University of Minnesota Press, 2012), 14, 57.
107 For more on the popular appeal of the economic progressivism that animated Jackson's presidential campaigns and his Rainbow Coalition, see John Nichols, *The Fight for the Soul of the Democratic Party: The Enduring Legacy of Henry Wallace's Antifascist, Antiracist Politics* (New York: Verso, 2020), 198–203.

EPILOGUE: NEW POLITICS, NEW DEMOCRATS, AND AMERICAN LIBERALISM IN THE TWENTY-FIRST CENTURY

1 Robin Toner, "Perot Quits Race, Leaving Two-Man Field; Clinton Vows Change and 'New Covenant' as He and Bush Court Abandoned Voters," *New York Times*, July 17, 1992; Thomas B. Edsall, "Democrats' Middle-of-the-Road Theme Winning Over Voters Tired of Old Deal," *Washington Post*, July 17, 1992; *1992 Democratic Platform: "A New Covenant with the American People"* (Washington, DC: Democratic National Committee, 1992), 1–2, 13; Stuart Auerbach, "Overcoming a Continental Divide; North American Free-Trade Pact Talks Reach Tough, Final Stage," *Washington Post*, July 25, 1992.
2 R. W. Apple Jr., "Anti-Bush Sentiment Could Break Colorado's Tradition of Loyalty to G.O.P.," *New York Times*, September 21, 1992.
3 *State of Colorado Abstract of Votes Cast, 1992* (Denver: Office of the Secretary of State, 1993), 86–87; Robin Toner, "Bush Pledges Help: Governor Given an Edge of 43% to 38%, with Perot Getting 18%," *New York Times*, November 4, 1992.
4 Jeff Gerth, "Liberal Group Backs Clinton in Effort to Unify Democrats," *New York Times*, January 7, 1996; David E. Rosenbaum, "Democratic Platform Shows Shift in Party's Focus," *New York Times*, July 14, 1992; Philip Dine, "Joe Rauh's Been Lifelong Battler for Unpopular Causes," *St. Louis Post Dispatch*, July 31, 1992;

Marshall Ingwerson, "Tsongas, Clinton Results Indicate Historic Shift in Democratic Party," *Christian Science Monitor*, February 21, 1992.

5 "Text of the State of the Union Address," *Washington Post*, January 24, 1996; Alison Mitchell and Todd S. Purdum, "Clinton the Conciliator Finds His Line in Sand," *New York Times*, January 2, 1996.

6 Of course, Clinton's signing of the 1996 Defense of Marriage Act—which banned federal recognition of same-sex marriages—makes clear that his commitment to gay rights was anything but ironclad. Forty-five days before the 1996 presidential election, Clinton sought to prevent Republicans from placing him beyond the pale of mainstream social values and avoid alienating gay voters by quietly signing the legislation into law at 12:50 AM. John F. Hale, "The Making of the New Democrats," *Political Science Quarterly* 110, no. 2 (1995): 223, 229; Peter Baker, "President Quietly Signs Law Aimed at Gay Marriages," *Washington Post*, September 22, 1996.

7 Daryl A. Carter, *Brother Bill: President Clinton and the Politics of Race and Class* (Fayetteville: University of Arkansas Press, 2016), 26; Hale, "The Making of the New Democrats," 215; William Schneider, "No Modesty Please, We're the DLC," *National Journal*, December 12, 1998, 2962.

8 Hale, "The Making of the New Democrats," 207, 225; Nicol C. Rae, *Southern Democrats* (New York: Oxford University Press, 1994), 141; Schneider, "No Modesty Please, We're the DLC," 2962.

9 Hale, "The Making of the New Democrats," 229, Elizabeth Drew, *On the Edge: The Clinton Presidency* (New York: Touchstone, 1994), 42; Kenneth S. Baer, *Reinventing Democrats: The Politics of Liberalism from Reagan to Clinton* (Lawrence: University Press of Kansas, 2000), 212.

10 For more on the politics of Bill Clinton and the DLC, see Lily Geismer, *Left Behind: The Democrats' Failed Attempt to Solve Inequality* (New York: Public Affairs, 2022), esp. 1–13, 287–89. Geismer offers a valuable study of the DLC and its impact on American liberalism that challenges the notion that the New Democrats were simply reacting to Republican electoral success. She argues that while Clinton's efforts at "triangulation" were based on appropriating ideas from the right to appeal to moderate swing voters, his "third way" politics owed much to the efforts of the Watergate babies to reimagine government and liberalism prior to the Reagan Revolution. Nevertheless, Geismer's inattention to the Watergate babies' roots in the New Politics movement obscures the important ways in which the politics of the DLC, the Atari Democrats, and the Watergate babies owed much to the New Politics. Carter, *Brother Bill*, 3–4, 187, 193; Thomas Frank, *Listen, Liberal: Or What Ever Happened to the Party of the People?* (New York: Metropolitan, 2016), 101–3.

11 Robert Shogan, "Cracks Appear in Democrats' Unity Façade," *Los Angeles Times*, August 26, 1996.

12 ADA Finance Committee meeting minutes, July 15, 1975, folder 38, box 6, M97–135, ADA; Americans for Democratic Action, Profit & Loss Budget vs. Actual, box 5, M2013–116, ADA.

13 Leon Shull, "National Director's Report to National Board," December 7, 1968, box 498, JKG.

14 For more on the importance of direct mail campaigns to conservative groups during the 1970s, see Rick Perlstein, *Reaganland: America's Right Turn, 1976–1980*

(New York: Simon & Schuster, 2020), 35, 96–98, 385, and 399. Leon Shull to Winn Newman, April 24, 1980, folder 3, box 6, M97-135, ADA.

15 Gertrude Riger to Abner Levine, July 10, 1973, folder 38, box 6, M97-135, ADA; ADA Finance Committee meeting minutes, July 15, 1975, folder 38, box 6, M97-135, ADA.

16 Nelson Lichtenstein, *State of the Union: A Century of American Labor* (Princeton: Princeton University Press, 2002), 16.

17 Frank Newport, "Democrats More Positive about Socialism Than Capitalism," Gallup News Service, August 13, 2018, https://news.gallup.com/poll/240725/democrats-positive-socialism-capitalism.aspx (accessed February 4, 2022).

18 Arthur M. Schlesinger, Jr., *The Crisis of Confidence: Ideas, Power, and Violence in America* (Boston: Houghton Mifflin, 1969), 248–49.

19 Harold Meyerson, "The First Post-Middle-Class Election," *American Prospect*, Summer 2016, 24–25.

20 Alissa Quart, *Squeezed: Why Our Families Can't Afford America* (New York: Ecco, 2018), 50–53.

21 For examples, see Daniel Denvir, "Hillary Clinton's Cynical Race Appeals: The Revenge of Neoliberal Identity Politics," *Salon.com*, February 19, 2016, https://www.salon.com/2016/02/19/hillary_clintons_cynical_race_appeals_the_revenge_of_neoliberal_identity_politics/ (accessed February 4, 2022); and Greg Grandin, "Bernie's Challenge to American Exceptionalism," *The Nation*, July 29–August 5, 2019, 25.

22 Amanda Hess, "'In this House' Yard Signs, and Their Curious Power," *New York Times*, October 29, 2021; Jared Clemons, "'From 'Freedom Now!' to 'Black Lives Matter': Retrieving King and Randolph to Theorize Contemporary White Antiracism," *Perspectives on Politics* 20, no. 4 (2022): esp. 1297.

INDEX

Italicized page references followed with *f* indicate photos.

Abel, I. W., 144
abortion: and ADA's 1970 resolution, 185–86; National Abortion Rights Action League, 252; and neoliberalism shift, 5, 6, 222, 226; New Democrats and Clinton presidency, 245–46, 248–49
Abrams, Elliot, 203–4
Abzug, Bella, 174, 259n19
ADA World (ADA): Curtis Gans as editor of, 140; on Freedom Budget, 119; on national security and military-industrial complex, 177; on poverty, 107–8; on Vietnam War, 65, 76, 85
affirmative action, 167, 186–87, 201, 203
"affirmative government," 227–28
The Affluent Society (Galbraith): on Cold War and military production, 36–37; on consumer demand, 42; and New Class, 137–38; on postwar economic growth and social balance need, 25, 32, 34; on poverty and civil rights, 101–4, 110; on qualitative liberalism and social balance, 46–53; sales of, 44
African American Brotherhood of Sleeping Car Porters, 105

Agnew, Spiro, 288n33
Aid to Families with Dependent Children, 112, 249, 277n60
Allende, Salvador, 8
Amalgamated Clothing Workers of America, 215
American Capitalism (Galbraith), 240, 241
American Federation of Labor–Congress of Industrial Organizations (AFL-CIO), 170, 212, 215–17, 230–31
Americans for Democratic Action (ADA): on ABM, 180–81; Carter endorsement debate by, 225; civil rights resolution (1964), 106–9; Clinton endorsed by, 247; Cold War and Wallace's 1948 presidential campaign, 20–21, 71–73, 81, 87, 260n9, 261n14; congressional voting records rated by, 5–6, 211, 250; conservative portrayal of, 7; convention (1954), *2f*; convention (1965), 65–66; convention (1966), 66, 131; convention (1980), 206; decline in influence by, 250–52; Duffey as national director of, *6f*, 130, 159–65, 251, 284n89; Dukakis endorsed by, 237; economic policy

Americans for Democratic Action (*cont.*)
resolution (1954), 26–27; Edwards as former national chairman, 87; Galbraith as national chairman, 140, 159–60; Isaacs as national director, 250; liberal intellectual leaders and legacy of, 2–3, 6–7, 251; liberalism and shift toward social/cultural issues, 1–5; Lowenstein as national director of, 7f, 130, 159–65, 251, 284n89; McCarthy endorsed by, 1, 10–14, 127–30, 136–45, 214, 251; McGovern as president of, 221; and McGovern's presidential campaign (1972), 1, 11, 14; membership statistics (1947–1980s), 21–22; and NDC inception, 169–75; neoliberalism criticized by, 237–43; on NLF, 272n96; on polycentric communism and US national security, 61, 66–69, 90, 128, 167, 175–77; as preeminent liberal organization in the United States, 19–23; Roosevelt Day Dinner (1959), 49; Roosevelt Day Dinner (1965), 66; Shull as national director, 4f, 75–76, 119, 180, 216; state and local chapters of, 22, 76, 84, 97, 129, 145–51, 180, 220; Ted Kennedy endorsed by, 221; on Truman presidency, 22–23, 271n14. *See also ADA World*; Galbraith, John Kenneth; neoliberalism; New Class; New Politics movement; poverty and civil rights; qualitative liberalism; Schlesinger, Arthur, Jr.; Vietnam War; "vital center"
Anderson, John, 226–28
anti-ballistic missile (ABM) (Safeguard) system, 180–81, 288n33
anti-establishment sentiment, 152–58
A. Philip Randolph Institute, 94, 115, 118–19. *See also* Freedom Budget
Arab countries, Six-Day War, 133
Aron, Raymond, 41
Ascoli, Max, 39
"Atari Democrats," 5, 14–15, 207–10, 230, 231, 234–35, 237–43
Auerbach, Carl, 47–48, 144
Averbeck, Robin Marie, 272–73n2

Bank of Japan, 234
Bayh, Birch, 227
Bazelon, David, 192
Beer, Samuel, 77–78, 191
Beirne, Joseph A., 144
Bell, Daniel, 192, 196, 201–2, 211, 239–41
Bell, Jonathan, 183
Bellamy, Carla, 254
Bennett, Roy, 65
The Bitter Heritage (Schlesinger), 68–69
Black Lives Matter, 255
Bloodworth, Jeffrey, 260n21
Bond, Julian, 169–70, 171
Bookbinder, Hyman, 196
Bowles, Chester, 6
Braun, Louis, 78–79
Broder, David, 231, 232
Brown, Jerry, 243
Brown, Sam, 169–70, 178
Browne, Robert, 122
Brown v. Board of Education (1954), 96
Brzezinski, Zbigniew, 196, 200
Burnham, James, 7, 138, 280n21
Bush, George H. W., 246
Bush, George W., 205

California, New Class of, 242–43
Campus Americans for Democratic Action, 159
Carmichael, Stokely, 117
Carr, Bob, 210–11
Carswell, G. Harrold, 227, 295n62
Carter, Jimmy: CEA, 218; and FEAC coalition, 219–20; presidential campaign (1976), 213, 219; presidential campaign (1980), 206, 207; and "Reagan Revolution," 225–29; Ted Kennedy's challenge to, 206–7, 209, 220–27, 244
Central Intelligence Agency (CIA), 38
Chicanos, civil rights of, 183–84
The Children of Light and the Children of Darkness (Niebuhr), 72–73
China, Vietnam War and US policy on, 62, 63, 67–69, 90

Chomsky, Noam, 59, 153
Christian Century, on Vietnam War demonstration, 80
Christianity and Crisis, Duffey's writing for, 162
Church, Frank, 81, 141, 225, 227, 229
City University of New York, 80, 191
civil rights movement: Civil Rights Act (1964), 92, 105–6, 274n24; Civil Rights Act (1968), 153; Freedom Summer (1964), 97, 161; and qualitative liberalism debate, 22, 40, 51; and Vietnam War demonstrations, 66, 79, 81, 84, 91. *See also* poverty and civil rights
Clark, Joseph S., 178
Clean for Gene (Rising), 283n64
Cleveland Americans for Democratic Action (ADA), 98
Clinton, Bill, 10f, 207, 245–50, 253, 298n6, 298n10
Clinton, Hillary, 1, 5, 15, 255
Coalition for a Democratic Majority (CDM): "Come Home, Democrats" manifesto of, 195–201, 203; inception of, 167–69; as neoconservative movement, 202–5
Coalition on National Priorities and Military Policy, 168, 178, 179
Cohen, David, 119, 187
Cold War and military spending: ABM system, 180–81; Galbraith on "Cold War mystique," 66–70; and qualitative liberalism debate, 27, 34–40, 49; and Wallace's 1948 presidential campaign, 20–21, 71–73, 81, 87, 260n9, 261n14. *See also* communism; Vietnam War
Collins, Robert, 25
Common Cause, 215
Communications Workers of America, 144
communism: ADA on polycentric communism and US national security, 61, 66–69, 90, 128, 167, 175–77; anticommunist containment principle, 6, 13, 58, 61, 67–71, 127–28; and qualitative liberalism debate, 20–21, 23, 34–41, 45, 54, 58; Second Red Scare, 123–24
Community Action Program (CAP), 107
Conference on Economic Progress, 123
Congress: ADA ratings of congressional voting, 5–6, 211, 250; Congressional Black Caucus, 215; Congressional Budget Office, 217–18; Congressional Conference on the Military Budget and National Priorities, 175–78; and neoliberalism rise, 207, 209, 213–21, 230–31. *See also individual names of senators and representatives*
Congress for Cultural Freedom (CCF), 37–38, 41, 240–41
Congress of Racial Equality (CORE), 117
"constituency of conscience," 152, 156–57, 171–74, 192, 242. *See also* New Class
consumer culture: *The Affluent Society* on social balance, 46–53; and Cold War, 34–40; and Schlesinger on "spiritual unemployment," 40–46
Corona, Bert, 171
The Correspondent, on liberalism vs. anticommunism, 65, 267n20
Council of Economic Advisers (CEA), 18, 24, 25
"countervailing power," 240
Cowie, Jefferson, 281n25

Davies, Gareth, 276n53
Davis, Lanny, 156–57, 163
Decter, Midge, 196, 201
Defense of Marriage Act (1996), 298n6
Dellinger, David, 79
Democratic Leadership Council (DLC), 245–49
Democratic Party: Democratic Advisory Council (DAC), 51–52, 55–57; McGovern candidacy and reform of, 188–95; midterm election losses (1966), 122; midterm "mini-conventions" of, 222; Midwestern Democratic Conference (1960, Detroit), 55; National

Democratic Party (*cont.*)
    Convention (1948), 96; National Convention (1964), 95–101, 273n8; National Convention (1968), 169, 189, 193; National Convention (1972), 188–90, 193–94, 197; National Convention (1992), 245, 246; and NDC inception, 169–75; neoconservatives' response to McGovern's loss, 188–95; New Democrats and Clinton presidency, 245–50, 253; primaries and state caucuses, 172, 189–90, 290n55; and qualitative liberalism debate, 19–20, 22–23, 28–34, 44, 45, 51–52, 55–56; *Quiet Revolution* on reform of, 289n52; twenty-first-century public opinion on social issues vs. economic issues, 252–56. *See also* neoliberalism; *individual names of political candidates and leaders*
Democratic Socialist Organizing Committee, 222
Diem, Ngo Dinh, 62–63
Diggs, Charles, 99
Đilas, Milovan, 138, 280n21
Dissent, neoconservative term first used in, 201–2
The Disuniting of America (Schlesinger), 187
Doherty, Gerard, 223
Douglas, Paul, 47, 49, 263n75
Douglas, William O., 261n14
Dubinsky, David, 132
Duffey, Joseph: and ADA leadership, 6f, 79, 130, 147, 159–65, 251, 284n89; on liberalism and affluence, 173
Dukakis, Michael, 237, 243

economic issues: economic growth consensus, 23–28; Economic Opportunity Act (1964), 107, 116; Glass–Steagall Act, 233–34, 249; GNP growth (1948–1952), 24; Humphrey–Hawkins bill (1976, Full Employment and Balanced Growth Act), 209, 213–21, 230, 231; Japan and economic growth of 1980s, 233, 234; neoliberals on entrepreneurship in technology, 234–36; New Democrats and Clinton presidency, 245–50, 253; "stagflation," 9, 213, 216, 253; twenty-first-century Democrats on social issues vs. economic issues, 252–56; Vietnam War, financial cost, 130, 135. *See also The Affluent Society*; employment; Employment Act; neoliberalism; New Deal; poverty and civil rights; qualitative liberalism
Edgar, Bob, 210–12
Edwards, Don, 76–78, 82, 87
Ehrenreich, Barbara, 281n25
Eisenhower, Dwight D.: and ADA on Truman presidency, 261n14; election of (1952), 138; New Look foreign policy, 27, 35–36; and qualitative liberalism debate, 25, 26–28, 44–45, 52
Eizenstat, Stuart, 223
employment: automation fears about, 111–15; Freedom Budget on, 94–95, 115–25; full employment debate and neoliberalism, 212–20; guaranteed annual income initiatives, 111–15, 276n53, 277n60; March on Washington for Jobs and Freedom (1963), 3f, 4f, 92, 104–6, 275n32. *See also* Employment Act; poverty and civil rights
Employment Act (1946): and ADA on poverty and civil rights initiatives, 108, 112, 114–17; and Humphrey–Hawkins bill, 213; passage of, 276n45; and qualitative liberalism debate, 23–24
"end of ideology" thesis, 239–44
Equal Rights Amendment (ERA), 215, 226
Executive Order Number 8802 on racial discrimination, 105

Fair Deal policy, 18, 28, 42–43, 58, 117
Fair Employment Practices Committee, 105

Family Assistance Plan (FAP), 277n60
Federal Reserve, Carter administration, 221
Federation of American Scientists, 178
Fields, Sam, 211
Finley, Murray, 215
Ford, Gerald, 209, 222
Ford Foundation, 184
"Four Freedoms" (Roosevelt), 116
France, Vietnam colonialism by, 61, 62
Fraser, Donald, 189–91, 193, 200, 214, 215, 222, 290n55
Freedom Budget (Randolph Institute): initiative, 94–95, 115–19, 177; and middle-class values, 277–78n71; and Vietnam War, 120–25, 216
Freedom Summer (1964), 97, 161
From, Al, 248
From Opportunity to Entitlement (Davies), 276n53
Fulbright, William, 81
Full Employment Action Council (FEAC), 215–16, 219–20
Full Employment and Balanced Growth Act (1976, Humphrey–Hawkins bill), 209, 213–21, 230, 231
Full Employment and Balanced Growth Act (1978), 220
full employment initiative. *See* Employment Act

Galbraith, John Kenneth: ADA legacy of, 2–3, 6, 251; and ADA's McCarthy endorsement, 10–12; as ambassador to India, 59, 153; *American Capitalism*, 240, 241; and anti-establishment sentiment, 153–56, 158; on "Cold War mystique," 66–70; on "countervailing power," 240; Minority Advancement Plan of, 186; as national ADA chairman, 140, 159–60; and Negotiation Now!, 90, 134, 136–37, 281n84; and neoliberalism, 210, 218–19, 239–43; on New Class, 15, 130, 139–44, 253; and new generation of ADA leadership, 159–61, 164–65, 284n89; and

New Politics movement, 167–69, 173–79, 192–94, 198–200; and *New Republic* on Negotiation Now!, 286n104; photos, *5f, 8f, 10f*; on poverty and civil rights, 93–95, 101–4, 109–11, 120, 125, 126; and qualitative liberalism debate, 12–13, 17–19, 22–23, 32, 34–42, 45–57; as Stevenson's speechwriter, 22–23; testimony to Senate Committee on Banking, Housing, and Urban Affairs, 218–19; on Vietnam War, 59, 64–71, 82–85, 88–91, 272n98. *See also The Affluent Society*
Galbraith, Kitty, *10f*
Gans, Curtis, 85–86, 88, 140–41, 169–70
Gans, Herbert, 121
Geismer, Lily, 33, 208, 298n10
Geneva Accords (1954), 63
Gephardt, Dick, 248
Gillon, Steven, 9–10, 127, 136, 265n3, 274n24
Gingrich, Newt, 249–50
Gitlin, Todd, 182
Glass–Steagall Act, 233–34, 249
Glazer, Nathan, 196, 200, 201–2
Goldwater, Barry, 64, 98
Goodwin, Richard, 10–11, 70, 143, 179
Gottlieb, Sanford, 75–76, 79
Graham, Frank Porter, 163
Great Society programs. *See* War on Poverty
gross national product (GNP), growth (1948–1952), 24
"growthmanship," 23
Gulf of Tonkin Resolution (1964), 63–64

Halberstam, David, 153, 154, 156, 203
Hamer, Fannie Lou, 98, 100
Harkin, Tom, 246
Harrington, Michael: and NDC, 169–70, 173, 201–2; *The Other America*, 102–4, 112–13; and presidential campaign (1980), 222; as socialist, 102, 252, 270n75; *Toward a Democratic Left*, 192

Harris, Seymour, 32, 265n102
Hart, Gary, 4–5, 9f, 207, 210, 226, 229–31, 234–39
Hart, Jeffrey, 229
Hawkins, Augustus, 213
Haynsworth, Clement, 227, 295n62
Henderson, Leon, 6
Henry, Aaron, 98–100
Ho Chi Minh, 69, 77
Hollander, Edward, 48
House Education and Labor Committee, 218–19
Huerta, Dolores, 215
Humphrey, Hubert: ADA legacy of, 6; as CDM co-chairman, 196; and Gary Hart's criticism, 210; and Mondale, 238; on poverty and civil rights, 95–96, 98–100, 273n8; presidential campaign of, 169, 189, 203, 213, 223; and Schlesinger's criticism, 155
Humphrey–Hawkins bill (1976, Full Employment and Balanced Growth Act), 209, 213–21, 230, 231

identity politics, and New Politics movement, 1–2, 4, 15, 181–88, 200–201, 257n2, 258n6. *See also* social issues
inflation, and Humphrey–Hawkins bill (1976, Full Employment and Balanced Growth Act), 209, 213–21, 230, 231. *See also* economic issues
International Association of Machinists, 222, 224
International Days of Protest (NCC), 70–71
International Ladies Garment Workers Union (ILGWU), 131, 144, 196
"In This House" yard signs, 255–56. *See also* social issues
Iran hostage crisis, 223–24
Isaacs, Amy, 250
Israel, Six-Day War, 133
Isserman, Maurice, 271n95

Jackson, Andrew, 43–44
Jackson, Henry "Scoop," 196

Jackson, Jesse, 5, 15, 243, 244
Japan, economic growth of 1980s, 233, 234
Javits, Jacob, 22, 215
Jefferson, Thomas, 43–44
Johns Hopkins University (1965 speech, Johnson), 65, 70
Johnson, Lyndon B.: Budget Bureau of, 218; and CDM, 203; Civil Rights Act (1964), 92, 105–6, 274n24; Civil Rights Act (1968), 153; on Freedom Budget, 119; Galbraith and Schlesinger in administration of, 153; Johns Hopkins University speech (1965), 65, 70; on Kerner Report, 125; presidential campaign (1968), 13, 127, 130–36, 140–43, 145–48, 175–76; presidential election (1964), 98–101; and qualitative liberalism debate, 18, 58; on Vietnam War, 60, 63–66, 68, 70, 80, 84, 87, 120, 126, 214, 265n3; War on Poverty, 93–95, 106–10, 112–16. *See also* poverty and civil rights

Kampelman, Max, 196–97
Katznelson, Ira, 274n24
Kemble, Penn, 196–97, 199
Kennedy, John F.: on civil rights, 275n32; conservatives on ADA influence on, 7; Galbraith in administration of, 59, 153; legacy of, and New Politics movement, 194; legacy of, and "Watergate babies," 210–11; legacy of, as "Camelot," 10; and *The Other America*, 103; and qualitative liberalism debate, 18, 52, 53; Schlesinger as special assistant to, 101, 103, 153; on Vietnam War, 59, 62–63, 67
Kennedy, Robert: and labor movement, 215; legacy of, and NDC, 168; presidential campaign (1968), 129, 141, 146, 149; on Vietnam War, 81
Kennedy, Ted, presidential campaign (1980), 5, 15, 206–7, 209, 220–27, 244
Kerner, Otto, 124
Kerner Report (1968), 124–25

Keyserling, Leon: and ADA's split from labor unions, 144; and CDM, 196; as CEA chair, 18; and FEAC, 216; at joint Economic Committee (1949), *1f*; on poverty and civil rights, 94–95, 108, 113, 115–19, 120–23, 126; on presidential campaign (1968), 132, 133–34; and qualitative liberalism debate, 13, 18, 19, 22–33, 39, 43–44, 48, 50–58, 274n86. *See also* Freedom Budget
Keyserling, Mary Dublin, 123
Khrushchev, Nikita, 38
King, Coretta Scott, 79, 215, 231
King, Ed, 99–100
King, Martin Luther, Jr.: Martin Luther King Jr. Center for Social Change, 231; on poverty and civil rights, 96, 99–100; and presidential campaign (1968), 148–49; Selma march, 160; on Vietnam War, 82, 84, 85
Kirkland, Lane, 230–31
Kirkpatrick, Jeane, 196
"Kitchen Debate" (Nixon), 38
Korean War, 24, 26
Kristol, Irving, 199
Kuh, Edwin, 186

labor unions: ADA's split from, 131–37, 139, 142–45, 149, 156, 165, 251; on NAFTA, 245; and neoliberal Democrats, 206, 212–20, 224, 230–31; and New Politics movement, 170, 172, 196, 201; on Vietnam War, 60, 91. *See also individual names of labor unions*
La Raza Unida, 184
Lasch, Christopher, 45
Latinos, civil rights of, 183–84
Left Behind (Geismer), 298n10
Lekachman, Robert, 53
Levison, Andrew, 281n25
Lewis, John, *3f*, 97, 100, 105
Lewis, Penny, 281n25
LGBTQ rights: and Defense of Marriage Act, 298n6; identity politics and New Politics movement, 181–88, 200–201; neoliberals on, 224, 237, 243; New Democrats and Clinton presidency, 245–46, 249, 298n6
Liberalism Is Not Enough (Averbeck), 272–73n2
Lichtenstein, Nelson, 274n24
Lindsay, John, 22, 124
Lippert, Edward, 178
Lipset, Seymour Martin, 196
Loeb, James, 6
Look magazine, on McCarthy candidacy, 157
Losing the Center (Bloodworth), 260n21
Lowenstein, Allard: and ADA leadership, *7f*, 130, 140–41, 159–65, 251, 284n89; and NDC, 169–70
Lucey, Patrick, 227
Lugar, Richard, 232
Lynd, Staughton, 79

Macdonald, Dwight, 103
Magnuson, Warren, 225
The Managerial Revolution (Burnham), 280n21
March on Washington (1965), 74–82, 269–70n63
March on Washington for Jobs and Freedom (1963), *3f*, *4f*, 92, 104–6, 275n32
Martin Luther King Jr. Center for Social Change, 231
Massachusetts Americans for Democratic Action (ADA), 97
Mattson, Kevin, 262n41
Matusow, Allen, 54, 257–58n4, 259–60n20, 265n3, 266n7
May 2nd Movement, 79
McCarthy, Eugene: ADA endorsement of, 1, 10–14, 127–30, 136–50, 214, 251; *Clean for Gene*, 283n64; and New Class, 145–52, 156–58, 160, 164–65; and New Politics evolution, 166, 168, 175–76, 204, 283n62; photo, *5f*
McCarthy, Joseph, 29
McClure, James, 232
McGovern, George: as ADA president, 221–22; Democratic Party reform and

McGovern, George (cont.)
  candidacy of, 188–95; McGovern–Fraser commission, 189–91, 193, 200, 214, 215, 222, 290n55; neoconservatives' response to 1972 election, 195–201; New Politics movement evolution and 1972 campaign, 14, 157–58, 166–68, 199–200, 203; on presidential campaign (1968), 141; presidential campaign (1972) of, 1, *8f*, 11, 210, 223, 225, 231, 238–39; Senate seat and 1980 election, 227, 229; on Vietnam War, 81
Meany, George, 218, 230–31
Meigs, Henry, 76–77, 78
Mexican American Political Association, 171
middle-class America: American liberalism oriented to, 58; Freedom Budget and values of, 277–78n71; and March on Washington (1965) participation, 78, 79; New Class, defined, 138; suburban vote and Republican Party, 29–30, 33. *See also* New Class
Middle East, Six-Day War, 133
military budget. *See* Cold War and military spending
military bureaucracy, anti-establishment sentiment against, 154, 176
Miller, Richard, 159–60
Minority Advancement Plan, 186
Mississippi Freedom Democratic Party (MFDP), 95–101
Mondale, Walter, 221, 238–39, 243, 248
Morgenthau, Hans, 164
Morse, Arthur D., 6–7
Moses, Bob, 97, 99
Moynihan, Daniel Patrick, 196, 202
Muravchik, Josh, 199
Muskie, Edmund, 166

Nathan, Robert, 49–50, 132, 164
National Abortion Rights Action League, 6, 252
National Advisory Committee on Civil Disorders, 124
National Association for the Advancement of Colored People (NAACP), 103–4, 117
National Association of Manufacturers, 23
National Committee for a Political Settlement in Vietnam, 272n98, 286n104
National Committee for a Sane Nuclear Policy (SANE), 74–75, 78, 80, 122, 178, 268–69n46, 285–86n103
National Conference for a New Politics (1967), 148–49
National Coordinating Committee to End the War in Vietnam (NCC), 70–71, 73, 74, 78–79
National Liberation Front (NLF), 69, 80, 83, 89, 272n96
National Mobilization Committee, 86
National Organization for Women (NOW), 185–86, 215–16
National Review, ADA criticized by, 7
National Rifle Association, 5–6
national security: anti-establishment sentiment against, 154, 176; National Security Council Report 68 (NSC-68), 36; neoliberals on military preparedness, 234–35. *See also* Cold War and military spending
National Urban League, 117
National Welfare Rights Organization, 172
Negotiation Now!, 82–90, 134–35, 266n5, 270n75, 271n95, 286n104
Negotiation Now! Bulletin, on discredited opponents to Vietnam War, 271n91
Negro American Labor Council, 105
Nelson, Gaylord, 226, 227, 229
neoconservatives: and liberalism mantle, 201–5; response of, to McGovern candidacy, 195–201
neoliberalism, 206–44; and "Atari Democrats," 5, 14–15, 207–10, 230, 231, 234–35, 237–43; criticism of, by ADA and its veteran leaders, 237–43; defined, 208; and

Democratic primary (1984), 231, 238–39, 243–44; and Democratic primary (1988), 239, 243–44; and full employment debate, 212–20; as New Politics legacy, 14–15, 206–7; and "Reagan Revolution," 225–30; rise of, in Democratic Party, 230–37; Ted Kennedy and 1980 presidential campaign, 220–25; and "Watergate babies," 209–13, 214, 217
"Neoliberals, Paleoliberals" (*New Republic*), 238
"A Neo-Liberal's Manifesto" (Peters), 236
New America, and Harrington, 102
New Class, 127–65; and anti-establishment sentiment, 152–58; and California politics, 242–43; CDM criticism of, 199; as "constituency of conscience," 152, 156–57, 171–74, 192, 242; defined, 138, 280n21; educational attainment and individual's political views, 138–40, 150, 156; McCarthy campaign and New Politics movement, 145–52; and McCarthy endorsement by ADA, 13–14, 127–30, 136–50; and NDC membership, 170–75; in twenty-first century, 252–56; Vietnam War as transcendent issue of, 130–36; white working class on Vietnam War, 281n25
The New Class (Đilas), 280n21
"A New Covenant with the American People" (1992 Democratic Party platform), 245
New Deal: "Atari Democrats" and neoliberalism in comparison to, 207; end of political coalition, 138; middle-class values of, 186; and qualitative liberalism debate, 17–18, 20, 28–29, 33, 42–43, 55, 58; Schlesinger on, 71
A New Democracy (G. Hart), 234–38
The New Democrat, and New Politics movement, 172
New Democratic Coalition (NDC), 168, 170–74, 194, 223

The New Leader, Schlesinger on Vietnam War, 134–35
New Left: and identity politics, 182; neoconservatism as response to, 195; vs. New Politics movement, 145, 149–50; and Schlesinger on "spiritual unemployment," 40, 46; and Vietnam War, 60–61, 266n7
New Look foreign policy, 27, 35–36
Newman, Paul, 6f
New Politics movement, 1–16, 166–205, 245–56; and ADA's decline in influence, 250–52; and ADA's role in, 5–11; and CDM, 167–69, 195–205; Democratic Party reform, McGovern candidacy, and New Class, 188–95; evolution of, overview, 14, 166–69; guiding principles of, 11–16; and identity politics, 1–2, 4, 15, 181–88; and individualism, 276n53; liberalism and shift toward social/cultural issues, 1–5; NDC inception following 1968 election, 169–75; neoconservatives and mantle of liberalism, 201–5; neoconservatives' response to McGovern candidacy, 195–201; neoliberalism as legacy of, 14–15, 206–7; and New Class in twenty-first century, 252–56; New Democrats and Clinton presidency, 245–50, 253; and qualitative liberalism debate, 18, 19, 39–40, 46, 58; Schlesinger on initial revolt, 145; two-party system circumvented by, 148; Vietnam War and call to reorder national priorities, 175–81, 200. *See also* qualitative liberalism
New Republic: on ADA's McCarthy endorsement, 136; on Keyserling and Humphrey-Hawkins, 216; on Negotiation Now!, 286n104; "Neoliberals, Paleoliberals," 238; on qualitative liberalism, 51, 55
The New Yorker, on *The Other America*, 103
New York State Social Studies Review and Development Committee, 187

New York Times: on ADA's McCarthy endorsement, 146; and CDM, 195, 203; on Tsongas, 232; on Vietnam War, 75–76, 79–80

New York Times Magazine, Galbraith on Vietnam War, 134

Niebuhr, Reinhold, 6, 7, 72–73, 159, 162

Nixon, Richard: on ABM system, 180–81; election (1972), 195, 223, 239; FAP, 277n60; "Kitchen Debate" (1959), 38; resignation of, 209–10; Supreme Court nominees of, 227, 295n62; on Vietnam War, 179, 281n25

North American Free Trade Agreement (NAFTA), 245, 249

North Vietnam. *See* Vietnam War

Nourse, Edwin, 24

Novak, Michael, 196, 199

Obama, Barack, 3–5, 15, 250

Occupy Wall Street, 15

Oglesby, Carl, 79, 84

Ohio Democratic Party convention (1964), 98

The Other America (Harrington), 102–4, 112–13

The Other American (Isserman), 271n95

Peace Corps, 210, 235

Pearson, Drew, 20

Pells, Richard, 45

Peters, Charles, 207, 230, 235–36

Peterson, Don, 7f, 147, 170–71, 172, 174

Phillips, Channing, 171

Pinochet, Augusto, 207

Podhoretz, Norman, 166–67, 196, 197, 200, 201

Politics and Vision (Gillon), 9–10, 265n3, 274n24

Popular Front, 6, 20–21

Port Huron Statement (SDS), 62

poverty and civil rights, 92–126; ADA on race and poverty relationship, overview, 13, 92–95, 128; and ADA's civil rights resolution (1964), 106–9; and ADA's dissent on Vietnam War, 125–26; *The Affluent Society* on, 101–4, 110; "case poverty" vs. "insular poverty," 102–3; and diversity awareness, 183–84; Freedom Budget initiative, 94–95, 115–19, 277–78n71; Freedom Budget initiative, and Vietnam War, 120–25; and guaranteed annual income initiatives, 111–15, 276n53, 277n60; and Humphrey-Hawkins bill (1976, Full Employment and Balanced Growth Act), 213; Kerner Report and Vietnam War opposition, 124–25; and March on Washington (1963), 92, 104–6, 275n32; and MFDP at National Convention (1964), 95–101; qualitative liberalism and divergent perspectives on, 109–11; regulation of private industry, 94, 111, 249, 273n5

poverty and social balance concept, 46–53. *See also* qualitative liberalism

Prinz, Joachim, 3f

Progressive Citizens of America (PCA), 20–21

Progressive Party, 20–21, 71–73, 81, 87, 260n9, 261n14

Proposition 13, 242–43

Purdum, Todd, 1

qualitative liberalism, 17–58; and *The Affluent Society* on social balance, 46–53; Cold War and consumer culture, 34–40; defined, 17–19, 32; divergent perspectives on poverty, 109–11; and economic growth consensus, 23–28; identity politics and New Politics movement, 181–88; and middle-class orientation of American liberalism, 58; as New Politics origin, 167–69, 173–74, 181–88, 201, 204; presidential election (1952) and growth of, 28–34; vs. "quantitative" approach, 18, 19, 31–34, 57–58, 181; and Schlesinger on "spiritual unemployment," 40–46; as source of divergence, 53–57

Quart, Alissa, 254
Quiet Revolution (Shafer), 289n52

racial capitalism, 92, 272–73n2. *See also* poverty and civil rights; social issues
Raggio, Grier, 172
Randolph, A. Philip, 3f, 105, 113, 115, 119, 122
Randolph Institute, 94, 115, 118–19. *See also* Freedom Budget
Rauh, Joseph: ADA legacy of, 6, 10–11; as ADA vice chairman, 88–91; on Democratic Party during Clinton presidency, 246; at March on Washington (1963), 3f; and neoliberalism, 221, 225, 227–28, 239; and *New Republic* on Negotiation Now!, 286n104; on poverty and civil rights, 93, 96–100, 122, 273n8; on presidential campaign (1968), 136, 140–43, 148, 153, 161, 164–65; on Vietnam War, 82, 87–91
Reagan, Ronald: CDM's influence on, 205; and neoliberalism, 207–9, 225–29, 230–31, 233, 239; "Reagan Revolution," 3–5, 14, 225–30
The Real Majority (Scammon and Wattenberg), 197
Referendum '70 campaign (midterm elections), 179–80
regulation of private industry, 94, 111, 249, 273n5
Reporter, and qualitative liberalism debate, 28, 31
Republican Party: on business community's power, 71; CDM manifesto on, 199; free market fundamentalism of, vs. neoliberal entrepreneurship, 236–39; and 1968 presidential election, 131–32; and suburban vote, 29–31, 33. *See also individual names of political candidates and leaders*
Reuther, Victor, 164
Reuther, Walter, 6, 95, 98–100
Rising, George, 283n64

The Road from Here (Tsongas), 228–29, 231–33, 237, 242
Robinson, Cleveland, 3f
Roche, John, 60, 92, 132, 144, 196
Rolling Thunder policy, 64
Romer, Roy, 246
Roosevelt, Eleanor, 6, 20, 163
Roosevelt, Franklin, Jr., 20
Roosevelt, Franklin D.: Executive Order Number 8802 on racial discrimination, 105; on "forgotten man," 2, 8; "Four Freedoms," 116; qualitative liberalism debate, 18–20; Tsongas on, 229. *See also* New Deal
Rossinow, Doug, 54, 176
Rustin, Bayard: and ADA's McCarthy endorsement, 132; and CDM, 196; as March on Washington deputy director (1963), 4f, 275n32; photo, 4f; on poverty and civil rights, 96, 100, 104, 115, 119, 121–22

Safeguard ABM system, 180–81, 288n33
Sanders, Bernie, 1, 5, 8, 15, 250, 252–55
SANE (National Committee for a Sane Nuclear Policy), 74–75, 78, 80, 122, 268–69n46, 285–86n103
Scammon, Richard, 197
Schifter, Richard, 196–97
Schlesinger, Arthur, Jr.: ADA legacy of, 2–3, 6, 251; and ADA's McCarthy endorsement, 10–12; and ADA's new generation of leadership, 160, 161, 164–65; on "affirmative government," 227–28; Anderson endorsed by, 227; *The Bitter Heritage*, 68–69; at City University of New York, 80, 191; *The Disuniting of America*, 187; on historic disunity among communist nations, 268n29; on identity politics, 187–88; in Kennedy administration, 101, 103, 153; on "Me-Too" Reaganites, 237, 239; on Negotiation Now!, 134, 136–37; and neoliberalism, 207–8, 210, 222, 223, 225–29, 237, 239–43; on New Class, 15, 253,

Schlesinger, Arthur, Jr. (*cont.*)
281n28; and New Politics movement, 145, 167–69, 173–75, 180–82, 187, 191–94, 199–204; and *New Republic* on Negotiation Now!, 286n104; photos, *2f, 10f*; on poverty and civil rights, 93–95, 100–101, 109–11, 120, 126, 273n8; on presidential campaign (1968), 128, 130, 132–40, 142, 143, 145, 148–50, 153–56, 158; and qualitative liberalism debate, 12–13, 17–19, 22–23, 28–42, 51, 53–55, 57; and qualitative liberalism debate, on "spiritual unemployment," 40–46; "spiritual unemployment," 40–46; as Stevenson's speechwriter, 22–23; on Vietnam War, 59–60, 65–66, 70–75, 78, 80–83, 88–91, 266n6, 272nn97–98; *The Vital Center*, 7–8, 71–74, 81; "vital center" concept of, 266n4

Schlesinger, Arthur, Sr., 44
Schlesinger, James, 232
Schlesinger, Stephen, 171–72
Schrade, Paul, 170–71, 172
Schultze, Charles, 218
Schwartz, Louis, 113–14
Seabury, Paul, 77–78, 132, 144, 196
Selective Service System, 224
Senate Committee on Banking, Housing, and Urban Affairs, 218
Sexton, Brendan, 281n25
Sexton, Cayo, 281n25
Shachtman, Max, 271n95
Shafer, Byron, 190, 289n52
Shanker, Albert, 196, 201
Shrum, Robert, 223
Shull, Leon: and ADA legacy, 11; as ADA national director, *4f*, 75–76, 119, 180, 216; and ADA on Vietnam War, 75–77, 84, 87; and neoliberalism, 216, 219, 221, 222, 232; and New Politics movement, 178, 180; and *New Republic* on Negotiation Now!, 286n104; on poverty and civil rights, 119; on presidential campaign (1968), 142, 144, 160, 163
Silone, Ignazio, 41

Simpson, Alan, 232
Six-Day War, 133
Smeal, Eleanor, 215–16, 231
social issues: identity politics and New Politics movement, 1–2, 4, 15, 181–88, 200–201, 257n2, 258n6; New Democrats and Clinton presidency, 245–50, 253; qualitative liberalism on social balance, 46–53; social balance and taxation, 27, 46–57; social democratic approach to poverty, 106–9; twenty-first-century Democrats on social issues vs. economic issues, 252–56. *See also* poverty and civil rights; qualitative liberalism
Socialist Party of America (SPA), 89, 102, 270n75, 271n95
Solidarity Day (1981, AFL-CIO), 231
Southern Christian Leadership Conference, 117, 178
South Vietnam. *See* Vietnam War
Southwest Council of La Raza, 184
Soviet Union: Afghanistan invasion, 223–24; Sputnik program, 34; Vietnam War and US policy on, 62, 63, 67–68, 265n3
"spiritual unemployment," 40–46
Spock, Benjamin, 79, 84, 85, 148
Spring Mobilization Committee, 83–86
Sputnik program (Soviet Union), 34
Squeezed (Quart), 254
"stagflation," 9, 213, 216, 253
Stalin, Joseph, 34
Stanley, Timothy, 225
Stearnes, Rick, 223
Steinem, Gloria, 216
Stevenson, Adlai, 22, 28, 35, 129, 138, 150–51
Student Nonviolent Coordinating Committee (SNCC), 97, 100, 117
Students for a Democratic Society (SDS), 62, 70, 73, 74, 79
Students for Democratic Action, *2f*
Stulberg, Louis, 144, 196
suburban voters. *See* middle-class America; New Class

Supreme Court: and 1980 presidential election, 227–28; Nixon's nominees to, 227, 295n62

Tamiment Institute Annual Book of the Year Award, 47
taxation: and *The Affluent Society* on social balance, 46–53; and qualitative liberalism debate, 27, 49–57
teach-ins, 70
Temporary Assistance for Needy Families, 249
Thatcher, Margaret, 207
Thomas, Norman, 79
Thurow, Lester, 186
Toward a Democratic Left (Harrington), 192
Trilling, Lionel, 71–72
Truman, Harry: ADA influence on election of, 6; ADA on presidency of, 22–23, 271n14; China "lost" by, 90; on civil rights, 96; on conservative parties, 239; election (1948) of, 71; and Employment Act (1946), 276n45; and Fair Deal policy, 18, 28, 42–43, 58, 117; Keyserling at joint Economic Committee (1949) of, *1f*; and qualitative liberalism debate, 18, 20, 22, 23, 24, 27, 36
Tsongas, Paul: and neoliberalism, 4–5, 206–7, 210–11, 217, 226, 228–38; photo, *9f*; *The Road from Here*, 228–29, 231–33, 237, 242
Tyler, Gus, 60, 131–33, 144, 204

Union for Democratic Action (UDA), 19–21, 72, 94, 108, 276n45
United Auto Workers (UAW), 95, 98, 170, 224
United Farm Workers, 215
United Federation of Teachers (UFT), 196, 201
United Steelworkers of America, 144
University of Chicago, Department of Economics, 47, 273n75
University of Michigan, Ann Arbor, 70

The Unraveling of America (Matusow), 257–58n4, 259–60n20, 265n3, 266n7
U Thant, 82

Veblen, Thorstein, 138, 280n21
Vietcong. *See* National Liberation Front
Vietnam Moratorium Committee (VMC), 168, 178–80
Vietnam War: ADA on unilateral withdrawal, 60–63, 74–82, 87–90, 135; ADA's dissent against US policy, 13, 62–66, 125–26; and anti-establishment sentiment, 152–58; *The Bitter Heritage* on, 68–69; casualty statistics, 135, 157; early US involvement in Vietnam, 61–62; financial cost of, 130, 135; and Freedom Budget, 120–25; and Galbraith on "Cold War mystique," 66–70; Galbraith's letter to Kennedy about, 59, 62, 67; Gulf of Tonkin Resolution, 63–64; Kerner Report and opposition to, 124–25; March on Washington (1965), 74–82, 269–70n63; Negotiation Now! campaign, 82–90, 266n5, 270n75, 271n95, 281n84; and New Politics movement origin, 2, 4, 10, 13–16, 175–81, 200; and qualitative liberalism debate, 18, 40, 53, 58; Rolling Thunder policy, 64; SANE on, 74–75, 78, 80, 122, 178, 268–69n46, 285–86n103; and Selective Service System reactivated by Carter, 224; Tet Offensive, 143; Vietnam Summer (1967), 84–87; VMC, 168, 178–79. *See also* New Class; "vital center"
"vital center": CDM's goal for, 202–3; defined, 59–61, 71, 73–74, 90–91; and "end of ideology" thesis, 239–41; political boundaries of, 70–74; Schlesinger's first reference to, 266n4; *The Vital Center* (Schlesinger), 7–8, 71–74, 81
Volcker, Paul, 221

Wallace, Henry, Cold War and 1948 presidential campaign of, 20–21, 71–73, 81, 87, 260n9, 261n64
Wall Street Journal: on CDM's manifesto, 203; Schlesinger's column in, 227, 232
War on Poverty, 93–95, 106–10, 112–16. *See also* Johnson, Lyndon B.; poverty and civil rights
Washington Monthly, on neoliberalism, 230, 235–36
Washington Post: on ADA's McCarthy endorsement, 146; and CDM advertisement, 195; on National Convention (1972), 193–94; "A Neo-Liberal's Manifesto," 236; on Solidarity Day rally (1981), 231
Washington Star, Rauh's endorsement of Anderson, 227
"Watergate babies," 209–14, 217, 233. *See also* neoliberalism

Wattenberg, Ben, 196–97
W. E. B. Du Bois Clubs, 79
Wechsler, James, 6, 143, 158, 160, 161
When America Was Great (Mattson), 262n41
Wiley, George, 172
Wilkins, Roy, 96, 100
Winpisinger, William, 222, 224
Women's International League, 80
women's rights, identity politics and New Politics movement, 181–88, 200–201. *See also* abortion
Women Strike for Peace (WSP), 78, 80
World War II, period following. *See* Cold War and military spending

Young, Kenneth, 212, 217

Zucker, Ron, 247

www.ingramcontent.com/pod-product-compliance
Lightning Source LLC
Chambersburg PA
CBHW030008240426
43672CB00007B/874